From the Lighthouse: Interdisciplinary Reflections on Light

What is a lighthouse? What does it mean? What does it do? This book shows how exchanging knowledge across disciplinary boundaries can transform our thinking. Adopting an unconventional structure, this book involves the reader in a multivocal conversation between scholars, poets and artists. Seen through their individual perspectives, lighthouses appear as signals of safety, beacons of enlightenment, phallic territorial markers, and memorials of historical relationships with the sea. However, the interdisciplinary conversation also reveals underlying and sometimes unexpected connections. It elucidates the human and non-human evolutionary adaptations that use light for signalling and warning; the visual languages created by regularity and synchronicity in pulses of light; how lighthouses have generated a whole 'family' of related material objects and technologies; and the way that light flows between social and material worlds.

Veronica Strang directs Durham University's Institute of Advanced Study and is the author of *The Meaning of Water* (2004), *Gardening the World: Agency, Identity and the Ownership of Water* (2009) and *Water: Nature and Culture* (2015).

Tim Edensor belongs to the Geography Department of Manchester Metropolitan University and is the author of *From Light to Dark: Daylight, Illumination and Gloom* (2017), *Industrial Ruins* (2005) and editor of *Geographies of Rhythm* (2010).

Joanna Puckering works for Durham University's Institute of Advanced Study. Joanna completed her PhD at the Department of Anthropology, Durham University.

From the Lighthouse: Interdisciplinary Reflections on Light

Edited by Veronica Strang,
Tim Edensor and Joanna Puckering

LONDON AND NEW YORK

First published 2018
by Routledge
2 Park Square, Milton Park, Abingdon, Oxon OX14 4RN

and by Routledge
711 Third Avenue, New York, NY 10017

Routledge is an imprint of the Taylor & Francis Group, an informa business

© 2018 selection and editorial matter, Veronica Strang, Tim Edensor and Joanna Puckering; individual chapters, the contributors

The right of Veronica Strang, Tim Edensor and Joanna Puckering to be identified as the authors of the editorial material, and of the authors for their individual chapters, has been asserted in accordance with sections 77 and 78 of the Copyright, Designs and Patents Act 1988.

All rights reserved. No part of this book may be reprinted or reproduced or utilised in any form or by any electronic, mechanical, or other means, now known or hereafter invented, including photocopying and recording, or in any information storage or retrieval system, without permission in writing from the publishers.

Trademark notice: Product or corporate names may be trademarks or registered trademarks, and are used only for identification and explanation without intent to infringe.

British Library Cataloguing-in-Publication Data
A catalogue record for this book is available from the British Library

Library of Congress Cataloging-in-Publication Data
A catalog record has been requested for this book

ISBN: 978-1-4724-7735-4 (hbk)
ISBN: 978-1-315-58357-0 (ebk)

Typeset in Times New Roman
by Swales & Willis Ltd, Exeter, Devon, UK

Printed and bound by CPI Group (UK) Ltd, Croydon, CR0 4YY

Contents

List of figures xii
List of plates xv
List of contributors xvi
Acknowledgements xxiv

360° OF ILLUMINATION 1
VERONICA STRANG

LIGHT MATTERS 5
VERONICA STRANG

An early sun 5
FOKKO JAN DIJKSTERHUIS

Light and matter 7
ROBERT FOSBURY

LIGHT AS A MATTER OF LIFE AND DEATH 10
VERONICA STRANG

Shedding light on the limitations of microalgal production 11
KEVIN FLYNN

Sunflowers 15
JOANNA PUCKERING

In the Cambrian light . . . 16
GLENN A. BROCK

Light and the evolution of vision: a conversation with Rob Barton 20
JOANNA PUCKERING

ON THE EDGE OF THE DARK 23
VERONICA STRANG

Lighting space   25
FOKKO JAN DIJKSTERHUIS

ATTRACTIVE AND REPULSIVE LIGHT 27
VERONICA STRANG

Biological lighthouses   27
MARGO HAYGOOD AND BRADLEY TEBO

Cosmic signallers   30
ULISSES BARRES DE ALMEIDA AND MARTIN WARD

Lighthouses of the insect world   34
JOANNA PUCKERING

PHENOMENOLOGICAL LIGHT 37
VERONICA STRANG

Visual rays: the light within the eye   40
FOKKO JAN DIJKSTERHUIS

DIVINE RAYS 41
VERONICA STRANG

Lighthouses in the Bible: symbols of enlightenment and salvation   45
JOANNA PUCKERING AND DAVID WILKINSON

The aesthetics and ethics of visible and inner light: a conversation with Douglas Davies   47
JOANNA PUCKERING

Light as metaphor and as technology, c.1700–1900   51
TOM MOLE

Guiding light: the early modern lighthouse as image and emblem   54
RICHARD MABER

LIGHTHOUSES IN TIME AND SPACE 59
VERONICA STRANG

The Colossus of Rhodes according to Giacomo Torelli   60
JAN CLARKE

'Places of light': lighthouses and minarets   66
JOANNA PUCKERING

*'On lofty cliffs, where the sea pounds the rock . . .':
   lighthouses in early medieval England*   70
DAVID PETTS

The redistribution of light and dark at sea   74
TIM EDENSOR

TECHNOLOGIES OF LIGHT AND POWER   77
TIM EDENSOR

Technologies of light   78
BRIAN BOWERS

The Fresnel lens: enabling lighthouse technology   83
GORDON D. LOVE

Early lighthouse lamp technology   86
STEVE HOON

BUILDING THE LIGHTHOUSE   89
TIM EDENSOR

The physicality of lighthouses   89
STEVE HOON

The modern lighthouse: a sculpture by accident   91
STEVE MILLINGTON

Sky-tower as icon   96
DAVID COOPER

Turner's lights   99
JAMES PURDON

*Illuminating science: scientific expertise and lighthouse
   reform in 19th-century Britain*   103
HANNAH CONWAY

Light offshore: governing dark waters in shipping straits   109
KIMBERLEY PETERS

A personal view from the lighthouse   112
RICHARD WOODMAN

The materiality of lighthouses 114
STEVE HOON

Shining a light on lighthouse resilience in the 21st century 117
PATRICIA WARKE

Enmeshed in geographies of sand, sea and war: the lighthouses of Skagen Odde 122
TIM EDENSOR

Lightships 128
KAREN SAYER

MATERIAL RELATIVES 131
VERONICA STRANG

Wish image 132
PETER ADEY

The extraterrestrial lighthouse: St John's Beacon, Liverpool 137
DAVID COOPER

THE BODY OF THE LIGHTHOUSE 139
VERONICA STRANG

The lighthouse at Cape Reinga 144
VERONICA STRANG

Horn section: John Tyndall's 1873 foghorn testing sessions 147
JENNIFER LUCY ALLAN

Disturbing the peace: the Cloch foghorn and changing coastal soundscapes in the 19th century 149
JENNIFER LUCY ALLAN

Foghorn Requiem *154*
JOSHUA PORTWAY AND LISE AUTOGENA

Death of a lighthouse 157
CAITLIN DESILVEY

LIGHT MESSAGES 161
TIM EDENSOR

Ambiguous beams 161
TIM EDENSOR

Lights across the sky   164
FOKKO JAN DIJKSTERHUIS

Coming in on a wing and a prayer   166
JOANNA PUCKERING

Trinity House and the formation of the modern British state   168
STEVE MILLINGTON

The lit archipelago   171
ERIC TAGLIACOZZO

The Albion Lighthouse: from Dutch shipwrecks to British colonialism and US imperialism   175
DINI LALLAH

The lighthouse without a light: lighthouses, exploration and geography   177
ROBERT SHAW

The lighthouse as survival   179
PHILIP STEINBERG

The lighthouse as a site of refuge and welcome   184
UMA KOTHARI

A vigil: Disappearance at Sea, Tacita Dean, 1996   *187*
JULIE WESTERMAN

The deadly lighthouse beam   189
TIM EDENSOR

Moth hunting in Sumatra   192
CHARLES COCKELL

SPACE AND PLACE   194
TIM EDENSOR

The rhythms of place, the rhythms of the lighthouse   194
TIM EDENSOR

The watcher at the edge   198
PHIL WOOD

Relational places: lighthouses and networks of mobility 201
ROBERT SHAW

No keepers 204
CHRIS WATSON

THE ART OF LIGHTHOUSES 207
VERONICA STRANG, JOANNA PUCKERING AND TIM EDENSOR

'The Last Lighthousekeeper' 207
LINDA FRANCE

'There'll be no landing at the lighthouse tomorrow': Virginia Woolf and the Godrevy Lighthouse 208
PATRICIA WAUGH

The centenary celebrations of Grace Darling and the Longstone Lighthouse 214
YSANNE HOLT

Going round the twist 219
PETER ADEY

The haunted lighthouses of death 223
PETER HUTCHINGS

Uncanny architecture: Lighthouse, Catherine Yass, 2011 228
JULIE WESTERMAN

'The Weather is Lovely' 232
JULIE WESTERMAN

the encircling of a shadow: *the house of light made dark* 233
RONA LEE

360° 236
VERONICA STRANG

The metaphor, metaphysics and music of light in medieval and modern thought 236
TOM MCLEISH

Wonder and the lighthouse 240
H. MARTYN EVANS

CONCLUDING COMMENTS 243

The shifting multiplicity of the lighthouse 243
TIM EDENSOR

Interdisciplinary reflections 244
VERONICA STRANG

References 248
Index 270

Figures

1	*Giant Wave at Seaham Lighthouse, County Durham, UK*	xxiv
2	North Ronaldsay Lighthouse	1
3	Cast-iron lighthouse (1865) at Whiteford Point, Gower Peninsula, South Wales	9
4	Sunflowers, Raichur, India	15
5	The trilobite Redlichia takooensis from the lower Cambrian Emu Bay Shale, Kangaroo Island	19
6	Waves emanating from a candle, taken from Huygens' *Traité de la Lumière*, 1690	25
7	Bioluminescent jellyfish	28
8	Spinning pulsar – the 'cosmic lighthouse'	32
9	Imentet and Ra from the tomb of Nefertari, 13th century BC	41
10	18th-century monstrance from Bemposta palace chapel, Portugal	43
11	*Hildegard of Bingen receiving the Light from Heaven*, c.1151 (vellum) (later coloration), German School	44
12	Hermann Hugo's *Pia Desideria, 1624* (Antwerp, Hendrick Aertssens)	57
13	*Prologue: The Harbour with the Colossus of Rhodes* (oil on canvas), by Giacomo Torelli (1608–1678) / Pinoteca Civica di Fano, Fano, Italy	61
14	Detail of Map of Calais, Malta, Rhodes, and Famagusta, from *Civitates Orbis Terrarum*, by Georg Braun (1541–1622) and Frans Hogenberg (1535–1590), c.1572, engraving by Joris Hoefnagel (1542–1600)	63
15	Set design with Venice in background from *Apparati Scenici per il Teatro Nuovissimo dell'Opera Pubblica di Venezia* (set designs for the Teatro Novissimo in Venice), by Giacomo Torelli from Fano (1608–1678), 1644	64
16	Grand Mosque of Kairouan	68
17	The Roman lighthouse at Dover Castle	71
18	Argand improved oil lamps in 1782 by introducing a circular wick with air flowing inside as well as outside	79

19	Fresnel lens, Point Arena Lighthouse, California	83
20	The Fresnel lens and its effect on a beam of light	85
21	The Stanislav Range Front Light, a 'sister' lighthouse echoing the design of the Adziogol Lighthouse in the Ukraine	90
22	Dungeness New Lighthouse in Kent	95
23	*Bell Rock Lighthouse*, by J. M. W. Turner, 1819	100
24	Longships, Cornwall: an example of a rock tower lighthouse	117
25	Stratification of air within towers reflecting temperature and relative humidity	119
26	The Vippefyr, Skagen Odde	124
27	The Engulfed Lighthouse, Rubjerg Knude	126
28	*Galloper* in a bottle, by Elise&Mary, 2013	130
29	Liverpool Speke Airport, now the Crowne Plaza Hotel Liverpool	132
30	Radio City Tower, St John's Beacon, Liverpool	136
31	'A Lighthouse – Not Professor Tyndall', from *Moonshine*, published 20 December 1884 (wood engraving), English School	140
32	St John's Anglican Church, Ashfield, New South Wales: 'I am the Light of the World' (John 8:12). Stained glass by Alfred Handel	141
33	Souvenir lighthouses from Helsinki	143
34	Cape Reinga Lighthouse, near the northern-most point of the North Island of New Zealand	145
35	Sculpture based on Cape Reinga Lighthouse, by Blue Powell, 2009 (ceramic)	146
36	Brass band playing in *Foghorn Requiem*	155
37	Map of Wadden Sea lighthouses	165
38	The Hoad	178
39	Asylum seekers and migrants descend from a large fishing vessel used to transport them from Turkey to the Greek island of Lesbos, 11 October 2015	180
40	Image of off-duty soldier, Antonis Deligiorgis, pulling Wegasi Nebiat from the surf in Rhodes, 2015	183
41	*Wish you were here – Gratiot Light*, by Julie Westerman, 2017	188
42	'Time–space compression', from Harvey, D. (1989: 241)	201
43	*The interior of Longstone Lighthouse, Fern Islands.* Engraving by A. J. Isaacs, from a painting by Henry Perlee Parker, 1866	215
44	Cape Bruny Lighthouse interior	219
45	*Wish you were here – Douglas Head*, by Julie Westerman, 2017	228
46	*Lighthouse (East)*, by Catherine Yass, 2011	229
47	*Phare*, by Ron Haselden, 2008	230
48	*Harbour Scene, Newhaven*, by John Piper, c.1937 (watercolour, body colour, gouache, collage, pen, brush and black)	231

xiv *Figures*

49	*The Weather is Lovely – George Olson aground at Cape Disappointment Lighthouse,* by Julie Westerman, 2017	232
50	*The Weather is Lovely – Shipwreck by Lighthouse,* by Julie Westerman, 2017	232
51	*the encircling of a shadow,* by Rona Lee, 2001	233

Plates

1 Bioluminescent jellyfish
2 Spinning pulsar – the 'cosmic lighthouse'
3 *Hildegard of Bingen receiving the Light from Heaven*, c.1151 (vellum) (later coloration), German School
4 *Prologue: The Harbour with the Colossus of Rhodes* (oil on canvas), by Giacomo Torelli (1608–1678) / Pinoteca Civica di Fano, Fano, Italy
5 *Bell Rock Lighthouse*, by J. M. W. Turner, 1819
6 *Wish you were here – Gratiot Light*, by Julie Westerman, 2017
7 *Wish you were here – Douglas Head*, by Julie Westerman, 2017
8 *Lighthouse (East)*, by Catherine Yass, 2011
9 *Phare*, by Ron Haselden, 2008
10 *Harbour Scene, Newhaven*, by John Piper, c.1937 (watercolour, body colour, gouache, collage, pen, brush and black)
11 *The Weather is Lovely – George Olson aground at Cape Disappointment Lighthouse*, by Julie Westerman, 2017
12 *The Weather is Lovely – Shipwreck by Lighthouse*, by Julie Westerman, 2017

Contributors

Veronica Strang directs Durham University's Institute of Advanced Study (IAS). She is an environmental anthropologist whose research focuses on water and sustainability, and includes work with the United Nations. From 2013–2017, she was Chair of the Association of Social Anthropologists of the UK and the Commonwealth. She is regularly involved in major collaborative projects, and has written extensively on interdisciplinarity. In 2017, she was appointed to the Higher Education Funding Council for England's national Interdisciplinary Advisory Panel.

Tim Edensor is the author of *Tourists at the Taj* (1998), *National Identity, Popular Culture and Everyday Life* (2002), *Industrial Ruins: Space, Aesthetics and Materiality* (2005) and *From Light to Dark: Daylight, Illumination and Gloom* (2017) as well as the editor of *Geographies of Rhythm* (2010). Tim has written extensively on national identity, tourism, ruins and urban materiality, mobilities and landscapes of illumination and darkness.

Joanna Puckering is a Research Associate at Durham University in the Department of Anthropology, where she completed her PhD thesis on volunteering and community engagement in UK Higher Education, seen through the lens of reciprocal gift exchange. Research interests include contested meanings and uses of community, and the intersection of material culture with mental health. She currently works for Durham University's Institute of Advanced Study.

***

Peter Adey, Professor in Human Geography at Royal Holloway, University of London, works at the intersections of space, security and mobility and within the blurring boundaries between Cultural and Political Geography. He has published widely in academic journals and edited collections; books include *Mobility* (2009) and *Air* (2013). In 2011, he was awarded a Philip Leverhulme Prize. Peter was an IAS Fellow in 2014, developing his research on aerial security.

Jennifer Lucy Allan is a writer and researcher who works with physical archives, unearthing sensory material in the historical record. She is writing a PhD at Creative Research into Sound Arts Practice, University of the Arts London, on the social and cultural history of the foghorn, and is also a journalist, specialising in experimental and underground music. She contributes regularly to *The Guardian* and *The Wire*, and co-founded the reissues record label Arc Light Editions.

Lise Autogena is a Professor of Cross-Disciplinary Art at the Cultural Communication and Computing Research Institute (C3RI), Sheffield Hallam University. In 2013, she worked with Joshua Portway to develop *Foghorn Requiem*, a requiem for a disappearing sound, performed by the Souter Lighthouse foghorn, three brass bands and fifty ships on the North Sea.

Ulisses Barres de Almeida is an astrophysicist at the Brazilian Center for Physics Research (CBPF), leading the Astro-particle Physics Group. He graduated from the University of São Paulo in 2003 and obtained his PhD in Astrophysics from Durham University in 2010. From 2010–2012, he was a post-doc at the Max-Planck-Institut for Physics and is currently leader of the Cherenkov Telescope Array Consortium in Rio. Ulisses Barres was an IAS Fellow in 2014.

Rob Barton studied Psychology and Zoology at Bristol University. He has been interested in research at the intersection of evolutionary biology, psychology and cognitive neuroscience. He is Professor of Evolutionary Anthropology, founder of Durham's Evolutionary Anthropology Research Group, and has been President of the European Human Behaviour and Evolution Association. His PhD was on the behavioural ecology of wild baboons, but he now focuses on the evolutionary biology of the brain.

Brian Bowers, a chartered engineer and historian of technology, was Curator of the lighting, electrical engineering and domestic technology collections in the Science Museum, London. He has written and lectured extensively on these subjects in Britain and abroad. He has served on various committees including the Council of the Royal Institution, and been an Examiner for the Open University. Publications include *Lengthening the Day: A History of Lighting Technology*.

Glenn A. Brock is Associate Professor of Palaeobiology at Macquarie University in Sydney, Australia. His interdisciplinary research programme aims to untangle the roots of early animal evolution to better understand the origins and relationships of the major animal phyla. He focuses on the Cambrian 'Explosion' of animal life. He was an IAS Fellow in 2013 and is a Visiting Professor at the Nanjing Institute of Geology and Palaeontology, China.

Jan Clarke is Professor of French in the School of Modern Languages and Cultures at Durham University. She has written on all aspects of 17th-century theatrical production, and published three monographs on the Guénégaud Theatre (1673–1680), examining its design, management and production policy. She is currently working on an edition of Thomas Corneille's ten operas and machine plays and a monograph on the early years of the Comédie-Française.

Charles Cockell is Professor of Astrobiology in the School of Physics and Astronomy at the University of Edinburgh, and Director of the UK Centre for Astrobiology. His research group studies life in extreme environments and the implications for habitability on other planetary bodies.

Hannah Conway is pursuing her PhD in the History of Science at Harvard. She examines the history and anthropology of infrastructure and regulation in the post-war US. Current projects focus on scientific and legal architecture of clean air legislation and advancements in bio-concrete production and manufacture. She holds a BA in Photography from Appalachian State University, an MA in History from College of Charleston, and an AM in History of Science from Harvard.

David Cooper is a Senior Lecturer in English at Manchester Metropolitan University. He focuses on contemporary literary geographies, and leads on the Manchester Writing School's MA/MFA in Place Writing. He has published widely on digital literary mapping: he is the co-editor of *Literary Mapping in the Digital Age* (2016) and a co-investigator on the major project 'Creating a Chronotopic Ground for the Mapping of Literary Texts' (Arts and Humanities Research Council, October 2017–2020).

Douglas Davies studied Anthropology and Theology at Durham and Oxford. Publications include work on the interface of those fields, especially ritual, symbolism and belief, notably concerning Mormonism, the Church of England, death, cremation, and traditional and woodland burial practice. He is a Fellow of the UK Academy of Social Science, of the Learned Society of Wales, an Oxford D. Litt., and an honorary doctor of theology of Sweden's Uppsala University.

Caitlin DeSilvey is Associate Professor of Cultural Geography at the University of Exeter, and researches the cultural significance of material and environmental change. She has worked on a range of interdisciplinary projects, supported by UK research council funding, the Royal Geographical Society, the Norwegian Research Council and the European Social Fund. Recent publications include *Visible Mending* (2013, with Steven Bond and James R. Ryan) and *Curated Decay: Heritage Beyond Saving* (2017).

Fokko Jan Dijksterhuis is Associate Professor in the History of Science and Technology at the University of Twente, Netherlands. He studies the early modern roots of science and technology. His recent work has focused on early modern cultures of innovation with a particular interest in the way Enlightenment collectioneurs, savants, artists and printers developed new conceptions of light and vision. He was an IAS Fellow in 2013.

H. Martyn Evans is Principal of Trevelyan College, Durham University. He was founding joint editor of the UK *Medical Humanities* journal, co-director of the Durham Centre for Medical Humanities, and holder of a £2m Wellcome Trust Strategic Award (2008). He is an honorary Fellow of the Royal College of General Practitioners, and of the Royal College of Physicians of London. In 2017, he became Professor of Philosophy of Music, Durham.

Kevin Flynn is an expert in the construction, testing and use of mechanistic plankton function type models for commercial and oceanic settings. His PhD (algal physiology) is from the University of Wales. He was the first recipient of the Natural Environment Research Council's (NERC) 'Advanced Fellowship' award. He holds a Chair in Marine Microbiology at Swansea University. Kevin was an IAS Fellow in 2011, researching *Biofuels, Science and Society*.

Robert Fosbury is an astrophysicist who studied at Warwick and Sussex/RGO and then worked in Australia, Switzerland and latterly in Germany where, for three decades, he has been working for the European Space Agency (ESA) on the Hubble project. After retiring from ESA in 2011, his interests have included how to characterise earth-like planet atmospheres with the next generation of large ground and space-based telescopes. He was an IAS Fellow in 2013.

Linda France is an award-winning poet, with eight poetry collections published since 1992, including *The Toast of the Kit Cat Club* (2005); *book of days* (2009) and *Reading the Flowers* (Arc, 2010). She edited *Sixty Women Poets* (1993) and won the 2013 National Poetry Competition. Linda was an IAS Fellow in 2013, Creative Writing Fellow at Leeds University, 2015–2016, and researches and teaches at Newcastle University.

Margo Haygood (PhD, Marine Biology, Scripps Institution of Oceanography, University of California, San Diego) is a Research Professor at the University of Utah. Dr Haygood is a marine microbiologist with an interest in symbiotic associations between bacteria and marine animals. She has studied symbiotic bioluminescence, and contributed to our understanding of the way microbes can provide defensive chemicals to their hosts, some of which have potential as drug candidates.

Ysanne Holt is Professor of Art History and Visual Culture at Northumbria University. Her research focuses on 20th- and 21st-century visual culture in Britain, its critical discourses and institutions, and particularly the broader processes and practices that cohere within northern cultural landscapes. She has a strong interest in the social and historical relations between forms of cultural production and was founding editor of the Routledge journal *Visual Culture in Britain*.

Steve Hoon is a physicist and Professor of Applied Science at Manchester Metropolitan University. He gained his PhD from the University of Bangor in 1980 studying nanomagnetism. His research publications and teaching expertise span magnetic materials, the design and automation of scientific instrumentation, physics education, the physics of music and environmental science. More recently, he has studied bio-physical and bio-geographical feedback in dryland systems, in the Kalahari in particular.

xx *Contributors*

Peter Hutchings was Professor of Film Studies at Northumbria University. He is the author of *Hammer and Beyond: The British Horror Film* (1993), *Terence Fisher* (2002), *The British Film Guide to Dracula* (2003), *The Horror Film* (2004) and *The Historical Dictionary of Horror Cinema* (2008) (republished as *The A–Z of Horror Cinema* (2009)). He also published numerous journal articles and book chapters on horror cinema, British film and television, science fiction cinema and television, and the thriller. Sadly Peter died shortly before the publication of this book.

Uma Kothari is Professor of Migration and Postcolonial Studies in the Global Development Institute at the University of Manchester. Her research interests include global humanitarianism, migration and refugees. Publications include *Development Theory and Practice: Critical Perspectives* (2001) and *A Radical History of Development Studies* (2005). She is a Fellow of the Academy of Social Sciences and received the Royal Geographical Society's Busk Medal for contributions to research in support of global development.

Dini Lallah, a story writer and graphic designer, teaches English and Mauritian Creole, and works as a translator. She is presently engaged in activist campaigns relating to mother-tongue language, land rights and data protection issues. From her house in Albion, she has a view of the bay from the lighthouse to the beach at which pieces of porcelain from the wreckage of 17th-century Dutch ships can still be found.

Rona Lee is an artist and Professor of Fine Art at Northumbria University; a specialist in critically engaged fine art practices she works in an expanded manner combining different media, forms of intervention and engagement. Over the last twenty years a number projects have adopted the sea/water as an investigative locus, while recent works are concerned with the politics/poetics of the phenomenal world.

Gordon D. Love is an interdisciplinary scientist working on the boundaries of physics, vision science, computer science, astronomy and engineering. A common theme to his work is adaptive optics. Much of his early work was on liquid crystal Fresnel lenses which can electrically adapt their optical properties. He now works on the optics of the eye, and runs projects involving understanding the mechanisms behind vision and creating improved 3D technology for displays.

Richard Maber is Emeritus Professor of French at Durham University, and was for twenty years Director of the university's interdisciplinary Research Centre for 17th-Century Studies. He is founder and general editor of the journal *The Seventeenth Century*. His principal research interests are 17th-century French poetry and early modern intellectual history. He is currently editing the complete correspondence of Gilles Ménage (1613–1692), to be published in six volumes by Honoré Champion.

Tom McLeish recently started a new role as Professor of Natural Philosophy in the Department of Physics, at the University of York. He works with chemists, engineers and biologists in universities and industry to connect material properties with their molecular structure. He also works on connections between science and policy, history and theology, resulting in the recent books *Faith and Wisdom in Science* (2014) and *Let There Be Science* (2017). He was Pro-Vice-Chancellor for Research at Durham (2008–2014) and is Chair of the Royal Society's Education Committee.

Steve Millington is a Senior Lecturer in Human Geography at Manchester Metropolitan University and a Director of the Institute of Place Management. Steve is co-editor of *Spaces of Vernacular Creativity: Rethinking the Cultural Economy* and *Cosmopolitan Urbanism*. Working with Tim Edensor, Steve has written about household Christmas light displays and Blackpool Illuminations.

Tom Mole is Reader in English Literature and Director of the Centre for the History of the Book at the University of Edinburgh. He received his PhD from the University of Bristol in 2003. With Michelle Levy, he wrote *The Broadview Introduction to Book History* (2017) and edited *The Broadview Reader in Book History* (2014). Other books include *Byron's Romantic Celebrity* (2007) and *What the Victorians Made of Romanticism* (2017).

Kimberley Peters teaches Human Geography at the University of Liverpool, where her research seeks to better understand the governance of maritime space. She is co-editor of the volumes *Water Worlds: Human Geographies of the Ocean* (2014), *The Mobilities of Ships* (2015), and *Carceral Mobilities* (2017). She has published extensive articles and book chapters and the discipline-wide textbook, *Your Human Geography Dissertation: Doing, Designing, Delivering* (2017).

David Petts is a Senior Lecturer in Archaeology at Durham University. He specialises in the archaeology of early medieval Northern Europe, particularly Northern Britain. His current research focuses on early monastic sites and their wider landscape contexts both terrestrial and maritime.

Joshua Portway is an artist and game-designer. He is known for his collaboration with Lise Autogena, who he has worked together with since the early 1990s. Their recent works have explored uranium mining as a means to independence in Greenland (*Kuannersuit; Kvanefjeld*, 2016), real time visualisation of the world's financial markets as a night sky (*Black Shoals; Dark Matter Stock Market Planetarium*, 2015/16) and visualisation of real time climate data to find the world's bluest skies (*Most Blue Skies*, 2009).

James Purdon teaches Modern and Contemporary Literature at the University of St Andrews, and co-edits the open-access book series *Technographies* (Open Humanities Press). He writes regularly on modern painting and sculpture for the art magazine *Apollo*, and his *Modernist Informatics: Literature, Information, and the State* (Oxford University Press) was published in 2016.

Karen Sayer is Professor of Social and Cultural History at Leeds Trinity University. Her work addresses light, illumination and the flows of energy connecting country and city in the 19th and 20th centuries. She has received funding from the Society of Nautical Research to engage with the archival holdings and object collection at the National Maritime Museum, Greenwich, and works with artists Mary Hooper and Elise Liversedge on the 'Last Station' project.

Robert Shaw is a Lecturer in Geography at Newcastle University. With his research interests in city life at night, he has explored street-lighting technologies in the UK and most recently the Nuit Debout protest movement in Paris. His first book, *The Nocturnal City*, is due to be published with Routledge in 2018.

Philip Steinberg is Professor of Political Geography at Durham University, where he directs IBRU: the Centre for Borders Research and edits the journal *Political Geography*. He focuses on spaces and processes that cross, or exist outside, land-territory. Publications include *The Social Construction of the Ocean* (2001), *Managing the Infosphere* (2008), *What Is a City? Rethinking the Urban after Hurricane Katrina* (2008), *Contesting the Arctic* (2015), and *Territory beyond Terra* (2018).

Eric Tagliacozzo is Professor of History at Cornell University. He is the author of *Secret Trades, Porous Borders: Smuggling and States along a Southeast Asian Frontier* (2005), and more recently of *The Longest Journey: Southeast Asians and the Pilgrimage to Mecca* (2013). He is also the editor or co-editor of nine other books. He is Director of Cornell's Modern Indonesia Project (CMIP), and editor of the journal *Indonesia*.

Bradley Tebo (PhD, Marine Biology, Scripps Institution of Oceanography, University of California, San Diego) is a Distinguished Professor of Marine and Biomolecular Systems at Oregon Health & Science University (OHSU). Dr Tebo is a marine microbiologist whose research focuses on microbe–metal–mineral interactions and how microorganisms gain metabolic energy from them in the absence of light. His research has applications for pollution remediation, bioenergy and synthesis of new materials.

Martin Ward is an astrophysicist, and holds the Temple Chevallier Chair of Astronomy at Durham University. His research interests include black holes and quasars. He was a consultant for the European Space Agency and is involved in the next generation Hubble Telescope project. He is also interested in science public outreach, and has been a guest on Patrick Moore's *The Sky at Night*, Melvyn Bragg's *In Our Time*, and Andrew Marr's *Start the Week*.

Patricia Warke is a Senior Lecturer in the School of Natural and Built Environment, Queen's University Belfast. Early research on rock weathering in arid regions led to a focus on climate change impacts on decay dynamics of stone in built structures covering a wide range of ages, and she has worked with the Commissioners of Irish Lights and Trinity House General Lighthouse Authorities on condition issues in offshore lighthouses.

Chris Watson is a composer and sound recordist with a passionate interest in the wildlife sounds of animals and habitats around the world. Watson has presented many BBC Radio 4 programmes and his music is regularly featured on the BBC Radio 3 programme *Late Junction*. In 2013, Watson received a Paul Hamlyn Composers Award. Recent commissions include: Opera North, Leeds; The National Gallery, London; The Louvre, Paris; and the Aichi Triennial, Japan.

Patricia Waugh is a Professor in the Department of English Studies at Durham University, and a Fellow of the British Academy. She has written and edited extensively on modern fiction, (post)modernism, feminist theory, contemporary fiction and literary theory. She is completing a book with Marc Botha, *Critical Transitions: Genealogies of Intellectual Change*, and working on a new monograph examining Virginia Woolf's experiments in relation to theories of voice and hearing voices.

Julie Westerman, artist, researcher and lecturer in Fine Art, Sheffield Hallam University, works across sculpture, drawing, film, animation and as a curator. Cross-disciplinary research projects include: collaborations in art/science, *Fly Birdie Fly* for the Olympic year; IAS Fellowship, exploring light; *Trigger Point*, interdisciplinary city guides, walking as a research methodology; art/engineering/social anthropology; *Hard Engineering*, exploring attitudes towards climate change and seismic activity (Lisbon, Natural History Museum/Instituto Superior Técnic, Lisboa).

David Wilkinson is Principal of St John's College and Professor in the Department of Theology and Religion, Durham University. His background is research in theoretical astrophysics, where he gained a PhD in the study of star formation. His current work involves the relationship of the Christian faith to contemporary culture. Recent books include *Science, Religion and SETI* (2013), and *When I Pray What Does God Do?* (2015).

Phil Wood is an urban therapist and psychogeographer from Yorkshire.

Richard Woodman went to sea aged sixteen in 1960 and in 2006 became an Elder Brother of Trinity House. A prolific author, his histories include studies of merchant shipping, convoys and lighthouses. Richard is a Fellow of the Royal Historical Society, the Nautical Institute, and a Freeman of the Honourable Company of Master Mariners. In 2014, he was appointed a Lieutenant in the Royal Victorian Order.

Acknowledgements

Figure 1 Giant wave at Seaham Lighthouse, County Durham, UK. Photograph: Paul Kingston / Northern News and Pictures.

This book owes its existence to the Institute of Advanced Study at Durham University. In a year focused on the research theme of *Light* (2013–2014), the IAS organised the public event *To The Lighthouse: an experiment in interdisciplinary creativity*, which initiated the project. Its directors and visiting Fellows (including Tim Edensor) took forward the experiment of trying to capture an interdisciplinary conversation in text.

The IAS has provided practical and creative support to this experiment throughout, and the editors would like to express their warm thanks for this assistance, and their appreciation of the imaginative confluence of people and ideas that is fostered in Cosin's Hall. As well as drawing on the editors' wider academic networks, this endeavour has benefited greatly from being able to call upon the IAS's international College of Fellows and their shared enthusiasm for interdisciplinary adventures.

This book is therefore dedicated to those scholars whose intellectual curiosity carries them beyond their own disciplinary areas, and whose generosity enables the open exchanges of knowledge upon which real interdisciplinarity depends.

360° OF ILLUMINATION

Veronica Strang

Figure 2 North Ronaldsay Lighthouse. Photograph: Marion E Muir, North Ronaldsay.

The beam of the lighthouse sweeps in an arc, reaching out to illuminate different points of the compass. In this book, which is the product of a series of interdisciplinary conversations, that searching beam is reflected back from multiple directions to consider the lighthouse itself. It focuses on what a lighthouse is and what it does, but it is, simultaneously, an experiment in thinking about what happens when diverse perspectives are brought to bear on shared questions. It explores how exchanges of knowledge across disciplinary and experiential boundaries transform not only the object of study but each other.

2   360° of illumination

Most edited volumes bring together different viewpoints from within particular disciplines. Some mix it up more and invite authors from contiguous areas. The general aim is to employ related kinds of expertise to examine a specific topic. But the curiosity that impelled this volume was not merely about the topic itself but about the dynamic effects of interdisciplinary conversations where radically different kinds of expertise meet, often for the first time. It is a rather organic process: as one of our contributors put it, 'its genuine interdisciplinary nature comes from the short, concise chapters which allow more of a dialogue' (Kimberley Peters). Rather than replicating the neat sequence of chapters in conventional collections, therefore, the text roams freely across disciplinary terrains. There are multiple short excursions into specialised contributions, but the overall aim is not to traverse from A to B, but to circle the lighthouse to consider the advantages of a 360° view.

A hundred years ago, scholars strolled across different areas of knowledge without a qualm, borrowing whatever seemed useful to inform their thinking. But as disciplinary specialisms emerged it became more challenging to encompass the sheer wealth of information that they generated. The academic world became a more competitive professional arena, and specialist knowledges 'divided into (putatively) distinct and mutually incomprehensible areas' (McLeish and Strang, 2014). With the emergence of well-defended disciplinary territories, such relaxed trespassing was less welcome. And while the deep knowledge afforded by disciplinary specialism has been – and remains – hugely valuable, mutual exclusivity has tended to subsume the essential unity of a shared endeavour to seek and advance knowledge.

There are some advantages to this intellectual fission. Like cultural diversity, disciplinary specificity has created particular forms of knowledge that, when compared, can radically transform each other. This is the point of an interdisciplinary conversation: that interlocutors find their own thinking altered, as well as co-producing new ideas that would not have been arrived at independently. Interdisciplinarity is not an over-arching superstructure trying to bolt disciplines together: it is, as Lash observed, the ultimately connected structure that underlies all of them (1996). Genuine exchanges of knowledge – on any topic – should generate understandings that are more than the sum of their parts.

The Institute of Advanced Study (IAS) at Durham University was founded upon this premise and, in the decade following its foundation in 2006, it focused on a series of annual research themes such as *Being Human*, *Water*, *Emergence*, *Evidence*. This project was sparked by its year on *Light*, in 2013–2014, with the topic of the lighthouse itself chosen simply to provide a specific focus for a public conversation about human (and non-human) relationships with light. It was a quite (literally) light-hearted experiment, which wildly underestimated the fascination with lighthouses that would draw IAS Fellows and members of the public into an interdisciplinary discussion that included the development of optical lenses; the luminescent signals of marine creatures; pulsars from outer space; and a contribution from a member of the public, who, as the conversation turned to territoriality and the notion of a lighthouse as a homologue, asked 'what about

The Spooky Men?', a band whose song *Lightpole* – it turns out – precisely encapsulates this idea.

From the Lighthouse is an experimental attempt to represent and expand that conversation and to ensure that, as another participant put it, 'interdisciplinarity is embedded as a practice throughout' (Peter Hutchings). Many of the contributions are from visiting Fellows at the IAS (not necessarily during 'the *Light* year'). Others are from people invited to push the conversation in different directions. Rather than imposing a strict narrative structure, the editors have aimed at a light touch that allows disciplinary voices to speak in their own ways and foreground what matters most to them. Our major aim, in the linking sections, has been to draw out the connections between the perspectives offered, and to provide some narrative underpinning.

Thus, the conversation begins by discussing light itself: how different disciplines understand its material properties; its role in evolution, and its biological effects. Contributions explore human and animal responses to light, the process of seeing, and phenomenological experiences of light. They show how material engagements with light generate the plethora of symbolic meanings attached to light, and to darkness, in different historical and cultural contexts.

There are examples of how different species make use of light – to signal, to attract and seduce, and to prey on others. Regularity in signals, and synchronicities between them, seem to convey intentionality in efforts to communicate, and this applies not only to light, but also to sound, for example in the foghorn signals that identify lighthouses.

Appearing in the conversation is a range of objects that could be described as the lighthouse's 'material relatives': other technologies for surveillance and warning, and for bringing people home safely, such as beacons and airport control towers. Geographical rather than disciplinary territoriality emerges as a key theme, as does the importance of the location of the lighthouse in the liminal space at the edge of the land, marking a critical boundary between concrete form and formless fluid. This leads towards ideas of the lighthouse as a symbol of enlightenment and consciousness, illuminating the mind with religious epiphany or lighting the path to reason.

As this implies, the idea of the lighthouse is an ancient one, and there are contributions exploring classical examples, such as the Colossus of Rhodes, as well as transitions from 'enlightening' minarets to light towers, and from medieval to modern lighthouses. The history of lighthouses is also an account of changing technologies for building lighthouses, and for creating and distributing light. These historical perspectives serve to illustrate the changing purposes of lighthouses: their increasing importance as the seas became more intensely navigated, and their decline as new electronic technologies for navigation and surveillance appropriated their functions.

More recently, lighthouses have undergone a renaissance, providing a focus for local community identity and cultural heritage. As such, their replication as souvenirs becomes comprehensible. Attention to identity also allows us to explore the ways in which, both materially and symbolically, the 'body' of the lighthouse is a homologue that enables the expression not just of a community's *persona*, but also its territorial agency and ownership.

Lighthouses are a perennial source of fascination: their centrality to coastal communities, their critical functions, their dramatic interior spaces and their exterior punctuation of the landscape, as well as the frisson of fear or desire elicited by their liminal position, means that they feature regularly in art, film and literature. Examples range from the deep symbolism of Woolf's *To the Lighthouse* to the joyful anarchy of *Fraggle Rock*. The arts, as ever, shed new light on the layers of meaning and function uncovered by the social and natural sciences.

From the Lighthouse takes us through each of these areas, exploring not only specialised knowledges but also the connections through which these knowledges transform into each other and lead to new understandings.

LIGHT MATTERS

Veronica Strang

The lighthouse is only possible because of the material properties of light. Light travels outwards from a source of energy in the form of waves, and it is the way that these waves are reflected by objects that makes the world visible to the human eye. It is the particular characteristics of material surfaces and their capacity to reflect, refract or absorb light, in conjunction with the evolution of the eye, that enables humans – and other species – to perceive form and in many cases colour. This not only provides a beautiful example of how the evolution of biological organisms emerges from intimate engagement with the material environment, it leads to a host of ideas about vision and seeing, which affect how we think about lighthouses.

Refraction

When light waves pass through materials, such as water or glass, they are refracted. Indeed, it is through interaction with materials that light itself becomes visible (O'Shaughnessy, 1984). In what is called 'the Tyndall effect', a light beam is only visible to the extent that it is reflected by materials such as mist, rain, dust or insects. 19th-century physicist John Tyndall was interested in how atmospheric molecules affected both light and sound waves, so his work not only informs thinking about light beams, but also the capacity of foghorns to penetrate the mist (DeYoung, 2011). Earlier navigators had already provided a clue that the atmosphere affects the Sun's rays. Historian of science and technology, Fokko Jan Dijksterhuis, describes how three 16th-century Dutchmen and their faith in their celestial reading pushed scientists to understand the refraction of light.

An early sun

Fokko Jan Dijksterhuis

On 24 January 1597, three Dutchmen stood on the south shore of the north tip of Nova Zembla (Novaya Zemlya), above the Arctic Circle, watching the sky expectantly. For a few days, the weather had improved, and in the

(continued)

(continued)

dark sky, the first shining beam of the Sun could be seen. They were eager for the Arctic night to be over, so that they could at last go home. The previous August, on an expedition to find the northern passage, their ship had become stuck and was destroyed in the Arctic ice. It was their third failed effort in three years. Seventeen men had survived the harsh winter by building a 'safe house' on Nova Zembla from the remains of their ship, and they wanted to try and cross over to Kola. They would succeed eventually, only losing their captain, Willem Barentsz (c.1550–1597).

Officer Gerrit de Veer (c.1570–1598) was on the shore that day, and recorded his excitement at this glimpse of light. 'There I was the first to see, against all our expectations, the brim of the Sun' (*alwaerbuytenonsgissinge, ick aldereerstsach de kimmevander Sonne*). The men on the shore could not believe it, because, according to their data, it was two weeks too soon. At the latitude of 76 degrees the Sun was still 5 degrees below the horizon and would rise only two weeks later. (The date was corroborated by the observation of a conjunction of Jupiter and the Moon a couple of hours later.) Three days later the weather was once again good enough to permit them to go outside and 'then we all together saw the Sun in its full roundness above the horizon' (*doensaghenwyaltesamen de Son in zijnvollerondichheytboven den Horizont*) (van der Werf et al., 2003). This was still ten days early, it seemed, but the end of the Arctic night had been announced by the Sun, the supreme lighthouse of the cosmos.

Upon the crew's safe homecoming, De Veer's report immediately raised doubts and his observations have been debated by many scientists since. Possibly the men had erred in determining their position, in recording the date, or in their measurements. Or perhaps they had simply been misled by a wishful longing for the light to appear. In his ground-breaking treatise on optics, *Paralipomena* (1604), Johannes Kepler (2000: 151–155) discussed the 'observations of the Dutchmen in the frozen North' and defended their astronomical and observational competence. He argued that the phenomenon was a result of a refraction of light rays upon entering the atmosphere, and a subsequent reflection at convection layers in the atmosphere. In this way, the Sun could be seen from below the horizon.

Not many followed Kepler, and numerous alternative explanations were offered to account for the Dutch crew's observation. But now the Groningen physicist, Siebren van der Werf, has solved the mystery. He developed a computer model of the optical properties of the atmosphere that includes the effects of inversion layers. With this he can analyse all kinds of phenomena like 'fata morgana': effects of refraction and reflection in atmospheric layers making objects beyond the horizon visible. Van der Werf has succeeded in replicating the Dutch expedition's observations on Nova Zembla. Kepler lacked a modern understanding of the composition and dynamics of the atmosphere, but he did have the basics right: the Dutch men standing on that cold winter shore saw the Sun reflected against the atmosphere.

The Dutch observations on Nova Zembla, and Kepler's prescient explanation, remind us that light finds its way to Earth through the atmosphere. There is no direct, rectilinear connection between light source and observer: the path of light is always mediated. In this way, the lighthouse of the Sun can make its presence clear, even when it lies below the horizon.

By the early 19th century, scientific understandings of refraction enabled engineer and physicist Augustin-Jean Fresnel to demonstrate that light could be captured and concentrated via optical technologies – lenses and reflectors – to form intense beams that would travel a considerable distance (Ostdiek and Bord, 2013).

The lighthouse literally 'houses' a source of light that is concentrated in this way. Like most technological advances, lighthouse technology depends both on an understanding of the material world – in this instance the energies of the Sun, and the way that light interacts with objects and surfaces – and a capacity to be inventive in replicating what the world does. Fresnel's creative efforts led to a plethora of technologies using light beams which, as astronomer Robert Fosbury observes, can be used to illuminate the inner workings of materials themselves.

Light and matter

Robert Fosbury

In the lab, we point beams of light at all kinds of stuff for all kinds of purposes. This is one of the – maybe the most – important tools in physics, chemistry and biology for figuring out what the stuff is and how it works. It can also be beautiful.

If someone hands you an object of interest, you will feel it, heft it, possibly smell it, but certainly you will look at it. If you have any inclinations towards physics or chemistry, your visual examination may become more serious. You may illuminate it with various kinds of light from ultraviolet, to visible and to infrared, and you might also use the tightly collimated (aligned) beams of lasers. You will shine these lights through the object (or through a slice taken from it) and you will reflect the light from the surface.

The interaction of light with matter has been one of the most important drivers of discovery across the sciences. The richness of this interaction has attracted such concentrated attention from curious minds that, during

(continued)

(continued)

the last century or so, the intensive study of its physical nature has resulted in the exquisitely successful theory of Quantum Electro Dynamics (QED).

This scientific study of light and matter has spread far beyond the laboratory. It has created a plethora of industrial and artistic applications and has, in the study of astrophysics, reached to the limits of the known Universe. Consider the gemstone called emerald, a crystal of beryl coloured green by a trace of chromium replacing the occasional aluminium atom in a crystal built from beryllium, oxygen, aluminium and silicon (a beryllium aluminium silicate). This may be in the form of a beautifully cut green stone set in a ring, or it may be a water-washed pebble picked up from a stream bed.

In addition to being remarkably beautiful, gem emerald is of particular interest in two ways when we ponder the history of the Universe and of the planet Earth. The atoms of beryllium which form an integral part of the crystal structure were forged neither in the Big Bang, by nuclear reactions in the interiors of stars, nor even in the supernova explosions that end some stellar lives. If any beryllium is created in such locations, it is rapidly destroyed before it gets the chance to escape into less hostile environments. No, the beryllium in that ring is a product of nuclear fission occurring when a high-energy cosmic ray collides with an atomic nucleus drifting through interstellar space.

The mineral beryl is called a *cyclosilicate* because of the particular arrangement of the silicon and oxygen atoms within the crystal: they form cylindrical, open channels within the crystal structure that are large enough to capture occasional volatile atoms or molecules from the volcanic magma in which the crystal grew. These volatile interlopers, commonly helium, argon and water, can be trapped in their little 'vials' for geological periods as long as the age of the Earth. Indeed, the majority of the occurrences of beryl are in the oldest rock formations, so measurements of these interlopers can tell us about conditions prevailing in young Earth magmas. This subject was first investigated by the 4th Baron Rayleigh (Robert John Strutt) who realised that there was too much helium to be explained by the decay of radioactive elements within the original crystals (Rayleigh, 1933). It was eventually shown in 1958 that the helium and argon came from radioactive decays in the surrounding magma rather than from the beryl crystals themselves (Damon and Kulp, 1958). Today extractions from beryl minerals provide helium for physics laboratories, and for party balloons.

By shining a beam of red and infrared light through a beryl crystal, we can actually see the water molecules trapped in their channels from these early magmas. The water molecules can be stimulated to vibrate and absorb the incident light at wavelengths corresponding to the main vibrational frequencies within the molecule (caused by stretches and bends of the interionic bonds). This produces an easily recognised 'signature' of ancient water in the rock.

This is but one example of how shining a beam of light at or through a material can reveal its composition, its structure and its history. Many different measurement techniques have been developed to explore the richness and complexity of light-matter interactions.

Figure 3 Cast-iron lighthouse (1865) at Whiteford Point, Gower Peninsula, South Wales. Photograph: Thomas Guest, CC BY 2.0 (https://creativecommons.org/licenses/by/2.0/) via Wikimedia Commons.

LIGHT AS A MATTER OF LIFE AND DEATH

Veronica Strang

The idea of light as necessary to life is so powerful that it is often assumed that all organisms depend on it. This is mostly true, but there are 'extremophiles' deep in the oceans that can make use of other energy sources. Chemist Chris Greenwell explains:

> You don't need light at all to create life and for ecosystems to be sustained and driven; you just need a chemical gradient and that's what you get at these deep sea hydrothermal vents . . . Extremophiles creep into our discussions around origins of life and evolution of life on Earth . . . A lot of these organisms tend to be from older groups of organisms [and] they also expand the regions of habitability that we might have previously considered, whether they are very tolerant of extremes of pH, or whether they are tolerant of extreme pressures and temperatures. But certainly, lots of them can use very different substrates and energy sources than you might originally imagine . . . they don't rely on photosynthesis to be able to split up water and generate electrons, and be able to build their building blocks from basic molecules: they use different mechanisms to do that.
>
> (2016: np)

Nevertheless, the scientific 'origin story' focuses on the magical interaction of light and water as the basis for biological life in which, 4 billion years ago, light streaming from the Sun met water carried to Earth in a 'heavy bombardment' of water-bearing asteroids. As I have noted elsewhere:

> Even today, there is no scientific consensus about the origin of water on Earth. However, the ideas initiated by Charles Darwin and Louis Pasteur offer a compelling vision of chemical evolution, in which sunlight and radioactivity provided sufficient heat and energy for the creation of water, and a feisty interaction of amino acids, carbon monoxide, carbon dioxide, nitrogen and other organic matter enabled the emergence of living cells with their own metabolic and reproductive processes.
>
> (Strang, 2015a: 12)

Thus, the presence or absence of light has been critical since the beginning, as illustrated by marine biologist Kevin Flynn's exploration of the intricate relationship that phytoplankton have with light.

Shedding light on the limitations of microalgal production

Kevin Flynn

The world's fisheries, our aquaculture, and recent interests in exploiting biotechnology for biofuels all have a common feature – namely the growth of microalgae using energy from sunlight that, like light from a lighthouse, is delivered in pulses. Unicellular microalgae are not plants, but in common with those multicellular organisms they photosynthesise, using light to help fix carbon dioxide (CO_2) to enable growth. These microscopic algae (typically c.0.01 mm diameter) have been largely responsible for producing the oxygen that we breathe, and for locking away much of the CO_2 that was in the atmosphere into vast limestone deposits that dominate certain geological features (such as the 'white cliffs of Dover'). Collectively then, microalgae have helped transform Earth from a planet more like Venus to that which we see today. And their fatty acids, geologically contained and transformed over millennia, also gave us crude oil.

Most microalgae are marine, inhabiting the upper few tens of metres of oceans that are, on average, some 4 kilometres deep. For biotechnology applications, we may grow them in pea-soup-like suspensions in 'bioreactors' only a few centimetres in depth. Interestingly, though, the maximum rate of photosynthesis expressed as CO_2-fixation per square metre per day is much the same in the most fertile areas of the oceans and in bioreactors. That rate (3–5gC/m^2/d; Kenny and Flynn, 2015) results from several interconnected factors limiting microalgal growth suspended in water.

While providing a source of energy, light is dangerous. Every packet of light (photon) that hits a photosynthetic organism, while being exploited to generate energy, also shakes, heats and otherwise damages the photosynthetic apparatus. An organism unable to utilise the energy streaming into it becomes damaged more rapidly. Using sunlight is literally like tapping into a nuclear reactor over which the organism has very little control, and certainly none that can be exerted quickly. For one of the features of light is that the quantity of it can change very rapidly, in milliseconds, and typically over minutes as clouds move over the sky. In contrast, microalgae and plants can only respond by altering their biochemistry over the course of many tens of minutes, if not hours. They cannot 'close the blinds' if there is

(continued)

(continued)

too much light: they must simply endure the excess energy input. So how do these organisms balance the costs and benefits, and what are the evolutionary consequences?

The challenge

Light is a necessary evil for photosynthetic organisms. To succeed competitively, the net growth rate of the individual needs to be higher than that of the neighbouring microalgal cell. As a population of microalgae grows, the light for the individual cell gets shaded out by the other cells around it. To compensate, cells make more photosystems (they become greener), but collectively all these photosystems further shade out the light – it is a vicious circle and light-limitation of population growth can develop rapidly, which limits the potential for commercial microalgal growth in bioreactors (Kenny and Flynn, 2016). On the face of it, a cell with a large photosynthetic capacity would seem to have the advantage. However, if/when the nutrient supply (ammonium, nitrate, phosphorous, etc.) becomes exhausted, then possession of such a large photosynthesis capacity becomes a liability: one that can literally fry the organism. Suddenly the light energy has no useful biochemical role, and damage to the photosystems then occurs more rapidly; and because the nutrient status of the organism is low, such photodamage cannot be repaired rapidly.

In common with the light beam from a lighthouse, the light experienced by microalgae flashes with refraction and reflection as the light meets the rippling surface of the water. For microalgae, the light field is even more variable in quality and quantity than that experienced by terrestrial plants. Unlike the slow competition between terrestrial plants played out over weeks and years, microalgae compete with each other by the minute and by the hour. And then there are the periods of day and night to contend with; for an organism with a life cycle of a day or so, each night is a long time. Some microalgae can migrate vertically in the water column: flagellates of c.0.01 mm diameter swim 5–10 metres up and down every day, thus balancing their need for energy from light during the day and for the nutrients available at a greater depth at night. Water is very viscous for a microbe, so this migration is akin to a human swimming hundreds of kilometres in treacle.

Once light energy and nutrients are acquired, the microalgae need to make new biomass. This starts with 'dark reactions' that use the photo-generated chemical energy from the 'light reactions' for CO_2-fixation. This critical process is limited by the activity of the most common, and arguably most important, protein on Earth: the enzyme ribulose bisphosphate carboxylase (RuBisCO) (Raven, 2013). RuBisCO is a rather inefficient enzyme, but its activity is further adversely affected by the presence of the waste product of the light reactions (namely oxygen) and because its substrate (CO_2) is not very abundant in water. RuBisCO also lies dormant at night. While it may contribute as much as 20 per cent of total cellular protein, its activity places a cap on the potential rate of microalgal growth, and hence on the ability of the organisms to exploit light (Flynn and Raven, 2016).

Why has evolution not selected for a more efficient form of RuBisCO? It seems that it is not worth it. There is no evolutionary logic (selective pressure) in having physiological components that can run far ahead of the rest of the organism's physiology and which cost the cell so much material (Flynn and Raven, 2016). Furthermore, recently we have come to realise that all is not quite what it seems in the oceans: natural microalgae are not as reliant on light or on inorganic nutrients as we thought.

The new paradigm for primary production in the oceans

The oceans cover over two-thirds of the Earth's surface, and contain a food chain dominated by photosynthetic primary producers (microalgae termed phytoplankton) and their consumers (zooplankton). This traditional paradigm has been accepted for over a century. Now, however, research has shown that most phytoplankton are not just photosynthetic, relying on light and inorganic nutrients: they are mixotrophic, combining both plant-like photosynthesis and animal-like predatory activity. The success of these microscopic triffids is less dependent on the dangers of too much, or indeed too little, light than we thought. In fact, the evolution of the eukaryote (protist) microalgae stems from organisms that acquired a photosynthetic capability by stealing photosystems from their prey (Mitra et al., 2016). The only major protist microalgae that conform to the traditional phytoplankton configuration are the diatoms, which have glass-like cell walls (and which we use, incidentally, in toothpaste, which contains the rock 'diatomite' made from ancient deposits of those cell walls).

Diatoms evolved to rely solely upon the dangerous light for energy, surrendering the ability to eat in order to benefit from a tough transparent cell wall. Diatoms cannot swim: they typically live in turbulent water columns that supply them both with nutrients pushed up from the depths, and with a rapidly varying light supply as sunlight is mixed through the water column. They have also evolved ways to handle too much light, with mechanisms to help vent the excess biochemical energy and prevent it from damaging the cell. Diatoms do best in the spring and autumn when the higher inorganic nutrient availability helps maintain a healthy fast physiology. In contrast, mixotrophs dominate in better-lit summer waters that contain fewer nutrients to pair with newly fixed CO_2; mixotrophs obtain extra nutrients from their prey, and need less photosynthesis in the first place.

(continued)

> *(continued)*
>
> **Conclusion**
>
> Microalgae have shaped the Earth and human experience of it. Their legacy is everywhere: in the atmospheric O_2 we breathe, in the limestone we walk upon, in the oil we extract and burn to warm and transport us, and in the fisheries that sustain us. They have evolved in an environment of fluctuating light that changes over seconds, over day and night, and over seasons, maximising their potential for growth exploiting light, while balancing the dangers of being fried by capturing too much light energy. The way they handle the challenges of light constrains rates of primary production both in nature and in bioreactors. That we have only very recently realised that many also eat for a living is also (excuse the pun) illuminating, for mixotrophy allows them to stay further away from the dangerous environment signposted by the lighthouse that is the Sun.

Similar responses to the presence or absence of light are readily apparent in larger organisms and, as with phytoplankton, too much light can be as harmful as too little.

Seeing the light

As well as relying upon photosynthesis to manufacture glucose and thus energy, plants are responsive to patterns of movement in light. Most are photoperiodic, responding to fluctuating levels of light at various times of the year, using photoreceptors that sense the wavelengths of sunlight available. In this sense, botanist Daniel Chamovitz says, plants may be said to 'see':

> They don't see pictures. But they see colors, they see directions, they see intensities. But on a certain level, plants might think that we're visually limited. Because plants see things that we can't see. They see UV light and they see far red light, and we can't see that at all. So I think we can say that plants see.
>
> (2012: np)

Picking up on this, Kevin Flynn (pers. comm.) notes that 'certainly motile phytoplankton "see"; some even have eye spots; and they navigate using "sight"'.

While slower seasonal responses to light are more common, some flowering plants respond to diurnal changes in light: examples include daisies ('day's eyes', or more formally *Bellis perennis*); chickweed (*Stellaria media*); poppies (*Eschscholzia californica*); hibiscus (*Hibiscus syriacus*); the magnolia (*Magnolia grandiflora*); and water plants such as the white waterlily (*Nymphaea odorata*).

Figure 4 Sunflowers, Raichur, India. Photograph: Mike Lynch, CC BY-SA 3.0 (https://creativecommons.org/licenses/by-sa/3.0/deed.en), via Wikimedia Commons.

Sunflowers

Joanna Puckering

Called *tournesol* in French and *helianthus* in Greek, the wild sunflower (*Helianthus annuus*) was domesticated, primarily for its edible seeds, about 5,000 years ago, by the indigenous peoples of Mexico and the southern United States. Spreading gradually through what is now Western Europe, it has had many horticultural, medicinal and culinary uses and, in 18th-century Russia, farmers began to cultivate it commercially, to produce oil (Schneiter, 1997).

Although it is not the only plant that moves with the Sun, the sunflower is the best known, made famous in van Gogh's painting and the lines of William Blake (2011): 'Ah Sun-flower! weary of time, Who countest the steps of the Sun'. The solar tracking displayed by sunflowers and similar plants originates in a chemical and cellular response called phototropism. Photosynthetic organs, which use the energy from sunlight to turn carbon

(continued)

(continued)

dioxide into food, align themselves with the direction of incoming light. It is not sunflower blooms themselves that follow the Sun, but cellular growth in the neck and leaves of the sunflower stem. This is achieved when the hormone auxin, found in plant cells furthest from the light, reacts to light stimulus by causing asymmetric growth on that side of the plant, causing it to tilt towards the Sun (Atamian et al., 2016).

Solar tracking, or heliotropism, is a more dynamic form of phototropism where a plant responds to the changing signal of the Sun as it moves throughout the day, rather than to a static external light source. It returns to a neutral position or closes during the night in preparation for the next day's journey. Once a flower has matured, it ceases to follow the Sun and usually – but not always – continues to face east (Atamian et al., 2016; Kutschera and Briggs, 2016).

As the sunflower illustrates, some plants are able to move faster than others in responding to what they 'see'. But ambulatory organisms need to see and respond much more quickly, and thus the story of evolution contains a fascinating thread about how species developed eyes (and other sensory mechanisms) enabling them to see and respond to light immediately. Palaeobiologist Glenn Brock's work on the 'explosion' of life in the Cambrian era is just such a story.

In the Cambrian light . . .

Glenn A. Brock

> The glorious lamp of heaven, the radiant sun,
> Is Nature's eye
>
> (John Dryden, 'From the Thirteenth Book of Ovid's Metamorphoses', 1779: 129)

Light from Dryden's 'radiant sun' has shaped the evolution of life on this planet for more than 3.7 billion years. The origin and subsequent evolution of photosynthesis, the fundamental process by which light energy from the Sun is harnessed by microbial cellular machinery and synthesised into food (sugars) from carbon dioxide, releasing oxygen as a waste product, has largely been responsible for the blossoming of the biosphere (Blankenship, 2010). The preservation of fossilised stromatolites, the laminated, domical and conical constructions of photosynthesising cyanobacteria in the oldest sedimentary rocks on the Earth, is an incredible testament to the importance of radiant light energy on life processes. The fact that c.99 per cent of all primary productivity and storage available for consumption by organisms occurs within the 'photic zone' – the upper 200 metres of the oceans through which light can effectively penetrate – illustrates just how intimately organisms rely on light. The dominance and diversity of these microbial mountains (some built kilometre-sized reef structures) produced the oxygen that saturated the oceans, and then the atmosphere which eventually enabled more complex multicellular life to prosper.

The exuberant evolutionary 'explosion' of animals during the Cambrian Radiation, over half a billion years ago, is a case in point. This was undoubtedly one of the most significant events in Earth history. The ancestors of nearly all animal groups (which we call phyla) that dominate the biosphere today have roots in the Cambrian period, and the novel body plans that emerged during this interval eventually resulted in the construction of the first animal-dominated marine ecosystems. Some of the morphological features established during this astonishing evolutionary milieu included well-developed neural systems, an incredible diversity of biomineralised hard parts, burrowers with flexible, contractile musculature and swift, manoeuvrable free-swimming predators with specialised appendages that could capture, crush and shred prey with tooth-rimmed jaws. All are interconnected, part of a complex evolutionary mosaic, and light plays a central role in explaining how such diverse connections transpired.

Perhaps the most extraordinary anatomical novelty that evolved during the early Cambrian are the first 'eyes'. For the first time in geological history, organisms developed specialised anatomical features that could effectively harness, focus and direct light in order to perceive the watery world around them. Andrew Parker developed the 'light switch theory':

> The initial introduction of vision to the behavioural system of animals caused the Cambrian explosion. Vision was introduced with the evolution of the very first eye, capable of producing visual images, which took place around 521 Ma.
>
> (2011: 327)

The first complex eyes were the compound eyes of trilobites. These consisted of multiple closely packed lenses (ommatidia) made of longitudinally arranged calcite crystals located on the anterior part of the head, sometimes as large crescentic or bulbous turrets. They produced well-resolved images of the surrounding environment and the organisms sharing these early shallow marine environments. The ability to focus light to form an image led directly to major changes in animal behaviour, feeding and mobility, and the evolution of the visual system and the associated neural machinery to process the light stimuli evolved extremely rapidly in arthropods.

(continued)

(continued)

For instance, in 2011, my colleagues and I found large (2–3 cm) isolated, flattened but beautifully preserved compound eyes in the 515-million-year-old Emu Bay Shale on Kangaroo Island, South Australia. The individual lenses are superbly preserved, and the size of the eyes suggested they could be confidently assigned to *Anomalocaris* (Order Radiodonta), the largest predatory arthropod known from Cambrian seas (Paterson et al., 2011). These eyes are remarkable because the number of lenses exceeds 16,000 on the exposed surface (and possibly double this number if more lenses are hidden on the unexposed surface). The size of the visual field, and the number and arrangement of the lenses suggest that this animal had extremely acute vision that, in combination with multiple swimming flaps and large, menacing frontal appendages, would have made it a very effective predator in early Cambrian oceans. Indeed, recent evidence reviewed by Strausfeld et al. (2016) strongly indicates that the evolution of the four different types of arthropod eyes can be traced back to the ground pattern represented in the Radiodonta.

Along with the beautifully preserved compound eyes in *Anomalocaris*, the fossil record has also revealed, with astounding clarity, the neural cortex of a number of early Cambrian arthropods (see Ma et al., 2012; Cong et al., 2014). For example, Cambrian brains in arthropods from the famous Chengjiang fossil deposit in South West China provide the first direct evidence for how the nervous system actually 'enervated' the segments of head and connected to the eyes.

The rise of visual predators in shallow, warm, well-lit marine waters led prey to respond with a cascade of evolutionary responses to avoid being devoured. Ornate suits of biomineralised armour – in a variety of forms – were developed by a range of phyla (many fixed sessile filer feeders or slow-grazing herbivores) that had no other means of escape. Some worm-like forms also developed armour, but many remained soft-bodied, evolving contractile muscles along the length of the body that allowed them to burrow vertically, seeking sanctuary in the soft substrate. Other animals developed specialised appendages or body plans that allowed them to swim swiftly or change direction rapidly as a means of escape. This evolutionary and ecological escalation is at the heart of the Cambrian explosion and the implications are potentially profound – there is now a real prospect that we will be able to chart the evolutionary fate of individual character traits, including labile tissues such as brains.

I remember traversing a high unexplored ridge in the Holyoake Range, in the central Transantarctic Mountains in 2011. Our small team was having a fruitless morning searching for signs of ancient life in Cambrian limestones laid down 510 million years ago as carbonate sediments in warm, tropical seas near the equator. Because of the slow tectonic dance that followed, these rocks are now within 6 degrees of the South Pole. Most of the team kept searching along the ridge, and they were getting frustrated with the lack of finds. I had found a thin layer of limestone containing a few tiny fragments of fossil, so I stayed behind to spend more time cracking open the rock. I was alone. The silence was overpowering: no hum of insects; no bird calls; no water flowing. The sunlight bounced off the ice. The crack of the hammer on rock sounded like a gun shot. And then, with one strike, the rock fell open like a page from archive Earth to reveal the pristine head of a trilobite. Its eyes stared back from deep time.

Literally, reflectively and philosophically, light is indeed 'Nature's Eye' and one of the main drivers of animal evolution.

Figure 5 The trilobite Redlichia takooensis from the lower Cambrian Emu Bay Shale, Kangaroo Island. The large crescentic shaped eyes on the cephalon (head) are among the earliest visual systems on Earth. Photograph: © David Mathieson. Specimen from the collections of the South Australian Museum. Scale bar = 3 cm.

Light and the evolution of vision

A conversation with Rob Barton

Joanna Puckering

Evolutionary anthropologist Rob Barton has a keen interest in the evolutionary effects of light. This leads back to a more fundamental question about what may have caused the diversification of our close primate relatives as they developed many specific physical characteristics, and a range of social behaviours, in different ecological niches. As he says, the senses are central, 'and one of the very fundamental ecological factors in primate evolution has been the transition between a nocturnal and a diurnal way of life'.

Among mammals, primates have the most elaborate and sophisticated visual systems, and the transition to a diurnal way of life has been a key driver in this evolutionary and cognitive development. Primates are the only mammals that typically have trichromatic colour vision. Three kinds of cone cell in the retina enable the animal to make more colour-based distinctions. Colour has therefore become an important cue for primates, including humans, and is used in various forms of display. It is trichromatic colour vision, for example, which enables the distinction between red and green.

However, colour cues can only be used in daylight, and animals that are specialised for a diurnal way of life will often need to find a safe refuge at night, perhaps up a tree or in a cliff, and that is when they sleep. Nocturnal species tend not to have colour vision, but there are also cathemeral species, including some species of lemur, which are irregularly active during the day or night and can forage at any time. They have some adaptations for diurnal vision, some for nocturnal vision, and some for half-way between, which enables greater activity at dawn and dusk.

'Seeing red' – colour and perceived dominance in sport

Barton's research into the colour red has been expanding, particularly in relation to perceptions of dominance in sport: 'It started as a conversation over coffee [with a colleague] just over ten years ago'. Emerging from this conversation was the recognition that in many species of anthropoid primate – a group including humans and apes, as well as Old and New World monkeys – and in some bird species, the colour red seems to be used in male–male competition as a badge of status. This is particularly apparent in patches of red skin produced by oxygenated blood coming near to the surface of the skin through the blood vessels. It is also possible to elicit a response to artificial colour stimuli. For example, placing a red leg band onto a male zebra finch in an aviary makes it more dominant.

> With Russell Hill, another anthropologist, Barton decided to look for a similar psychological effect in humans. The Olympic Games provided an opportunity to test their idea experimentally, using combat sports in which individuals are randomly assigned to wear either red or blue. Data were collected from the 2004 Olympic Games, and analysed for colour bias in the outcomes of matches. 'Much to our surprise', said Barton, 'there was an effect'. Results indicated a consistent and statistically significant advantage for contestants wearing red in matches between individuals of similar ability (Hill and Barton, 2005).
>
> While this and subsequent studies suggest that 'seeing red' has a strong psychological effect on how men react to perceived dominance in sport, it has been harder to demonstrate its effects with women. For example, Barton and his colleagues published a recent experimental study, asking people to rate colour stimuli in photographs of individuals for dominance and aggressiveness (Wiedemann et al., 2015). Only men perceived red as a signal for dominance. However, a similar effect has yet to be found on sporting outcomes involving women.

Tim Edensor (pers. comm.) draws attention to the critical relationship between vision and interpretation:

> Humans see *with* light by combining the specific optical equipment we possess, the ways in which the light reflects, deflects or is absorbed by the elements of the material environment, and the ways in which prevailing cultural values influence how we direct our vision and make sense of what we see. As with all animals, the entanglement of light and perception foregrounds the dynamic interaction between the external and internal. Thus vision is facilitated when the eye's convex lens focuses light to produce an inverted image of a scene on the retina. The iris expands and contracts in controlling the amount of light admitted. The image is sent via the optic nerve to the brain, which processes this information. The two kinds of light-sensitive receptors on the retina, cones and rods, respond to different wavelengths of light, with cones functioning in normal levels of (day)light allowing the experience of a colour spectrum, and rods operating when there are low levels of light. But crucially, we always interpret what we see – in the case that Barton discusses, the colour red – in accordance with psychological and cultural dispositions.

Other animals have evolved eyes that see light and colour in accord with their particular needs for reproduction and predation. The latter takes many forms: false attraction (angel fish), traps (spiders), and camouflage (many fish and amphibians); but one of the most critical divisions between predators and preyed upon is the former's enhanced capacity to see in the dark. It is here that the great cats excel: one of the few species to hunt humans, their eyes are designed to make use of minimal levels of light and to discern the tiniest of movements.

Light is not merely a matter of life and death in the longer term of biological evolution, but a critical factor in a shorter timetable of cultural evolution, in which, with limited abilities to produce illumination throughout their early history, humans had every reason to be afraid of the dark. There was the safety of the campfire and the danger of moving beyond its pool of light into the darkness, where predators could lurk unseen. This brings us to one of the major cross-cutting themes of this book, as it becomes plain that the dualism of light and dark, safety and danger, is ever-present in ideas about what lighthouses do and what they mean.

ON THE EDGE OF THE DARK

Veronica Strang

The potential for lighthouses to encapsulate ideas about light and dark as a matter of life and death is compounded by another major dualism: their position at the edge of safe and solid land where it meets the dark, formless deep (Bachelard, 1983; Strang, 2004). The location of the lighthouse between land and sea places it at the boundaries between light and dark and life and death, actively defying the latter with its beam of light. The sea – the fluid realm with its dark underworld – is depicted in multiple origin myths as the stuff of primeval chaos (a word which derives from the Greek *khaos* (abyss)). It is the Great Sink into which material corporality dissolves; the final stage in the life journey of the river. There are resonances too with multiple religious narratives that describe death as a descent into dark underworlds involving a loss of embodied form, of memory and the self, with spiritual enlightenment offering the only hope of a 'return to the light' and – in some cases – reincarnation into material form. The lighthouse is a sentry that defies the chaos of death, a concrete material bastion against fluidity, against dissolution into non-material being.

Philosophers Michael Levine and William Taylor (2016) note Clifford Geertz's anthropological observation that:

> [Man] can adapt himself somehow to anything his imagination can cope with; but he cannot deal with Chaos. Because his characteristic function and highest asset is conception, his greatest fright is to meet what he cannot construe.
> (Geertz, 1973: 99)

The sturdy lighthouse, hewn out of and sometimes built deep into the rock at the edge of chaos, brings into focus the contrast between material and non-material states of being. As Levine and Taylor (2016) later added (in discussing disaster movies), dissolution into chaos is often signified by the destruction or collapse of the certain materiality of buildings: '"Catastrophe" and disaster are emblematic of darkness. They "put out the light" so to speak. The "disorders" ingredient in catastrophe may be seen as metaphors for disintegration, darkness, change, and transformation.'

This highlights the role of lighthouses as part of the essential infrastructure that maintains both material and social order. Anthropologists Penny Harvey and

Hannah Knox's ethnographies of roads and power stations show how such order is literally 'made concrete' through such technologies (2010, 2012). Through this lens, the lighthouse can be seen both as a defender of practical navigational order, and as something that contributes to wider visions of social and moral order.

The notion of the sea as 'original' chaos, or at least uncontrolled formlessness, carries over into ideas about the mind, where it provides a metaphor of the unconscious Id with its deep, dark primal urges and waves of emotions which ebb and flow, and sometimes overwhelm. The solidity of the lighthouse is a powerful counter-statement of security, and its beam of light provides a beacon across the dark waves: an image of consciousness, reason, rationality and 'enlightenment'. Yet at the same time, it is ambiguous: the Id is also a creative urge, and the sea, the deep, is not merely darkness and chaos, it is also generative, a force through which life is renewed. Thus, the lighthouse also represents the other half of a hydrotheological cycle too, its beam lighting the way towards regeneration.

These are all powerful reasons for a universal recognition that light is a source of life. Societies over the ages have connected the rising of the Sun with the coming of life, have seen that sunlight and water are the most fundamental ingredients of all organic processes, and have worshipped or at least valorised light accordingly. There are concomitant associations between death and darkness, to the extent that the extinguishment of light often stands, symbolically, for the 'snuffing out' of life itself. Whether in spiritual or secular terms, light is a 'spark' that animates living beings, signalling a living, conscious, active presence: thus, like Dylan Thomas (2010), we 'rage, rage, against the dying of the light'.

Shine

The vision of the dark sea as a metaphor for the unconscious also highlights some important connections between ideas about life, light and animation. There is some intriguing work on the cross-cultural importance of 'shine', for example in the work of anthropologist Howard Morphy (1992, 1994). This highlights an understanding that the moment of death involves the loss of shining animation: the eye dulls, the skin greys. Fish that, in life, glitter with multicoloured shimmering scales turn dark and dull. A loss of 'shine' is also linked with ill health, which similarly involves a dulling of the eyes, the hair, and the skin. It is therefore logical that one of the recurring aesthetic themes to surface cross-culturally is an appreciation of shine as a signal of health and well-being – of 'liveliness'. Morphy describes how the sparkle of Aboriginal Central Desert dot paintings is believed to imbue them with the vitality of ancestral force (*bir'yan*); how the gleaming bodies of ritual participants in Papua New Guinea, greased with pig fat, and the glowing ochre colours of Nuba body art, are all reaching towards an idea of shining animation and health.

A celebration of light is also evident in multiple forms of art and architecture: in the gold bedecking Egyptian Pharoahs, in shining Celtic jewellery, in the gleaming domes of Islamic mosques. The glittering triptyches of the Early Church were made in three parts so that, when they were opened, the gold, shimmering in the candlelight, seemed startling and miraculous. And, as historian Fokko Jan Dijksterhuis observes, the animation of light is also well celebrated in Western art (see also Dijksterhuis, 2004).

Lighting space

Fokko Jan Dijksterhuis

Light does not travel in straight lines. In general, light rays bend according to the atmosphere's varying density. As the experience of the Dutch expedition in 1574 showed (pp. 6–7), in special circumstances, rays of light can be reflected and inverted around the Earth's surface. But light sources make their presence known primarily through the diffusion of light caused by its scattering in the atmosphere. Light is simply everywhere.

Figure 6 Waves emanating from a candle, taken from Huygens' *Traité de la Lumière*, 1690.

Natural scientists have had to work hard to explain this everyday experience. The first to do so was Christiaan Huygens (1629–1695), and to do so he had to break radically with the primacy of the concept of the light ray in optics, which had held sway since antiquity. In *Traité de la Lumière* (1690) Huygens argued that light consisted of waves propagating through the ether. He envisaged innumerable tiny wavelets which produced visible light when they converged according to exact rules. Thus, in his terms, a ray of light was no longer the essence of light, but merely the property of light waves and their direction of propagation. This might be straight, but could also be oblique or curved. It all depended upon the circumstances, which were determined by the state of the medium traversed by the light waves. His contemporary Newton resisted Huygens' idea that

(continued)

> *(continued)*
>
> waves could bend around corners. But the straight rays Newton preferred make it difficult to explain other things (such as the Sun's shimmering in the morning). Huygens recognised that space is filled with light, and that every point of a medium is a source of wavelets of light.
>
> A contemporary of Huygens expressed the idea of space filled with light through completely different means. Rembrandt van Rijn (1606/7–1669) wanted to create images exclusively with natural light. There was no random illumination, no divine light; in his pictures, the source of light can be identified and its spatial effects reconstructed. Rembrandt was a master in creating and depicting luminous effects. He didn't make things easy, for he preferred scarce and secluded light sources. Light enters a room, rebounds between objects, acquires tints and tones, colours surfaces. The whole scene participates in processes of illumination. Space is not an empty area between objects, but a luminous medium.
>
> Despite the conspicuous parallels between Huygens' and Rembrandt's understanding of light and space, and the proximity of their lives, there was no interaction between them. Huygens' father was a great admirer of Rembrandt and an early and important promoter. Huygens even copied a Rembrandt painting in his youth. But he managed to keep his artistic expertise separate from his scientific research.

This focus on the meaning of shine, and its powerful association with the spark of life, tells us something quite fundamental about the lighthouse beam shining across the sea. It says, in no uncertain terms, that 'we are here'; 'we are alive'; 'we are sentient'.

ATTRACTIVE AND REPULSIVE LIGHT

Veronica Strang

Humans are not alone in their appreciation of 'shine': many species, such as magpies and bower birds, have a penchant for bling. In the latter case, the male bower bird, having built his little love nest, seeks shiny things to scatter around it like jewellery to attract a mate. Some species, such as moths, are fatally attracted to light, as Tim Edensor observes later in exploring the impact of lighthouses on local wildlife.

But equally relevant in thinking about 'attractive light' is the range of species which use light not only to entice members of the opposite sex, but also to attract prey and confuse or warn off predators. David Attenborough's elegant synthesis of research on bioluminescence (2016a) provides a helpful summary. There are literally thousands of species in every group of organisms – approximately 50 different strands of evolution – that produce light for a variety of purposes. There are fungi that shine to attract insects that will distribute their spores; fish that capture and harvest luminescent bacteria so that the light will confuse predators; and millipedes that use chemicals to produce a glow that deters nocturnal hunters. Dinoflagellates, the largest single-celled marine organism, combine two chemicals to produce a flash of warning light when disturbed, providing what Attenborough describes as a 'burglar alarm' and ensuring that smaller predators, such as shrimps, will be revealed to the larger ones that prey on them. Marine biologists Margo Haygood and Bradley Tebo provide some deeper insights into marine light signallers, with some obvious echoes in the various purposes of lighthouses.

Biological lighthouses

Margo Haygood and Bradley Tebo

Light from the Sun, absorbed by plants, is the major source of energy for life on Earth. However, some organisms are capable of producing light themselves. Light produced biologically is based on chemical reactions. The energy available is never sufficient for biological light to be as strong

(continued)

(continued)

as sunlight, so such bioluminescence is only visible, and thus useful, in the dark. At the Earth's surface the darkest conditions occur at night when the Moon is not present in the sky. Bioluminescence is a minor phenomenon at the Earth's surface, and only a few organisms on land rely upon it, though they produce light with a wide range of colours.

But the major part of the ocean's volume is perpetually dark: it is the dark biosphere. Here bioluminescence comes into its own as a major mode of interaction among organisms. Because water absorbs all colours except blue-green, almost all bioluminescent sea creatures emit a single blue-green colour. The open ocean is a world without hiding places. At the top of the dark biosphere is the twilight zone, a region where very dim sunlight penetrates during the daytime. Here predators hunt by looking upward, seeking the shadow produced by their prey. Many prey creatures defend themselves by producing light emitted from the underside of their bodies to match the

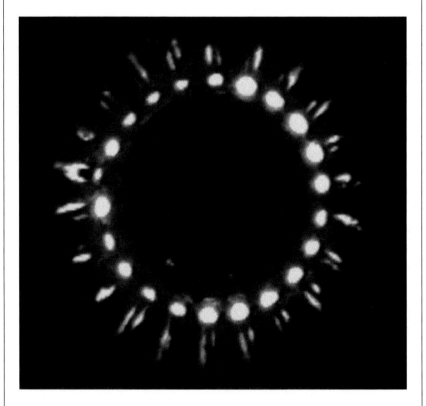

Figure 7 Bioluminescent jellyfish. Credit: National Oceanic and Atmospheric Administration's National Ocean Service, CC BY 2.0 (https:// creativecommons.org/licenses/by/2.0/).

Also see Plate 1.

downwelling light, to cause them to disappear. This strategy is known as counterillumination, and is similar to the camouflage colouring used by animals on land. This common strategy uses bioluminescence as a form of defence. Another form of defence, used by deepwater shrimps, is a flash or cloud of light that startles and blinds the predator, allowing the prey to escape. In some cases, the bioluminescence display functions as a 'burglar alarm'. When disturbed, the prey flashes brightly, attracting a larger predator to attack the enemy.

Bioluminescence is also used offensively by predators in the deep ocean. A well-known example is the deep-sea anglerfish, which has a specialised spine on its forehead which dangles a bioluminescent lure in front of its enormous toothy mouth. Some kinds of deep-sea fish produce light from organs just below their eyes, which may allow them to see their prey when hunting. Remarkably, some of these fish emit red light that is invisible except to themselves. Deep-sea fish lack photoreceptors sensitive to red light, since all red light is absorbed near the ocean surface. But these red-emitting fish have red-sensing photoreceptors that enable them to see the light reflected from nearby prey.

Bioluminescence is used for communication in the ocean just as it is by fireflies on land. Displays, in the form of small puffs of bioluminescent material released sequentially as the animal moves upward, are used by small crustaceans called ostracods to attract mates around coral reefs. Ponyfishes have an internal light organ, and the males have a transparent window on their sides that allows them to flash light to attract mates.

Most bioluminescent animals make light themselves, using enzyme catalysts they produce and chemicals they make or obtain from their diet. A few, such as the anglerfishes and ponyfishes, have bioluminescent bacterial partners that they cultivate in special organs to provide their light. In all these cases, this light production comes at an energetic cost to the organisms: producing light requires a lot of metabolic energy. However, the evolutionary advantages of light production explain why most organisms in the dark oceanic biosphere are bioluminescent.

Like lighthouses, constructed to ensure the safety and survival of seafarers, the main function of biological light is to aid the ability of bioluminescent organisms to survive. However, in the latter case it is clear that the uses of bioluminescence extend far beyond a simple signalling function, enabling organisms to locate food, find a partner, and to employ light as a defence mechanism.

Research located in areas such as biology and animal behaviour demonstrates that there is a huge range of animals doing 'lighthouse' kinds of things with light: employing light as a homing device; to warn each other of danger; to warn others off; or even, like 'wreckers', using light to confuse others.

Wreckers represent the application of human ingenuity to the use of false lights, with the positive functions of lighthouses subverted to prey on hapless mariners. Romantic tales about such activities, particularly in the 18th and 19th centuries, in Scotland and Cornwall are famously depicted in the novels of Robert Louis Stevenson and Daphne du Maurier. Historian Bella Bathurst records stories about local opposition to the building of the Stevenson family's lighthouses, and opportunistic 'salvaging' that was more like piracy: 'There were stories of false lights and false foghorns, false harbours, false rescuers, false dawns; even stories of entire coastlines rigged meticulously as stage sets' (2005: xv). Similar stories are recounted in Florida and the Bahamas (Wilkinson, nd), and in both the UK and the USA the 1800s brought extensive legislation against wrecking, suggesting that the use of false lights was at least perceived to be a genuine problem. While such stories may have been largely mythical, their recurrence suggests an underlying anxiety about disingenuous uses of light.

By placing historical narratives alongside other disciplinary perspectives on uses of light, it becomes possible to locate human light signalling in a shared evolutionary context with a host of other 'light signallers' who use the languages of light to communicate with each other for a variety of friendly or unfriendly purposes. Lighthouses are thus revealed as an expression of impulses that are both human and animal, with deep roots in shared evolutionary engagements with light.

Synchronies of light

A particularly pertinent example is provided by fireflies which, as Joanna Puckering observes below, are readily described, with their steady blinking signals, as 'the lighthouses of the insect world'. Like individual lighthouses, each local subspecies has its own particular code or dialect of flashes, as David Attenborough (2016a) puts it, 'rather like Morse code'. This evidence of patterned communication connects with two key points about lighthouses: that their particular codes serve to identify them, and that the regular patterns through which they signal distinguish them from random lights and are readily discerned as intentional communication. As Puckering points out, it was this assumed tie between regularity and conscious intentionality that led to widespread excitement about the pulsars discovered by astrophysicist Jocelyn Bell Burnell in the 1960s, and to their labelling as 'the lighthouses of outer space'. Fellow astrophysicists Ulisses Barres de Almeida and Martin Ward describe how this came about.

Cosmic signallers

Ulisses Barres de Almeida and Martin Ward

Lighthouses are designed to act as benevolent signallers. Strategically positioned along Earth's coastlines, for centuries they have guided sailors, indicating the path of their vessels and marking out their intended destinations.

The cosmic analogue of a lighthouse is the pulsar, discovered in 1967 by a graduate student at Cambridge University, Jocelyn Bell Burnell. Like other notable discoveries in astrophysics, such as the cosmic microwave background (the echo of the Big Bang), the discovery of pulsars was serendipitous, because the radio telescope used to detect them was designed to look for something else.

Notably, for a short interval immediately after their discovery, they were called 'LGM', the acronym for Little Green Men, because of their regular clock-like radio signal. Other signals from cosmic radio sources were either constant or randomly variable in strength, so it seemed plausible that some intelligent life form must be responsible. However, a more prosaic explanation for their regular pulses was soon proposed. We now accept that they are generated following the gravitational collapse of their giant star progenitors, when the dense remnants explode to create a luminous, multicoloured gas cloud that expands into interstellar space at speeds of thousands of kilometres per second. This expelled gas forms the beautiful nebulae that modern astronomers call 'supernovae remnants', and whose birth has been witnessed throughout human history, for example by the Chinese in 1054, by Kepler in 1604, and recently with the famous supernovae SN1987A, whose neutrino emission was the basis for the Nobel prize-winning work awarded in 2015 to T. Kajita.

The collapsed remnant left at the centre of the glowing gas cloud is a compact object composed of neutrons. This 'neutron star' marks one of the endpoints of stellar evolution. Compressed during its collapse to a sphere of little more than a few tens of kilometres in radius, this object contracts like a figure skater curling arms and body to spin faster and faster on the ice, sometimes completing several thousand turns every second and, in the process, signalling its presence.

When matter is compressed during the star's collapse, the magnetic field embedded within it is concentrated to an extreme degree. From the star's magnetic poles a beam of charged particles emerges, radiating light in a powerful stream across the electromagnetic spectrum, from long wavelength radio to the shortest wavelength gamma-rays. These are relatively narrow beams, and unless by some incredibly unlikely coincidence an observer was aligned precisely along this axis of rotation, then the beam of light from one or other pole will appear only briefly, once every rotation. The metaphor of pulsars as 'cosmic lighthouses' is thus very apt.

Pulsars are now used to study aspects of fundamental physics. A key recent event was the announcement, in February 2016, of the direct detection of gravitational waves. However, back in 1974 two astronomers, Joe Taylor and Russell Hulse, used observations of the super-accurate clock defined by the signals emitted from the 'double pulsar' to prove a fundamental prediction of the theory of gravity: that gravitational waves carry away energy, and thus the pulsar clock should slow down.

(continued)

(continued)

Figure 8 Spinning pulsar – the 'cosmic lighthouse'. Credit: NASA.
Also see Plate 2.

A message to the cosmos

When Neil Armstrong and Buzz Aldrin landed the Apollo module 'Eagle' on the surface of the Moon in 1969, they marked a new era in terms of human efforts to explore the cosmos. In the following decades, space missions visited or approached every planet in the solar system and many of its most prominent minor bodies and moons. Today there is renewed interest in a mission to Mars. With much less fanfare than the Moon landing, but with comparable importance, another fundamental border was crossed in 2012, when the *Voyager I* spacecraft, launched some 36 years before, after a journey of 18 billion kilometres, finally crossed the heliopause, the magnetic and plasma barrier which defines the boundary between Earth's solar system and the rest of the Galaxy. Entering the realm of interstellar space, it reminds us that the ships we send into space must also navigate the unknown, guided by signals communicating from afar. Thus, the *Voyager* spacecraft carried equipment essential to the mission's success: a parabolic antenna for communication with Earth; a battery powered by plutonium with a radioactive half-life of about 40 years, to generate energy; twelve scientific instruments, and finally a golden disc – a message to the cosmos from humankind.

In about 2020, the lack of power will gradually shut down all of *Voyager*'s instruments, but it will continue to drift across interstellar space carrying this golden record of images, sounds, greetings and music from Earth, accessible to any form of life sufficiently evolved to have the technological equivalent of a gramophone. There is no planned destination, it is simply 'a message in a bottle'. On the cover of the disc, the mission designers inscribed basic information explaining how the message embedded in the disc could be decoded, as well as offering a schematic depiction of a man and a woman. And they drew a map locating Earth within the Galaxy, using its pulsars as 'cosmic lighthouses'.

Like lighthouses on Earth, which can be identified by the frequency of their light beams, each pulsar is individually recognisable by its particular spin rate. Pulsars are the most accurate clocks in the cosmos, maintaining the same rate of spin over millions of years. So, with a measurement of its rate of flashes, any cosmic lighthouse can be singled out from all the others in the Galaxy. This is how scientists in the Voyager programme created a 'cosmic map'. Earth is at the centre from which fifteen lines of different lengths emerge, each leading to a pulsar. However, the lengths of the lines do not represent distances: instead they define the pulsar's identity, its fingerprint spinning rate. The angle between the lines shows the relative direction of each pulsar from the Earth. Thus, by locating these fifteen unique cosmic lighthouses, and by reading their repeating, monotonous signals, an intelligent extraterrestrial being would be able to find the Earth. So, the *Voyager*'s 'message in a bottle' not only communicates much about humans, it shows LGM where to find them.

Cosmic navigation

Pulsars are the basis of the most successfully theorised Galactic navigating system beyond the frontiers of the solar system. Earth-bound techniques using radio-wave receptors have their limitations, and a spaceship needs to be able to track its position autonomously, relative to a known referent, without having to rely on Earth-bound systems. Scattered throughout the Galaxy, pulsars' unique spinning rates potentially provide the cosmic reference points needed to navigate in space.

The idea of using pulsars in navigation systems emerged when these objects were discovered in the 1960s, but it is only recently that it has seemed feasible to implement such a cosmic navigating system. Such a system would use the pulsars' signals like a GPS system, in which simultaneous measurements of the pulse of a few (at least three) pulsars would enable the triangulation of the spacecraft's position. Such a technique substitutes the mathematical tables carried onboard ships with a matrix of pulsar profiles, which, like the signals from terrestrial lighthouses, can be compared and recognised.

(continued)

(continued)

In 2001, a German astrophysicist, Werner Becker and his collaborators, proposed making such an interstellar GPS system feasible by using the X-ray emission component of the pulsing beams emitted from pulsars, as the use of the better-known radio component would require antennae too large to be feasible (Becker et al., 2015). Initial calculations suggest that this technique will vastly improve the precision of current space navigation, as well as extending it to virtually anywhere in the Galaxy. If these new ideas become a reality, cosmic lighthouses could guide future human missions to the distant reaches of outer space.

Returning to Earth, and to the smallest of lighthouses, Kevin Flynn reminds us that microscopic plankton (c.1 mm and smaller) light up the sea when they are disturbed. Such organisms represent a danger to the security of otherwise stealthy nuclear-powered submarines, because collectively (like millions of microscopic lighthouses) they illuminate the passing vessel in the darkness.

Fireflies also highlight the intriguing matter of synchronicity: there are times when they all blink in harmony, creating collective pulses of light. Joanna Puckering's conversation with ethnomusicologist Martin Clayton provides some insights into this tendency to synchronise which – as anyone who has attended a large concert will know – is very much shared by humans, who easily fall into clapping in rhythm or waving candles in firefly-like unison. From an anthropological perspective, this resonates readily with many cultural rituals involving light, sound and rhythm, which have much to do with bringing individuals into harmony with their communities and forging a collective sense of identity.

Lighthouses of the insect world

Joanna Puckering

John Ruskin had a lifelong fascination with fireflies that was frequently reflected in his work. He once wrote to his mother from Siena: 'Last night the air was quite calm, the stars burning like torches all over the sky, the fireflies flying all about, literally brighter than the stars' (Ruskin, 1870: liii). Such a fascination with, and affection for, real and metaphorical fireflies has appeared in many forms and in many cultures over the years, in science, literature, art and poetry.

Fireflies – actually a type of winged beetle – are part of the group known as photophores: bioluminescent animals with a light-emitting organ. Their light is produced through a chemical reaction whose components are named after Lucifer, the fallen angel of light. A combination of luciferin (the fuel) and luciferase (an enzyme which triggers the bioluminescent reaction) mixes with different levels of oxygen to start and end the light emission.

The scientific classification for fireflies is *Lampyridae*, which means 'torchbearer' (Turpin, 2009); but they could equally well be described as the lighthouses of the insect world. There are approximately two thousand subspecies of firefly, and they are not merely composed of individual insect lighthouses emitting regular blinks of light. Each of these subspecies has a collective species-specific pattern of light flashes that creates beautiful rhythmic group displays. It is this astonishing example of synchronicity and entrainment that most intrigues the scientific world.

Entrainment occurs when rhythmic physiological or internal behaviours – mechanical or biological – become synchronised with a regular external stimulus. As well as developing theories about the properties of light, physicist Christiaan Huygens observed that the rhythm of pendulum clocks synchronises when they are placed on a common support: the same effect can be achieved with a pair of metronomes (Clayton, 2016). A frequently cited biological example is the entrainment of circadian rhythms to the daily light–dark cycle in an evolutionary 'rhythm of life' shared by the majority of living beings (Ball, 2016). Fireflies offer another example: each one is capable of producing an independent, regular pulse of light, while also being influenced by the signals from others, resulting in large clouds of fireflies flashing in unison (Clayton, 2016).

Lighthouses and fireflies often feature together, or with related metaphors, in both science and literature. One of the earliest written references to fireflies is contained in the *Shih Ching* or *Book of Odes* (c.1500–1000 BC; Karlgren, 1950), and Longfellow (1855: 41–42) paints a lyrical picture in *Hiawatha*: 'Little, flitting, white-fire insect; little, dancing, white-fire creature'. Ruskin was more ambivalent in his views: depending on his mood, fireflies were regarded with either 'foreboding or delight', either infernal or angelic in their intensity (Arrowsmith, 1982: 202). The English physicist and astronomer, Sir James Jeans, commonly used metaphors in his work to reach popular audiences: 'In comparing the different luminosities of stars, for instance, if the Sun is a candle, the faintest stars are fireflies, the brightest is a lighthouse' (cited in Whiting, 2011: 234).

Such cosmological analogies have retained their currency, and are regularly employed by the scientists working with NASA in the search for exoplanets beyond our own system. NASA's Kepler Mission, designed to survey our region of the Milky Way, has confirmed the existence of over 1,200 new exoplanets since July 2015. This achievement has been described as 'the single largest finding of planets to date' (NASA, 2016: np). Ironically, it is the very presence of light in space that impedes this search, because the light that is reflected from planets that are orbiting other stars is so much dimmer than that of direct starlight. As one scientist observed, it is like 'trying to distinguish a firefly next to a lighthouse' (NASA, 2008: np).

The search for exoplanets often focuses on their potential to support life, which reminds us that Jocelyn Bell Burnell's discovery of the first pulsar in

(continued)

(continued)

1967 gave rise to much public and media speculation about the possibility of extraterrestrial intelligence, based on an assumed association between signal regularity and intelligence (Bell Burnell, 2011). While assumptions of agency, intelligence and communication could not be met in the case of pulsars, the same sorts of questions often arise in discussions about the synchronicity of fireflies, which have been paradoxically described as 'autonomous agents . . . that flash together' (Clayton et al., 2013: 19).

But what is meant by agency in relation to human and non-human entrainment and synchronicity? In his work on musical entrainment, Martin Clayton explains that for individual things to entrain, they must first be self-sustaining: each must have their own internal rhythm and energy source, and then they may interact and synchronise. However, he notes that Huygens' pendulums offer a very simple example of entrainment with no more than a mechanical connection, a vibration being passed between the individual devices. This differs from the complex intentions and interactions that exist between individual people, or even fireflies, as they bring multiple sources of rhythm together into synchronous coordination.

Scientific descriptions of firefly behaviour often convey a sense of wonder that extends beyond the idea of synchrony as a mechanistic stimulus response. Clearly such collective regularity in the emission of light captures the imagination of scientists as much as it does for authors, philosophers and poets. In a television documentary, Sir David Attenborough talks about the idea of 'living light' and the technological advances that enable new ways of exploring how and why bioluminescence is created. The 'flash code' that is unique to each subspecies of firefly, formed from a combination of flash signal and flight pattern, is described as a conversation in which we can participate, by responding with artificial lights of our own. Translating the glow of fireflies into a 'language of light' is extended to include what Attenborough calls 'local dialects': a preferred time of evening or night for fireflies to glow, and locations that show light flashes to the best advantage (Attenborough, 2016b). These species-specific flash patterns also resonate with the 'character' of many lighthouses, which must also act as a unique identifier to communicate their location accurately.

And so, with this maritime comparison, we return to another evening walk, surrounded by the characteristic patterns of dancing fireflies: 'One hardly knows where one has got to between them, for the flies flash, as you know, exactly like the stars on the sea, and the impression to the eye is as if one was walking on water' (Ruskin, 1908: 562). Almost a century and a half after Ruskin wrote to his mother from Siena, these tiny lighthouses of the insect world continue to offer insights into the evolutionary mechanisms linking light, rhythm and synchronicity.

PHENOMENOLOGICAL LIGHT

Veronica Strang

The capacity of light and – especially rhythmic – movement to fascinate opens up some interesting questions about phenomenological experiences of light. As well as engendering a sense of *communitas*, rituals involving light often aim to induce an altered or transcendental state of being. This relates – no doubt recursively – to the religious meanings of light, which we explore shortly. But there are also some phenomenological issues which intersect with aesthetic and religious experiences and help to explain the special interest that lighthouses seem to elicit.

Ethnographic research focusing on human engagement with the material world regularly generates comments from informants about the 'mesmerising' or 'numinous' effect of light shimmering on water, and the similarly magnetic attraction of fire:

> It sort of mesmerises you doesn't it, looking at fire . . . I suppose fire and water are the basic elements of life.
> (Michael Rule quoted in Strang, 2004: 51)

> It's wonderful, then you start to get the breeze which just ripples the surface, and that's always changing . . . It's not dissimilar [to looking at a fire] . . . it certainly has a magic and a fascination.
> (Edward Dawson quoted in Strang, 2004: 103)

In developing the earlier discussion about uniquely human capacities for seeing with light, scientists have long recognised that the retinal cells of the eye are more sensitive to changing visual stimuli than they are to static objects, and that the eye is drawn particularly to flickering movement (Vernon, 1962; Schiffman, 1996). Specialists in art have similarly observed that shimmering and visually exciting patterns, such as those in the Central Desert Aboriginal art mentioned earlier, or in the Trobriand canoe paintings analysed by Alfred Gell (1992), can stimulate affective responses in many different cultural contexts.

With water or fire, or stimuli that in some way replicate their qualities, the eye is presented with a luminescent image it cannot 'hold'. Instead, it must simply absorb all of the rhythms of movement and the tiny shifts and changes. Water also 'creates' light: as Watt says, 'we do not see light; we see the world as it is revealed

38 *Phenomenological light*

by light . . . [Water] behaves like a light source' (1991: 3, 43). With an apt analogy to explain physiological responses to visual input, psychologist Magdalen Vernon provides a further clue as to why water may be mesmeric:

> The visual pattern that impinges on the brain is not static; it continually moves and flickers. The light and shade and colour of the pattern alter as the light reaching the eyes changes in colour and brightness . . . If we were conscious of this pattern, we should see something like shimmering lights reflected from moving water.
>
> (1962: 13–14)

Equally important in creating altered states of mind are water's acoustic effects: the trickling of moving water and the swash and backwash of waves, which clearly add to the appeal of lighthouses as objects of contemplation.

The combination of light and sound is now a standard part of therapies using hypnosis (Freitag, 2005), particularly in new treatments for attention deficit disorders (ADHD) (Micheletti, 1999) and to assist children with learning disabilities. And – suggesting that Vernon was onto something in pointing to resonances – it appears that synchronicity may be both a neurological and a social response. Neuroscientist Ruth Olmstead describes the therapeutic uses of light in entrainment:

> Auditory and visual stimulation (AVS) is a method of brain stimulation and brain wave 'entrainment' that is applied through the ears and eyes by means of headphones and specially designed glasses inset with white light-emitting diodes (LEDs). These lights flash at predetermined frequencies, and are coupled with tones that are received through headphones. The light emitting from the glasses and rate of the flickering affect the brain through the optic nerve, and cause the brainwaves to 'entrain' or match the rate of flickering to a desired frequency, depending on the preferred outcome. The external flicker of light at specific frequencies has been found to induce the brainwave activity to fall into specific frequencies by becoming entrained or synchronised.
>
> (2005: 51)

Ritual light

While neuroscience has revealed the mechanisms of entrainment, the historical ubiquity of rituals making use of light and sound suggests that human societies have long recognised the importance of affective responses to light. There are many and diverse historical and cultural examples. The Athenian torch race, one of several *lampadedromia*, ritually honoured Athena and the relighting of the sacred fire (Stewart, nd). Plato refers to the race (2012, I:328a) and, highlighting the inextricability of light and life, employs it as a metaphor for passing the torch of life from generation to generation (2008, 6:776b). For Judaism, light in the Holy of Holies not only signals the presence of Yahweh in the Ark of the Covenant, it is vital for Shabbat celebration and in preparing for Passover. Hanukkah, the 'Festival of Lights', involves the ritual lighting of a Hanukkiyah (a candelabra holding nine candles or oil containers). Memorial candles (yahrzeit) are crucial in the mourning period of Shiva, the seven days following a funeral, and on the anniversary of a death, as they are for the annual collective remembrance day of the Holocaust, Yom HaShoah, which has taken place since 1949 (Cohn-Sherbok, 2003).

Another Festival of Lights, Diwali (also known as Deepavali, 'lighting lamps'), is celebrated by Hindus, Sikhs and Jains, and although each religion adheres to its own mythological sources, it broadly celebrates the triumph of good over evil, and new beginnings. It is marked with firework displays and lanterns, and, in some instances, these are lit to pay tribute to Lakshmi, the goddess of wealth, and to guide her into people's homes.

There are many such rituals celebrating life or marking death in which light – whether as shimmering art or as a candle or lamp – is used to lead the participants to an altered state of being. Whether religious or secular, all are permeated by the meanings of light and by its capacity to elicit affective responses. For some people, this entails a spiritual experience and, for others, an uplifting aesthetic engagement with the beauty of light. And there is a physiological dimension too, which reminds us that heightened perception is not merely induced by religious practices. As any keen runner knows, physical exertion, and its capacity to produce a rush of endorphins, also rewards exercisers with a shift in visual perception that makes the world appear brighter and more colourful.

The apparently magical effects of light were certainly of interest to early scientists. Michael Hutchison observes that:

> Ancient scientists were fascinated by the phenomenon of flickering lights. Apuleius experimented in 125 A.D. with the flickering light produced by the rotation of a potter's wheel, finding that it could reveal a type of epilepsy. Ptolemy studied in 200 A.D. the phenomenon of the flickering generated by sunlight through the spokes of a spinning wheel. He noted that patterns and colors appeared in the eyes of the observer and that a feeling of euphoria could be experienced.
>
> (1990: 2)

Such scientists were also deeply interested in light itself. For example, an interdisciplinary team in Durham has been examining the work of medieval polymath Robert Grosseteste (c.1170–1253) (see McLeish, this volume). Grosseteste wrote treatises on light (*De luce*), on the rainbow (*De iride*) and the colour spectrum (*De colore*), and was the first to introduce the notion of refraction into an explanation of the physics of the rainbow (Dinkova Bruun et al., 2013; Smithson et al., 2014; Tanner et al., 2016). There were also early ventures into understanding visual perception, producing a belief that pertained for many centuries about the 'visual ray': an idea that, like the Sun or other light sources, the human eye emitted a light beam, much like a lighthouse. And this – as the later section on homologues reveals – serves beautifully to connect Ptolemaios of Alexandria (c.90–c.168) with The Spooky Men and their 'lightpole' (Morrison, 2004).

Visual rays

The light within the eye

Fokko Jan Dijksterhuis

The greatest astronomer of antiquity was Klaudios Ptolemaios (c.90–c.168) of Alexandria. His major work, the *Almagest*, collected astronomical knowledge from Babylonian times and transformed it into a comprehensive mathematical system of celestial motions that would remain authoritative well into the 17th century. Ptolemaios also contributed to the mathematical science of optics, the optical part of astronomy dealing with the analysis and reconstruction of visual observations. His optics built upon Euclid's *Optica* (3rd century BC) and formed the basis for Alhazen's 11th-century synthesis of optics (Smith, 2014).

At the heart of the optics of Ptolemaios is the concept of the 'visual ray', which suggested that visual perception is accomplished by rays of light emitted by the eyes. They touch objects illuminated by sources of light, such as the Sun or a candle. The idea of visual rays had a long ancestry even before it was articulated by Ptolemaios. Empedocles proposed it in the 5th century BC as part of his four elements theory; Plato adopted it in *Timaios*; and it may go back to the Pythagoreans. It remained the preferred concept among mathematicians well into the early modern period, and Alhazen harmonised it with the philosophical theory of intromission, giving the latter priority but maintaining the idea of the beam-like essence of light.

Plato (2015: 45b) described the origin of the visual ray as 'the pure fire that is within us . . . to flow through the eyes in a stream smooth and dense'. The notion of the 'fire within the eye' effectively conceptualises humans as having the characteristics of a lighthouse. The Pharos was part of Ptolemaios' everyday world: the world-famous lighthouse of Alexandria built in the 3rd century BC. A lighthouse, a distant light in the night, an artificial star that the human observer could detect and locate – for Ptolemaios, Pharos emitted a shaft of light that intersected with the beam coming from the human eye.

DIVINE RAYS

Veronica Strang

Figure 9 Imentet and Ra from the Tomb of Nefertari, 13th century BC. Courtesy of Wikimedia Commons.

42 Divine rays

The notion of the visual ray – a beam of light making the world discernible and emanating life-giving power – raises the vital question of causality. From whom or what did this power derive? For many ancient societies sun gods and goddesses provided a way of describing the creative power of light and the movements of celestial light sources. There is no shortage of examples: the Greek Helios (and then Apollo), the Persian/Iranian Mithras, the Aztec Huitzilopochtli, the Egyptian Amun-Ra, the Hittite Arinna, the Norse Sol (Sunna).

Of particular note are the ancient Egyptian gods Ra, the sun god (represented by an image of the Sun and solar rays) and Horus, god of the sky, generally depicted as a falcon whose right eye was the sun and his left eye the Moon. Some representations of Ra combine these images, to depict a falcon with the sun above its head. This sharp-eyed embodiment conveys two key ideas which have regularly recurred in religious belief systems: the notion of a major god as the creative, generative source of light and power; and – in accord with the idea of the visual ray – the assumption that this vast beaming divinity would also have omniscient powers 'to see'. The latter idea is equally evident in Hinduism (where it appears as the 'third eye' of Shiva) and Buddhism, in which the *Maha-parinibbana Sutta* refers to Buddha as the 'Eye of the World' (Koenderink, 2014).

There is a minefield of debate about the extent to which religions absorb and recycle the ideas and images of other belief systems. But this serves as a reminder that all human societies think *with* the material worlds they inhabit. There is thus a persistent logic between their symbolic representations and the things that provide the imaginative fodder for these representations. Thus, images of the sun as the generative source of vital light and life are never going to be passé.

Emile Durkheim's 'projection theory' is also useful here. This modern polymath, who combined sociology, psychology and philosophy, suggested that humans created gods in their own images but with magnified powers – in this instance magnified capacities for 'seeing' (Durkheim, 1912).

Certainly, images of the sun and emanating rays of light have a very prominent place in Christian rituals and material culture, as exemplified by the monstrance (an object or image depicting the sun) which situates God as the 'light of the world', and by images of the 'all-seeing' Eye of God. Murray et al. describe the latter:

> An equilateral triangle with a single eye inside it, and with rays emanating from it (rarely without them) is a symbol of the all-seeing Eye of God. Such a triangle is itself a symbol of the Holy Trinity, and usually also has rays emanating from it, for example in the lantern of the dome of San Carlo alle Quattro Fontane in Rome, or in Federico Zuccaro's *Angels Adoring the Trinity* in the Gesù, Rome. There are several Biblical references to the all-seeing Eye of God; in the Psalms (34:15 (VG. 33:16)): 'The eyes of the Lord are on the righteous' and similarly Prov. 15:3: 'The eyes of the Lord are in every place'.
>
> (2013: 196)

Figure 10 18th-century monstrance from Bemposta palace chapel, Portugal.
© José Luiz Bernardes Ribeiro, CC BY-SA 3.0 (https://creativecommons.org/licenses/by-sa/3.0/), via Wikimedia Commons.

The image of the all-seeing eye is best known today as the 'Eye of Providence' in the Great Seal of the United States (represented on the dollar bill) and as a masonic symbol which refers to an initiation ritual described by theologian Douglas Davies and anthropologist Joanna Puckering below (Chornenky, nd).

Enlightenment

This perspective offers the idea of the light beam as a representation of conscious and powerful surveillance (later discussed by Tim Edensor), which illuminates not only what a lighthouse does in practice, but how it is used to express ideas about social and religious 'watching'. Such surveillance is not invariably positive: the 'evil eye' has long been a powerful image in many cultural contexts, as have the 'good' eye motifs used in charms (*nazars*) to repel it. The evil eye attracted much interest in classical antiquity, and Plutarch's explanation is telling. It came about, he suggested, because the eyes were the source of the deadly rays that spring up like darts from within the recesses of the person possessing such

44 *Divine rays*

powers (Dickie, 1991). A more modern imagining appears in Tolkien's *The Lord of the Rings* (1955), in which the deadly Eye of Sauron's malevolent gaze rakes the landscape and blasts the goodness from it.

Primarily, however, the presence of a sentient deity is linked, through the image of the light beam, to positive notions of communication and the acquisition of wisdom, and the lighthouse, or beacon, has been used across time and space to express the idea of enlightenment and an enhanced capacity 'to see'. If we consider this as an affective response to the receiving of light, there is obvious resonance with some of the earlier conversation about sensory and phenomenological experiences of numinous light and its state-altering effects upon the person.

Figure 11 Hildegard of Bingen receiving the Light from Heaven, c.1151 (vellum) (later coloration), German School. Credit: Private Collection / Bridgeman Images.

Also see Plate 3.

A nice historical and theological example is offered by Saint Hildegard of Bingen (1098–1179), a German Benedictine Abbess. As well as delving into philosophy, writing and composing, Saint Hildegard is widely regarded as the founder of scientific natural history in Germany. From her childhood, though she did not disclose this till later, she received enlightening visions. As medical historian Katherine Foxhall observes, several scientists have suggested that these were caused by migraines, based on the similarity of her experiences and those of migraine sufferers (Foxhall, 2014). To Hildegard, however, the shafts of light were of heavenly origin:

> Heaven was opened and a fiery light of exceeding brilliance came and permeated my whole brain, and inflamed my whole heart and my whole breast, not like a burning but like a warming flame, as the sun warms anything its rays touch.
>
> (Griffin, 2005: 59)

The light imparted theological doctrine, which she communicated in a detailed set of treatises. These established a powerful image of penetrating and transforming light, which has since recurred in multiple images of enlightenment throughout many centuries, as a transmission of faith, hope and wisdom, and as a cleansing light scouring the body and mind of darkness and leading to moral purity and salvation. But as theologian and physicist David Wilkinson observes, symbols change as religions do.

Lighthouses in the Bible

Symbols of enlightenment and salvation

Joanna Puckering and David Wilkinson

In Media City, in Salford, stands The Lighthouse. Though rounded in form, it does not conform to how one might expect a church to look; nor is it where one would usually expect to find a lighthouse, being located in an industrial park. Since 2010, it has built a congregation of about five hundred people from over forty-five different nations. It is one of many churches throughout the world to adopt the name of The Lighthouse. The same name is used for various Christian counselling services, church holiday clubs, home schooling networks and deliverance ministries; it can also be found on numerous encouraging posters and cards: 'In the storm of your life, let Jesus be your lighthouse'.

What is fascinating about this phenomenon is why the lighthouse has become such a powerful religious symbol for so many people, when they

(continued)

(continued)

may know little about lighthouses themselves. There are key images even in the earlier parts of the Bible. Within the Jewish tradition, the people were led to the Promised Land by the glory of God in the form of a pillar of cloud by day and a pillar of fire by night (Exodus 13:21–22). The law was a 'light to guide the path' (Psalms 119:105) and, as Conzelmann suggests, 'Light is Yahweh in action' (1995: IX, 320).

In more recent iterations of Christianity, however, the beacon of light became more associated with Jesus. In the New Testament, and especially in John's Gospel, Jesus is described as 'the light of the world', and light appears as a strong motif throughout accounts of his life, death and resurrection. At the beginning of the Gospel, the context is cosmological, but later it becomes soteriological – connected to notions of salvation. In an echo from Genesis 1:3 ('Let there be light'), Jesus is described as the divine Word: 'In him was life, and that life was the light of all' (John 1:4). Thus, Jesus was a light in himself and the agent by which God bestowed life and light upon the world. The following verse, 'The light shines in the darkness and the darkness has not overcome it' (John 1:5), presents a dualistic universe in which light and darkness, good and evil, are equally matched, and creates the broader context within which Jesus makes his path through life, revealing not just the truth of God but also serving as the source of salvation.

The combination of light and salvation relates specifically to lighthouses. Lighthouses were little mentioned within the Christian scriptures, despite the famous presence of the Pharos Lighthouse, built in Alexandria Harbour in 290 BC. But since the 19th century – perhaps because of their more frequent presence in the landscape – lighthouses have become a dominant metaphor in expressions of popular spirituality, appearing in 19th-century hymnody, and stories of both salvation and disaster that were fused with scriptural images. Philip Bliss (1871) wrote a hymn (which remains popular with Methodists) following a shipwreck in Cleveland Harbour, 'caused by the extinguishing of the lower lights of a lighthouse during a storm' (Bradley, 2005: 170).

> Brightly beams our Father's mercy from His lighthouse evermore;
>
> But to us He gives the keeping of the lights along the shore.
>
> Let the lower lights be burning! Send a gleam across the wave!

Evangelists such as D. L. Moody use the hymn to talk about the Christian responsibility to bear witness to the good news of Jesus: to keep the light burning so that others are not destroyed by the rocks of sin. This vision of the lighthouse as an embodiment of the individual Christian giving light to others reflects the words of Jesus from the Sermon on the Mount: 'You are the light of the world' (Matthew 5:14). It is also present in the early

20th-century hymn, 'Standing like a lighthouse on the shores of time'. But, in the later part of the 20th century, the imagery of the lighthouse shifts to represent not the individual Christian but Jesus himself. This can be seen in 'Never fades the name of Jesus' by David Welander, a hymn included in the Salvation Army songbook (1953):

> In the night his dear name shineth
>
> Like a lighthouse evermore,
>
> Guiding lonely shipwrecked seamen
>
> Safely to salvation's shore.

These themes of Jesus as the light of creation and salvation overcoming the darkness, were subsequently reiterated in much Christian hymnody, liturgy and poetry, not least in the poetry of T. S. Eliot (Asciuto, 2015).

It is useful to conceive the lighthouse as a symbol rather than a physical structure: thus, if a church calls itself 'The Lighthouse', the image is not about coming in to find secret illumination but about wanting to shine for the whole world. The theme is about giving light to others, not by inviting them into our religious or physical structures but by saying that we are called upon to shine that light out. This resonates with the understanding that the light referred to in John's Gospel and throughout the New Testament is illumination for everyone. Thus, in the Sermon on the Mount (Matthew 5:14–16), Jesus goes on to say, 'Let your light so shine before men, that they may see your good works and glorify your Father in heaven'. It is perhaps in such passages of the New Testament, about sharing the light of salvation and making it a public rather than an inner spiritual light, that the strongest links may be found to the guiding, illuminating and warning beam of the lighthouse.

The aesthetics and ethics of visible and inner light

A conversation with Douglas Davies

Joanna Puckering

The theme of light in Christianity frequently revolves around belief in guidance and salvation and light as a symbol of goodness: a beacon of faith, central to life and death. Similar themes are found in other world religions and spiritual communities, explored here in relation to an aesthetic and ethic of visible and hidden light.

(continued)

(continued)

In the Old Testament, it is common for Yahweh to be manifested as fire, particularly through the iconic image of the burning bush (Exodus 3:1–4), which is the symbolic evidence of a divine presence. Then there is the role of light in Christian liturgy, with the intersection of theology and ritual in the kindling of fire in the darkness of Easter morning, linking light with resurrection. However, there is an ambiguity to fire throughout Christian history. The 'newly kindled fire' and candles of the Easter Vigil, that form part of the service held in traditional Christian churches to celebrate the resurrection, contrast starkly with a more negative and punitive role of fire (Davies, 2008). On the one hand, it is regarded as a symbol of divine and creative love; on the other, a 'purifying agent' that delivers both earthly and purgatorial punishment (Davies, 2005, 2008).

A vast number of hymns and liturgies dwell upon the theme of 'fiery purification and illumination' (Davies, 2005: 192–193). In his hymn, 'Eternal Light', Thomas Binney explores the idea of spiritual blindness and salvation, asking how we, 'whose "native sphere is dark, whose mind is dim" [can] appear before the eternal light of God' (Davies, 2008: 89). Another well-known example is 'Come Holy Ghost Our Souls Inspire', a 9th-century hymn about enlightenment and divine love translated in the 17th century by the Bishop of Durham, John Cosin. In this, too, the blind are made to see through the illumination of divine light (Davies, 2005).

Similar themes of light and enlightenment can be found in Sikhism, with the concept of the 'guru' (Davies, 1984), whose nature is compared to light, passing from guru to guru, as though there is a single flame passing through many candles. There is a whole notion of power in relation to light in traditional Hinduism. The idea of Hindu cremation is a familiar one, but for someone who is really holy, it is believed that there is no need to put a match to the fire: holiness is such a great thing that it cremates itself (Davies, 2005). In this context, fire becomes a matter of purification and illumination, important not only as a source of heat but through its visible qualities as a guiding light and a symbol of spiritual sacrifice.

Returning to Christianity, the visual importance of fire – and by extension, light – lies in rituals of purification and in manifestations of the Holy Spirit, such as that described in Acts (2:3) when 'tongues as of fire' descended on Jesus' disciples at Pentecost (Davies, 2005: 192). The image of the purifying flame has also been used extensively since the 19th century for the rite of cremation, but in this case fire becomes a 'hidden symbol' of light since it tends not to be visible in Christian crematoria (Davies, 2008: 143).

What these examples share is a relationship to the moral dimension of light, and the intersection of aesthetics and ethics. Aesthetics consider the art of light, and ethics enquire about the consequence of light. This aesthetic and ethical tradition is represented in the Old Testament through the divine light, and in the New Testament where the divine light becomes channelled into the image of Jesus, as a light that shines in the darkness and which the darkness does not put out (Davies, 2008). This is the key text of the Prologue to John's Gospel (John 1:1–18), known to many as part of the Christmas Mass.

Similarly, in the iconography of Sikhs, gurus are represented as glowing; they shine. Extending the light metaphor further, while the word 'guru' is translated as 'teacher' or 'guide' in Sanskrit, other interpretations include 'dispeller of darkness', and Guru Nanak (1469–1538) was described as 'the Light and the Teacher of Mankind' (Singh, 1994: 113). The image of the halo is the artistic, aesthetic representation of an ethical fact that these men are holy, linking the ethical and moral dimension with aesthetic, artistic, literary and iconographic forms of expression.

Two obvious examples illustrate the motif of light within the Christian world. Firstly, there are the Quakers, whose founder George Fox (1624–1691) developed the idea of the 'inner light' as a personal experience of God (Quakers in Britain, nd). This raises an interesting issue since the light is hidden. The aesthetic and the ethical cohere within the self, and this notion of inner light as an ethical guide persists within Quaker culture to this day. At a more communal level, Collins (2009) describes how political and spiritual resistance among 17th-century Quakers was supported by their belief in an inner light. 'The Quaker movement was primarily a radical religious movement' (Collins, 2009: 18), guided by that light towards an ethical framework of democracy and equality.

The second example considers Mormonism. As a Christian innovation, it takes many of its iconographic motifs from pre-existing Christianity and reconfigures them, reorganising concepts and practices so that they make sense within its own terms. The idea of 'inner light' plays an integral role in the process. The grand narrative that turned a group of six people in 1830 into the 15 million contemporary followers of the Church of Jesus Christ of Latter-day Saints (Davies, 2003) has at its heart a story. This focuses upon a young man, Joseph Smith (1805–1844), going into the woods at a time of Protestant revivalism in New York State in the 1830s, in an area which was said to have been the 'burned-over district' (Davies, 2003). It was called the 'burned-over district' because there had been so many Protestant revival movements going on; in other words, movements of the Holy Spirit.

Joseph Smith went into the woods to ask God what the true church is. When God said that all churches are false, the divinely influenced Joseph Smith became enshrouded in darkness – not just blackness, but an almost tangible darkness. When he was almost at the point of death, a pillar of light appeared above his head, and in that moment of salvation he saw the two divine figures of the Heavenly Father and the Heavenly Son (Davies, 2003). Thus, darkness and light become the birth scenario; it is a paradigmatic scene. The birth of Mormonism is invariably associated with what is called the First Vision, which is both the experience of destructive darkness

(continued)

(continued)

and the encounter with a redemptive light of salvation. As Joseph Smith wrote in 1869, 'the Lord still continues His mercy, manifests His grace and imparts unto us His Holy Spirit, that our minds may be illuminated by the light of revelation' (Smith, 1869: 12.347). More recently, the inner light of Mormonism has been described as 'the light of Christ', whose beams can 'warn and guard and guide' (Packer, 2005).

Moving away from mainstream and nonconformist Christianity towards a more mystical tradition, 'light' is one of the key words in Freemasonry (Masonic Dictionary, nd), with texts and rituals focusing on both visible and inner light, and a strong emphasis on spiritual and intellectual illumination. Freemasons have been called 'the Sons of Light', and initiates are led from the darkness of ignorance into the light of knowledge (Garey, 1869). The first-degree initiation ritual into Freemasonry is one of symbolic death and rebirth, in which visible and hidden light play a crucial role. The initiate is blindfolded before being brought into the lodge, 'as one in darkness seeking the light of truth' (Davies, 2003: 19). After being laid in a symbolic tomb, with the lodge in complete darkness except for a light that falls upon the sacred book and the Master of the lodge, the initiate returns to life, emerging from darkness into light as the blindfold is removed.

While lighthouses rarely feature as physical structures in religious texts or teaching, their illuminating presence as metaphorical sources of surveillance, warning and inspiration is readily apparent in liturgy, hymns and creation stories. The examples of Quakers, Mormons and Freemasons offer just three interpretations of 'inner light' and the idea of a watching, guiding presence that is variously expressed through moral conscience, divine revelation and paths to spiritual or intellectual enlightenment. The aesthetics and ethics of visible and hidden light are apparent in rituals of birth, life and death; in the moral and ethical frameworks that we live by; and as a shining beam from the lighthouse that cuts through the darkness of ignorance and despair.

Religious images of light still constitute one of its most powerful metaphorical interpretations but, with the emergence of science and more secular modes of thought, a parallel – some would say contending – image is that of scientific enlightenment, in which illuminating light becomes a symbol of reason and rationality. English Literature scholar Tom Mole makes an important point: that metaphorical histories are invariably interlinked with social and material changes. And modern language specialist Richard Maber's account of lighthouse imagery in the early modern period shows how even the most pious religious metaphors stray readily into ways of describing more down-to-earth experiences.

Light as metaphor and as technology, c.1700–1900

Tom Mole

The archive of European literature and culture from the 18th and 19th centuries is illuminated by shifting metaphors of light at every turn. The Enlightenment identified itself through twin metaphors of illumination: shining light into the dark corners of superstition on the one hand, and walking towards the light of reason on the other. The light in question was literal as well as figurative. The Birmingham Lunar Society was a network of progressive thinkers, including Joseph Priestley and Erasmus Darwin, that met regularly between 1765 and 1813, and became one of the principal intellectual centres of Enlightenment thought in Britain. It got its name because its members met at the full moon, which lit their way home. London street lighting improved significantly as smoky tallow candles were replaced with Argand oil lamps from the 1780s and gas lamps from the 1800s. One visitor claimed, 'In Oxford Street alone there are more lamps than in all Paris' (cited in Porter, 2000: 44).

This was also a period of great lighthouse development. An early landmark of lighthouse design was the Eddystone Lighthouse built by Henry Winstanley. The first lighthouse to be open to the sea on all sides, it was lit in 1698 but destroyed by a storm in 1703. In his mock-epic poem *Trivia* (1716), John Gay (2007: III.345–350) recalled the event:

> So when fam'd Eddystone's far-shooting ray,
>
> That led the sailor through the stormy way,
>
> Was from its rocky roots by billows torn,
>
> And the high turret in the whirlwind born,
>
> Fleets bulg'd their sides against the craggy land,
>
> And pitchy ruines blacken'd all the strand.

Gay was using the image of the uprooted lighthouse and the resulting shipwrecks as a mock-epic simile for an overturned carriage in London's busy streets. When the light fails, chaos rules. The first Eddystone Lighthouse was replaced by one designed by John Rudyard, which lasted from 1709 to 1755, when it burnt down and was replaced in turn by one designed by John Smeaton, which remained in place from 1759 to 1877.

As Enlightenment became Romanticism, this literal and rational light was displaced both by darkness and by a new set of metaphors for light. Darkness reigned in the many obscure dungeons, galleries

(continued)

(continued)

and passageways of gothic literature, where the built environment and its sources of light were often instrumental in driving the plot. Ann Radcliffe uses the word 'darkness' 276 times in her seven gothic novels, and the word 'light' only thirty-five times. Compare this to Jane Austen, who uses 'darkness' six times in her gothic parody *Northanger Abbey* and only once in her other five novels (figures from Literature Online (nd)). Darkness in the gothic novel is both an imaginative tool to heighten the sense of horror in characters and readers, and a metaphor for the gothic's fascination with the dark places of the psyche. Byron's apocalyptic poem *Darkness* (1816) imagines the end of the world not as a product of war, famine or disease, but as the result of the Sun going suddenly dark (Byron, 1986). As implied by Gay, without light – both literal and metaphorical – civilisation collapses.

At the same time, a new metaphorics of light began to appear. Now light could be visionary, as in the 'innumerable company of the heavenly host' that William Blake saw streaming from the Sun (1988a: 566), and the 'light that never was, on sea or land' that illuminated Wordsworth's (1984) imagination. Its source could lie within the individual, as in the many figures in Blake's illuminated books that seem to light up their surroundings. This shift in metaphors of light was famously labelled by M. H. Abrams (1953) as a shift from poetry as 'mirror' to poetry as 'lamp'. Light was also, however, a political issue. Blake's assertion that 'Some are born to sweet delight, / Some are born to endless night' (1988b: 492), may have been not only a metaphysical claim, but also a political statement about privilege, a reminder that the window tax and the unmanaged development of London slums, in which buildings sprung up close together, made light a scarce resource for the poorest city dwellers.

The Romantic period also witnessed the birth of modern celebrity culture (Mole, 2007, 2009), which entailed another set of light metaphors. In 1761, the theatre critic Benjamin Victor described the actor David Garrick as 'a bright Luminary in the Theatrical Hemisphere' (1761: I.61–62). In 1819, a journalist remembered Samuel Taylor Coleridge arriving in Bristol in 1794 'like a comet or meteor in our horizon' (Holmes, 1990: 92). In the two most important theatres of London, Covent Garden and Drury Lane, lighting technology greatly improved at the beginning of the 19th century, as tallow candles were replaced with high-quality wax ones equipped with polished reflectors to direct the light onto the stage. The Theatre Royal in Drury Lane installed gas lighting in 1817. 'Limelight' was first introduced at Covent Garden theatre in 1837 and rapidly spread to other theatres (Lambert, 1993). Produced by heating a cylinder of quicklime (calcium oxide) with a mixture of burning hydrogen and oxygen, limelight creates a bright light that can be focused tightly on a particular spot. This allowed individual star performers to be picked out from other actors and the surrounding scenery. Being 'in the limelight' quickly became a general-purpose term for celebrity, which could be applied beyond the theatre, and which retained its currency even after limelight was replaced by electrical followspots at the end of the 19th century.

These metaphors of light, in their turn, began to shift as the first generation of celebrities became canonical writers, included in anthologies, editions and the earliest university syllabi for courses in English Literature. Now, their writing was increasingly identified as containing the 'sweetness and light' that Matthew Arnold, in *Culture and Anarchy* (1869), made the catchphrase of cultural value, opposed to the darkness that beset 'barbarians' and 'philistines', who saw in it only another kind of light: 'moonshine' (Arnold, 1932: 22). In making 'light' one of his key terms, Arnold made an important change in the history of light imagery. He sought to revive and re-sacralise the Enlightenment image of light as rational and secular, and to put it into the service of a Victorian, Christian vision of culture.

But even as Arnold made light a metaphor for what we might call literature's renewable energy, light was also becoming an agent that helped transmit literature to new audiences. The new technology of photography was rapidly adopted to produce images illustrating or associated with Romantic writing, 'obtained', in Fox Talbot's words, 'by the mere action of Light' (2011: 2). Now light was not simply a metaphor; it was a factor in the production of cultural artefacts. There are many connections between early photography and literature. William Henry Fox Talbot (1800–1877), inventor of the negative-positive process, had an interest in Romantic writing that was – forgive the pun – well developed. Fox Talbot knew at least one Romantic writer well. Thomas Moore lived at Sloperton Cottage, near Bromham, Wiltshire, from 1816 until his death in 1852 (Kelly, 2008). This made him one of Fox Talbot's neighbours at Lacock Abbey and the two became close friends. Fox Talbot photographed Moore in April 1844, when Moore was 65 (Jordan, 1979). Fox Talbot's second book, *Sun Pictures in Scotland* (1845), was inspired by the writings of Sir Walter Scott. Fox Talbot visited a number of Scottish places associated with Scott's poems and novels, capturing them in landscape photographs as well as photographing the Scott Monument in Edinburgh, then under construction. He also photographed one of Byron's manuscripts (Burkett, 2015).

Throughout this period then, light – as both a metaphor and a technology – was remarkably changeable. We can trace interlinking histories of its material and metaphorical shifts. In night-time streets, lighthouses, theatres and homes, light altered materially and took on new shades

(continued)

(continued)

of meaning in the process. In poems, novels and prose works, it was deployed metaphorically in shifting ways for different purposes. If this history is not always easy to see, it may be because even as light changed materially and metaphorically, it was also used as a symbol for unchangingness. Henry Wadsworth Longfellow wrote his poem *The Lighthouse* in 1849, in which he describes the lighthouse as a figure of steadfastness and self-sacrifice. The mariner remembers his first sight of it as a child and greets it like an old friend when returning from a long voyage. It stands:

> Steadfast, serene, immovable, the same
>
> Year after year, through all the silent night
>
> Burns on forevermore that quenchless flame,
>
> Shines on that inextinguishable light!
>
> (Longfellow, 2000: lines 33–36)

In this poem, Longfellow elides the shifting history of light, as a metaphor and as a historical reality, in order to present light, and the lighthouse, as a figure for Providence: unchanging, enduring and benevolent, giving its light equally to all, freely and forever.

Guiding light

The early modern lighthouse as image and emblem

Richard Maber

The lighthouse, with all its emotional and symbolic connotations, forms a powerful and versatile image which becomes particularly prominent from the early modern period onwards.

Lighthouses became a topic of considerable interest. The great development of seaborne trade had led to a corresponding focus on mariners' aids of all kinds, with the provision of lighthouses prominent among them. They are of course highlighted in the innumerable publications of charts and coastal guides for sailors published all over Europe, while the 17th century is noteworthy for the number of petitions, prospectuses and royal warrants for the construction or repair of lighthouses around the most hazardous parts of the coast, for example in Northumberland, Yorkshire, Norfolk, Suffolk, Kent, Cornwall and Pembrokeshire. So, when praising a mathematics textbook that emphasises its own usefulness for navigation, it was natural for the author of a commendatory poem to write: 'Thy Book's a Light-house Mariners to guide' (Barrow, 1687).

The image is especially effective because of the immediacy and drama of its visual appeal, and its appropriateness to different contexts. The clearest and most frequent metaphorical applications are, as one would expect, moral and theological. The lighthouse guides, and it warns; some guide into port, while others warn away from dangerous rocks or shoals; its light is followed to safety or ignored with terrible consequences.

There are emotive and widely familiar phrases in the scriptures and by the Church Fathers that are expressly designed to evoke a visual image of the light shining in the darkness or the beacon on a hill: lights that guide the ship safely to harbour (from the storms of life) or lead the wanderer to the safe path (of salvation). To quote just one typical exhortation from the mid-17th century (Denny, 1653: lines 19–28):

> Refuse not Then so good Advise,
>
> As points from Hell to Paradise.
>
> So have I seen A Lighthouse stand
>
> In sable Night with burning Hand
>
> Directing from Wracke's Shelf, Rock, shoar
>
> The sayling Pilot blind Before;
>
> By which, escaping Danger's Tort,
>
> He well arrives at Safetie's Port.
>
> So maist Thou too; If Thou seek'st Grace
>
> And up to Heavenward Eye doest place.

The image can be appropriated to any confession. For the faithful Protestant, the lighthouse of true faith warns of the treacherous shoals of popery (Pett, 1688: 357); while for the Roman Catholic, it guides the convert into the bosom of the Church (Morel, 1675: 25). Indeed, in an earlier example, it becomes the Church itself, as the author engages in excruciating word-play to support the image of the Catholic Church as the bride and temple of Christ: 'But the Catholique Church is Christs huswife and his house too, his *Spouse* and his *Temple* also [. . .] Shee is a *light* house (but no light huswife) and Christ is the *Light* thereof' (Tuke, 1617: 71–72).

The moralising potential of the lighthouse is especially effective in that it has its own evil antonym, the wrecker's light, as evoked by Thomas Turner (1674) in a pamphlet on bankers, creditors and the national debt that is not without some 21st-century resonance:

(continued)

(continued)

> If a false Light-house be erected near a dangerous Rock in the Sea, and in a dark and tempestuous night the Ship is steered that way, as to a safe Port, and thereupon suffereth wrack, no body can with any reason impute this misfortune to the error or incogitancy of the *Pilot*, or governor of the Vessel, but rather to the malice and falsity of this wicked invention.

This false lighthouse was also much used by the religious writers, providing a favourite trope of moralising antithesis. Richard Hearne (1640: 45) presents it as an established contrast in the collection of aphorisms that he published in 1640:

> A virtuous man shining in the purity of a righteous life, is as a light house set by the Sea side, whereby the Mariners both saile aright, and avoid danger: But hee that lives in noted sinnes, is as a false Lanthorne, which shipwrackes those that trust it.

Hearne's collection was particularly influential, and we find the identical words being adapted to illustrate the warning posed by the penitent sinner, and the contrast between the godly minister and the false preacher.

The visual immediacy of the image of the lighthouse gives it especial appeal in this golden age of the emblem book, when readers' imaginations were conditioned by the constant interplay between the verbal and the visual. Such works constituted an international repertory of images used in both poetry and prose all over Europe: emblem books were frequently published with the accompanying text in at least two or three languages for their easy diffusion. The striking visual image can give a forceful new twist to a familiar phrase: thus, in Jacob Cats' influential work (1627), the injunction *Luceat lux vestra coram hominibus* ('Let your light shine before men', Matthew 5:16) is illustrated with the picture of a cherub at the foot of a beacon at the end of a breakwater, guiding a ship through the darkness and stormy seas into the port.

In the most celebrated emblem book of the century, Hermann Hugo's famous *Pia Desideria* (Antwerp, Hendrick Aertssens, 1624), the nautical scenes, whether of salvation or destruction, very often feature a symbolic lighthouse in the background. This work had forty-two Latin editions, was very widely translated, and its engravings were copied in numerous other compilations, including the most popular English emblem book, Francis Quarles' *Emblemes* (London, 1635). One of Quarles' emblems, taken directly from Hugo, combines the nautical and the terrestrial to illustrate the text *Utinam dirigantur viæ meæ ad custodiendas justificationes tuas!* ('O that my ways were directed to keep thy statutes!' Psalm 119:5) – the multi-tasking lighthouse simultaneously shines forth to direct a ship at sea and provides a guide-rope to direct the pilgrim soul through the maze of life.

Figure 12 Hermann Hugo's *Pia Desideria, 1624* (Antwerp, Hendrick Aertssens). Courtesy of Emblem Project Utrecht. Cropped from original.

However, the image of the lighthouse is not confined to such predictable religious and moralising contexts. Jacob Cats developed an amusingly secular application in a separate section of his *Proteus*, a verse dialogue in Latin and French between two young women, Anna and Phyllis, who exchange views on men and marriage. Anna is older and more experienced, at twenty-seven, and advises the over-eager Phyllis on how to catch and keep her man. Girls should not run after young men: it is the young man's job to come after the girl. The young woman is the lighthouse, the young *amoureux* is the ship: the ship comes to the lighthouse, not vice versa. Anna starts properly enough – the mariner can't get his hands on the lighthouse – but the image soon evolves in a rather more *risqué* direction: as the light guides the ship into the harbour, so the loving suitor should slide gently in to the maiden's bosom:

(continued)

(continued)

> Tout ainsi que le Phare escleire aux matelotz [. . .]
>
> Pourtant le nautonnier n'y touche de sa main [. . .]
>
> C'est aux jeunes garçons de chercher les pucelles
>
> Et de les requerir fort amoureusement
>
> En se laissant couler vers leur sein doucement,
>
> Ainsy que vers le port abordent les nacelles.
>
> (Cats, 1627: Untitled section,
separate pagination, p. 14,
no line numbers)

The humour is enhanced by the use of a familiar image in an unexpected context; yet however it is employed, as this illustrates, the image of the lighthouse always retains its exceptional visual and emotional impact.

LIGHTHOUSES IN TIME AND SPACE

Veronica Strang

With the diverse ways of thinking about light explored above, we are now well equipped to focus on the lighthouse itself, and to recognise in its historical development important resonances with related ideas about light and all-seeing power. Building on the foundations of religions describing their light-bearing gods in human form, what could be more logical, as societies became more materially instrumental, than to construct gigantic human figures carrying torches aloft? The quintessential example is the lighthouse of Alexandria, or as it was known in ancient Greece, *Pharos*, named for the island in the Nile Delta on which it was constructed.

Built by the Ptolemaic Kingdom between 280 and 247 BC, Pharos was one of the seven wonders of the ancient world listed by Hellenic travellers (Clayton and Price, 1988). It was made of large blocks of stone, sealed with lead to withstand the waves. At its apex, light came from a mirror reflecting the sunlight during the day and from a fire at night. It was at least 400 feet tall, and it held its place as the tallest human construction for centuries, prior to irreparable damage caused by three earthquakes between AD 956 and 1323 (McKenzie, 2007). It was crowned by a statue of Zeus, king of the Greek gods, and associated, appropriately, not only with the sky and lightning, but also the imposition of law and order.

In its historical context, Pharos was magnetic. Like a giant firefly, it drew people to what was seen as a centre of civilisation and salvation, a metaphor that has persisted in other material renditions of vast torchbearers, most recently the Statue of Liberty. Pharos had much to say about the power of its creators: their divine capacities to enlighten the world, and hold the line between order and the abyss of chaos. In this sense, it became the archetype for many lighthouses/torchbearers, as is readily apparent in theatre historian Jan Clarke's account of images of the Colossus of Rhodes. Following Clarke's discussion, in drawing upon examples from North Africa, Joanna Puckering details how the lasting influence of Pharos also shaped the development of the Islamic architectural form of the minaret.

The Colossus of Rhodes according to Giacomo Torelli

Jan Clarke

When reflecting on how to address the trope of the lighthouse in a manner appropriate to my discipline of French 17th-century theatre history, I did not immediately foresee any difficulties. After all, ports, the sea and seashore scenes abound in the spectacular drama of the period, with the most notable of the latter undoubtedly being that in which Perseus flies down on Pegasus to rescue Andromeda from the monster in Pierre Corneille's *Andromède* of 1650. Moreover, scenic designers relished the challenge of imitating waves, as we see from Nicola Sabbattini's *Pratique* of 1638, where he describes three different ways of 'causing the sea to appear', 'rise up, swell, become agitated and change colour', and make vessels seem to glide across it (Sabbattini, 1994: 110–113, 115, 117, 120). However, when I came to look for examples of lighthouses, at first, I found none – a fact I found all the more surprising given that lighting effects were also extremely popular (Clarke, 1999, 2007, 2011a). The only explanation I could offer was that the majority of these effects sought to reproduce the grandeur of the natural world, with the rising of the Sun and Moon, and the appearance of stars, planets and constellations being particularly appreciated.

After some searching, though, I did find one striking image (Figure 13): a representation of the decor for the prologue of the opera *Deidamia* performed at the Teatro Novissimo in Venice in 1644 (libretto by Scipione Herrico, music possibly by Laurenzi Filiberto, although frequently attributed to Francesco Cavalli) (Whenham, 2001). The decors for this production (like those subsequently for *Andromède*) were produced by Giacomo Torelli, 'the magician of Fano', who worked at the Teatro Novissimo from 1641 to 1644, before moving to Paris in 1645. Engravings of three of them, together with those of the decors for another of Torelli's Teatro Novissimo productions, *Venere gelosa* (1643), have been identified in a volume published the same year entitled *Apparati scenici* (Bisaccioni, 1644) (Bjurström, 1962: 122).

The decor for the prologue of *Deidamia* features two towers, one square and one round, to either side of the stage, with the Colossus of Rhodes set slightly further back in the centre. The prows of vessels can be seen beyond, ranked to either side of the harbour, with waves between them, and a painted backcloth representing the city of Rhodes closes up the rear of the stage. Cupid hovers above, his bow clearly visible, while two female figures are borne upon the waves, one supported by a kind of lily pad and the other on a machine featuring a large wheel. These are the nymph Thetis and the goddess Fortune, who appear along with the god of love in the opera's prologue.

The Colossus of Rhodes is said to have been a representation in bronze of the sun god Apollo, the archetype of light and power, and this is what Torelli depicts: his statue bears a golden staff, his head is surrounded by

The Colossus of Rhodes 61

Figure 13 Prologue: *The Harbour with the Colossus of Rhodes* (oil on canvas), by Giacomo Torelli (1608–1678) / Pinoteca Civica di Fano, Fano, Italy. Credit: Bridgeman Images.

Also see Plate 4.

rays of light, and he holds aloft a flaming beacon to guide vessels into the port. But although fire and firework effects were frequently used on the Renaissance stage, it is probable that a painted scenic element would have represented not only the beacon, but also the whole figure. Similarly, the vessels in the harbour would have been depicted on a series of progressively smaller stage flats running parallel to the stage front on either side, painted to create the impression of perspective.

The Knights Hospitallers captured and established their headquarters on Rhodes in 1307, and were confirmed in possession of it by Pope Clement V in 1309. In 1522, after beating off Ottoman attacks over many decades, the Knights and Suleiman the Magnificent agreed terms and the Knights left the island. Thomas Corneille, in the third volume of his *Dictionnaire universel géographique et historique* of 1708 (III. 273), describes the main port of Rhodes as follows:

> At the entrance to this port, on the right, there can be seen a new tower, that the Turks constructed in the place of an old one that had been there previously, and that was called the Saint Nicholas tower. It is square, and at the top there is a very beautiful donjon, with a look out post at

(continued)

(continued)

> each corner [. . .] [O]pposite this tower is an old castle that was known as Saint Ange, from the time when the Knights were the masters of the island. This castle and this tower, which are more than fifty toises apart, are built on the two spots where were placed the feet of the great bronze Colossus, one of the seven wonders of the world, between the legs of which vessels passed in full sail.

We see, therefore, as Bjurström notes, that the tradition according to which the Colossus bestrode the harbour entrance persisted into the 18th century, 'in spite of the knowledge that the harbor entrance was three hundred feet wide whereas the statue was only one hundred and sixty feet high' (1962: 91). Also, that the tower and castle were said to have been built on the place where the Colossus' feet had stood, whereas Torelli shows tower, castle and Colossus as existing simultaneously.

Bjurström traces the development of the image of the Colossus via Maerten van Heemskerck's 1572 engraving to that of Marten de Vos (1614), concluding that 'the *contrapposto* [OED: 'the arrangement of a figure so that the action of arms and shoulders contrasts as strongly as possible with that of hips and legs; a twisting of the figure on its own axis'], so pronounced in Heemskerck and less so in de Vos, is still noticeable in Torelli's structure' (1962: 93). Another imaginative illustration of the Colossus, by Georg Balthasar Probst, this time from the 18th century, similarly purports to show this wonder in operation with a boat exiting the harbour through its legs. While the engravings of van Heemskerck and de Vos feature only a single tower, Probst includes two, but sets one back from the other, thereby giving the impression of greater depth. Torelli's choice, on the other hand, of two parallel towers is rational in a theatrical sense, in that the two towers serve to mask the edges of the side flats on which the vessels are depicted. And Bjurstöm emphasises the fact that Torelli's positioning of the structure at the front of the stage, with a tower on either side, and the proscenium arch above, would have increased its stability (1962: 93). The domed buildings that can be seen to the rear in the depictions of van Heemskerck and de Vos, and indeed that of Probst, are echoed by a similar dome just visible in Torelli's work. This may have been included merely as a source of oriental exoticism, or may have been (anachronistically) intended to represent the mosque of Suleiman, constructed in Rhodes in 1522 after the Ottoman conquests.

The two towers described by Corneille are visible in a map of Rhodes made in the 16th century by Georg Braun and Frans Hogenberg (Figure 14), although it is not possible to distinguish here the domed building seen in the two engravings. Nonetheless, we can conclude that Torelli is presenting for his Venetian audience a 17th-century conception of Rhodes,

The Colossus of Rhodes 63

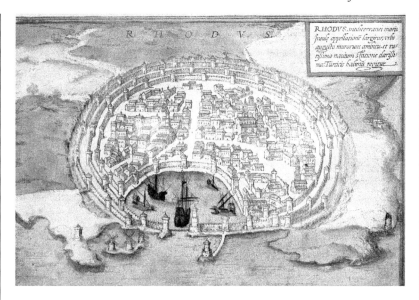

Figure 14 Detail of Map of Calais, Malta, Rhodes, and Famagusta, from *Civitates Orbis Terrarum*, by Georg Braun (1541–1622) and Frans Hogenberg (1535–1590), c.1572, engraving by Joris Hoefnagel (1542–1600). Credit: Private Collection / The Stapleton Collection / Bridgeman Images.

onto which he has superimposed the Colossus. The main question, therefore, is why.

Torelli's primary objective must have been to set the scene for his spectators. Herrico's Deidamia must not be confused with Achilles' lover, the heroine of operas by Cavalli, Campra and Handel. Our Deidamia is daughter of Aeacides, King of Epirus and his wife, Queen Phthia, and sister of Pyrrhus, who also appears in the opera, which tells the convoluted story of how she came to be married to Demetrius, son of the King of Asia Minor. The prologue to *Deidamia* tells the reader that it is set in 'Le port de Rhodes'. How better to render this for the spectator than by the representation of the Colossus? In fact, Rhodes itself is mentioned only infrequently in the opera: four times in the front matter, five times in stage directions and seven times in the text. More importantly, though, given its central position in Torelli's decor for the prologue, the Colossus is not mentioned at all. Possible insights into why this figure was nevertheless made so central are provided by comparing Torelli's decor for the prologue of *Deidamia* with an engraving showing his set for *Bellerofonte*, produced at the Teatro Novissimo in 1642 (Figure 15).

(continued)

Figure 15 Set design with Venice in background from *Apparati Scenici per il Teatro Nuovissimo dell'Opera Pubblica di Venezia* (set designs for the Teatro Novissimo in Venice), by Giacomo Torelli from Fano (1608–1678), 1644. Credit: De Agostini Picture Library / A. Dagli Orti / Bridgeman Images.

Elements of decor were frequently re-used, and the appearance of ships with curved prows on the left in Torelli's Colossus depictions and on the right in the *Bellerofonte* engraving can be explained by the fact that images in engravings are automatically reversed. However, perhaps more striking in the latter is the view of Venice itself to the rear of the stage. According to Ellen Rosand, during the course of the opera, a 'model' of the city was caused by Neptune to emerge from the sea (Rosand, 1990: 134); although, in my view, this was more probably represented by a painted backcloth.

In her book on opera in 17th-century Venice, Rosand describes how, in the 1640s and 1650s, these works reflected the current political situation, as authors of librettos moved away from the Trojan–Roman founding myths that had formed their previous subjects:

> If less concerned with the legendary origins of Venice, [these librettos] seem to bear an even more specific relationship to current events. References to and personifications of Venice continue to cultivate or expand upon her image as a stronghold of freedom and haven against

the barbarians, but the barbarians are now pointedly Turkish, as if in response to Venice's growing preoccupation with the Ottoman threat to her maritime power.

(Rosand, 1990: 143)

Indeed, 1645 saw the outbreak of the sixth Ottoman–Venetian War or Cretan War, which was to continue until 1669.

In these librettos, and as would subsequently be the case for the France of Louis XIV (Clarke, 2011b, c), Venice is praised not only as a haven of liberty, but also as a promoter of the arts – a sentiment echoed by Herrico in his dedicatory epistle to *Deidamia*:

> This great city has, as much as by her site, always shown herself to be admirable and exceptional in public and private activities. Nowadays, the foreigner is amazed to see richly decorated theatres where so many works of musical drama are performed that are ingeniously planned and full of varied and wonderful things to see. So many great geniuses are there given the opportunity to exercise their talents and attract praise, either in poetry, or music, or the construction of machines, or in other fields that are just as honourable with regard to this art form.

Similar themes are developed in the text of the opera, as when the President of the Rhodes Senate declares (I, 8):

> I will be justly praised
>
> If for our dear liberty
>
> I must risk, if necessary, my life.
>
> In truth, a wise perspicacity is necessary,
>
> Because all around us,
>
> On one side the untrustworthy Greek,
>
> And on the other the lords of Asia and Egypt
>
> Show by many signs
>
> That our liberty annoys them and makes them envious.

As noted above, Torelli's decor for *Deidamia* is in many ways a mash-up of old and new elements: towers from the 14th and 16th centuries, a vaguely Ottoman domed building, together with an entirely anachronistic Colossus, since the latter was felled by an earthquake in 226 BC. Indeed, the Colossus in Torelli's decor is still more anachronistic than might immediately appear, since Herrico's opera deals with the marriage of Deidamia to Demetrius,

(continued)

(continued)

the son of Antigonus. This is the same Demetrius who, in 305 BC, besieged Rhodes on the instructions of his father, but then relented and departed a year later, leaving behind a huge store of military equipment. The Rhodians then sold this and used the revenue to construct the Colossus (Pliny the Elder, xxxiv.18). Herrico was right, therefore, in omitting the Colossus from his libretto, since it did not exist at the time of the events he is relating, and there is a profound disjunction between text and decor in this respect. Perhaps more importantly in the context of this discussion, there is evidence to suggest that the Colossus did not actually straddle the harbour (and may not even have been constructed near it) and did not carry a torch (Jordan, 2014: 22–33). In other words, it was not a lighthouse. But, of course, we can hardly blame Torelli for following the accepted wisdom of his time.

I would suggest that, by deliberately echoing the decor of the earlier *Bellerofonte*, which had revealed Venice in so magical a fashion, and onto which he has superimposed the Colossus in order to suggest Rhodes, Torelli is making a conscious parallel between the two states. The Knights had constructed Rhodes City as a model of the medieval European ideal, only to see it fall beneath the Ottoman onslaught. How very pertinent, then, this must have seemed to the members of the Venetian audience of *Deidamia* as they geared themselves up for yet another episode in their own titanic struggle against the same forces.

Even if the real Colossus was not a lighthouse (and let us not forget that there was another lighthouse among the seven wonders of the ancient world: the Pharos of Alexandria), and even if its representation within Torelli's decor did not actually serve to emit light, the *Deidamia* Colossus could, nevertheless, be said to be a beacon in another regard, alerting contemporary spectators to the danger of the Ottoman threat and thereby representing Venetian (and by extension Christian) values of liberty, art and culture in the face of a perceived encroaching Muslim 'darkness'.

'Places of light'
Lighthouses and minarets

Joanna Puckering

Chania was the capital of Crete between 1898 and 1971. Located at the site of the ancient Minoan city of Kydonia, on the island's northwest shore, it is one of the world's oldest inhabited cities. Chania Lighthouse was built by the Venetians in the 16th century and lies at the end of a long 'harbour of refuge'. The lighthouse is no longer in use, despite being renovated in

2005, but still provides an architectural landmark. With its 21-metre-high tower, it 'resembles a minaret rising from a Venetian bastion' (De Wire and Reyes-Pergioudakis, 2010: 149).

While this resemblance appears to be no more than aesthetic in the case of Chania Lighthouse, in many other instances, the link between lighthouses and minarets is much stronger. There are several recent histories describing the architectural, religious and cultural developments of the minaret throughout the Islamic world (Bloom, 2013; Behrens-Abouseif, 2006), as well as earlier work (e.g. K. A. C. Creswell, 1926). Drawing on archaeological and historical research, these suggest an important link between maritime lighthouses and early minaret design.

The Pharos Lighthouse had a lasting influence upon art, architecture and language. The word for 'lighthouse' is *phare* in French and *faro* in Italian. Reflecting Alexandria's position as a centre for civilisation and enlightenment, Pharos has inspired artists through the ages. In this volume, James Purdon writes 'of the blood-red silhouette of the Pharos' (p. 102) that illustrated Thomas Moore's 1837 novel, *The Epicurean*, and Uma Kothari describes the work of artist Thomas Kilpper, whose 2008 project focused on refugees crossing the Mediterranean and involved creating a lighthouse structure in Lampedusa that 'refers to the Alexandria Pharos' (p. 187). Many earlier and more permanent lighthouses in the Mediterranean were modelled on Pharos (Salem, 1991) and it has been argued, not without controversy, that this influence extends to the design of other types of tower, particularly the early minarets in the Mediterranean and North Africa.

The lighthouse of Alexandria was 'different in function and proportions from the minarets. Its main function was to guide the ships to safety' (Salem, 1991: 150), whereas the minaret served to carry the message of the *adhan* over long distances, although this could also 'help travellers in finding their way by day or by night' (ibid: 150). Jonathan Bloom observes that the earliest mosques did not have minarets, and that the *adhan*, or call to prayer, was chanted from high walls and rooftops (1991: 55). He concludes that the minaret was probably invented towards the end of the 2nd century of Islam (8th century AD) and has controversially suggested that it 'had little – if anything – to do with the call to prayer' (Bloom, 2013: xvii).

Although there is a lack of consensus over the relationship between lighthouse design and North African minarets, 'it should perhaps be recalled that the Arabic word for lighthouse, *manār*, also means "minaret" in Egypt' (Behrens-Abouseif, 2006: 11). 'Minaret' has been a part of the English language since the 17th century, and has its roots in the Persian *minār* and *mināre* and Arabic *manār* or *manāra* (Bloom, 2013). The primary meaning of *manār* is 'place of fire' or 'place of light': in effect, lighthouses, beacons or towers, which might be attached to Islamic fortresses along coastal and desert routes, and used to guide caravans or individual travellers. It can also

(continued)

(continued)

describe a signpost or a boundary stone, but in all cases the emphasis is on literally or figuratively lighting the way (AlSulaiti, 2013). For those travelling at night, an illuminated minaret might similarly offer the services of a 'landlocked lighthouse' (Bosworth et al., 1987: 365).

In addition to this linguistic evidence, a more concrete historical relationship between lighthouses and the architectural development of minarets can be found on the Mediterranean coast of North Africa, particularly in the cities of Kairouan and El Jadida.

Founded in AD 670, the city of Kairouan lies in northern Tunisia, between the mountains and the sea. While not a coastal city, the minaret that now forms part of the Great Mosque of Kairouan is closely associated with ancient lighthouse design (UNESCO, nd). Dating from the early 9th century and approximately 32 metres in height, its imposing three-storey minaret was the tallest in the Maghreb until the 12th century, when the Kutubiyya minaret in Marrakesh was built (Qantara, nd).

In addition to its religious purpose, the presence of arrow holes as well as windows in the main structure of the square, stone-built minaret suggests a military role (Qantara, nd). The 9th-century, 30-metre fortified Aghlabid tower of Khalaf al-Fata, situated in Sousse to the east of Kairouan, is often

Figure 16 Grand Mosque of Kairouan. Photograph: Citizen59, CC BY-SA 2.0, (https://creativecommons.org/licenses/by-sa/2.0/), via Flickr.

> cited to support the idea that the Kairouan minaret served a defensive purpose, since it was used as a lookout point and lighthouse (Harrison, 2004; Bloom and Blair, 2009). The Kairouan minaret is also believed to have been modelled on a Roman lighthouse at Salakta, which in turn echoed the lighthouse of Alexandria (Harrison, 2004). These architectural links suggest an indirect relationship between Pharos, the minaret of Kairouan and minaret design more generally in North Africa.
>
> Moving forward in time and further west into what is now Morocco, El Jadida lies 90 kilometres to the south-west of Casablanca, on the Atlantic coast. Initially built by the Portuguese in the early 16th century as the fortified settlement named Mazagan, it was a key port for Portuguese mariners sailing round Africa towards India. The minaret of El Jadida's mosque was converted from a five-sided lighthouse, originally built on the town's fortified ramparts in the 19th century, and is 'the only pentagonal minaret in Islam' (Ellingham et al., 2010: 319).
>
> While pre-dating Islam by many centuries in its original form, the lighthouse at Alexandria not only played a crucial strategic and maritime role as watchtower and guiding beacon; it also 'became a beacon of Islam' (Behrens-Abouseif, 2006: 12), as Muslim rulers gradually adapted its form through successive restoration projects, before its final destruction in the 14th century. The role of Pharos as an Islamic symbol of enlightenment and culture contrasts with Jan Clarke's description (this volume) of the Colossus of Rhodes as 'a beacon' that represented the Christian 'values of liberty, art and culture in the face of a perceived encroaching Muslim "darkness"' (p. 66).
>
> Writing about the influence of the Pharos in the Muslim West, Salem observes that 'Alexandria was the principle maritime base in Egypt' and for travellers arriving after a long voyage, its lighthouse 'was the first thing they saw amongst its distinguished land marks' (Salem, 1991: 153). It is therefore unsurprising that other structures were modelled on Pharos, especially forts and other lighthouses, providing an architectural link between navigational aid and the spiritual guidance associated with the minaret as a 'place of light'.

While many lighthouses aimed to emulate Pharos' influence in shining a guiding light, some developments reflected its powers of surveillance and its symbolic and practical role in maintaining law and order. Archaeologist David Petts describes how early medieval lighthouses focused primarily on keeping the land safe, only turning to navigational concerns when threats from the sea decreased and fishing and trade expanded beyond local waters. Subsequently, Tim Edensor discusses how the lighthouses emerged out of a history in which after nightfall, little light was available, reinforcing how the advent of illumination was materially underpinned as a powerful metaphor of enlightenment.

'On lofty cliffs, where the sea pounds the rock . . .'
Lighthouses in early medieval England

David Petts

In the late 7th century, the Anglo-Saxon scholar Aldhelm wrote a collection of riddles or mysteries (*enigmata*). Among the diverse subjects he addressed, including peacocks, book-cupboards and ostriches, was 'the lofty lighthouse', which he described as standing on high cliffs assailed by storms while it guided wandering ships to safety (Lapidge and Rosier, 1985: 90). This appears to be the first early medieval English description of a lighthouse.

It is not clear whether it was based on a direct observation of a lighthouse, and it is possible that Aldhelm based it on the work of earlier writers, such as Isidore of Seville (ibid: 254, note 82). It has been suggested that a small chapel at Worth Matravers in Dorset may have had its origins as an Anglo-Saxon beacon with which he may have been familiar (Lepard and Barker, 2004). However, Aldhelm also visited Dover, where he must have viewed the remains of the great stone Roman lighthouse that stood over the Western Approaches. The *pharos*, which still stands, worked in concert with another (now missing) lighthouse on the western heights to aid navigation into the Roman port (Booth, 2007). On the other side of the Channel, stood another lighthouse at Boulogne, the Tour d'Ordre, reputedly built in AD 39 by the Emperor Caligula (Suetonius, 2007: 46).

While the Dover *pharoi* may have had a functional role in the Roman period, it is likely that these two structures also had monumental significance. At a height of over 20 metres, they would have been some of the tallest buildings in Roman Britain. One of the few competitors for this title would have been the great four-way monumental arch just up the coast at Richborough, at around 25 metres in height. Like the Dover port, Richborough was a 'gateway' to Roman Britain, a major military base throughout the period. Indeed, in the 3rd century, the Richborough monument was converted into a signal station before its final demolition.

In the 4th century, a series of new signal stations was built along the eastern coast of *Britannia* (Bell, 1998; Hind, 2005). These ran from the Humber, possibly to South Shields. Standing on commanding coastal positions, the stations acted as watchtowers and communication nodes. They guarded against coastal attack and, on sighting hostile forces, communicated through beacons with the other such installations along the shore, and inland. However, unlike the Dover and Boulogne lights, they had limited navigational function. They were more directly intended as nodes in a network, collating observations and passing on data. Again, although functional in design, they had a monumental aspect – at least one carried an inscription referring to a high-level military officer (Collingwood and Wright, 1965: *RIB* 721).

Lighthouses in early medieval England 71

In his description of the important synod of Whitby in AD 664, Bede gives an alternative name for Whitby as *in sinus fari* (the bay of the lighthouse). It may well be that he was referring to the ruins of a former Roman structure (Bede, 1907: 3.25; Bell, 1998), although others have argued for a more allegorical understanding of the name (Hunter Blair, 1985).

While the Anglo-Saxons probably continued to use beacons, the use of monumental structures to house them appears to have decreased. Although Charlemagne restored the Tour d'Ordre in AD 811, the Dover *pharoi* remained derelict. It was not until the 10th century that the surviving lighthouse was annexed by the construction of a church (Taylor and Taylor, 1980: I.214–217; II.figs 451–452).

Figure 17 The Roman lighthouse at Dover Castle. Photograph: Chris McKenna (Thryduulf), CC BY-SA 4.0 (https://commons. wikimedia.org/w/index.php?curid=44108), via Wikimedia Commons.

(continued)

(continued)

In the absence of documentary records, it is not easy to discern the use of lighthouses in the early Anglo-Saxon period. It is not until we reach the 'documentary horizon' in the 7th century that there is clear evidence for signalling using lights in a coastal context. It is far from certain whether Aldhelm ever saw a lighthouse in action, and there is no evidence that the Dover lights were in use when he visited. However, there is other evidence of the use of lights. In his description of the death of St Cuthbert on Farne Island in AD 687, Bede wrote in his *Vita Sancti Cuthberti*:

> One of the monks went without delay and lit two candles and went up, with one in each hand, to a piece of high ground to let the Lindisfarne brethren know that Cuthbert's holy soul had gone to the Lord . . . The brother in the watch tower [*specula*] at Lindisfarne, who was sitting up all night awaiting the news, ran quickly to the church.
>
> (1969: c.40)

While these were clearly special circumstances, the mention of a watch-tower implies a permanent observation point, if not a lighthouse *per se*.

By the later 1st millennium AD, much of southern and eastern England had an extensive and systematic network of beacons and watchtowers built in response to the threat of seaborne raiding, particularly by the Vikings (Baker and Brookes, 2014; Gower, 2002). The raiders came both directly from Scandinavia and from increasingly permanent bases elsewhere in Britain and in France. These coastal beacons, like those of the Romans, were linked to inland networks of signal points and not intended to mark navigational dangers for shipping but to warn of coastal threats to those inland, allowing them to prepare for attacks and protect important nodal points. Their presence is recalled in early place-names with the term *tote (a lookout) being used in toponyms, such as Tote Copse (Aldingbourne, Sussex) and Toddington (Lyminster, Sussex) (Mawer et al., 1929–1930: I.64, 171). They often had good coastal visibility, but were also able to observe roads and other communication routes. In many cases, they were simply located on high places with good visibility. In other cases, it is probable that such structures were used in conjunction with other strong points. For example, the residences of local lords (*thegns*) at Portchester (Hants) and Bishopstone (Sussex) were both equipped with tower-like structures which would have provided vantage points and observation positions (Thomas, 2008; Cunliffe, 1975: 49–52). It is in this context that the 10th-century refurbishment of the Dover *pharos* may have occurred (Booth, 2007).

Obligations to watch the coast also appear in the 10th-century charter of King Edward giving land to Ealdorman Aethelweard. The charter frees the new landholders of all royal dues except military service, the fortification of fortresses, and maritime guard (Whitelock, 1979: I.115, 522–523). Given the other exceptions, maritime guard appears to have been seen primarily as a military duty rather than one focused on safeguarding navigation. The 10th/11th-century *Rectitudines Singularum*, a schematic overview of the duties of individuals of different ranks, recorded that *thegns* were expected to be able to equip a guard ship and guard the coastline, while the lowly *cottars* were expected to keep watch on the sea coast (Douglas and Greenaway, 1981: II.813–814).

It is clear that these coastal watch networks reflected royal policy in response to external military threats. However, as the quotation about the death of Cuthbert makes clear, there were probably many informal systems of signalling and observation that took place on a more localised and contingent level.

The relatively late development of lighthouses focused on communicating navigational information may indicate the changing nature of coastal shipping. In the early medieval period, the majority of sea travel would have been in small boats sailed by men with a good knowledge of the local coastlines. While there were clearly some boats making longer voyages, these would have been limited in scale and extent. Most exploitation of marine resources would have focused on local inshore and shallow-water areas.

However, at the turn of the first millennium, the scale and nature of sea fishing underwent an important change, with major expansion and a move towards species such as cod, which were found further offshore (Barrett et al., 2004; Barrett et al., 2011). This required frequent fishing trips beyond the sight of land, and led to an overall increase in coastal traffic. Over the 13th and 14th centuries, fishermen searched further for fish supplies, moving away from local waters. Alongside the wider increase in international trade, there was a slow but significant increase in the number of non-local seafarers who, with less detailed knowledge of local waters, created more need for external navigation markers and lighthouses to protect shipping.

Over the thousand years from the beginning of Roman control in Britain to the arrival of the Normans, lighthouses underwent an important transition. In Roman Britain, signal stations and towers were primarily lookout stations plugged into a network of communications that fed inland, warning those in the interior of ship-born threats. And over the Anglo-Saxon period, this terrestrial warning function still took priority. But with changes in the wider use of shipping and shipping lanes, particularly for trade and fishing, the purpose of lights slowly transformed from warning those on land of the threat from the sea to warning those at sea of the threat from the rocks and shoals of the coastline.

The redistribution of light and dark at sea

Tim Edensor

The global distribution of illumination has changed beyond recognition since the lighthouse first cast its beam across the night sky. Because we have become so habituated to the ubiquity of electric illumination, it is difficult to imagine the pervasive darkness that formerly saturated most space after nightfall; yet only in the last two centuries has this gloom been ameliorated. In deeply dark marine environments, on nights when the Moon did not cast its light, the illumination of the lighthouse would have pierced the darkness dramatically.

The dangers and discomforts that suffused everyday life before the emergence of widespread illumination are described by Roger Ekirch. In towns, rubbish, filthy ditches and overhanging timbers posed nocturnal risks, while beyond city walls, travellers might stumble into 'fallen trees, thick underbrush, steep hillsides and open trenches' (Ekirch, 2005: 123). Footpads, murderers, burglars and arsonists might lurk in the darkness, and to keep such perils at bay, householders performed a daily ritual of 'shutting in', firmly bolting doors. Towns organised watches to guard against fire and interlopers. For most householders, rudimentary candles lit meagre patches. At sea, dangerous rocks and reefs, turbulent waters and oncoming storms were imperceptible in the darkness: hazards that the lighthouse sought to alleviate.

In these times, fear of the unseen imagined a host of spectral, ungodly forces. In Europe, it was believed that Satan carried out his work at night. Other malign spirits – imps, hobgoblins, ghouls, boggarts and witches – fed on ghost stories, folk beliefs and religiously inspired terrors. At sea, krakens, leviathans, sea sprites, ghost ships and serpents might seethe below the waves. In contrast to these forces of darkness, associations of light with divinity and goodness saturated Christian belief, along with notions that a metaphorical darkness preceded the advent of Christ and was synonymous with death. Craig Koslofsky (2011) identifies the continuing struggle of the devout through 'the long night of the soul', in which faith was threatened by temptation and terror.

These ideas subsequently merged with narratives describing a transcendent shift from dark to light that symbolised passage from medieval ignorance to rationality and science. The Enlightenment was explicitly concerned to 'shed light on all things' in the pursuit of 'truth, purity, revelation and knowledge', embodying the ideals of 'illumination, objectivity and wisdom' (Bille and Sørensen, 2007: 272–273). Darkness was not only construed as a hindrance to efficient modern regulation and health, but as an obstruction to moral behaviour. The lighthouse was thus an important modern signifier of science, safety and rationality at the edge of the wild sea, a 'cultural' symbol deployed to counter the 'natural' threats of turbulent seas and darkness.

Nevertheless, while dominant Western concepts suggested that light should vanquish darkness, defeat ignorance, reveal immorality and rationalise space, alternative meanings of darkness have invariably coexisted. At a practical level, pervasive darkness necessitated the development of competencies. Expertise about the stellar constellations and the phases of the Moon was developed by the ancient Greeks and Phoenicians, and used to chart routes through dark seas. Familiarity with the constellations also stimulated the invention of the Arabian *kamal*, a device that measured the distance between the North Star and the horizon, while later sailors relied on the astrolabe, an appliance that measured the height of an astronomical body.

Nyctophobia has never been culturally or historically universal, and even during times of scarce illumination, has been accompanied by multivalent understandings. Koslofsky (2011) identifies how darkness has been conducive to conviviality, intimacy, experimentation and excitement. He discusses the mystical Christian theology of 16th- and 17th-century Europe that promoted meditation within caves whose murk metaphorically encapsulated the religious struggle from earthly gloom to illuminated afterlife. Darkness was valued as conducive to mystery, profundity and beauty, connoting the ineffability of God.

In modern times, as William Sharpe notes, a 'second city – with its own geography and its own set of citizens' emerges when daylight fades (2008: 14). Darkness permits clandestine, revolutionary and conspiratorial activities and challenges daytime norms of commerce, economic rationality and regulation. At night, the demi-monde comes to life, with witches, prostitutes, bohemians, beatniks, drug dealers, urban explorers, fly-posters and graffiti writers. Darkness is associated with libidinal desires, transgressive sexualities and mystical practices, promoting a nocturnal sublime, a 'realm of fascination and fear which inhabits the edges of our existence, crowded by shadows, plagued by uncertainty, and shrouded in intrigue' (ibid: 9).

These contrasts confirm Robert Williams' assertion that darkness is always mediated by human practices and values, 'constituted by social struggles about what should and should not happen in certain places during the dark of the night' (2008: 514). This remains the case as light banishes darkness from spaces in which it formerly persisted, as social and economic activity colonises the night (Melbin, 1978); all-night retail outlets multiply, television never ceases, and shift work and financial trading expand.

Excessive light pollution means that darkness is often deeply unfamiliar. Lurid skyglow surrounds urban areas, light trespasses into dark realms, and glare constrains the perception of dark space, reconfiguring the sensory and aesthetic experience of gloom (Edensor, 2013). There are still great swathes of darkness in the ocean, but in busy waters an abundance of buoys, windfarms, oil platforms and ships generate plentiful illumination, and this is intensified around the shore alongside fish farms

(continued)

(continued)

and harbourside developments. This surfeit of light has negative impacts upon migrating turtles, the life cycle of plankton and coral growth, and radically reshapes the human experience of marine darkness. An ability to see the night sky has been drastically curtailed. In response, there are new spaces in which darkness can be experienced: dark restaurants, theatrical experiences, tourist attractions and concerts – along with demands for dark sky parks on land and in marine areas.

In her quest to experience darkness 'for the love of its textures and wild intimacy', poet Kathleen Jamie took a ferry northwards along the east coast of Scotland from Aberdeen to the Orkney Isles, hoping to sail into the dark. As she writes:

> I'd been hoping for a moment at sea when there was no human light: 360° of winter sea, the only lights those carried by the ship itself. I wanted to be out in the night wind, in wholesome, unbanished darkness.

However, she was disappointed:

> There was always a light somewhere. From the port side, small towns, Brora perhaps, or Helmsdale, were an orange smudge against the darker line of land. From the starboard side I could look out at the moonlit, fishless sea. Some hours out, I saw three brash lights in a line to the east, the seaward side. I took them for other vessels, but they were too piled up and intense. They were North Sea oil-platforms, and even at this distance they looked frenzied.
>
> (2003: 30)

At one time, the lighthouse would have provided the only visible illumination for mariners, signifying the presence of land and other humans. Its beam would have been an immense source of relief. With the radical redistribution of light and dark across land and sea, the illumination dispensed by the lighthouse can no longer possess such potency. In an over-lit world, it is only one of many luminous marks along brightly lit coasts.

The over-illuminated world that now persists has led to a revaluing of darkness, which in many areas is now seldom experienced. The growth of dark sky parks, dark dining experiences, concerts staged in the dark, and forms of adventure tourism that take place during the night, testify to an unleashing of desires and practices that have until recently, been marginal. Challenging the reified cultural dualism of light and dark discussed earlier, these reappraisals of gloom stimulate the search for visual and non-visual encounters with space that diverge from normative sensory apprehension. They offer social engagements in which heightened experiences of intimacy and conviviality emerge, or direct participants towards quiet, meditative and imaginative practices (Edensor, 2017).

TECHNOLOGIES OF LIGHT AND POWER

Tim Edensor

As Tom Mole discusses, illumination was integral to notions of modernity and progress, a symbolic resonance further consolidated by scientific advances in illumination and construction. A radical transformation of space accompanied the introduction of gas and subsequently electric illumination. Urban inhabitants accustomed to remaining within their homes through fear of the dark flooded outside in search of amusement, spectacle, commerce and conviviality in shops, cafes and taverns, theatres and pleasure gardens (Brox, 2010).

By the end of the 17th century, though expansion was uneven, street lighting had been established in Amsterdam, Paris, Turin, London and Hamburg. Tallow candles were supplemented by cleaner and brighter Spermaceti candles from the whaling industry; lamps fuelled by paraffin and kerosene were succeeded by gaslight and, in the 1880s, by the incandescent electric bulb. Electric illumination spread throughout the late 19th and 20th centuries, as carbon, tungsten and subsequently ductile tungsten filament bulbs were successively replaced, and fluorescent and neon innovations were introduced. Nevertheless, this was an improvisational process, and the patchy, partial replacement of gas with electric lighting exemplifies how the history of illumination is characterised by 'multiple, overlapping perceptual patterns and practices rather than singular paradigms' (Otter, 2008: 10). Ad hoc arrangements, competing technologies and designs, corporate competition – notoriously between Thomas Edison and his competitors (Freeberg, 2013) – and disparities in wealth and power created variegated scenarios in which diverse forms of illumination coexisted, with obsolete technologies lingering in poor areas. As Cubitt (2013) asserts, illumination has always been a contested field in which, shifting according to cultural and historical contexts, meanings and practices are continuously negotiated between scientists, engineers, manufacturers, light designers, government officials, architects, businesses and inhabitants.

Nevertheless, illumination is synonymous with the industrial age, producing 'a new landscape of modernity' (Nasaw, 1999: 8), a nightscape of great white ways, illuminated driving spaces, shopping districts, leisure quarters and a new kind of theatrical realm, the illuminated shop window (Schivelbusch, 1988). This nocturnal reconfiguring produced uncertainty and fascination, transforming the city into a phantasmagorical realm abounding with 'the shadowy hauntings of the fleeting and insubstantial' (Collins and Jervis, 2008: 1). The modern city became 'a perceptual laboratory' (McQuire, 2008: 114), an oneiric setting, simultaneously enthralling and disorienting. According to Dietrich Neumann:

> No other artistic medium of the twentieth century has crossed the boundaries between art and commerce, technological display and utopian vision, easy entertainment and demagogic politics as effortlessly as this.
>
> (2002: 7)

The lighthouse was part of this radical defamiliarisation of space. The brilliance of the Alexandria Pharos must have astounded those encountering it for the first time, preceding and prefiguring this illuminated world. But the radiance of the modern lighthouse's beam and structural efficacy were transformed by modern technologies. In the following contributions, Brian Bowers explores the development of lighting technologies (see also Bowers, 1998); Gordon Love discusses the advent of perhaps the most momentous innovation in the history of lighthouse illumination, the Fresnel lens, which powerfully extended the transmission of the beam; and Steve Hoon discusses the evolution of the rotating devices that accommodated the weighty optical equipment. He also notes (pers. comm.) the effect of conversing with other disciplinary perspectives:

> With the physicality of the lighthouse as my primer, and knowing that this collection of essays was cross disciplinary, I found myself trying to encapsulate more than just inert matter and emotionless physics. I was affected by the knowledge that sociologists, historians and geographers of all hues, would have quite different takes upon lighthouses. This was a liberating experience. It let me write unconstrained by traditional subject disciplines. Specifically, I was able to reflect upon lighthouses as human agencies positioned temporarily and precariously within time and space in the natural environment, defined by more than just science and engineering, and specifically, appropriated by both microscopic and human life.

Technologies of light

Brian Bowers

Light when and where we want it is the main benefit of modern electric lighting. Until two centuries ago, the Moon determined night-time activity. Thus, in *Sense and Sensibility*, Jane Austen records a host trying to arrange a dinner at short notice, 'but it was moonlight, and everybody was full of engagements' (Austen, 1995: 17).

Oil lamps and candles

A simple oil lamp needs only a container and a piece of fibrous plant for a wick. Ancient Greeks and Romans made many pottery lamps, and their varied designs are used for dating archaeological sites and tracing patterns of trade. A larger wick consumes more oil and gives a larger flame, but not much more light. In Aristophanes' play, *The Clouds* (423 BC), Strepsiades rebukes his slave for putting such a hungry wick in the lamp that they ran out of oil. A candle is also an oil lamp: the wick stands in a pool of molten wax. Most candles were made of either expensive beeswax or cheaper tallow, derived from animal fat, until the late 19th century when paraffin wax was introduced.

Oil lamps were greatly improved in the 1780s, with circular wicks which gave more light (though also burnt more oil). For even brighter lights,

Figure 18 Argand improved oil lamps in 1782 by introducing a circular wick with air flowing inside as well as outside. For even brighter lights, as in lighthouses, several concentric wicks were used. Illustration: Figuier (1870) *Les Merveilles de la Science*.

(continued)

(continued)

including in some lighthouses, several concentric circular wicks were used. The paraffin that became available in the 1860s was cheaper and cleaner. Victorian paraffin lamps were often highly ornate, and given fancy names, such as the aneucapnic lamp (Greek: 'without smoke'). John Betjeman's (1977) children's story, *Archie and the Strict Baptists*, poked gentle fun at the idea that a paraffin lamp had no smell. But light without smell was really only possible with electric light.

Gas

For most of the 19th century, gas light meant light from a gas flame, which could be as bright as several candles, and not from a gas mantle. Gas light was demonstrated publicly in London in 1807 by Friedrich Albert Winzer, a German entrepreneur who subsequently established the world's first gas lighting company. This new technology was rapidly adopted, and by the end of the 19th century there were almost one thousand gas works in Britain. From the 1930s, however, gas lighting declined and the industry shifted to its modern role as a provider of heat.

A particularly brilliant white gas light was obtained by playing a very hot gas flame on a piece of lime (calcium oxide). Used in theatres, it has left us with the phrase 'in the limelight'. Another variation was the use of acetylene gas in places – such as lighthouses – that were too far away from gas mains. Acetylene is produced by the reaction of water and calcium carbide, so only the solid calcium carbide has to be transported to where the light is required, and the apparatus is quite simple.

Until the latter half of the 20th century, most gas was produced by heating coal in gas works and distributing the gas through mains, but with the discovery of natural gas, most gas works closed. If it had remained reliant on such sources, gas light would have quickly been replaced by electricity, but Carl Auer von Welsbach found that a fine cotton fabric impregnated with a solution of certain rare-earth oxides produced a 'mantle' of oxides which glowed brilliantly when heated. Lighting that used gas mantles was used domestically and for some street lighting for most of the 20th century.

Arc lighting

In the arc lamp, first demonstrated by Sir Humphry Davy in 1802, two pieces of carbon connected to an electricity supply are brought together, and then pulled a few millimetres apart, drawing a spark, or 'arc'. So much heat is produced that the ends of the carbon pieces glow white hot. As they burn away, a mechanism is needed to keep the gap constant. The Jablochkoff Candle, devised by the Russian engineer, Paul Jablochkoff, had parallel carbon rods separated by a thin layer of plaster of Paris. A thin link of graphite joined the upper ends. A live current fused the connecting link and an arc was struck, then, as the carbon rods burnt, the plaster crumbled away. In 1878 Jablochkoff Candles were installed along the Avenue de l'Opéra in Paris and London's Victoria Embankment. More reliable arc lamps with automatic regulators soon became available, but the brief period when Jablochkoff Candles were used made the public aware of the possibilities of electric light. Demand grew rapidly.

Incandescent filament

The brilliant light of the arc lamp could illuminate large areas and seemed ideal for lighthouse use. Michael Faraday experimented with arc lights for Trinity House, but reliable generating equipment was not available. The first incandescent filament lamps possessed carbon filaments, but several high-melting point metals were tried, with tungsten proving most successful. The essential requirements are a filament that can be heated and cooled repeatedly, connections sealed in a glass bulb, and a pump removing enough air to prevent oxidation.

There was no single inventor of the filament lamp, though William Grove demonstrated its potential in the 1840s. His 'filament' was platinum – the only metal which can be made white hot without oxidising. An adequate vacuum became possible in 1865 with Hermann Sprengel's mercury pump, enabling several people to make workable lamps. Best known were those of the Englishman Joseph Swan, whose filaments were carbonised cotton, and the American Thomas Edison, who used bamboo fibre. Filament lamps were first presented on a large scale at the 1881 International Electrical Exhibition in Paris. The 1880s were a boom time for electric lighting, but an entire infrastructure of public electricity supply had to be in place before it could be widely adopted.

Metal filaments, introduced in the early 20th century, have to be longer and thinner than carbon ones and require elaborate support. The coiled filament, from 1934, was often coiled again, giving the 'coiled-coil' filament. A carbon filament lamp gradually becomes blackened by a sooty deposit of carbon evaporating from the filament. J. A. Fleming's research in the mid-1880s led to the development of the diode valve, and other attempts were made to prevent blackening by including a small amount of chlorine, or other halogen, in the bulb, which reacted with the evaporated carbon to form a transparent compound. With 'quartz iodine' lamps, iodine was used rather than chlorine, and the bulbs were made of quartz. Soon the quartz was superseded by hard glass, and other halogens were used in 'tungsten halogen' lamps. These lamps were marketed for domestic use, both as general-purpose, mains-voltage lamps, giving higher brightness and a longer life than ordinary lamps, and as low-voltage spotlights.

(continued)

(continued)

Discharge and fluorescent lamps

In 1675 the French astronomer, Jean Picard, carrying his mercury-in-glass barometer at night, noticed a glow in the tube as the mercury slopped about. Francis Hauksbee investigated and concluded that the effect must be electrical, produced by the friction of the mercury on the glass. In the 1850s, when the Rühmkorff induction coil was available, researchers, notably Heinrich Geissler, studied electrical discharges in gases. Multicoloured 'Geissler tubes', with a Wimshurst machine supplying high voltage, were a favourite late Victorian scientific amusement.

The first practical 'discharge' lamps employed mercury vapour. In about 1900, Peter Cooper Hewitt introduced lamps with tubes a metre long. Although more efficient than filament lamps, they flickered and had an unattractive colour. In 1907, Georges Claude obtained a light with neon which, although reddish, wasted even less energy in heat. Early discharge lamps were more efficient and cheaper to run than carbon filament lamps, but their size, high operating voltage and poor colour were serious disadvantages. High-pressure mercury discharge lamps giving a bluish but steady light were introduced in 1932 and first used for street lighting at Wembley, Middlesex. To reduce heat losses, the discharge tube was mounted within an outer bulb. The low-pressure sodium discharge lamp works in a similar way and is even more efficient, but gives a very yellow light. The problem was to find materials able to withstand highly reactive hot sodium. In the 1970s, the high-pressure sodium lamp proved almost as efficient as the low-pressure lamp, but gave a wide-spectrum light, sometimes described as 'salmon pink'. The development which made this possible was a translucent ceramic material, alumina (Al_2O_3), for the arc tube.

In the second half of the 20th century, the most common electric light in shops and offices was the fluorescent tube, in which an electric discharge in mercury vapour produces ultraviolet light which is converted into visible light by an internal phosphor coating. Although efficient, early fluorescent lamps were not popular because of their poor colour rendition and tendency to flicker. An initial high cost also discouraged their adoption. But modern fluorescents have largely overcome these problems and, with low running costs, rapidly increased their share of the market.

Lighting now and in the future

Today lighting is changing yet again: the 'light-emitting diode' – the LED – is rapidly becoming the preferred light source for all purposes. It was known for over a century that some semiconductor devices could emit light, and red LEDs have long been used as indicators. Further development has produced very efficient LEDs giving white light, ideal for general illumination.

> Lighting technology has come a long way. Early lighthouses, such as that at Alexandria in the 3rd century BC, burnt wood. Contrast this with the intensity and efficiency of the modern lighthouse beam, whose luminous glow can be seen even beyond the horizon.

The Fresnel lens
Enabling lighthouse technology

Gordon D. Love

Which technological advance throughout history has had the greatest impact on the world? There are many laudable candidates. My own favourites include, in chronological order, the wheel, the lens, penicillin, and finally

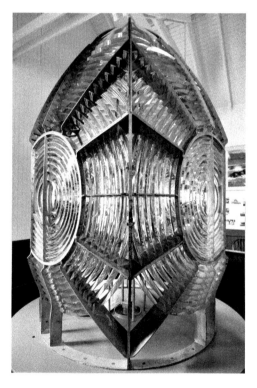

Figure 19 Fresnel lens, Point Arena Lighthouse, California. Photograph: Gabelstaplerfahrer at English Wikipedia, CC BY 3.0 (http://creativecommons.org/licenses/by/3.0), via Wikimedia Commons.

(continued)

(continued)

the transistor, which opened up the possibilities for electronic technology and our current information revolution. My argument for including the lens in this list is twofold. First, its deployment has enabled developments in many fields of science. We learn about the physical world through a variety of sources, but by far the largest source is via light and imaging. The lens has enabled the development of microscopes and telescopes which have opened up whole new – vast and minuscule – worlds. Second, lenses are one of the most widely used medical aids, in the form of spectacles. Poor vision affects the vast majority of people, especially as they age, and the ability to correct it is enormously important for both our productivity and well-being.

Lenses have been integral to the development of lighthouses. The evolution of modern lighthouses in the 18th century, as shipping expanded, required two key pieces of technology: a source of light and a mechanism for directing the light. Light sources changed from fire to oil and, in the 19th century, to electricity. However, all light sources, except lasers, emit rays in all directions and therefore require some kind of focusing mechanism to concentrate the light and send it in the required direction. Systems were designed using both mirrors and lenses to focus light. But a major challenge was how to build a very large high-powered lens. French scientist Augustin-Jean Fresnel addressed this problem. A giant in the history of optics, he made contributions to understanding the nature of light as a wave, polarisation and diffraction of light, and crucially, implemented a number of practical applications such as the lens that bears his name.

In order to make a parallel beam of light (one which is neither converging nor diverging), a lens is placed in front of the light source exactly one focal length away. A broad beam of light requires a large lens – typically a metre or so in diameter. The thickness of a lens relates to this length. A lens has a lenticular (biconvex, lentil-like) shape – if we increase its diameter then its thickness must also increase. To build a large lens that is not enormously thick would demand a very long focal length, placing the lens a long way from the light source. Such a lighthouse would need to have a huge diameter. This is impractical, so a method of making a large lens with a short focal length was needed. Fresnel's design is shown in Figure 19. The operation of a Fresnel lens can be understood in a number of ways, according to different theories for describing light. The simplest is ray optics, in which light is thought of as beams that travel in straight lines. This theory is commonly used in analysing optical systems. However, it does not account for the fact that light is a wave, or explain certain observations such as diffraction and interference (for instance, as with the colours we see on the road when oil is spilt onto water). Wave, or physical optics, is used to describe these phenomena (and also the whole of ray optics). A third theory is called quantum optics – employed in dealing with extremely faint sources of light (but not when analysing lighthouses).

The Fresnel lens: enabling lighthouse technology 85

The simplest way to consider a Fresnel lens is with ray optics, and by noting that a lens operates by bending rays of light, and that this bending occurs at the lens surface where light travels through air to glass and *vice versa*. This is described by Snell's law. Accordingly, if the focusing ability of a lens is caused primarily at its surface, can we remove much of the glass? Fresnel's design removed much of the bulk of the glass to produce a lens which essentially replicated just the surface of the lens, making it possible to have a lens of almost arbitrary size which is very thin. As well as in lighthouses, such lenses are used in overhead projectors (now somewhat obsolete) and as simple magnifying glasses.

So, why aren't all lenses made this way to avoid making bulky heavy lenses? The first practical reason is that the surface of the lens possesses numerous discontinuities which can distort and scatter the light if not made properly, and these discontinuities also limit the ability of the lens to focus light from a range of angles. A more fundamental reason is that ray optics is only an approximation for wave optics, and our assumption that we can remove large chunks of glass without affecting the performance of the lens is only correct for light of a single wavelength. Thus, a Fresnel lens has a number of different focal lengths, and focuses light of different colours differently. It is not a very high-quality lens. This is fine for lighthouses and overhead projectors, but less useful in things such as cameras where the undesirable effects would be evident.

Lighthouse lenses today work on the principle of Fresnel lenses, but with some modification. They have elements that both reflect and refract (bend) light. The aim is to take light from the light source – which is radiated in all directions – and redirect it into a beam of light, as shown in Figure 20.

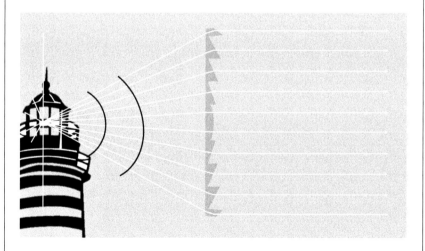

Figure 20 The Fresnel lens and its effect on a beam of light.

(continued)

(continued)

In the Fresnel lens, the jagged lens structure is conventional except that large, superfluous, chunks of glass have been removed. The lens is placed close to the light source – but is shown here outside of the lighthouse for clarity.

Fresnel lenses have been important in the history of science for a host of reasons. Fresnel was one of the key players in the development of the wave theory of light – and a full understanding of a Fresnel lens needs a comprehension of this crucial theory. Critically important in the development of the lighthouse, it enabled the construction of huge lenses from smaller glass elements. Modern lighthouses no longer necessarily use Fresnel lenses, but Fresnel structures are used in many other technologies, for example to direct light in car headlights and, more recently, in TV projection systems. One of the most exciting modern developments in lenses is spectacle lenses for correcting presbyopia. Affecting most people over the age of 45, this is caused by hardening of the eye lens, resulting in an inability to change focus. This can be fixed with reading glasses, but then requires a change of glasses for near and far vision, or varifocal lenses, which some people struggle to use. Spectacles or contact lenses with varying optical power – either varying power across a single lens, or a lens that can switch in time – has the potential to help many people. Emerging companies trying to push this technology generally use some variation of Fresnel's lens.

The lens is therefore one of the most important technologies in history, and the Fresnel lens has enabled a number of important variations on the basic lens design – the lighthouse being the most famous of them all.

Early lighthouse lamp technology

Steve Hoon

The lights of the earliest lighthouses were weak, comprising only towers upon which fires were built. Even the illumination of the tallow candles of the 18th-century Eddystone Lighthouse was faint, unable in storms to warn mariners until they were almost upon the hazard. Although 19th-century acetylene gas lamps, electric carbon arc lamps and high-power electric filament lamps increased the efficacy of lighthouses and so maritime safety, it was the invention of the 18th-century Argand oil lamp that enabled the development of modern lighthouse optical components.

In a homogeneous material, rays of light travel in straight lines. But the Earth is curved, and light from an unfocused beam weakens in proportion to the reciprocal of distance squared. Thus, a lighthouse needs both a powerful lamp and a tall tower. A powerful lamp atop a 50-metre tower can (in a clear atmosphere) be seen on the horizon 25 kilometres away. The way to achieve such a beam proved to be to employ a large focusing concave parabolic mirror behind the light, and an equally large convergent convex lens in front of it. The luminously stable Argand oil lamp, which could be mounted at the centre of a large optical system, was the genesis of the modern lighthouse. The fabrication of a lightweight mirror was not problematic. But making a lightweight glass lens a metre or more in diameter is more problematic. As Gordon Love has explained, the solution was to employ Fresnel lenses which emulated the active optical surface of a lens but omitted its passive centre. By omitting the lens core and repositioning the resulting segmented surface as a sheet of concentric annular prismoidal arcs, a Fresnel lens reduced its weight by 75 per cent.

But a focused light can only be seen over a narrowly defined sector, rendering the lighthouse invisible to all outside the narrow angle of its beam. The solution is to rotate the focusing mechanism by incorporating occluding shutters, which also meant that every lighthouse could be given a locally distinctive optical signature. Rotation also avoids the technological challenge of switching high-powered lamps on and off and imposing thermal shock that shortens their life.

The lighthouse optical system must rotate precisely or its code of light pulses will be unrecognisable to mariners and its unique signature lost. The sweeping beam of traditional lighthouses creates the illusion of an optical flash. Early lantern rotation systems were driven by large weights hanging from cables within the tower. Their descent was regulated by an escapement mechanism echoing that of a longcase clock, similarly designed to rotate regularly to mark the passage of time. It fell to the 18th-century lighthouse keeper to wind up these weights each day and replenish the expended gravitational energy. So, was the light's rotation actually gravity powered? One might say that it is the carbohydrate content of porridge and potatoes that are the intermediate bio-energy sources driving the ATP (Adenosine triphosphate) cycles within the keeper's muscles. These plants in turn derive their energy via photosynthesis from the Sun. Thus, through biotic and human agency, solar energy has morphed from pure sunlight into a rotating light!

Whatever its physical source, considerable energy has to be expended to overcome friction and inertia and rotate the carriage supporting the lighthouse lantern, which can easily weigh five tons or more. Such a weight generates significant frictional load upon the carriage bearings. Iron wheels running on circular rails were frequently employed to support the carriage, as the small point contact between the rim of a circular metal wheel and its supporting rail possesses very low rolling friction: a fact well understood by railway engineers.

An alternative and favoured solution was to float the optics and carriage on a pool of liquid mercury contained in a cast-iron trough. This provided a

(continued)

vibration-free low-friction rotational bearing upon which the entire lantern could be rotated with little energy loss, even by hand in an emergency. Although low-loss mercury bearings were an inspired choice, their use today would be completely unacceptable due to mercury's bio-toxicity. But highly motile metallic mercury, with a density 13.6 times greater than water and a similar viscosity, can float solid concrete, stone, glass and iron. In the past, it was not just the mariners that floated.

BUILDING THE LIGHTHOUSE

Tim Edensor

In turning to consider the technologies deployed to build lighthouses, it is pertinent to acknowledge both their adaptability to spatial context and purpose, and the sheer variety of forms they have assumed: conical, cylindrical, rectangular, pyramidal or tapered in shape, and composed of brick, stone, wood, steel or concrete. More sheltered shore-based lighthouses are usually shorter and constructed out of wood or brick. Those situated in hurricane-threatened environments also tend to take stockier and shorter form, but are composed of sturdier materials.

Where they are more exposed or sited offshore, lighthouses usually possess a thick base or take the form of skeleton towers, less affected by wind and easily disassembled. In such unprotected locations, diverse technologies have been enlisted to maximise their stability. Steel cables embedded in lead have been deployed to reinforce stone bases, but this has been largely superseded by the sinking of iron screwpiles deep into the rock strata or the construction of a concrete-filled iron caisson. As Steve Hoon shows, the application of physics through which the lighthouse form and structure has been developed has been critical in ensuring that these often-exposed structures endure.

The physicality of lighthouses

Steve Hoon

Lighthouses embody the defining parameters of science: mass, length, time and energy, and, more cryptically, life itself. Lighthouses are interfaces between the natural world and human endeavour. Interfaces, where much fascinating science lies, are 'between-surfaces', neither surface '*a*' nor surface '*b*' but their ad-joint. Soils are the interface between geology, life and planetary atmosphere. The planet's thin crust is the interface between molten magma and the domain we call Earth. It is into this interfacial crust that lighthouses are keyed.

(continued)

(continued)

Figure 21 The Stanislav Range Front Light, a 'sister' lighthouse echoing the design of the Adziogol Lighthouse in the Ukraine. Photograph: AL, CC BY-SA 3.0 (http://creativecommons.org/licenses/by-sa/3.0), via Wikimedia Commons.

The smooth, asymptotically tapering, axially symmetric columnar form of the classic lighthouse is modelled upon the hyperboloid, exemplified by the tubular steel lattice Ukrainian Adziogol Lighthouse. The internal, circular, walled living spaces of a lighthouse may challenge the placement of rectangular furniture, but the clean, steep-sided hyperbolic tower is so designed for good reason. Its form comprises a smooth, low-resistance structure. It lets wind and wave flow easily over it, deflecting rather than opposing the violence that would be unleashed by resisting the momentum of massive storm waves. Just as the tapered prow of a ship parts the sea, so the smooth, rounded cross-section of the lighthouse's tower deflects with least resistance a vengeful storm wave in a way that a flat obdurate surface could not. As Newton understood, the rate of change of momentum (the product of velocity and mass) is the origin of all kinematic force. For a structure to oppose, in a short time, even a slowly moving wave weighing over a tonne per cubic metre and further laden with sand and cobbles, is to experience an enormous reactionary force. A lighthouse obstinately designed to oppose or reverse the motion of the sea would experience ferocious, abrasive and destructive forces, while one designed to let the sea and wind flow around and over it does not.

> As attested by the smooth pebbles on a beach, nature sculptures unregimented curves. Even the awe-inspiring pinnacles of the Alps are in time eroded, smoothed, flattened and returned to the sea in an endless bio-hydro-geological cycle. Lighthouses too erode into the brine. Humankind's desire for security and permanence enters into uneasy terms with elemental forces acting over time to smooth rough interfaces.
>
> While the earliest land-based lighthouses were often rugged 'four-square' masonry structures, building on wave-washed islets and exposed rocks posed significant physical and civil engineering challenges. Like the first wooden 1698 Eddystone Lighthouse, many were transitory structures later replaced by durable stone. To withstand the pounding of the sea, John Smeaton and Robert Stevenson, 18th- and 19th-century pioneers of British lighthouse design, developed a technique of interlocking dovetailed and reinforced masonry in ringed courses, the mortar chemically bonding and sealing each dressed block with another. Smeaton also developed hydraulic lime mortar which set underwater. Due to the self-sustaining exothermic chemical bonding reaction, the mortar continued curing even when covered by an incoming tide. The collective bulk of the tapering stone tower secures it by gravitation, chemistry and morphology to the foundational bedrock. A physicality that is a harmonious synthesis of gravity, earth history, geology, engineering, chemistry and the stonemason's craft results in a structure protecting lighthouse keeper and seafarer alike.

Returning to the ways in which illumination has been emblematic of modern science and enlightenment, Steve Millington suggests that it was not merely light technologies that symbolised modern progress but that the functional form of the lighthouse itself is proto-modern(ist), contradicting current interpretations that lighthouses are nostalgic emblems of maritime heritage. David Cooper then explores how a modernist structure, Liverpool's St John's Beacon, a giant homologue of a lighthouse, has been the focus of shifting assessments and functions.

The modern lighthouse

A sculpture by accident

Steve Millington

> On the coast waves break and salt foam scatters and denudes, gales blow stronger and the rain is more searching . . . Buildings must be sturdy and close to the earth.
>
> (John Piper quoted in Spalding, 2009: 135)
>
> *(continued)*

(continued)

This essay discusses the utilitarian qualities of the lighthouse, focusing on post-medieval lighthouse design, or what Hague and Christie (1975) describe as *secular lights*. John Smeaton's 18th-century Eddystone Lighthouse (1759) epitomises this more contemporary form, stripping away ecclesiastical symbols, cultural adornments and architectural indulgences to create a lighthouse marked by bold simplicity and functional design. Through the combination of innovative engineering, logical use of materials, and an emphasis on efficiency and economy, Smeaton (1724–1794) established the iconic lighthouse shape, typified by the wide, circular base supporting a tall, tapering tower. Through Smeaton, the lighthouse acquired architectural and functional qualities procreant of a modernist or the machine-age aesthetic. Considered both modern and a site of technological progress, the aesthetic qualities of the lighthouse have somehow slipped into a nostalgic realm of nautical gaiety or kitsch maritime heritage. This essay, therefore, re-examines the connection between lighthouse construction and the modernist aesthetic, and explores the other qualities associated with the lighthouse during the 20th century.

Unadorned functionalism: John Smeaton's Eddystone

In the most basic terms, a lighthouse is merely an architectural support for a lighting mechanism, which is its primary function. Drawing on the notion of *constructive intelligence*, Smeaton's utilitarian design was inspired by 'the trunk of an oak tree, which is equally remarkable for gracefulness and strength' (Anon, 1876: 31), in creating a structure where sturdiness, longevity and reliability were paramount.

Smeaton's engineering rationality therefore draws upon numerous technological innovations to enable the lighthouse to withstand climatic and topographical contingencies. The broad cylindrical mass at the base dissipates the energy from wave impact, while the taper encourages water to flow up the structure, absorbing the impact across a wider area of the granite exterior:

> At intervals of a minute and sometimes two or three; I suppose when a combination happens to produce one overgrown wave, it would strike the rock and the building conjointly, and fly up in a white column, enwrapping it like a sheet, rising at least to double the height of the house, and totally intercepting it from sight.
>
> (Smeaton, 1814: 40)

Eddystone's exterior was coated in a new water-resistant cement, while the internal structure combined a complex system of dovetailing, marble dowels, joggles, plugs, and cemented stonework. Bolting the structure to various rock types and precipices called for multiple engineering solutions, which generated a lexicography of functional terms: 'screwpile, skeleton, sparkplug, bottle, cupola, conical, cylindrical, square, pyramidal, hexagonal, octagonal, and integral' (Blake, 2007: 12).

Smeaton's blueprint differs from other Georgian–Victorian engineering projects, which often included adornments to add flavour, reflecting period design and taste. In general, lighthouses based on Smeaton's design were stripped of unnecessary decor to generate a utilitarian monotony. By contrast, the first two Eddystone lighthouses devised by Henry Winstanley were octagonal wooden structures festooned with 'projections and quaint contrivances' to resemble a Chinese pagoda (Davenport Adams, 1891). The second was washed away in 1703, after barely five years of operation. John Rudyard's replacement combined timber and masonry and operated from 1709, before burning down in 1755. The huge costs involved in constructing buildings in such perilous locations required structures that were made to last. In the words of Smeaton (quoted in de Mare, 1973: 45):

> You cannot fool the elements; you cannot play games with the sea – nor, indeed, with the ferocious force of water trying to find the tranquility of its own level in any place. When dealing with realities that can kill you have to build 'em right.

Ultimately, Smeaton's lighthouse endured: 'the house stood for over 120 years, before the rock itself gave way, so firm and functional was its design' (de Mare, 1973: 45). Smeaton's maritime engineering earned him the title 'the father of civil engineering' (Guichard and Trethewey, 2002). He influenced construction throughout the British Isles and the Colonies, including work by the great engineering families. Lighthouses including Robert Stevenson's Bell Rock (1811), James Walker's Bishop Rock (1858), James Douglass' Wolf Rock (1869) and William Douglass' Fastnet II (1904) all built upon and adapted Smeaton's initial design to establish the enduring iconic lighthouse.

Lighthouses as proto-modernist sculptures

Kurt Ackermann (1991) draws attention to a neglected appreciation of industrial architecture. We might celebrate the fusion of engineering and technology in the industrial classicism of Peter Behrens' AEG Turbine Factory (1909); the art-deco stylings of the Bauhaus; or the constructivist symbolism of Soviet factory design. But Ackermann discusses more prosaic industrial structures: chimneys, cooling towers, incinerators, electricity pylons and radio masts. The function of these structures is immediately apparent, and absolutely determines their design. For Ackermann, these structures possess *constructive intelligence*: they simply have to be the

(continued)

(continued)

shape they are to withstand the forces of gravity and nature. At the same time, they eschew economically unnecessary adornments that might also compromise their structural integrity.

Thus, the pylon or the chimney is a raw form of architecture: a building stripped to its abstract core, composed of bold geometries and shapes. They could be sculptures by accident. While the lighthouse is perhaps 'the most obvious of many functional buildings' (Piper quoted in Spalding, 2009: 138), it is rarely acknowledged as part of the modernist industrial landscape. This is surprising until we consider that, prior to the construction of 20th-century steel-framed skyscrapers, the world's great lighthouses were the tallest roofed structures ever constructed. The Corduan Lighthouse in France (1611) reached a lofty 223 feet, not quite surpassing the 250-foot Lanterna in Genoa. These structures, however, retain period architectural flourishes, including tiling and wood panelling, which places them firmly in a pre-modern realm, while Rayner Banham (1960: 131), in discussing Sant Elia's sketches, draws parallels between early 20th-century Futurism and lighthouse design:

> Their shapes are bare and smooth, rectangular or semi-circular in plan, often battered back in section to give a tapering silhouette, their vertical emphasis uninterrupted by string-courses and cornices, but reinforced by boldly marked vertical arrises [sic].

The clarity, simplicity and harmony of Smeaton's iconic design also resonates with the minimalist vocabulary identified by Robert Venturi and colleagues (1972) and associated with early 20th-century modernist architects such as Mies van der Rohe. Accordingly, the proto-modernist qualities of Smeaton's lighthouse should be considered alongside the architecture of the Industrial Revolution, as an iconic structure that helped to define a new age.

Perhaps the ultimate expression of Smeaton's lighthouse design – as described by Steve Hoon above (see Figure 21) – is Vladimir Shukhov's Adziogol (1911), located on the Dneiper River in the Ukraine. While retaining the iconic circular base and tapering tower, the structure not only does away with decor or colour, but also with the stonework and interior space. What is left is an abstraction of a lighthouse: a parabolic steel frame supporting a thin tubular post fixed to a simple circular concrete pad. The keeper resides in a cottage at the base of the structure. This fusion of Smeaton and Soviet Constructivism firmly locates this lighthouse design within 20th-century modernism.

Post-war lighthouse design has produced even starker brutalist structures. Hvalnes (1954), constructed in Iceland, is a simple square cylindrical concrete block, and Philip Hunt's fully-automated Dungeness (1961) is a minimalist tube-like structure, with no taper, constructed by stacking pre-cast, pre-stressed concrete rings.

Figure 22 Dungeness New Lighthouse in Kent. Photograph: Nilfanion, CC BY-SA 4.0 (http://creativecommons.org/licenses/by-sa/4.0), via Wikimedia Commons.

The descent of the lighthouse into nautical gaiety

Commissioned by John Betjeman in the 1930s, the *Shell Guides to Britain*, containing the paintings of John Piper, Peggy Richard and Paul Nash, endeavoured to capture Britain's recent-modernist landscape. They developed the notion of the *modern picturesque*, an appreciation of 20th-century landscapes which contrasts with 19th-century conventions regarding good planning and visual design. Britain's coastline communities are portrayed in Piper's *The Nautical Style* (1938) through a celebration of 'nautical gaiety', a notion developed by Eric de Mare's (1973) examination of coastal architecture in identifying a *functional tradition* within *sea-coast building*, foregrounding what he calls *the Sailor's taste*. This is a Britain of bright

(continued)

(continued)

regatta flags, striped signal masts and colourful dots, producing a colour symbolism that denotes gaiety through *unadorned functionalism*.

Crucially, from this point onwards, the iconic lighthouse form seems to slip into a landscape that is quaint, romantic or even gothic, associated with a nostalgic vision of Britain's maritime heritage that usurps the position of the lighthouse as an important site of innovation in visual technology and engineering experimentation (Otter, 2008). Despite maintaining a practical function, lighthouses, with their colourful black and white or red stripes, pass into a national design idiom that reproduces a notion of nautical gaiety, and qualities of sturdiness, strength and longevity become linked with visions of romance and beauty.

De Mare (1973) captures the ambivalence of this cultural representation, which combines aesthetics and utility, modernism and nostalgia:

> It's very unusual to see an ugly lighthouse. Unlike other buildings of a purely utilitarian nature, lighthouses are often located in places having a rugged beauty and this makes us think of them as picturesque even though they are not trying to be beautiful. Lighthouses are where they are because they need to be where they are.

Thus, by the mid-20th century, the lighthouse has passed far into the realm of nautical nostalgia, obscuring how, as sites of technological and engineering innovation since the late 18th century, they sit with mills and factories as defining symbols of the Industrial Revolution.

Sky-tower as icon

David Cooper

Lighthouses are exemplars of unshowy architectural efficacy: structures built for an unambiguous purpose and predicated on a harmonious marriage of modest form and necessary functionality. It would be erroneous, however, to assert that they are uncomplicated utilitarian structures. Rather, lighthouses are often the products of a knotty entanglement of social, political and cultural intentions, forming sites rich with emotional and spiritual symbolism. Sky-towers illustrate these more complex aspects. They comply with Iain Sinclair's definition of 'grand projects': 'vanity interventions' proposed by architects who appear to privilege concept over serviceability (Sinclair, 2011: 302–303). In other words, they are structures in which the symbolic has primacy over the practical.

Instead of the quiet architectural restraint of the liminal lighthouse, the sky-tower is an 'iconic' or 'beacon statement' in the centre of the urban landscape (Sinclair, 2011: 254); and, in contrast to the quotidian usefulness of the lighthouse, the sky-tower's principal function is to provide an elevated vantage point for gazing into and across the cityscape. The situated in-the-world-ness of the lighthouse, therefore, is replaced with an architectural space which provides the visitor with the opportunity to appreciate the topology of the built environment from a position of aerial detachment. As Michel de Certeau puts it in his famous discussion of the World Trade Center:

> When one goes up there, he leaves behind the mass that carries off and mixes up in itself any identity of authors or spectators. An Icarus flying above these waters, he can ignore the devices of Daedalus in mobile and endless labyrinths far below. His elevation transfigures him into a voyeur.
>
> (de Certeau, 1984: 92)

Where the lighthouse is to be viewed, the sky-tower is a site from which to view; but, as de Certeau makes clear, the granting of such panoptical perceptual experiences is invariably indexed to a demonstration of political and economic authority and power.

St John's Beacon, Liverpool, is a sky-tower of sorts. As Jon Murden explains, in 1959, Ravenseft – a property development company which had specialised in regenerating British provincial cities after the war – approached Liverpool City Council with a proposal to develop St John's Market into an American-style shopping 'precinct' (Murden, 2006: 399). Six years later, construction began on the market and the adjacent beacon to a design by Weightman and Bullen. The tower, rising 138 metres above sea level, was intended as a ventilation shaft for the market and was completed in December 1969. However, new legislation was passed which rendered this purpose redundant and signalled the start of the tower's spatial history as a site without a demonstrable *raison d'être*. Yet, despite this setback, the crow's nest opened in 1971 as a French restaurant, complete with a revolving floor. Diners were able to take a reassuringly smooth high-speed lift to enjoy a spatial and culinary experience offering an unprecedented elevation above the realities of the city. The beacon – which, as Joseph Sharples points out, was 'modelled on the Euromast at Rotterdam' – functioned as a glamorously exotic 'elsewhere', floating high above 1970s Liverpool: a site of social aspiration and a tantalising preview of the new forms of spatial experience which might – for a privileged few – constitute everyday life in the 21st century (Sharples, 2004: 188).

While a traditional lighthouse is both vulnerably embedded in, and resistant to, the often-extreme environmental conditions of its immediate

(continued)

(continued)

locale, this late 20th-century urban sky-tower was subjected to a radically different set of external pressures. In 1977, the fate of St John's Beacon was again shaped by legislation as a health and safety ruling forced the closure of the restaurant. A relatively long period of time followed in which the tower remained largely unoccupied. In 1983, the beacon's original potential as a lofty symbol of the future was self-consciously revisited through the opening of a Buck Rogers-themed restaurant. But this venture also failed to last and, for over fifteen years, the tower operated merely as a folly jutting above the city skyline. The rare occasions when members of the public were allowed to experience the 30-second elevator ride to the crow's nest in the 1980s and 1990s merely served to underscore the apparent pointlessness of the project.

In 2000, however, a commercial radio station ambitiously renovated and reconfigured the tower at a cost of just over £4 million. Ever since, Radio City – and its sister stations – have broadcast from studios in the crow's nest; and, in the spring of 2011, the company opened a viewing gallery to the (paying) public. Radio City's occupation of the space-in-the-sky for over fifteen years suggests that, at last, the beacon has found an explicable function. Crucially, it is also a use which – in spite of its unapologetically commercial imperatives – counters the earlier sense of exclusivity through a democratic appeal to the civic spatial imagination. For long periods of its history, St John's Beacon has operated, in different ways, as a closed space. Now, though, the tower broadcasts across Liverpool and its surrounding areas, providing a dominant spatial image of a centrifugal practice in which the station reaches its listeners from this elevated hub.

The intangibility of the radio wave means that Radio City has turned to light to materialise this practice, and the name and frequency of the main station is illuminated at night in giant yellow letters and numerals. The station has similarly used light to mark significant moments in the life of the city: for example, on 27 April 2016, the number '96' shone out on the night that the jury returned its verdicts at the Hillsborough inquests. That the radio signals aren't actually transmitted from the tower itself is a minor detail. The radio station uses light to show how, through sound, the identity of St John's Beacon is finally predicated on both geographical situatedness and social connectedness.

As discussed, the invention of the Fresnel lens and other innovations have been crucial to the technological development of the lighthouse. But technological developments in physics, optics and illumination did not merely circulate around scientific laboratories or the debating rooms of politicians but also suffused political and popular debate. Growing excitement about rapid technological developments is wonderfully illustrated by James Purdon's account of

J. M. W. Turner's enthusiasm for portraying the lighthouse as an exemplar of high-minded science but also as an estimable public good.

Turner's lights

James Purdon

Among the most radical transformations of the visual field in early 19th-century Britain was the technological assault on darkness. In factories, in homes, and in the newly gas-lit streets of London, innovations in lighting encroached on the night, replacing diurnal and seasonal rhythms of illumination with the possibility of eternal, industrialised visibility (Schivelbusch, 1988). But the most ambitious project of this new regime proceeded far from the heart of the metropolis. Beginning in the early 1780s, a new constellation of lights sprang up by the harbours of seaside towns, on remote clifftops, and far offshore. So dramatic was this expansion of illumination that in 1828 the lighthouse engineer Alan Stevenson took it upon himself to compile a book-length list with detailed descriptions of more than 180 coastal beacons. 'The Lights upon the shores of Great Britain and Ireland are now so numerous,' he explained, 'and additional ones are still so much called for by the mariner, that the difficulty of knowing one light from another is daily increasing' (Stevenson, 1831: vi–vii).

Throughout the early 19th century, Britain's most assiduous investigator of lights – of one sort or another – was the painter J. M. W. Turner. Following his death in 1851, Turner was canonised as the undisputed master of luminescence, an artist for whom everything, including form and colour, became secondary to 'the radiance of suffused light' (Hind, 1910: 119). Before he became known as a painter of light, however, Turner already had a reputation as a painter of *lights*. Between the 1790s and the 1840s, he made scores, if not hundreds, of sketches, drawings, watercolours, oil paintings and mezzotints depicting lighthouses around the coasts of Britain, France and Italy. From the early sketch, *Sunset at Sea with a Lighthouse and Ship* (1796–1797) to the late *Lighthouse at Dieppe* (1845), his work returns, again and again, to lighthouses, painted in all weathers and atmospheric conditions. In 1813, he executed a series of watercolours of the Eddystone Lighthouse, off the coast of Devon, showing one of Britain's best-known feats of maritime engineering in various conditions of storm and calm, night and day. Six years later he was commissioned by the engineer Robert Stevenson (the father of Alan) to design a frontispiece for his account of the construction of the Bell Rock Lighthouse in the North Sea off Angus. Engraved for the book by John Horsburgh, Turner's imaginative version of the scene – he never made the trip to see it for himself – depicts

(continued)

(continued)

Figure 23 Bell Rock Lighthouse, by J. M. W. Turner, 1819. Google Art Project via Wikimedia Commons.

Also see Plate 5.

waves creeping tendril-like up the stem of the tower as a ship passes safely in the middle-distance, guided by its warning beams.

Turner was particularly interested in the newly built and upgraded coastal lights which, along with improved roads, sanitation and other public works, heralded the expansion of Britain's 'infrastructure state' in the late 18th and early 19th centuries (see Guldi, 2012). His broader awareness of the changing appearance of maritime activity during the Industrial Revolution also illuminates the relationship between technology, national identity and aesthetics in the early years of Britain's imperial expansion.

In 1802, Turner crossed the Channel, touring France and Switzerland. His freedom of movement was then limited by the Napoleonic Wars, but after Waterloo he became a regular visitor to the continent. He travelled up the Seine in 1832 to gather material for a book of engravings, *Turner's Annual Tour*. For the 1834 volume, he produced a striking vignette of the twin light towers on the Cap de la Hève, of which he made several drawings; he also took views of the lighthouses at Honfleur – later to be a favourite subject for Boudin, Monet and Seurat – and at Quillebeuf-sur-Seine.

By that time, Turner would have been able to discern a marked improvement in the brightness of lighthouses on the Normandy coast, many of which had been upgraded with superior Fresnel lenses (Levitt, 2013). It would be another decade before the Fresnel lens, which focused beams of light by means of prisms rather than mirrors, was introduced to Britain.

Attuned as he was to the subtlest gradations of visible light, it would be surprising if Turner of all people had failed to notice these new French lights, which shone many times brighter than their British counterparts.

Lighthouses served Turner in his paintings in much the same way they served mariners at sea: by structuring the spatial field around a point of relatively high visibility. At la Hève, the towers form a common point of reference in views taken from multiple different perspectives. A lighthouse, for Turner, was never just a structure to be painted: although stationary, his lighthouses are active elements in the framing of the image even when their visibility is reduced to a minimum by his famous atmospheric effects. This can be seen clearly in the composition history of *Longships Lighthouse, Land's End* (1834–1835), a painting singled out by John Ruskin, Turner's most constant critical champion, for its production of a 'gloom, dependent rather on the enormous space and depth indicated, than on actual pitch of colour' (Ruskin, 1843: 240).

Whirling spray and rock and cloud together, Turner's squally watercolour looms out of the 19th century like a typhoon, capturing all the precariousness of the beacon palely glimpsed in the midst of an almighty gale. But the lighthouse, for all its obscurity, is the firm centre of the painting. In one of several colour studies he made in preparation, Turner depicted the viewpoint from the other side of the headland, with the northern coastline of Land's End looming up from the left-hand side of the image. But in the finished composition, his viewpoint has pivoted around the fixed point of the lighthouse itself, so that the jagged *southern* part of the coast, with its rough breakers and warning flare, appears on the right-hand side. The near foreground is occupied by a half-submerged wreck, its mass of sodden, splintered wood, broken metal and tangled rope balanced, in a different medium, by the whirling seabirds suspended between spray and sky at the top right. The painting is sharply divided between deep background, where the lighthouse imposes its ordering presence on seemingly featureless space, and a foreground consisting of nothing *but* feature. The evidence of nature's unpredictability, in the wreck and the whirling birds, is held in balance by the composition of the visual field. For Turner, such balance could only be held for an instant: where order could be achieved, it had to be made and maintained by the application of continuous effort.

For a more characteristically Victorian mind like Ruskin's, order suggested something reassuringly eternal. In the fourth volume of *Modern Painters* (1856), Ruskin describes three landmarks on the Calais coastline, in the arrangement of which he perceives a kind of symbolic harmony: 'the lighthouse for life, and the belfry for labour, and [the church tower] for patience and praise'. Turner, by contrast, was interested in lighthouses less as symbol than as *system*. In the right mood, he could certainly do the lighthouse as a version of the sublime – a preliminary study for an illustration of Thomas Moore's classicist novel *The Epicurean*, done in 1837,

(continued)

(continued)

shows the blood-red silhouette of the Pharos at Alexandria bursting out of a golden sunrise – but modern lighthouses were not to be confused with ancient wonders. Where Ruskin saw the lighthouse as an abstract representation of the contract between the secular and the sacred, Turner's copious pencil sketches make it clear that he saw individual lighthouses, sited and constructed with a practical view to their local functions. Taken together, these structures added up to more than their separate parts.

Accounts of Turner's interest in modernity generally focus on a few late works which overtly depict the contrast between modern steam power and the relicts of an older, less visibly mechanised, world: *The Fighting Temeraire* (1839), *Snow Storm: Steam-Boat off a Harbour's Mouth* (1842) or *Rain, Steam, and Speed – The Great Western Railway* (1844) (see Rodner, 1986). Although there is ample evidence of Turner's long-standing interest in a wide variety of tools and technologies, from spades and wheelbarrows to windmills and orthodontic instruments, his obsessive sketching and painting of lighthouses has usually been dismissed as part of the ordinary repertoire of the sea-painter, rather than further evidence of that interest.

To be sure, steam-powered transport also implies a kind of system: an industrialised order contriving a high degree of refinement both in mechanism and in the management of the materials and exchanges that enable the manufacture and assembly of such mechanisms. But the system that produces a steamship is the system of the market-place, governed by laws of supply and demand, and driven by the ingenuity of individual entrepreneurs. By contrast, the system that produces a network of lighthouses, supplied out of the public purse for the use of all seafarers, implies a mature polity, one that recognises the limits as well as the advantages of the free market, and works to supply its deficiencies.

Three years before Turner died, John Stuart Mill dealt with this point in his *Principles of Political Economy* (1848), when he considered the limits of laissez-faire capitalism. Most of a society's needs and wants, Mill thought, could and should be supplied by private enterprise. One exception – indeed, the model exception – was the government's duty to build lighthouses: 'for since it is impossible that the ships at sea which are benefited by a lighthouse, should be made to pay a toll on the occasion of its use, no one would build lighthouses from motives of personal interest, unless indemnified and rewarded from a compulsory levy made by the state'. Furthermore, Mill went on, the same principle could be applied to what he called the 'cultivation of speculative knowledge': those 'investigations and experiments', demanding 'not only a long but a continuous devotion of time and attention' and which 'engross and fatigue the mental faculties'. Such 'peculiar pursuits', uncertain of reward but necessary 'for the general interests of mankind' should, like a lighthouse, be supported as conducive to the public good (Mill, 1998: 364). Art, for Turner, was such a good. The Royal

> Academy, in which he had his training and where he served as Professor of Perspective for thirty years, had been founded with public money, and he in turn left his most accomplished paintings to the national collection.
>
> A lighthouse, like any potent symbol, is a tangle of contradictions. Emblematic of solitude, it is nonetheless part of a collective public work undertaken for the general good. Seen with that complex symbolism in mind, Turner's lights illuminate not just sea and spray, but a vision of art itself as such a project.

Later, Millington and other contributors discuss the functional and symbolic role of the lighthouse as an extension of state power. Yet this view has been contested by scholars for whom the lighthouse represents either praiseworthy state action or private enterprise and market efficiency. Taylor (2001) asserts that the incorporation of formerly private lighthouses by the British state stopped profiteering and inefficiency, curtailing the 'old corruption' of unhindered market exploitation, while Lindberg (2015) reveals a contrasting Swedish model whereby lighthouses were often owned by private interests, administered and overseen by the state, but paid for by ships who benefited from them, not taxpayers. Sechrest (2004) regards state control as inefficient, and calls for a reconsideration of the historic benefits provided by the private entrepreneurs who formerly profited as lighthouse owners. These debates are extended by Hannah Conway, who explores how in England, the lighthouse gradually became institutionalised as a state asset, administered by Trinity House. In her account, she shows how, in the midst of contesting political claims, the relationship between scientists and Trinity House was fraught and complex.

> ## Illuminating science
>
> Scientific expertise and lighthouse reform in 19th-century Britain
>
> *Hannah Conway*
>
> ### Introduction
>
> Between 1822 and 1861, Britain's lighthouses were debated by three parliamentary committees and one parliamentary commission. A long-standing system of private ownership was depicted by a struggling shipping industry as corrupt, and a two decade-long process of de-privatisation led to new understandings of infrastructure as a public good (Mill, 1848; Coase,
>
> *(continued)*

(continued)

1974; van Zandt, 1993; Taylor, 2001; Lai et al., 2008). Reformist scientists also blamed the private ownership system for slow technological advancement in Britain's lighthouses, particularly in comparison to those in France (Brewster, 1833). As regulators addressed the improvement of both lighthouse technology and management, they negotiated new connections between the central government and scientific, engineering and artisanal practitioners.

This period of lighthouse reform allows an examination of early relationships between state regulatory bodies and a nascent scientific profession. The grafting of scientific expertise onto legislative structures was slow and complicated, often defined more by bureaucratic procedure than by the ability of experts to provide practical guidance. In the United States and Europe, contemporary interconnections between scientific advisory bodies and lawmakers developed during the Cold War, but the roots of this cooperation are found in early projects that pushed legislators to act on subjects about which they had little knowledge (Krige and Guzzetti, 1997; Oreskes and Krige, 2014; Oreskes, forthcoming 2018). Parliamentary proceedings around lighthouse reform raised questions about the responsibilities of regulators to call on expert knowledge and who was best able to provide it.

Creating a public good

Historians examining the British lighthouse system have generally done so through the lens of economic history, focusing on the dichotomy of private versus public ownership and theories of public good and market failure. A lighthouse was a provider of information that proved difficult to secure on a contractual basis. Previously, there was no way for ships to communicate to land that a light was required, and no system to guarantee that non-paying ships wouldn't then also benefit from the light. There was no practical market for competition, and the erection of multiple lighthouses competing for fees from passing ships in the same location was unfeasible and dangerous. In the second half of the 18th century, leading economists argued that lighthouses were an example of the type of service that could only be provided as a public good (Mill, 1848; van Zandt, 1993; Lai et al., 2008).

However, prior to 1822, the majority of Britain's lighthouses were privately owned. Construction and ownership rights were granted by the Crown and Trinity House of London through a patent process. The patent granted the lessee rights to construct and maintain a lighthouse for a number of years with a fixed annual rent, stipulated the rate of dues the lessee was entitled to collect, and secured Crown support to enforce their collection. Further, governance of lights was divided between Trinity House, the Commissioners of Northern Lights in Scotland, and the Commissioners of Irish Lights, rather than a centralised body. Dues, collected by representatives from each lighthouse in ports and based upon the route a ship had taken, were both high and inconsistent. Once a lighthouse was erected, its owners also had little incentive to invest in improved technology. Shipwrecks caused high loss of property and life, and ship owners and reformers partly blamed lagging lighting technologies for these tragedies (Brewster, 1833; 'Report from the Select Committee on Lighthouses' (SC), 1834). In an age that embraced classic liberalism, and generated a broader British reform movement, lighthouse control stood out among a number of unregulated industries, attracting the special attention of reformers who saw the use of scientific rationalism as key to optimising social utility (MacLeod, 1965).

Parliament therefore convened three committees to address the centralisation of lighthouse control in 1822, 1834 and 1845. Comprised of representatives from Parliament, the Royal Navy and the shipping industry, the committees organised oral witness testimonies from lighthouse managers, merchants, naval officers, ship owners and engineers. Each published a report with recommendations for reform. While these emphasised the necessity of deep and uniform reductions in dues and the reclamation of lighthouses from private hands by Trinity House, they also explicitly stated that the technological aspects of the structures were in need of improvement, and that this process would require the incorporation of experts not yet involved with either the boards or the committees (SC, 1834, 1845; Brewster, 1835; 'Report of the Commissioners appointed to Inquire into the Condition and Management of Lights, Buoys, and Beacons' (RC), 1861).

The process of de-privatisation was completed prior to the proceedings of 1845, aided by legislation passed in 1836 requiring resistant lighthouse owners to surrender property to Trinity House. Further, the 1845 report was the first in which interviewees were asked if they would rather sail the coast without lighthouses than continue to pay the dues: they answered with a resounding 'no'. This testimony highlighted the publicly perceived value of Britain's expanding lighthouse system: the lights were an important aspect of the nation's growing shipping industry and its rapidly developing economy, and a necessary safeguard against the loss of life and property along its treacherous shores.

When reforms began, no scientific practitioners were included in the three lighthouse boards, and none of the members of the commissions charged with assessing the state of the lighthouses had engineering or scientific experience. When the 1834 committee began its proceedings, engineers were employed by both Trinity House and Northern Lights, although neither was paid enough to devote all their time to the works of the boards (SC, 1834). Testimony from them was slim, and official recommendations relied on the opinion of a handful of experts. Of these, only English polymath and inventor Thomas Drummond (1797–1840), and Scottish engineers Robert (1772–1850) and Alan Stevenson (1807–1865) had direct experience

(continued)

(continued)

with lighthouses. While not called to testify, the publications of Scottish polymath David Brewster (1781–1868) also provided evidence of the committees' limited knowledge of how to implement technological reform.

Thus, prior to 1845, innovations in lighthouse illuminants in Britain were the outcome of private ingenuity and design. Independent practitioners developed improvements or new designs and then encouraged the Royal Society and the boards to test them. The most extensive testing was undertaken by Drummond, Brewster and Stevenson, but was grossly underreported and replete with discrepancies, leading to indecisiveness and a lack of clarity in how best to improve lighthouse technology (Drummond, 1830; Brewster, 1833; SC, 1834). Much work was needed throughout the middle of the century to incorporate the expertise of scientific and engineering practitioners, as exemplified in the final Parliamentary Commission on Lighthouses and report published in 1861.

Crafting light

The major scientific and technical questions raised by the reform of Britain's lighthouses were concerned with the production of a reliable, consistent, and bright flame, and the best way to direct the light into a powerful ray visible at great distances. Following the report of 1834, and building upon the early experimental work of Brewster, Drummond and the Stevensons, Trinity House appointed English physicist and chemist Michael Faraday (1791–1867) as its consultant on lighthouse management following a series of lectures he presented to the Royal Society and published in the *Philosophical Transactions* on the development of optical glasses (Faraday, 2008; Porter, 1998). His first experiments for Trinity House were alongside the scientist brought in to continue Drummond's work. Their experiments ultimately concluded that the limelight apparatus in question was unfit for lighthouse installation, but not before both men – as well as Drummond – became frustrated with what they regarded as wasteful repetition of failed experiments (Porter, 1998). Faraday was never officially employed by Trinity House, but occupied a salaried advisory position. Consequently, his endeavours remained largely detached from lighthouses, and his experimentation was limited to those inventions recommended to him. Nevertheless, his cooperation with the board prompted important changes in its relationship to scientific study.

The Commissioners of Northern Lights in Scotland maintained a long association with the engineering family most famously associated with the development of lighthouse construction, the Stevensons: Robert and his three sons Alan, David (1815–1886) and Thomas (1818–1887). Following a visit to France in 1834 where he met Léonor Fresnel (1790–1869), brother of the late Augustin (1788–1827), Alan experimented extensively with the implementation of polyzonal lenses; a technology his father had previously resisted (SC, 1834; Brewster, 1835). He made significant changes to the shape of the apparatus and its individual refractors, and recommended adding fixed reflecting prisms around the bottom to further concentrate the light. The first redesigned apparatus was built in Paris and installed in the Skerryvore Lighthouse in 1844. Following successful testing, others were installed in seven of Scotland's fixed lights and almost half of its revolving lights by 1847 (Bathurst, 2010).

In 1859, the first meeting of the Parliamentary Commission on Lighthouses was headed by three naval officers, a ship owner, and chemist John Gladstone. Instead of oral testimonies, circulars containing questions on the state of lighthouse management and maintenance were sent to naval officers, merchants, ship owners, foreign offices, steam companies, and scientific practitioners. This allowed them to 'procure returns from 114 Authorities having the management &c of Lights, Buoys, and Beacons in the United Kingdom, the evidence of 1,184 witnesses, and returns from 13 foreign countries' (RC, 1861). The 1861 Commission therefore undertook the most thorough assessment of matters related to lighthouses in British history. The Commissioners also visited all British lighthouses, as well as several in France and northern Spain, to compare operating systems and the effects of the lights from the sea. They concluded that the science of lighthouse illumination was in a transitional state. Most lighthouses by this time used the new dioptric lens systems, but a number of illuminants were employed, including the first electric generator system being tested at Foreland.

When the earliest British dioptric light systems were installed in the 1830s and 1840s, lens apparatuses were produced in France, although some domestic glass manufacturing began in the 1830s. Early British lamp production was undertaken under the direction of Léonor Fresnel, but the French lenses remained superior (Brewster, 1835; Chance, 1902). In 1850, glass company Messrs. Chance Bros. and Co. of Birmingham enlisted the aid of Fresnel's former assistant to produce a light that was shown at the Great Exhibition of 1851, where jurors deemed it equal in quality to French lenses. The company continued to perfect its craft over the following two years, completing seven apparatuses and attracting the attention of Faraday, who, in 1854, reported to Trinity House that this product indeed matched that of the French (Chance, 1902). James Chance (1814–1902) took over as chief manufacturing partner in 1854, and his cooperation with the boards led to a decade of experimentation.

There remained significant flaws in the installation of lens apparatuses. After visiting the lights at Whitby, Astronomer Royal George Airy (1801–1892) declared, 'it really gave me a feeling of melancholy to see the results of such exquisite workmanship entirely *annihilated* by subsequent faults in the mounting and adjustment' (Chance, 1902: 14, original emphasis). In December 1859, the Commissioners and Airy visited the three companies engaged in the production of dioptric lenses – two in Paris

(continued)

(continued)

and Chance Brothers in Birmingham. During the meeting with Chance, the Commissioners discovered that few of the crucial details about the size or elevation of the lighthouse and the measurement of the horizon were provided when the order for lenses was placed. Airy wrote to Faraday, who appealed to Chance for aid in remedying the situation.

The Whitby lights were chosen as the site for a series of tests to establish formulaic measurements for the proper installation and adjustment of the lenses. Airy hypothesised that during the lens' first development, Fresnel's rule of adjustment had invariably proved to be wrong, and wrote to Chance proposing tests to remedy the situation. Eager to aid the Commission, Chance calculated the necessary adjustments to optimise the use of his lens apparatus at Whitby. With Airy he produced new tables and calculations for the Commission, and, in August 1860, members of the Commission, Faraday, Thomas Stevenson, and Chance assembled at the Whitby lights to observe them prior to any adjustments and summarised fifteen ways in which they were inefficient. Upon returning to London, Faraday began a lengthy correspondence with Chance about how to resolve these shortcomings (Faraday, 2008). Subsequently, Faraday and Chance worked together in Chance's shop in Birmingham and at Whitby, making adjustments and revising their formulae.

In January 1861 Chance submitted to the Commission a full report on the adjustment of lenses, the results of his experimentation, and the tables and mathematical processes for calculating the correct position of the apparatuses. He retained his connection to the development of lighthouse technologies to the end of the decade, working continuously with the Stevensons and Faraday on the production and improvement of lighting systems.

While the report acknowledged the work of these individuals and the improvements introduced, it asserted that the boards still 'betray an evident want of scientific thought' (RC, 1861). However, the boards continued to maintain unstable relationships with their scientific advisors. In 1865 Faraday was replaced by his protégé John Tyndall, again in an advisory position. The relationship between Tyndall and the board was rocky. His experimentation with new electrical technologies became increasingly complex, slow-paced and expensive, and the board's reluctance to invest restricted his work. A sustained public argument between Tyndall and David and Thomas Stevenson led him to resign his position in 1883. Trinity House did not name a replacement scientific advisor until a decade later (MacLeod, 1969).

Conclusion

While the 1860s seemed to promise a closer relationship between the state and scientific and technological practitioners, the honeymoon was short-lived, and the incorporation of advisors into the state apparatus remained temporary and ad hoc. Faraday and Tyndall advanced systematic processes of experimentation, but their purely advisory roles impeded development. Further, Trinity House's funding enthusiasm waned towards the end of the century, and slow progress in bringing electricity to lighthouses, along with a series of technological disappointments further discouraged them (MacLeod, 1969). Research into the applications of electricity as a replacement for gas or oil, therefore, largely took place in the private sector. No further committees or commissions of Parliament were organised to address Britain's lighthouses until 1908.

The deployment of technologies of marine illumination has not ceased. Though lighthouses are no longer the pre-eminent form of illuminated guidance for mariners, Kimberley Peters confirms that a broader expansion of maritime lighting technologies shows that illumination remains essential to the seas, especially along busy shipping traffic routes. Marking out maritime space after dark in new ways, such lights also reveal emergent configurations of commerce and administration.

Light offshore

Governing dark waters in shipping straits

Kimberley Peters

Navigating darkness

Offshore, when night falls, it is truly dark. The stars and the Moon comprise the oldest and most trusted aids to navigation (Edensor, 2013), but the blackness can be consuming. A cloudy sky can obscure all means of locating oneself on the ocean. Even a glimpse of natural light from the sky might confuse rather than comfort (Peters, 2012).

Lighthouses, casting light out into the blackness, have long ensured the safety of life at sea. Pinned to the edges of land or on rocky outposts, each with a unique pulse of light, they enable seafarers to be certain of their whereabouts in relation to the land and hazardous coastlines. With increased shipping traffic, the necessity for clear pointers, identifiable by *light*, continues to be vital for safe passage. This is especially true for vessels that hug the coast, those navigating to port or those that have strayed off course.

But for those further from land and its rocky shores – in spite of a sky littered with extraterrestrial shipping guides – there remains a need for light to

(continued)

(continued)

navigate dark seas. There are multiple invisible hazards for vessels traversing the oceans: floating detritus, hidden reefs or shifting sandbanks under the water's surface, and other vessels. There may be failures in observation due to fog, darkness or faulty radar technology.

1971

In the diminishing evening light on Monday 11 January 1971, a major maritime collision occurred in the Dover Strait, 6 miles from Folkestone. The motor vessel *Texaco Caribbean*, weighing 13,604 gross tons and registered in Panama, collided with a sandbank below the sea's surface. The vessel began to sink. Then, some hours later, the merchant vessel *Paracas*, weighing 9,481 gross tons and registered in Peru collided with the partly submerged wreck. The ships were sharing a channel littered with hidden dangers – ridges and sandbanks. The *Texaco Caribbean* was heading down-channel with ballast, set for Trinidad. The *Paracas* was motoring up-channel to the ports of northern Europe.

To add to these disasters, in the muted morning light on 12 January, similarly unable to see the hazards ahead, the *Brandenburg*, a vessel of 2,695 gross tons, registered in the Federal Republic of Germany, was involved in a further collision and sank in the vicinity of the earlier accidents (The National Archives, 1971). The decisions that followed focused on the provision of light offshore and the need to govern the movements of vessels in the dark waters of global shipping straits.

Guiding lights

Compared to the densely populated spaces of land, seas and oceans are often configured – at least by Western societies – as empty spaces, 'perfect and absolute blanks' as described by Lewis Carroll in his famous poem, *The Hunting of the Snark* (see Anderson and Peters, 2014: 1). Maps have been used as political tools, constructing the 'blue-between' as an unmapped void, a space emptied of meaning and only useful in its role as a smooth *surface* of connection (Steinberg, 2001). Accordingly, the sea has often been perceived as a dark space where all identifiable features are obscured.

This distinction – setting the sea apart from the land – is echoed in another dualism. Seas and oceans are often perceived as disordered, chaotic and unlawful spaces, in contrast with the ordered, rational and regulated spaces of land (Langewiesche, 2004). In these murky spaces of unruliness, illicit activities can flourish (Peters, 2012).

But many seafarers would refute such terra-centric accounts. Oceans and seas are in fact intricately mapped (Raban, 1999) and highly governed

(Steinberg, 1999, 2001). Since the era of global expansion – through voyages of exploration and colonial enterprise – questions of how to map and govern maritime space have been central to the concerns of nation states and to entrepreneurs keen to exploit them (Steinberg, 1999, 2001). Today, over 95 per cent of trade travels by ship (see Lavery, 2005; George, 2013). Shipping companies, marine organisations and government agencies strive to ensure safe and secure oceanic transport links. The 'just-in-time' economy and the advent of containerisation has resulted in the explosion of sea transport, and supposedly 'empty' seas are busier than they have ever been.

The governance of this traffic is especially necessary in geophysically confined conduits of maritime space: pinch points, such as straits, where there is limited room for the manoeuvre and channelling of vessels. Here – even with radar – there is a heightened risk of accidents, collisions and associated environmental harm. To ensure that shipping moves smoothly and safely, the dark ocean is mapped and governed in many ways and in particular through the provision of guiding lights.

Illuminating depth

The Dover Strait is one of the busiest maritime channels in the world (Maritime Coastguard Agency (MCA), 2014). Lying between Britain and France, it is a natural geographical 'pinch point' but also a vital trade route connecting the North Sea and the Atlantic. In 1962, over 80 per cent of shipping through-traffic in the Channel navigated an area less than 5 miles wide (The National Archives, 1961–1962). Today, over 400 vessels above 300 gross tons negotiate it every day (MCA, 2014), and these are subject to stringent regulations.

Following the trio of sinkings in 1971, the Dover Strait became the first marine passage to be regulated via a Traffic Separation Scheme (TSS) creating channels or motorways at sea. There is a north-eastbound lane on the French side of the strait and a south-westbound lane marked on the English side. Versions of such schemes to map and govern maritime movements have now been implemented around the world. In Dover (and other waterways), such regulations are often designed to circumnavigate the dangers that exist under the surface of the ocean, as well as upon it.

The Dover Strait presents particularly complex conditions. Tidal changes to water depth, the presence of sandbanks and the impacts of weather mean that only a small part of it is usable for deep-draught shipping. The Sandiette, Varne and Bullock Banks; the Goodwin Sands, South Falls and Ruytingen Ridge are all areas of dangerously reduced depth. While mapping makes navigation around these hazards possible, in practice, it is light that shows the way.

Light is used to define separation schemes, with lighted buoys, light vessels and automated light structures marking routes and shallow zones. On

(continued)

(continued)

the evening of January 11 in 1971, the lightship *Siren* was sent to mark the wreck of the *Texaco Caribbean* and *Paracas*. The inability of the *Siren*'s crew to locate them in the dark resulted in the loss of the *Brandenburg* the following day. But, once there, the *Siren* and additional light buoys kept other vessels safe.

Light offshore

Just as 'the night under artificial light makes a new world of different colours and sensations' on land, so it does in the deep and motionful spaces of the sea (Thrift, 1996: 269). Navigating the oceans and coastlines by designed light created new sensory experiences and perceptions, and developed different kinds of seafaring knowledge. Illuminating dark waters, lightships and buoys create a different seascape: complex lines of light enable ships to move faster, and support global supply chains. A history of a sea illuminated cannot stop at the shore. It cannot end with the lighthouse. The story must go offshore, into the ocean.

The lighthouse has thus relinquished its role as the pre-eminent technological source of lighting the seas and coastlines of the world. Commenting on the successive innovations that have enhanced the passage of mariners, naval historian and Trinity House official Richard Woodman offers a melancholy account of how lighthouses and other maritime equipment have become merely supplementary to navigation.

A personal view from the lighthouse

Richard Woodman

As a mariner, the lighthouse has two fundamental functions: firstly, it warns me of a navigational hazard, and secondly, it enables me to fix my position, possibly a very necessary thing to do if making a landfall after days at sea in bad weather, when observations of the Sun and/or stars have not been possible. At least that was their function when I first went to sea in 1960. Since then, advances in technology, particularly in satellite navigation, have made them less necessary. Their very existence is increasingly called into question and their numbers are being slowly reduced. Where, for complex reasons – for example increases in offshore power generation – the primitive buoy is likely to enjoy a long life, that once primary aid to navigation, the lighthouse, is not destined for so rosy a future.

Initially, I was but a passing seaman, if not homeward bound and making my landfall, then outward bound on my voyage, taking my 'departure' from the land with an accurate position based on one or more terrestrial objects, prior to a passage marked by dead-reckoning and regular astro-navigational fixes. Lighthouses were simply tools of which I made good use.

Later in my career I was employed by a General Lighthouse Authority (GLA), in my case Trinity House, the GLA for England, Wales, the Channel Islands and Gibraltar. I became a navigating officer in the Corporation's support vessels, and, for eleven years, I commanded several of these small but exciting ships. It was a fascinating, often very demanding and somewhat paradoxical job because we were expected to take our vessels into places in which the object of our attention was something others were specifically warned to avoid.

My years in harness spanned the most profound changes in what King Charles II supposedly called the 'art and mystery' of navigation, disarming it of both qualities. The sextant and chronometer have preceded the lighthouse into that depressing limbo of 'just-in-case' retention that is the forerunner of redundancy. Such sufferance has a profoundly regretful aspect, not just that of an acquired skill being made obsolete – or so it sometimes seems – in a single stroke, but a diminution of acquired skill: that sea sense that was bred into seafarers of the past and which is now entirely lacking among the young. It is not their fault, but the reliance that is placed upon digital data has almost entirely emasculated the ancient art and mystery of my craft. Hey-ho . . .

In due course, my practical involvement generated an intellectual curiosity, and I began to write about lighthouses and their associated aids to navigation (known in the trade as AtoNs). In doing so, I learned of their history, their construction and that of their various illuminating apparatuses. Global lighthouse construction has its heroes, many of them British, since it was Great Britain which largely pioneered their provision throughout our widespread, diverse maritime empire. There were the early mavericks like Henry Winstanley, Henry Whiteside and John Rudyerd: the first a trickster, the second a shipwright and the third a violin maker. After them came the great civil engineers of the 18th and 19th centuries: John Smeaton, Robert Stevenson, James Wyatt and Sir James Douglass. Their genius was coupled with the science of Argand, Fresnel, Faraday, Kelvin and others. Today, much reliance is placed upon the light-emitting diode, whose inventor's name I do not know – a comment upon how scientific progress is now taken for granted. Such grand endeavours, set against the indifference of the mighty ocean, had their setbacks and disasters. Though familiar to seafarers, such challenges came as a shock to those whose expertise had been developed onshore, but it was a measure of human persistence and individual courage that they overcame what – at the moment of impact – must have seemed insuperable.

(continued)

(continued)

> While the popular image of a lighthouse is the sea-girt rock-station defying the elements atop its seamount, the variety of their locations is matched by that of their architecture, mechanisms and history. When in 1822 a bevy of gentlemen selected the highest point on Lundy Island, deeming it a fit and proper place for a private lighthouse, they failed to take into account the reality that the island's summit was usually covered in orographic cloud. On acquiring the lighthouse some years later, Trinity House had to construct two short towers at either end of the rocky isle, just below the cloudbase. These isolated rock-stations, set on their dangerous outcrops amid the ever-changing swirl of the tide and subject to the waves and swells of the ocean, are unique, not least in the way one must decide how to approach them: in a support vessel or deploying a motor boat or helicopter.
>
> If I enjoyed a stimulating service career, I was even more fortunate later, for I found myself elected as an Elder Brother of Trinity House, responsible for the supervision of the Corporation's lighthouse service. When Trinity House celebrated its Quincentenary in 2014, I became its official historian. So, while I recognise that others find in the lighthouse an image, icon or metaphor, the lighthouse has for me been a fundamental cornerstone of my very existence. As the lighthouse, so symbolic of reliability and durability, ineluctably passes from being a practical tool to something acquiring more esoteric meanings, I am struck by the transience of all things.

Steve Hoon's final contribution focuses upon the stone, iron and concrete that compose the lighthouse, providing a hopefully durable materiality. Yet, as he observes, stone is not eternal in its constituency and over time becomes subject to the actions of a host of non-human agencies that will inevitably weaken the structural integrity of the lighthouse.

The materiality of lighthouses

Steve Hoon

Lighthouses are most frequently built of hard, dense and durable rock such as sandstone, limestone or granite. The actual choice of stone is important. Each block is a geological time capsule. The rock's mineralogy, grain size and molecular composition trace a unique geological history. Crystals and their dislocations record the stresses and strains that the rock has experienced and define its materiality. Granite is igneous, extruded from the Earth's magma. Prior to tectonic exhumation it has been reburied, tortured, reheated, recrystallised and compressed within the Earth's mantle over eons of time. Sandstones have a differing timeline that includes a previous maritime association. They are sedimentary deltaic deposits, derived from the eroded material of older mountains, washed out to sea, buried, cemented, heated and tectonically exhumed. Metamorphic limestone has an even closer association with the sea. Limestone is a biological marine sediment composed primarily of billions of calcium-based microscopic foraminifera, the skeletal fragments of marine animals cemented together after burial. Tectonic exhumation of limestone has formed the Alps and the southern English Pennines. The high physical rigidity, compressional strength and hardness of these natural materials makes them perfect for building storm-resilient lighthouses.

While natural stone is an excellent durable material, many lighthouses such as La Corbière, Jersey, have been built of steel-reinforced concrete, a manufactured material that balances contrasting physical properties. Concrete is a formable artificial stone, a mixture of sand and cement derived from limestone. It is strong in compression, excellent at bearing heavy loads but friable in tension. In contrast, steel, containing iron and carbon, is strong in tension but in the form of laterally unsupported thin rods is weak in compression, bending and flexing. Reinforced concrete, containing steel reinforcing 'rebars', ingeniously balances the compressive strength of concrete with the tensile strength of slender steel rods to form a robust building material that is both light and strong. But there is more to steel-reinforced concrete than physicality alone. A subtle electrochemical corrosion passivation-bonding reaction occurs between the iron in the steel rebars and the strongly alkaline calcium-rich cement environment created as the concrete sets. This confers strength and integrity: the steel-reinforced concrete is now a unified whole. However, even this material has its Achilles heel. Unless the concrete is dense and impervious to water, the latter will penetrate and corrode the rebars, rusting and expanding them, and spalling the concrete. Left unchecked, this will, in time, cause the structure to fail. No human ingenuity can confer permanence to manmade structures on a geologic timescale.

However, it is not just manmade concrete that bows to the forces of nature. Lighthouse stonework may appear solid to the eye, but it hides microscopic pores. In these pores, microbial life, less than a hundredth of a millimetre in size – far less than the finest hair's breadth – finds a home. To survive in this marine interface, the microbes must be halophytic: salt-tolerant organisms whose genetically related cousins are found on the saltpans and drylands of Australia, Africa and the high Atacama. Moisture, light and carbon dioxide-laden air all percolate into this pore space, providing the conditions necessary for carbon sequestration by photosynthetic cyanobacteria living within the rock. Like all autotrophic bacteria, these use water molecules and photons of light to sequester carbon from atmospheric carbon dioxide and release oxygen, enriching our atmosphere and turning inorganic carbon into living biotic carbon. In times of plenty, cyanobacteria

(continued)

(continued)

excrete sugary exopolysaccharides, both for protection and to store energy, a store which heterotrophic bacteria and fungi, incapable of photosynthesis, may pillage for their own purposes.

This plethora of biotic activity is not physically passive. It produces acids that attack the stone, breaking it down, releasing mineral micronutrients from the rock. And so, via a subtle physico-chemo-biological chain of events which, like all such events, involves light, the stonework weathers. As the pores enlarge, increased water penetration can occur. In sub-zero temperatures, the expansion of this freezing water may nucleate and propagate microcracks, slowly weakening the stone. *In extremis*, widening pores provide sufficient access for the tiny hardened root tip of an opportunistic fern or grass. After colonising a fissure, this root will form a symbiotic relationship via fungal mycorrhiza with the microbial community. Within the lighthouse's surficial pore space, an entire cryptic ecosystem flourishes. Indeed, much of the dark surficial staining on rock is biotic weathering, a sign of microscopic photosynthetic cyanobacterial life. What to one observer is the mature patina of a weathered rock is to another the very signature of life. In the natural world, this geobiotic interface has contributed to the formation and composition of the Earth's atmosphere. The epidermis of the apparently lifeless stonework breathes.

As Hoon shows, although lighthouses might seem to be durable structures, they are invariably weakened by the effects of non-human agents, and require unceasing maintenance, underlining how architecture is 'an ongoing process of holding together' (Jacobs and Merriman, 2011: 212). As well as regular supplies of oil to sustain lighting technologies, and water and food for their keepers, lighthouses required regular inspections and maintenance schedules, as I discuss later. Yet repair and maintenance itself can lead to structural and material failure, as evidenced by the deleterious effects of sandblasting which, aiming to achieve a pleasing smoothness, removes the protective crust that forms on stone. The agencies of destruction and the problems caused by prior endeavours to temper processes of erosion are directly confronted in Patricia Warke's discussion of the fate that has befallen many lighthouses since their decommissioning. Repair and maintenance also depend upon the value assigned to particular structures, exemplifying how buildings are restored or consigned to obsolescence. As Caitlin DeSilvey describes later in this volume, lighthouses are often valued as heritage, but she questions the expense and effort required to conserve them in perpetuity, suggesting that a policy of non-intervention might allow the lighthouse to slowly dissolve, honouring the processes of decay that affect all things.

Figure 24 Longships, Cornwall: an example of a rock tower lighthouse. Courtesy of Ronald Blakely, Trinity House.

Shining a light on lighthouse resilience in the 21st century

Patricia Warke

Introduction

Lighthouses have gained iconic status within coastal landscapes, marking the edge of terra firma and standing as symbols of permanence in ever-changing environments. Until the latter half of the 20th century, most lighthouses were manned and maintained to a very high standard, but technological advances have resulted in a programme of wholesale automation.

Automation and the removal of keepers marked a significant stage in the life of many of these structures, particularly the offshore stations, where daily maintenance was replaced by short visits at intervals of four to eight weeks. Following automation, reports of the deterioration of interior masonry (mainly stone and plaster) provided increasing indications that all was not well.

A vertical gradient of deterioration was evident, especially in tall towers, being most severe in the lower levels of the towers, while higher levels remained comparatively unaffected. Deterioration in shorter counterparts was evident at all levels (Warke et al., 2011). Identifying the reasons for this deterioration is akin to a detective story with a cast of potential suspects and

(continued)

(continued)

a complex 'crime scene' that requires forensic examination to identify the guilty parties. What causes the shift from conditions of apparent stability of interior stone to conditions of instability? Can the system be stabilised?

The following account is based on investigative work carried out in several granite and sandstone offshore island-based lighthouses around Ireland and the UK. Because of the variability of their architecture and materiality, it provides a general overview, recognising that deterioration may vary significantly because of site-specific factors.

Guilt by association?

Many decades of research have identified links between the action of salt and the breakdown of different stone types (Goudie and Viles, 1997), with different salts possessing different properties and varying impacts. In coastal environments, the most common salt is sodium chloride (or halite), a highly soluble salt with notable deliquescent properties. Given its abundance, it is not surprising that salt is assumed to be the guilty party in terms of stone breakdown. However, the deterioration of stone was most obvious in the interior of the towers, and not exhibited by the exterior stonework daily receiving salt from rain, fog or sea spray, so this 'guilt by association' may not necessarily be accurate. Salt may have been present at the scene, but the initiation of the crime was brought about by a more insidious villain, and like any good murder mystery the back-story often holds clues to the identity of the real culprit.

In the beginning . . .

For over 100 to 150 years, often for much longer, lighthouse towers have withstood extreme environmental conditions, with both exterior and interior stonework appearing immutable. Before automation, towers were maintained on a daily basis under well-ventilated conditions. Weather permitting, the entrance door at ground level and ventilation slats in the gallery (optic level) were opened to allow a flow of air upwards through the tower.

This form of passive ventilation reflects the operation of two factors: *Stack Ventilation* and *Bernoulli's Principle* (Fitzgerald and Woods, 2008). Both rely on differences in pressure to draw air through a building. *Stack Ventilation* is probably the simplest form of airflow, arising from differences in pressure caused by differential heating. As air warms and rises, it creates low pressure, drawing in cooler and denser air near ground level. This occurs even with little or no wind, and in a limited form even when no doors or ventilation slats are open.

Bernoulli's Principle describes the differences in air pressure that occur due to variations in wind speed, with faster moving air creating conditions

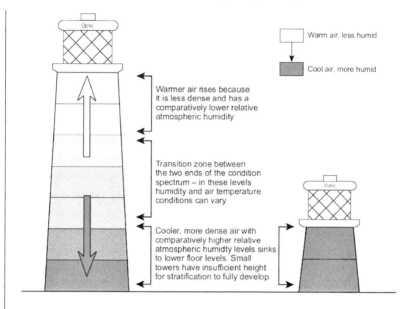

Figure 25 Stratification of air within towers reflecting temperature and relative humidity.

of low pressure. On windy days, air outside the lighthouse tower moves at different speeds, slower near the ground because of the frictional effect of an uneven surface, and faster higher up. The faster moving air draws air out of the upper levels of the tower through openings such as ventilation slats – which results in air being drawn in at the base of the tower. This form of ventilation is more effective than simple *Stack Ventilation* in the speed and volume of air moved. But the daily regimes of passive ventilation that ensured that lighthouse towers were well-ventilated changed with automation.

Pulling the trigger?

With the departure of keepers, offshore lighthouse towers were closed to keep water out between maintenance visits. This well-intentioned change had unforeseen consequences. First, the airflow regime within the towers changed from frequent ventilation to prolonged periods of still air with minimal movement between different floor levels. Second, in a coastal setting, ambient atmospheric humidity is typically high, even with stable warm weather conditions. When the towers are closed, the still air within them gradually becomes more stratified with cooler, denser, more humid air sinking to the lower levels. Then, during winter months when external

(continued)

(continued)

air temperatures are low, the masonry fabric cools, so that moist air in the lower levels of the tower overlies even colder stone and associated decorative surfaces for prolonged periods. The air in direct contact with the colder stone is cooled further, reducing its moisture-holding capacity. When air cools beyond its dew-point temperature, condensation begins.

With condensation, the salt dissolved within atmospheric moisture vapour can be transferred to stone surfaces. Once this begins, it is readily perpetuated, because certain salts, particularly sodium chloride, are strongly hygroscopic, drawing moisture from the air around them. So once salt accumulation starts, it attracts additional moisture and more salt.

The deposition and accumulation of salts and moisture can affect interior tower conditions in various ways. Damp surfaces allow the development of moulds, whose release of fungal spores have potential health implications for visiting personnel. The presence of moisture and salt may facilitate corrosive damage of exposed metalwork and electronics, and the presence of salt within condensed moisture can contribute directly to stone breakdown through a combination of physical and chemical processes. As salt absorbs moisture, it gradually dissolves to form initially a very concentrated hygroscopic solution, and salt in solution can pass more easily into the fabric of stone through pore spaces and other lines of weakness. This leaves the stone susceptible to physical damage related to crystallisation pressures if the atmospheric humidity drops below the critical value needed to maintain salt in its deliquescent state. And concentrated salt solutions typically create highly alkaline conditions (more than pH 7) which are detrimental to normally durable elements such as silica, and the minerals like quartz and feldspar that contain them, leading to a loss of structural integrity (Young, 1988). Quartz is an important component of granite and sandstone, and its deterioration has serious implications for their durability.

In contrast to the interior of the lighthouse, where condensation drives deterioration, it is the abundance of moisture that helps to retard the deterioration of exterior stonework. Regular washing by rain, and drying by wind and sunshine, prevents surface accumulation of salt and any retained on the surface from moving deeper into the stone. Sodium chloride in particular is highly soluble, and although natural stone surfaces in coastal locations frequently show evidence of salt-related weathering, they rarely contain high salt concentrations (McGreevy, 1985).

The finger of guilt

The deterioration within lighthouse towers since automation reflects complex interactions between several factors, with salt being one of several guilty characters. However, the trigger for the destabilisation of the system was the somewhat abrupt change in micro-environmental conditions within the tower which came with the shift from well-ventilated to static air conditions. At this point in the investigation, consideration has to be given to the second research question: can the system be stabilised?

Moving forward

It is not easy to identify the most effective way forward. In the lower tower levels, the penetration and accumulation of salts means that it is not possible to return stone to its pre-automation condition. Consequently, management intervention needs to focus on slowing and controlling future deterioration while reducing further salt accumulation. To achieve this, re-establishing effective ventilation is essential. However, this can be difficult in offshore towers that are closed for many weeks at a time and requires additional power to circulate the air. In the absence of heating, especially during the winter, even the effective movement of cool moist salt-rich air may not be sufficient to prevent condensation.

The challenges facing those responsible for ensuring the long-term resilience of these iconic structures are many and varied. Management is normally reactive, responding to problems when they arise or when detected during maintenance visits. Unforeseen consequences can be difficult to address when the changes incurred cannot easily be reversed. As with all heritage structures, climate change also presents challenges. In the UK and Ireland, there has been an increase in the frequency and intensity of severe storms, projected to increase still further over the coming decades (Murphy et al., 2009). This will present significant challenges for the future management of inaccessible offshore lighthouses where storm-related damage may not be dealt with promptly.

Ensuring a healthy environment within the towers is particularly challenging when frequent visits are not possible. Effective ventilation is important, but a compromise has to be made between the need to generate additional energy to power mechanical ventilation and the feasibility of venting air from the towers without letting moisture in.

Perhaps the greatest challenge facing lighthouses, with increasing reliance on satellites for navigation and communication, is ensuring a role for them in the future. Shore-based lighthouses can be seen and visited by the public, but the same cannot be said for offshore stations, precisely those that require the greatest, most costly management interventions. Lighthouses are deep-rooted in our appreciation of coastal landscapes. But they are ageing heritage structures located in often extreme environmental settings. Retaining all of them may not be possible.

Despite the huge endeavours to stabilise the material form of the lighthouse, to carry it through technological innovations and to protect through the ascription of heritage value and conservation, all may be in vain, for the powerful non-human

122 *The lighthouses of Skagen Odde*

agencies that surround it can thwart human intentions. The following contribution explores how successive technologies in northern Denmark have prompted new lighthouse developments, only to have them rendered obsolete, threatened by political contingencies or destroyed by the non-human agencies of tide and sand drift.

Enmeshed in geographies of sand, sea and war
The lighthouses of Skagen Odde

Tim Edensor

In Scott Reekie's (nd) website devoted to the heritage of Earlsferry in Fife, Scotland, a description of Elie Ness Lighthouse, on the north coast of the Firth of Forth, employs a familiar metaphorical trope: 'as (they) stand steadfast on windswept promontories, lighthouses make a statement of solidarity and permanence'. But this essay shows how several Danish lighthouses refute such assertions of intransience. In some locations, the vital agencies that surge around lighthouses mean that they are anything but solid and enduring.

The story of the lighthouses of North Jutland in Denmark testifies to a vibrant physical geography and a history shaped by their strategic military and commercial location. In this swirling, shape-shifting realm, the lighthouse has been refashioned by continuous technological adaptation, taking shape as obsolete remnants, historical reproductions and absent structures, or those about to vanish.

The Skagen Odde peninsula extends 20 miles north from Frederikshavn, a narrow finger of land, at the apex of which lies the town of Skagen. The spit's evolution has been influenced by the global eustatic sea-level rise that followed the last great Ice Age, and a corresponding isostatic uplift of the land following the departure of the heavy glaciers that covered it. The peninsula's particular form emerged around 15,000 years ago, as particles scoured from the Earth by the retreating ice drifted across the west coast of Jutland.

A mile beyond Skagen, at Grenen, lies the ever-fluid tip of the peninsula, where the Kattegat strait to the east joins the Baltic Sea and the western Skagerrak strait merges with the North Sea. The spit exists in an extraordinary state of flux: currents from the east deposit sand and extend the coastline by over 20 feet each year, while the North Sea's power erodes the western coastline. In addition, the inexorable movement of immense sand-created dunes in Skagen Odde has engulfed villages and farmland, driving the inhabitants of agricultural and fishing settlements into the interior. This encroachment instigated The Sand Drift Act of 1857, which empowered the state to expropriate or purchase areas of sand drift, with a further act allowing it to buy land adjacent to the drifts. Subsequently, dune grasses and extensive conifer forests were planted to stabilise the sands, allowing some sheep farming and fishing. By the 1950s, the dune drifts were largely – but not entirely – brought under control.

For centuries, the treacherous reefs, violent currents and storms that seethe alongside Skagen's peninsula have caused shipwrecks. Though an enduring hazard to ships, their crews and cargoes, the wrecks provided an economic opportunity for locals to profit from salvaging goods and from rewards for rescuing mariners. This income was threatened in 1560, when Denmark's King Frederik II commanded the head of the navy to erect a lighthouse in Skagen, marking the initiation of an organised Danish lighthouse authority. This was not simple benevolence, for the lighthouse tax imposed on passing vessels accrued valuable revenue for the Crown.

The lantern

The lighthouse, erected in the early 17th century, was a 'lantern': a simple two-storey, draft-proof, wooden building with glass windows and low, lead roof. The upper chamber – the candleroom – was initially equipped with six lamps fuelled by fish oil, and later with eight tallow candles, maintained by two men residing in the lower chamber. Though there were gradual improvements in luminosity, new approaches were sought to magnify radiance.

The Vippefyr

One solution was the Bascular Lighthouse or *vippefyr*, a device installed on Skagen's west coast in 1626. A pyramidal, tarred wooden scaffold was erected, carrying a simple lever with a metal bucket. Wood was burnt in this vessel, providing large flames that shot high into the air, allowing those at sea to see the glow from 6 miles away. Later, coal reduced the height of the flames, but posed less of a threat to the wooden structure. Today, a replica creates a striking sculptural form, honouring these early endeavours to provide safety for mariners. Each Midsummer's Eve, the relighting of a fire in the bucket celebrates both Skagen's role in Denmark's lighthouse history and the summer solstice.

The White Lighthouse

A significant advance arrived in 1747, with the construction of a 69-foot-high octagonal brick tower that soared above the *vippefyr*. In the early 19th century, the lighthouse was whitewashed to stand out better as a landmark in daylight, and a roof was added to protect the fire that created the light. Coal for the fire was laboriously hauled up through an internal shaft, using three times the quantity of fuel required by the *vippefyr*, but the resultant

(continued)

(continued)

Figure 26 The Vippefyr, Skagen Odde. Photograph: Tim Edensor.

flame greatly enhanced the lighthouse's visibility, projecting light for 25 miles. A further development was initiated in 1835, when less heavy rapeseed oil replaced coal, and a parabolic mirror was installed to focus the light more effectively. By 1858, superseded by a more advanced model, the lighthouse served solely as an orientation marker. Currently, still in a sound state of preservation, it is employed as a venue for art exhibitions.

The Kattegat side of the peninsula served as a gateway for foreign naval incursions, but powerful tides and hidden reefs meant that such voyages were fraught with danger. It was therefore essential for those attacking

Denmark to gain control of Skagen's lighthouse so that these maritime perils could be avoided. Thus, when the English navy attacked Denmark in 1807, all Danish lighthouses were ordered to extinguish their illumination to thwart the invaders' intentions, causing ships to run aground on what the English called Skaw's Reef and providing local residents with cargo to salvage. This tactic prompted the English to devise an alternative solution: to facilitate safer passage they anchored a lightship nearby, a vessel first created in its modern form in 1731.

The Grey Lighthouse

The White Lighthouse was replaced in 1858 by the Grey Lighthouse, an archetypal complex located less than a mile further north. Eighty feet tall, it initially installed a fixed light, but in 1905 this was replaced by a rotating apparatus. It proved highly effective in reducing the numbers of shipwrecks, delivering a final blow to the few local inhabitants whose livelihood still depended on rewards for assisting stranded ships and on salvaged cargo. Its beam continued to operate until recently.

This lighthouse, too, has been decommissioned, not because of technological inadequacies but due to its changing location. When first built, it was situated in a central position and cast light for ships sailing along both coastlines. But with vigorous coastal erosion on the east side, it is now very close to the Kattegat coast and too distant from Skaggerat. Yet the lighthouse remains a key local icon, and since Skagen Odde is an important site for migrating birds and the flight paths of eagles, it has been refurbished as an international bird station and observatory for visiting birdwatchers.

The site of Højen Lighthouse

With the shifting terrain around the Grey Lighthouse rendering it ill-equipped to warn shipping off the Skaggerat coast, the smaller Højen Lighthouse was established in 1892. This lighthouse was in service until 1956, when fears about erosion from the adjacent sea led to its closure. In 1976, with its foundations progressively undermined, a decision was taken to blow it up because of the dangers the crumbling fabric posed to visitors. The ensuing military operation was so efficient that little remains except a few concrete blocks.

Skagen West Lighthouse

Now Denmark's most northerly lighthouse, and currently the only operational facility sited on the Skagerrak coast, Skagen West was erected in 1956 to replace the undermined Højen Lighthouse. Unlike previous

(continued)

(continued)

Figure 27 The Engulfed Lighthouse, Rubjerg Knude. Photograph: Tim Edensor.

lighthouses, it is designed to be controlled remotely, obviating the need for resident keepers. Its unadorned, streamlined form exemplifies the high modernist style discussed by Millington in this book: a functional, cylindrical concrete tower rises high above the surrounding dunes in contrast to the vernacular flourishes of its predecessors. At its base, 1950s concrete meets 1940s concrete, for its foundations are formed by one of the mighty concrete bunkers that nestle within the dunes of Skagen's coastline. While some have been swallowed up by drifting sand or eroded by the sea, most remain intact by virtue of their architectural qualities and durable concrete. Part of Nazi Germany's formidable Atlantic Wall, devised to repel Allied invasion, these monoliths provide further evidence of the long-standing strategic importance of this coast.

Rubjerg Knude Lighthouse

Finally, about 20 miles south-west along the Skaggerak coast, lies another imperilled structure: the lofty, square Rubjerg Knude Lighthouse, standing 70 feet high. When first lit in 1900, the lighthouse was technologically advanced, equipped with its own gasworks to fuel illumination and a foghorn, though this was subsequently replaced by petrol and electricity. A lighthouse keeper, assistant keeper and light tender resided there.

The lighthouse was originally more than 200 metres inland, but over time the sea has eroded the friable 200-feet-high cliffs and moved ever closer. Simultaneously, the lighthouse has been surrounded by sand dunes. Though there were none nearby at the time of its construction, the wind blew huge quantities of sand, creating dunes so high that, occasionally, the sound of the foghorn was muffled and the lighthouse could not be seen from the sea. The sand swamped the kitchen garden and clogged up the well, and despite attempts to build pine gates and plant grasses, the engulfing dunes proved unstoppable. Consequently, the lighthouse ceased to operate in 1968 and housed a cafeteria and a museum, ironically devoted to sand migration. As the sand continued to advance, these two buildings too were engulfed, abandoned and eventually demolished.

Kaleidoscope sited in interior of Rubjerg Knude Lighthouse

The lighthouse now provides a compelling spectacle with its high white tower surrounded by large sand dunes. The local authority has recently provided a staircase that allows visitors to climb to the top of the building to witness the dramatic scenery. Although the light from the lighthouse lamp has been extinguished, a different form of light currently shines: a kaleidoscope casts a dancing sea of light into the tower's interior as it reflects the Sun's rays. This attraction will have a short lifespan though, as the lighthouse is expected to succumb to tidal incursion by 2023.

Over the past five centuries, the lighthouses of Skagen Odde have been continuously imperilled by the forces of tidal erosion and sand drift, and persistently implicated in economic and military strategies. The continuous drive for technological adaptations to these volatile social processes and non-human agencies is evident along the peninsula's coastline, with diverse historical artefacts that, although no longer functional as lighthouses, continue to serve as venues for artistic, heritage and touristic endeavours. They also demonstrate that, while lighthouses are readily deployed as images of physical and social stability, their material durability and their social meaning and use are always subject to larger, dynamic forces.

The innovative British military strategy of deploying lightships to overcome the absence of illumination in Skagen in the early 19th century signals the development of more mobile technologies to light the way in waters in which lighthouses could not be effectively established, as Karen Sayer describes. Like many lighthouses, some lightships have been decommissioned and are currently employed to serve different contemporary functions.

Lightships

Karen Sayer

Since they were introduced into the Thames Estuary in 1713 (Talbot, 1913), lightships provided a way to manage fluctuating spaces which never quite belonged to land, river or sea. Despite the heroic tales told of both lighthouses and lightships as conquests of Nature by Science (e.g. Talbot, 1913), lightships were not designed to control, but to place seafarers safely within wind and waves, fog, darkness, rocks, mud and sand. By mapping the margins of human danger, they have marked and mark otherwise invisible and changeable coastal margins. A tracery in light and sound of the borderlands of the British Isles, here is a way to see past leisured, leisurely beaches to histories of interconnection, trade and work (Dettingmeijer, 1996).

Lightships became significant and important 'seamarks' (Price Edwards, 1884). They are vessels guiding other vessels, anchored ships alerting sea-going ships in sight of port, unpowered, undocked. These vulnerable vessels were towed by tugs, moored securely and floated over submerged ridges and banks of mud. They could be found deep inland along tidal rivers and out into estuaries, over coastal shoals, reefs and sands, or by distant rocks, in locations too remote for a lighthouse. When staffed, by a small crew and a captain, they travelled nowhere for a month at a time. Anchored in places that needed constant surveying and charting, they offered, and still offer, guidance to shipping around land that is not land, and sea that is not sea. Located, yet dislocated, they could not be used as aids to navigation. Rather, by offering uniform, safe passage to all seafarers, illuminating the most untrustworthy coastal waters, they rewrote territorial waters as merely safe/hazardous to shipping.

At the time that light vessels developed, ship ownership was 'perhaps the riskiest form of business in Britain' (Armstrong and Bagwell, 1983: 167). But, investors continued to invest and, despite losses of all sorts, their profits increased. Larger and smaller ports, navigable waterways and canals were linked to shipping lanes in a complex transport network that complemented the expanding rail and road-haulage systems, and shifted farm and factory produce, raw materials and finished goods on a vast scale. The quantity and value of goods carried out to sea from the river ports and harbours, by sea around Britain and back inland, via a vast, complex array of horse-drawn barges, sailing vessels and steamships increased year on year (Freeman, 1983: 13–14; Bagwell and Armstrong, 1988; Doe, 2010; Owen, 2013: 198, Table 2). Stationed around the coast, the lightships became critical to safe passage of colliers, sailing barges, steam packets, anything travelling on coastal waters, passing inland through estuaries or on the open sea.

Until the 1960s, lightships were still stationed inland along navigable yet hazardous waterways, such as the Mersey and the Humber. Trinity House had won the right in the 1730s to control the first light vessel, the *Nore*, stationed in the Thames Estuary. But, intense investment mixing with high hazard and rapid change led to a more complex picture of legal oversight elsewhere. In the North of England, Hull Trinity House, established in the 16th century, gave way to the new Humber Conservancy Board in 1908, which was in turn replaced by the British Transport Docks Board in 1968 covering the area from (seaward) Goole on the Ouse and Gainsborough on the River Trent. Each operated in tandem with Trinity House in London.

As vessels were commissioned, so companies built them: Watson's of Gainsborough; Earle's of Hull; Cook, Welton & Gemmell Ltd. Each had to develop or buy patented technology for the ships' lights and address their fuelling, as well as building the ships themselves. The lights were generated, as with lighthouses, first by candles, then by vegetable-, sperm-, petroleum-, or gas-oil (the oil reservoirs being in the body of the ship). The built vessels generated expertise through decades of experience dedicated to their service – like yet unlike serving on a sea-going vessel, like yet unlike serving in a lighthouse. As with the lighthouses, after their early evolution, each lightship had its own 'character' of light flashes and pattern of fog signals sounded out by horn. Local maritime histories became entangled with histories of international trade, all reliant on the human effort to see and hear certainty within the topographical and climatic ambiguity of the tidal river, the estuary, the shore and the coast.

The vessels' stories and those of their crews have been captured in local histories, and reworked as art (Hooper and Liversedge, 2016). The dangerous features that they marked received a succession of vessels as lightships came and went for repair, refitting or replacement. More ephemeral than lighthouses, fragile structures, like their sea-going counterparts, they suffered wear and tear, could be run into or wrecked.

Most British lightships were decommissioned between the 1970s and 1980s. Many have had second lives as heritage sites, restaurants, workshops and studios, and have been used for church activities, for events and training. Some have been scrapped, others have sunk or lie stranded on mud banks between land and sea.

The remainder have been converted to automatic operation – the majority using solar power – and have continued to provide essential seamarks for international merchant shipping (Edgerton, 2008). Today, they mark danger and separate traffic in the Channel, gather data on weather and sea conditions, and watch wildlife. At sea, lightships have generated data for assessing the migration patterns of, among others, geese, herons, cormorants, gannets and petrels. Through them, we might revisit Britain's littoral histories. Manifestly human, artificial lights on the coast and at sea have influenced and revealed not just our own movements but also those of the seabirds that circulate and cross our borders (Barrington, 1900; Rojek, 2001).

(continued)

(continued)

Figure 28 Galloper in a bottle, by Elise&Mary, 2013.

Karen Sayer (pers. comm.) also reflected on how engaging with other perspectives shifted her own:

> Working on this project has led me to reflect on the flows of communication, the international messages of danger, carried by light across river, estuary and sea. Regarding that light, then reading about the evolution of its perception, drew me towards the evidence of gulls that struck lighthouses and the movements of seabirds: this was no longer just a human story, about human perception or safety; now it included the endangered and migrating members, and the agency, of other species. I looked 'up'.

MATERIAL RELATIVES

Veronica Strang

The image of the lighthouse, that plucky outpost perched on a vestigial afterthought of rock, is often one of isolation. But no constructed object is ever truly isolated. All – human and non-human alike – are material expressions of needs and desires, and of particular cultural, historical, geographical and species-specific ways of seeing, understanding and feeling. Some are the product of biological evolution, some the result of more rapid cultural adaptations, and many are both.

Lighthouses 'do' certain things for human communities. Their traditional function has been, through their unique light-signalling codes, to communicate information about shorelines, enabling sailors to reach safe harbour, and thus assisting the movement of people through marine environments. Their dual role in warning and assisting is entangled with their role as objects that 'survey' the unruly seas and mark the limits of terra firma, and with the development of navigation techniques and burgeoning marine travel.

As Steve Millington (above) observes, the form of lighthouses follows these functions. They must be extraordinarily sturdy and resilient, resisting the cruellest waves. They must be rounded and smooth, giving no purchase to the wind. They must be tall enough that their lights can be seen from far out at sea (and their foghorns heard). Their lights must be bright enough to penetrate the darkness, and distinctive enough to be recognisable.

Taking form and function as a starting point, disciplinary areas such as Design History and Archaeology reveal that the lighthouse sits within a whole genealogy of material relatives, ranging from the earliest of hilltop beacons to recent – and increasingly invisible – technologies of surveillance and communication. Some of their simpler functions are echoed in closely related technologies: semaphore signalling posts, or (sometimes illuminated) marine markers, whose sole function is to draw attention to hazards hidden beneath the waves and to mark the limits of safe passages.

However, if we broaden this view to consider the function of lighthouses in enabling safe movement, there are other material relatives: street and porch lights that guide people to their homes; 'cat's eyes' that keep cars safely on the road (and which use light refraction technology much like that employed in lighthouses); even the humble torch. There are more obvious relationships with the lights and 'control towers' that are used to guide aeroplanes safely into an 'airport'. The nomenclature alone is sufficient to illuminate a simple transposition of ideas into a new domain. Geographer Peter Adey's description of Liverpool's classic airport control tower also makes it plain that, while form necessarily follows function in this material relative too, the strong family resemblance equally demonstrates the aesthetic heritage of lighthouse architecture.

Wish image

Peter Adey

In June 1937, a group of Liverpool dignitaries were led into a vast hangar, one of two that would be positioned symmetrically either side of the art-deco masterpiece of Liverpool's first airport. The airport was on the outskirts of the city beside the Mersey at Speke (Butler, 2004). It is now a hotel, a few miles away from the new airport, built in the 1980s, also at Speke, and substantially redeveloped and rebranded in the 2000s.

The original hangars (one now a call centre, the other a gym) flank the control tower completed in 1937, with a passenger terminal following in 1938. The terminal's wings were gently angled inwards to embrace the apron upon which aircraft would taxi in. Spectators, enthralled by an earlier age of aviation, could visit the airport to take in the scene, sitting so close to the aircraft that it seemed they could almost touch them. Enthusiasts

Figure 29 Liverpool Speke Airport, now the Crowne Plaza Hotel Liverpool. Photograph: Calflier001, CC BY-SA 2.0 (http://creativecommons.org/licenses/by-sa/2.0), via Wikimedia Commons.

recall with nostalgia being able to feel the heat of the engines and taking in their fumes.

When the dignitaries arrived to open the first airport building, the massive hangar doors, manufactured by Esavian, opened slowly, powered by an electric motor. They revealed to the great and the good of Merseyside a dramatic view of the completed control tower. The tower was serviced by an elevator (in which the Lord Mayor of the city would unfortunately get stuck during a tour). What many of the spectators of this event of 'civic boosterism' aligned with a thirties idea of 'airmindedness' would realise (Adey, 2006), was that the tower was essentially a lighthouse. It was octagonal and built of decorative brickwork, but there, on top of the tower, was a glass lookout. Rather than containing a light, this was the lookout point, giving the air traffic controllers uninterrupted views of the apron and airfield. And, above all of the rooms in the seven-storey building, which included a telephone exchange, a records office, a meteorological department and radio telephone operators, was the tower's neon light, topped with a weather vane. Encased in glass, this light was visible, some claimed, even from Birmingham.

Liverpool's tower at Speke could be considered as what Walter Benjamin called a 'wish image' (Buck-Morss, 1991) when he identified, in the ironwork of imperial Paris, echoes of earlier architectural forms or naturally occurring shapes. The innovation of the airport, then, was not merely an expression of a new, more rational and technological future. Just as Corbusier observed a tendency to design aircraft like birds, the airport would build on images of the past to look to the future as, for many, international transportation would begin to move from the seas to the air.

For Liverpool's 1930s airport to borrow from what might seem to be outmoded architectural forms such as lighthouses (although the air age did not make maritime mobility obsolete), speaks to several things. First, it reveals how lighthouses have persisted in other structures and places, taking on a hybrid form in other sorts of buildings and other kinds of functions. Liverpool Airport's control tower-cum-lighthouse performed many of the same functions as the lighthouse design on which it was based. The beacon, combined with the radio transmitter, served to guide aircraft into the airfield and to warn others of their presence. The bulb would flash LV (Liverpool) in Morse code. Just as a lighthouse was designed to be seen, the control tower took advantage of its architectural prominence, using other lights (a searchlight and coloured light guns) to signal instructions to distant aircraft.

As demonstrated in the drama of the opening ceremony, Liverpool's control tower was clearly a landmark. Reports celebrated its construction and scale and, when the airport was de-requisitioned and returned to public ownership after the Second World War, the airport manager's son referred to it as Liverpool's own 'tower of Pisa'. Reporters marvelled at the breathtaking views from the control room:

(continued)

(continued)

> One is rewarded with one of the most loveliest views [. . .] to one's right the magnificent panorama of Wirral and the Welsh hills is unfolded, and stretching away in front of the tower is the great sweeping bend in the Mersey.
>
> (*Liverpool Daily Post*, 1946)

The building was to be seen, but it was also an important place to see from, allowing multiple perspectives to be experienced from within and without, distributing and shaping the visual through not only its height, position and architecture, but also through other technologies.

For some, the tower was the central nervous system of the airport, the locus of electrical and communication wiring that circuited its way from the building. The technology that drove information and control to the fingertips of the controllers was given emphasis as if they, the control tower and the airport's geography, composed a machinic assemblage of building, aircraft and a body electric. Reports focused on the tower's ability to concentrate multiple signals from distanced geographies. For example, obstruction lights at far reaches of the airfield were represented on a map lit up by electric indicator bulbs. The tannoy microphone made it possible to communicate orders within the building and outwards onto the apron.

As Latour writes of the astronomer's chart bringing 'celestial bodies billions of tons heavy and hundreds of thousands of miles away to the size of a point on a piece of paper' (Latour, 1987: 227), similar technologies were supplied to the controllers or meteorologists monitoring weather conditions, and to radio operators communicating with aircraft. The apparatus of building, machinery, bodies, charts and diagrams make the movements of disparate bodies knowable. Flows of movement were translated into information stored on graphs and charts. The information, in effect, became explicable and controllable, inscribing the incessant movement of the materials onto the electronic map. Thus, Liverpool's control tower/lighthouse provided what Lucy Suchmann has called a 'centre of coordination' (1997).

The control tower also expresses what Stewart Brand has called 'how buildings learn' from others. Like many airports of the time, the form and identity of the airport was not fixed, but drew upon the design and function of other buildings. Liverpool's leaders turned to Europe, especially Hamburg's Fulhsbuttel Airport. They sent a delegation to the United States. But they looked especially to the sea. With Liverpool's power brokers so invested in the city's port industries, this was not surprising. It was entirely logical to think of the airport, and its significant control tower, as an extension of the global maritime commerce that was so central to the city's identity.

City surveyors and engineers were similarly steeped in their own experiences of train station and port designs (Gordon, 2008). Municipal authorities elsewhere had made various attempts to merge the airport with the skyscraper. But in Liverpool's case it was thought that seaplanes offered the future for transatlantic travel, as they could stop and potentially replenish reserves at transatlantic refuelling points. The initial plans for the airport, designed by aviator Alan Cobham, included the creation of a lake so that sea planes could land and take off, even though the idea was eventually dropped.

And so, the lighthouse, in fusing with Liverpool's airport, lost part of its maritime identity. It was still open to the elements – to the wind whistling off the Mersey. It was a highly visible landmark, just as lighthouses remained, and still a beacon of light as well as emitting other waves in the electromagnetic spectrum. But in this form the lighthouse-cum-tower was mostly about control and coordination. The lighthouse was eventually wished away.

When we focus more closely on the function of lighthouses as communications devices, another family of material relatives emerges. Centuries ago, hilltop beacons composed a linked communication system. If we return to Greek history and the Athenian torch race (the *lampadedromia*), we find a reference to the Persians' use of a relay of horsemen to light signal beacons prior to the capture of Athens in 480 BC (Herodotus, 8.53–54 cited in Tracy, 1986). Audiences in classical Greek theatre were reminded of this in Aeschylus' *Agamemnon*, written in 458 BC. In the opening scenes, Clytemnestra uses light to signal the return of Agamemnon from the Trojan War (Rocco, 1997):

> From Ida's top Hephaestus, lord of fire,
>
> Sent forth his sign; and on, and ever on,
>
> Beacon to beacon sped the courier-flame.
>
> From Ida to the crag, that Hermes loves,
>
> Of Lemnos; thence unto the steep sublime
>
> Of Athos, throne of Zeus, the broad blaze flared.
>
> Thence, raised aloft to shoot across the sea,
>
> The moving light, rejoicing in its strength,
>
> Sped from the pyre of pine, and urged its way,
>
> In golden glory, like some strange new sun,
>
> Onward, and reached Macistus' watching heights.
>
> (Aeschylus, 2009: 16)

136 *The extraterrestrial lighthouse*

In a contemporary era, the technical scale of communications has massively enlarged, and it is radio masts, phone masts and other communications towers that take up and broaden the function of a lighthouse as a point source of messages. However, the human imagination has always been large in scale: ancient societies envisaged sentient celestial and solar deities watching and communicating with them from afar, and conducted rituals to send messages in response. Some – the Greeks and the Meso-Americans for example – constructed 'celestial architecture' through which particular alignments of celestial bodies were believed to open the way to underworlds or express the power of local deities.

In an era more literal in its interpretations of the world and 'outer space', popular imaginaries are more focused on signalling to alien others. In returning to his discussion of Liverpool's St John's Beacon, David Cooper recalls imagining how in the 1960s, the signals it transmitted might reach the 'little green men' believed – at that time – to be communicating with Earth via the spinning pulsar 'lighthouses' of outer space.

Figure 30 Radio City Tower, St John's Beacon, Liverpool. Photograph: El Pollock, CC BY-SA 2.0 (http://creativecommons.org/licenses/by-sa/2.0), via Wikimedia Commons.

The extraterrestrial lighthouse

St John's Beacon, Liverpool

David Cooper

As a child, for a long time I didn't like looking up. When I was dragged down Church Street before Christmas, I knew it was there. When trying on a school uniform in the department store, I could feel it. Sitting in the café on Williamson Square, I could sense it. Squeezed improbably between St John's Market and the Playhouse, the brutally concrete 'Tower' – as we all called it – loomed over the pre-regenerated cityscape. But seeing it involved standing at its base on Houghton Street and gazing straight up. It hurt as I tried to pull my head far enough back to take in its absurd verticality. My legs wobbled as the Tower seemed to sway in the unremitting wind coming in from the Mersey. It seemed to me that St John's Beacon – to give the tower its official name – might topple over and to crush the city streets and squares from which it rose. Close up, it was a vertiginous menace.

One day, however, I saw the Tower on television and, through this medium, from a distance. Instead of looking at the underside of the crow's nest on the top of the Tower, I could see the construction as a whole. TV also enabled me to see the Tower at night as a constellation of lights in the sky, signalling an enchanting other-worldliness. The Beacon acquired a new purpose. Seen on television, it became clear that the Tower's function was to provide the architectural anchorage for an alien spacecraft: a circular extraterrestrial vessel had moored at what was for me (to adopt Allen Ginsberg's myth-making assertion) 'the centre of the consciousness of the human universe' (Gruenberg and Knifton, 2007: 24). Why would beings from other planets, solar systems or galaxies wish to land anywhere else?

The next time we went to town, I looked up again. The Tower continued to swish and sway; but this time it was for a reason. Although I wasn't sure what they looked like, I was certain that the extraterrestrials inside the crow's nest were preparing to leave. It was obvious that the largely windowless tower was beginning to vibrate as the engines towards the top were fired up. It would be only a matter of minutes, before the circular structure would start to rotate at dizzying speeds, gathering sufficient momentum for the spacecraft to be released from the base mooring it to the centre of Liverpool. Any minute now the disc would shoot off, high over the city, clipping the Liver Birds as it spun violently across the mouth of the Mersey and beyond . . .

Cooper's delightful vision reminds us that lighthouses are not merely sending light signals, but also receiving them from ships at sea, just as aircraft communicate with control towers as they come in to land. This mutuality underlines the notion of the lighthouse as an active, sentient watcher, and points to another branch on the family tree: one that grows not only towards material relatives such as prison watchtowers and spy-towers at territorial borders, with their literal 'searchlights', but also to more benign lookouts – treetop hides for surveying wildlife or, in a metaphorical sense, the watching and illuminating 'eye of God' represented by the church tower and the minaret.

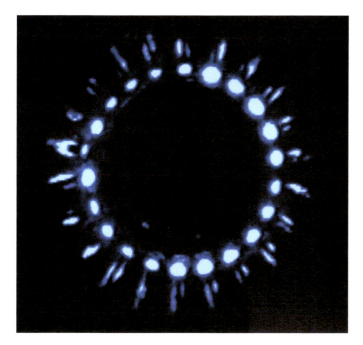

Plate 1 Bioluminescent jellyfish. Credit: National Oceanic and Atmospheric Administration's National Ocean Service, CC BY 2.0 (https://creativecommons.org/licenses/by/2.0/).

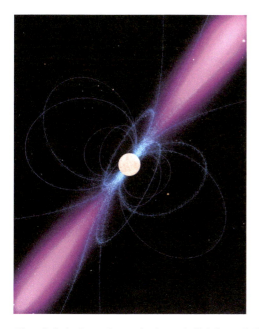

Plate 2 Spinning pulsar – the 'cosmic lighthouse'. Credit: NASA.

Plate 3 Hildegard of Bingen receiving the Light from Heaven, c.1151 (vellum) (later coloration), German School. Credit: Private Collection / Bridgeman Images.

Plate 4 Prologue: The Harbour with the Colossus of Rhodes (oil on canvas), by Giacomo Torelli (1608–1678) / Pinoteca Civica di Fano, Fano, Italy. Credit: Bridgeman Images.

Plate 5 Bell Rock Lighthouse, by J. M. W. Turner, 1819. Google Art Project via Wikimedia Commons.

Plate 6 Wish you were here – Gratiot Light, by Julie Westerman, 2017. © Julie Westerman.

Plate 7 Wish you were here – Douglas Head, by Julie Westerman, 2017. © Julie Westerman.

Plate 8 Lighthouse (East), by Catherine Yass, 2011. © Catherine Yass. All Rights Reserved, DACS 2017.

Plate 9 Phare, by Ron Haselden, 2008. A 60-metre-long sculpture constructed in fisherman's cord and steel rods. Au Pont Mévault. Plouër-sur-Rance, France.

Plate 10 Harbour Scene, Newhaven, by John Piper, c.1937 (watercolour, body colour, gouache, collage, pen, brush and black). Credit: Private Collection / Bridgeman Images. © The Piper Estate / DACS 2017.

Plate 11 *The Weather is Lovely – George Olson aground at Cape Disappointment Lighthouse*, by Julie Westerman, 2017. © Julie Westerman.

Plate 12 *The Weather is Lovely – Shipwreck by Lighthouse*, by Julie Westerman, 2017. © Julie Westerman.

THE BODY OF THE LIGHTHOUSE

Veronica Strang

Homologous forms

And so, to The Spooky Men and their 'lightpole'. To understand the form and function of a lighthouse fully, it is useful to consider the mental model-making that so intrigues psychologists, cognitive scientists and anthropologists. Implicit in previous sections is a sense that the lighthouse does some of the things that we do: it surveys; it sees; it has a coded rhythmic language of light that communicates ideas and information. Anthropologist Alfred Gell usefully observes that material culture is a 'prosthetic' extension of human agency (1998). By making objects that are stronger or more effective than we are, we expand our mental and physical capacities to act upon the world. A spade, for instance, is a bigger, stronger hand enabling us to turn the soil; an excavator is a larger digging avatar; a computer a (sometimes) more reliable brain and memory. A lighthouse, with its powerful beam of light, is like a giant person standing on a headland with a torch and shouting, 'Over here!' or 'Don't go near the rocks!', or scanning the sea for incoming shipping. In this sense, material culture inevitably represents extensions of human activities and aspirations.

The making of such objects emerges from specific cognitive processes in which the things we understand about ourselves – our physical capacities, and our behaviours – are transposed into other dimensions of our lives. Hegel describes this as a dialectical engagement in which humans imaginatively project themselves into the world, and then re-incorporate these projections into their conceptual schemes (1979). Bourdieu provides the notion of 'scheme transfers', in which the patterns of one domain are transposed into another (1977). More recent writing refers to 'environmental pattern recognition', a process through which people recognise similarities in forms and events. Through 'biomimicry', as Adey implies above, the patterns and forms observed in the surrounding world are employed imaginatively in designing architecture and material culture (Benyus, 1997).

In this way, the world is brought into the mind, and the mind extended outwards into the world and materialised (Clark, 2010). This includes 'the mind's eye' which, as well as surveying the internal landscapes of the conscious mind, looks outward, and in doing so provides the model for the lighthouse. The recursive nature of the process is encapsulated in Virginia Woolf's novel, *To the*

140 *The body of the lighthouse*

Lighthouse, which provides the inspiration for the title of this book. In her work – discussed later by Patricia Waugh – the lighthouse appears almost as a character in a story primarily concerned with exploring ideas about looking, seeing and perceiving (Woolf, 1927).

There is also a more prosaic physical dimension to this imaginative model-making. In transferring perceived patterns and forms from one frame to another, people make full use of the most familiar model: their own bodies. A house homologously becomes the domestic 'body' of the family; landscapes acquire arms, shoulders, necks; roads have legs; rivers and harbours have mouths. Such conceptual models are manifested at multiple scales: a household can have a 'head', but so too can organisations, whole nations and transnational

Figure 31 'A Lighthouse – Not Professor Tyndall', from *Moonshine*, published 20 December 1884 (wood engraving), English School. Credit: The Royal Institution, London, UK / Bridgeman Images.

Figure 32 St John's Anglican Church, Ashfield, New South Wales: 'I am the Light of the World' (John 8:12). Stained glass by Alfred Handel. Photograph: Toby Hudson, CC BY-SA 3.0 (http://creativecommons.org/licenses/by-sa/3.0), via Wikimedia Commons.

'corporations'. Because this is a recursive relationship, the material world is similarly incorporated into ideas about the human body. Thus, along with the inner sea of the Id, and the glittering light of the mind, people imagine the brain as fertile ground for emergent ideas, and circulating fluids as the hydrological flows of internal 'ecosystems'.

The lighthouse is homologous in several ways: in the broadest sense, with its mini-sun raised high, it expresses a celestial and vertical relationship between Earth and Sun. At a more immediate scale, it is a whole body, topped by a 'seeing' eye and so, implicitly, a mind. A member of the audience attending the public conversation about lighthouses that initiated this book observed that the idea of the lighthouse as a person is nicely encapsulated in depictions of 19th-century physicist John Tyndall as a lighthouse, and more recently in the song *Lightpole*, by The Spooky Men (Morrison, 2004):

>Think what you will
>
>I'm just a light pole
>
>Just a pole of light
>
>To brighten up your night.

As theologians know very well, in religious contexts the person or deity as a source of shining spiritual light is a recurring theme. Haloes of light and radiating rays of divine light illuminate iconic images of deities and saints across a range of religions, and appear in many texts stating, in one form or another, that 'I am the Light'. This vision of light embodied in the person, or in deities taking human form, underscores the importance of homologues in composing the meaning of things, and provides further insight into the lighthouse as a powerful metaphorical image of enlightenment.

Frontier monumentalism

At the risk of leaping too precipitously from the sacred to the profane, we must acknowledge that, as well as 'standing for' the whole person, lighthouses often bear a homologous resemblance to a more down-to-earth part of the human body. Their indisputably phallic form is partly explicable by the material requirements noted earlier: the need for a sturdy base; rounded wind resistance; visible height; and a distinct 'head'. But, if we place them among their material relatives, it is plain that there is more to it than this.

Lighthouses state, with some machismo, that not only are they sentinels marking the edge of safe land against the chaos of the sea; they also mark the limits of particular territories. Thus, they share both form and function with other monumental territorial objects aimed at stating national identities: the 'who's got the tallest' city tower, obelisk or spouting fountain. There is a conceptual logic to such homologous statements. These are not mere testosterone-laden messages about territorial ownership: they also offer generative symbolic rebuttal to the life-engulfing sea and provide a feisty phallic statement about the capacities of communities and nations to regenerate themselves and their social being. Lighthouses can be considered, therefore, as suitably upstanding manifestations of ideas about the physical location – and the physical limits – of what Benedict Anderson described as 'imagined communities' (2006). And understanding lighthouses in these terms provides insights into their importance as objects that embody and express identity and cultural heritage.

Lighthouses and cultural heritage

Every lighthouse embodies the cultural history and identity of a community and the place in which it is located. As new technologies have replaced lighthouses as navigational aids, many have acquired a new lease of life by emphasising their role as local identity markers. This is readily visible if we consider much smaller material relatives: the souvenir replica. Lighthouses that are now recast and promoted as tourist sites almost invariably have accompanying souvenir shops selling model lighthouse 'mini-mes', as well as lighthouse-shaped salt and pepper shakers, torches, bedside lamps, key-rings, hatpins, jewellery, lighthouse images on t-shirts, mugs, flags, table mats, photographs, calendars and postcards. There are even solar-powered lighthouse lawn ornaments. Such places also tend to specialise in traditional 'coastal foods': lobster bisque, clam chowder, lighthouse tea. And this array of votive offerings to an idea of cultural heritage is equally expressed in magazines such as *Lighthouse Digest* (Foghorn Publishing) and books with titles such as *Brilliant Beacons: A History of the American Lighthouse* (Dolin, 2016); and *Facing the Sea* (Chubbs and Kearley, 2013).

Figure 33 Souvenir lighthouses from Helsinki. Photograph: Veronica Strang.

These souvenirs compose a substantial lighthouse memorabilia industry, arising in part from people's enthusiasm for maintaining the lighthouses in their communities. Thus, Bill and Nancy Younger, the founders of Harbour Lights, observed that, although they hoped to make money through selling scaled-down replicas of particular lighthouses, 'the real reason we started Harbour Lights was to draw public attention to saving lighthouses and their history' (Harrison, 2006). Collectors' World (nd), which now distributes Harbour Lights' models notes that:

> There is a mystique and fascination with lighthouses. We see them standing firm against the most violent of storms while shining their powerful beacons to safely guide mariners as they have for hundreds of years.

On this miniature scale, too, there is a wider set of material relatives. The great majority of places with built objects that embody community or national identity sell similar kinds of material culture. For example, anyone who has visited the Eiffel Tower in Paris as a tourist will know that it is difficult to escape without a replicant key-ring. The appeal of such mini-replicas is that, like dolls' houses, or indeed dolls themselves, they encapsulate the homologous personhood of the lighthouse and its social and cultural meanings in a conveniently portable, ownable object, which literally provides the purchaser with a memorial – a souvenir – of what the lighthouse is and does. Back at home, on a mantelpiece or out on the lawn, such material culture speaks not only of the identity of that place and its community but of the collector's cosmopolitan connection with the lighthouse, the meeting of their eyes and its eye, and their miniature appropriation of its particular spirit of place.

The lighthouse at Cape Reinga

Veronica Strang

At the northern tip of New Zealand, where the Pacific Sea collides with the Tasman in frothing watery chevrons, is the lighthouse at Cape Reinga. Standing 961 feet above sea level, it marks a place that is important for both Māori and European New Zealanders. Its name comes from *Te Rerenga Wairua*: 'the leaping off place of the spirits'. According to traditional Māori beliefs, when people die, their spirits make their way to Cape Reinga, where they leave the world of light and life (*Te Rangi*) and slide down the roots of an ancient pohutakawa tree into the underworld, the dark fluid realm of non-material being, to return to their ancestral homeland of *Hawaiki*, and the regenerative womb of *Te Pō* from which new beginnings are conceived (Metge, 2004).

For the Europeans who built the lighthouse in 1941, it was vital in guiding shipping through the turbulent waters around the Cape and in providing

Figure 34 Cape Reinga Lighthouse, near the northern-most point of the North Island of New Zealand. Photograph: Gadfium, Public Domain, via Wikimedia Commons.

the nation with advance warnings about weather in a lively maritime climate (Beaglehole, 2006). But it was also a vital territorial statement, in this case aimed not only outwards to lay claim to the land in the eyes of foreign shipping fleets, but also inwards. Located at one of the most important sacred sites for local Māori tribes, it is historically entangled in the process of colonisation and contestation about the ownership and governance of New Zealand.

Today, despite – or perhaps because of – its remoteness, the lighthouse has become a popular tourist destination. As well as benefiting from modern technology (it was automated in 1987), the lighthouse site now reflects more enlightened cultural relations. The parking areas and facilities were

(continued)

(continued)

moved away from the sacred site in 2009, and some parts of Spirit Bay were placed 'off limits' to non-Māori visitors. Recognition that the lighthouse illuminates both Māori and European cultural identity has led to numerous calls for Cape Reinga to be listed as a UNESCO World Heritage Site. And, as Blue Powell's artwork below illustrates, with such a strong emphasis on identity, such sites continue to inspire homologous ideas that personify the lighthouse.

Figure 35 Sculpture based on Cape Reinga Lighthouse, by Blue Powell, 2009 (ceramic).

Soundscapes of the lighthouse

While the physical form of the lighthouse and its illuminating beam are the features that preoccupy the popular imagination, lighthouses have made another important contribution to marine communities. From the late 1800s, many were equipped with foghorns, whose deep, mournful bellowing added a further signal that guided mariners to safety and reminded local inhabitants of their presence. Jennifer Allan describes the careful tests made to maximise foghorns' abilities to reach out across the sea, and their impact on the 19th-century soundscape, while Joshua Portway and Lise Autogena's description of the musical composition *Foghorn Requiem*, composed to mark the end of this era, provides a sense of the nostalgia evoked by the sound of the lighthouse.

Horn section

John Tyndall's 1873 foghorn testing sessions

Jennifer Lucy Allan

John Tyndall is a major figure in Victorian science. He discovered greenhouse gases, explained why the sky is blue, was an accomplished mountaineer – the first to climb the Weisshorn. Steven Connor (2010: 190–191) credits Tyndall with initiating fundamental changes in the way we think about air: from seeing it as empty space to one teeming with imperceptible waveforms and energies. Tyndall was also the successor (and biographer) to his mentor and close friend Michael Faraday at the Royal Institution, and this led to him succeeding Faraday as scientific advisor to Trinity House.

While Faraday electrified the lighthouses, Tyndall's major contribution was to sound signals. He undertook the first large-scale foghorn testing sessions in Britain in 1873 (although three lighthouses in England – Dungeness, St Catherine's and Souter Point – had installed foghorns the decade before). His subsequent report *On Fog Signals* (RFS, 1874) has been generally ignored, however, and his biography makes scant mention of his work at Trinity House.

Tyndall's work on foghorns may have been dwarfed by other events: he delivered his life-changing Belfast Address in August 1874, and just before the tests began he published *Fragments of Science* (1872), an enormously popular book of scientific essays. However, the *Fog Signals* report is a remarkable document: detailed and descriptive, it created a bedrock of evidence that decided the character of fog signals along British coastlines.

The site chosen was the South Foreland Lighthouse, 5 miles from Dover, perched on top of the broad white cliffs roughly 90 metres above sea level. The tower is a whitewashed Victorian structure, an uneven octagon with a crenellated gallery, built in the 1840s to warn ships away from the Goodwin Sands, a treacherous 10-mile sandbank lying 6 miles off the Kent coast.

Tyndall's experiments began in May 1873. Different devices were tested each day, and included various horns, sirens, whistles and guns. On the first day, the committee tested two brass trumpets (11 feet and 2 inches long, sounded by vibrating steel reeds 9 inches long and 2 inches wide); a whistle,

(continued)

(continued)

of the same design as train whistles at the time; and a 12-inch steam whistle attached to a boiler. At the bottom of the cliff were two more trumpets and a 6-inch air whistle. Later on, guns were tested: a howitzer; an 18-pound cannon; and a mortar, worked by gunners from Dover Castle. Soundings were repeated and reported descriptively.

Tyndall writes skilfully about sound, using careful comparisons and economic vocabulary. In his 1867 book *On Sound* (from a series of lectures given at the Royal Institution), he describes the sounds of waves on a shingle beach as ranging from 'a scream to a noise resembling that of frying bacon' (1867: 55). In the 1874 foghorn tests, a whistle resembles 'the bellowing of a bull', and later, gun signals fired are described as 'sharp and dense, while others resembled the shock of a soft body against sheet iron' (RFS, 1874: 47).

Tyndall's objective was to find a signal that would operate reliably in fog at a distance of 4 miles. But trying to find a reliable sound signal to travel a useful distance out to sea proved almost impossible. The South Foreland was particularly susceptible to a number of extreme acoustic phenomena. There were soundless zones, 'acoustic clouds' where a ship would sail a mile out and hear a horn clearly, before the sound became lost for a distance of a few miles, only to reappear again. There were extreme and acute echoes when the sea was like a mirror and conditions were very still. The phenomena were mysterious: great reaches of water where sound was turned on its head, silenced, reflected back:

> From the perfectly transparent air the echoes came, at first with a strength apparently but little less than that of the direct sound, and then dying gradually and continuously away . . . the echoes reached us, as if by magic, from absolutely invisible walls.
>
> (RFS, 1874: 21)

A strong headwind, common to clifftop areas, was enough to carry weaker sounds away. Guns were lost on a gust of wind; whistles vanished a few hundred yards out. Echoes posed potentially the biggest problem: how would a mariner be able to locate the cliffs if echoes appeared to be coming from a different direction? The foghorn was intended to be a sonic substitute for the lighthouse when the light was obscured by fog. Could it be considered an effective acoustic replacement if it was so prone to distortion?

But known echoes and other sound sources were (and are still) used by mariners hoping to locate themselves in familiar channels. Penny McCall Howard retells an account in which a man 'described to me how in thick fog going through the narrows of Loch Hourn, his father would shout out of the wheelhouse window and use the echo of his voice bouncing off the cliffs to tell where he was' (2013: 63).

Tyndall's report, and these phenomena, show that sending a sound signal a useful distance out to sea reliably is difficult and subject to more distortion than a visual marker. Many attempts to control the sound transmission were made by Tyndall. Volume was increased; the effectiveness of 'beats' were tested, by sounding two horns simultaneously; sound reflectors were mounted behind the horns to augment the sound; the horns were rotated. But nature still gets in the way of Tyndall: the cliffs at the Foreland pose problems for sound signalling.

Just as the Industrial Revolution and increase in shipping trade was increasing the need for more coastal navigational aids, technological developments were also affecting the marine soundscape. The shift from sail to steam changed the sounds with which fog signals had to compete. In Eugene O'Neill's play, *Hairy Ape* (1922), Paddy the Irish stokehole laments the decline of the age of sail: 'Her sails stretching aloft all silver and white, not a sound on the deck, the lot of us dreaming dreams'. Paddy goes on to scorn the boats he now works on: 'Black smoke from the funnels smudging the sea, smudging the decks – the bloody engines pounding and throbbing and shaking'.

Tyndall quotes Faraday in the closing pages of the 1874 report: 'False promise to the mariner would be worse than no promise at all' (RFS, 1874: 64). Nevertheless, he recommended the installation of steam and compressed-air powered horns as, despite the hindrances, their sound travelled further and louder than existing sound signals. This heralded a decisive move in the installation of foghorns along the coast. Over the following decades, horns were installed at hundreds of lighthouses and harbours and, while the technology at each was applied on a case-by-case basis, and sounded with its own character, the metallic 'bellowing' was produced by the same basic means. Tyndall's report thus established the foghorns as a soundmark along British coastlines for the next hundred years.

Disturbing the peace

The Cloch foghorn and changing coastal soundscapes in the 19th century

Jennifer Lucy Allan

> The Doctors in Dunoon declare
>
> Their patients nightly mourn;
>
> They cannot get a wink of sleep,
>
> And blame the Cloch fog-horn
>
> (*Dunoon Herald*, 4 May 1897, in Cloch Foghorn papers and cuttings, 1897)

(continued)

(continued)

The Cloch Lighthouse is situated on a sharp bend in the Clyde, opposite the town of Dunoon, where the channel narrows and the land juts out into a point. In the 19th and into the 20th century, steam packets would race round the bend and collide, sometimes sinking in minutes.

In early 1897, a foghorn was installed in front of the whitewashed lighthouse. A steam-powered diaphone, it replaced a whistle sounded by a boiler. It was not well received. By 9 November that year, the Cowall District Committee (1897) of the County Council of Argyll had petitioned the Clyde Lighthouse Trust – the body that looked after local navigation – about the new foghorn. The petition complained that:

> (T)he sound emitted by the fog horn recently placed on the Cloch Lighthouse is a serious nuisance to the inhabitants of the district lying within its range, it being so loud and penetrating that to the inhabitants of Dunoon (which is about two miles distant from the lighthouse) it seems to be coming from a source a few yards outside their dwelling houses, and of such volume that in some parts of the Burgh where the configuration of the neighbourhood gives rise to an echo, it is so magnified by echoes and reverberation as to be almost overpowering.

The Cloch's horn sounded twice a minute, more frequently than many others, with four 2-second blasts – high low, high low – in quick succession. But it was the timbre and quality of the sound that caused the most disturbance. Complaints started from its installation, with letters and poems written into local newspapers. A W. B. P., who had made the mistake of moving near the Cloch, described it in a letter as though 'a gigantic bull and his gigantic mate, which had stolen noiselessly up to my chamber window, suddenly opened their mouths and emitted their characteristic notes – the male a hoarse roar, and 2 seconds afterwards the female a shrill skreigh' (Cloch Foghorn papers and cuttings, 1897).

There are other such complaints relating to foghorn noise in the archives of the Board of Trade and the various lighthouse bodies around the UK. This particular dispute lasted almost a year, and bounced between the Clyde Lighthouse Trust, the Northern Lighthouse Board, the residents of Dunoon and those further afield in earshot of the horn. The bundle of missives (Cloch Foghorn papers and cuttings, 1897) assembled in the offices of the Clyde Lighthouse Trust back in 1897 now gives us a rare primary account of the reception of a new foghorn: how did people react to new horns? How did the various authorities deal with conflicts between sound disturbance and maritime safety? What was the impact of the sound at the moment of installation? What did these horns sound like if you were a resident of Dunoon in 1897?

In the case of the Cloch, we have numerous first-hand descriptions: a bull, described above; a 'howling fiend' from another writer; but also a letter written in support of the horn, suggesting that it had 'at least as much melody in it as a Wagnerian opera'. The directors of Dunoon convalescent homes complained that the horn's 'unearthly yells' prevented their inmates from recovering: 'The tones emitted resemble very much the cries of one in sore distress, and are enough to upset the nerves of even those in robust health'.

The issue was not merely one of volume: the Cloch foghorn was thought to be 'shrill', so consideration was given not just to volume but also to whether the sound was pleasant or unpleasant and how it affected the local soundscape.

By November 1897, the Clyde Lighthouse Trust and the Northern Lighthouse Board had agreed that the signal could be changed. 'You will understand that we do not propose to diminish the power of the blasts, but to lower the pitch of both notes' (*Engineer's Department letter book*, 1897–1899). David Alan Stevenson wrote that 'this matter raises a very serious question, of which I fear we may hear more as fog signals extend, namely where the public and navigational interests are antagonistic, which is to give way?' (*Engineer's Department letter book*, 1897–1899).

The dispute about the Cloch foghorn happened at a crucial time in the developing coastal soundscape in the UK. The Industrial Revolution had rationalised the land, moving populations from rural to urban environments, and shipping had expanded. Steel and steam allowed ships to be bigger and faster, and competition increased. More collisions, sinkings and shipwrecks occurred due to a lag in regulation, coupled with the sheer number of boats on the water.

Oceans, seas and waterways, from the Clyde out to the North Atlantic and beyond, were unpredictable and inhospitable. Water took life and commerce. Goods sank. Accounts of wrecks frequently described vessels going down in under an hour. The foghorn, as a sonic extension of lighthouses, strove to make these trade routes safer. There was little consistency in their application; horns were installed in different shapes, sizes and arrangements, and were powered by a variety of engines in number and size, but the technology had an archetypal sound, rooted in the means by which it is produced: a sombre metal machine moan; the call of a cavernous metal lung. It is the sound that the lighthouse keeper in Ray Bradbury's short story 'The Fog Horn' (1953), describes as:

> A voice that is like an empty bed beside you all night long, and like an empty house when you open the door, and like trees in autumn with no leaves. A sound like the birds flying south, crying, and a sound like

(continued)

(continued)

> November wind and the sea on the hard, cold shore . . . a sound that's so alone that no one can miss it, that whoever hears it will weep in their souls, and hearths will seem warmer, and being inside will seem better to all who hear it in the distant towns.
>
> (Bradbury, 2001: 3)

Even in its construction, the foghorn is tied to this era: steam-powered and constructed largely in steel, its sound and its structure can be traced directly to Watt's improvement of the steam engine.

As church bells had done for centuries, the foghorn's sound populated and defined a territory. Alain Corbin describes bells as 'the spatial and temporal markers upon which individual and communal identities rested' (1999: 25). The foghorn similarly colonised space, expanding Victorian power out across the water via sound, and in the case of the Cloch, up to the doors of the residents of Dunoon.

This increase in the volume of the horn enabled by new steam-powered diaphones, as demonstrated at the Cloch, can also be read as an attempt to control the environment by filling it with sound. R. Murray Schafer, the originator of the study of acoustic ecology, saw industrial noise as an intrusion:

> Increase in the intensity of sound output is the most striking characteristic of the industrialized soundscape. Industry must grow; therefore its sounds must grow with it. That is the fixed theme of the past two hundred years. In fact, noise is so important as an attention-getter that if quiet machinery could have been developed, the success of industrialisation might not have been so total. For emphasis let us put this more dramatically: if cannons had been silent, they would never have been used in warfare.
>
> (1977: 77)

Michel Serres, whose early years involved working on boats and, later, serving in the Navy, writes that:

> The audible occupies ground through its reach . . . sound through its very ubiquity unites space in its entirety and makes of it a single phenomenon perceptible to all, whereas sight always remains multiple.
>
> (2008: 108)

'Power belongs to whomever has a bell or a siren', he continues, but while his point is partially metaphorical, we may take it literally – the foghorn, as a sound, is designed to extend across space. The case of the Cloch is a microcosm of a broader project to install steam horns: a Victorian display of power and an attempt to exert control over the sea.

Nineteenth-century foghorns disrupted the sleep of entire communities, were prone to giving misleading signals if the wind carried the sound in the wrong direction, and crucially, consumed fossil fuels. In their final, most powerful forms they aided what architect Paul Shepheard summarises as a '19th century landscape strategy of industrial exploitation of the earth' (1997: 9–10).

But what about now? The Cloch was a nuisance, and Schafer calls it noise. And yet the foghorn appears as a sonic motif in films, literature and music: John Carpenter's *The Fog* (1980); Ingram Marshall's *Fog Tropes* (1984); Martin Scorsese's *Shutter Island* (2010). Responses to it are often emotional, as evidenced by the *Foghorn Requiem* described below. How can a sound that once caused people to up sticks and leave town reduce audience members to tears on the cliffs at Souter Point over 115 years later?

Barry Truax suggests that 'sound phobias' may turn into 'sound romances', representing our changing feelings towards the sounds in our environments over time:

> The romance that builds up around the 'disappearing' sound from the past is the counterpart to the phobia that usually surrounds a new sound, particularly when it replaces an older, more familiar one ... The romance associated with a past sound arises from a nostalgia for a time and circumstance that no longer exists. The sound seems romantic because it has the power both to evoke the past context and to idealize it.
> (Truax, 2001: 29)

As a sonic motif, the foghorn has been used in films, literature and music to signify bad omens, but also as sombre memory music. Alvin Curran, in the notes to his large-scale radio project, *Maritime Rites*, called it 'the source of one of the most enduring minimal musics around us' (2004). The sound of steam-powered diaphone foghorns has become lodged in collective cultural consciousness.

In explaining this link between sentiment and sound, John Levack Drever expands on Yi-Fu Tuan's concept of topophilia. In an essay on the relationship between the sounds of Dartmoor and its inhabitants (Drever, 2007) he emphasises the relationship between place, the sensation of sound and sentiment. On the banks of the Clyde at the end of the 19th century, how did the sound of the foghorn relate to the landscape in which it was situated? How was the sense of place of the nearby inhabitants of Dunoon affected by such a drastic change in the soundscape?

Reports from the time note that people left the district because of the foghorn, and others worried that it would reduce the value of their property, but David Alan Stevenson, in his 25 November letter regarding the Cloch, carries a kernel of what Truax later detailed. 'Originally this signal was

(continued)

(continued)

produced by whistles blown by steam from a large boiler. Complaints were made of this signal which however ceased after the inhabitants of the district became familiar with the sound' (*Engineer's Department letter book*, 1897–1899). In other words, 'we will get used to it'.

In judging sound, we often fall into binaries: noise/music, pleasant/unpleasant, but the history of the foghorn at the Cloch allows us to take the passage of time into consideration and renders such binaries reductive and incapable of explaining experiences of the soundscape.

In the 120 years since the residents of Dunoon complained about the horn, the Cloch has been silenced, although its horn building still stands, a squat concrete structure directly in front of the old lighthouse. There is no signal now: it has been decommissioned as many were during the 1970s and 80s. Contemporary horns, like those at the Lizard in Cornwall, are higher pitched sirens. Human error in setting up GPS means that not all foghorns have been silenced. They perform a function in the most desperate circumstances but are of a very different sound character, and one which has not infiltrated cultural consciousness with such marked effect.

Meanwhile, some old horns are being restored and switched on again for tourists. Engine-powered diaphones can be heard at Sumburgh Head in the Shetlands, Souter Point in Sunderland and Nash Point in Wales. It is easy to get nostalgic for the old industrial beasts, but the residents of Dunoon would have welcomed a contemporary diaphone.

As a sound, the foghorn is uniquely connected to the maritime industrial history of the UK, representing a massive soundmark for that era. In its steel-trumpeted, steam-driven form, the foghorn is the purest sound of the Industrial Revolution.

Foghorn Requiem

Joshua Portway and Lise Autogena

When Margaret Thatcher privatised the shipyards in the 1980s, the subsequent collapse of maritime industries had a devastating impact on the North East of England. The region has yet to recover from the loss of an identity associated with centuries of maritime history and knowledge connected to the sea. It was in this context that we proposed the performance of *Foghorn Requiem* for Souter Lighthouse in 2012.

Situated on the cliffs above the North Sea, between the River Tyne and Sunderland, Souter Lighthouse has been calling out to mariners since 1871. It was the first purpose-built electric lighthouse in the world, and it has had a series of foghorns, culminating in the diaphone horns installed in the

Figure 36 Brass band playing in *Foghorn Requiem*. Photograph: © Adrian Don, 2013.

1950s. The horn was so loud that it could be heard 18 miles out to sea and sometimes far inland. But with advances in GPS navigation there was less and less need for the lighthouse, and in 1988 it was decommissioned and given to the National Trust, at which point a group of retired mariners and ship builders set out to restore the horn to create the original sound that they remembered so well.

When we realised that Trinity House was decommissioning the remaining foghorns across the UK, we set out to highlight the disappearance of their sound from the British coastal landscape. We wanted to explore the symbolic and emotional nature of the foghorn and how the sound becomes part of a particular landscape. In our childhood memories, the foghorn is a soft and melancholy voice in the distance, so we were surprised to find that, up close, it is actually a brassy, raucous, trumpeting noise. This change in the quality of the sound is caused by the innumerable reflections it gathers as it travels across the landscape. A foghorn is almost unique in that it is usually heard at a distance of several miles, and the tone is formed by the local environment as much as by the original horn. The sound is a unique encoding of time and distance, of atmospheric conditions and of the millions of echoes and reverberations of the physical landscape through which it travels. *Foghorn Requiem* was imagined as a celebration of this lost sound and its emotional significance to a particular landscape, memory and sense

(continued)

(continued)

of belonging, but it was also intended as a symbolic performance of the maritime culture in the North East of England that could only be performed by the maritime community itself.

Supported by producer Richard Hollinshead, the National Trust, South Tyneside Council, Customs House and Festival of the North East, we commissioned composer Orlando Gough to write a musical score for an orchestra consisting of the Souter Lighthouse Foghorn, the ship's horns of fifty ships on the North Sea, and three of the North East's finest brass ensembles: The Felling, NASUWT Riverside and Westoe bands. Such bands have existed since the 19th century and were part of the coal-mining tradition that complemented the maritime industries on the Tyne. They have a central place in the history and culture of the region. We wanted the presence of the brass bands to evoke these traditions, and during the performance we positioned them on the cliff top and hoped that the similarity of their instruments to the ships' horns would create a sense of unity between the sea and the land, the past and the present.

Developing the performance was a complicated year-long undertaking. We wanted the music to incorporate the sense of distance and landscape invoked by the foghorn and the timbral effects of distance. The idea was to create a piece of music blending sounds originating at different distances: from the ships' horns miles out at sea to conventional acoustic music just a few metres away. For this we needed technology that allowed the timing of distant sounds to be precisely controlled so that they would arrive in time with the music being played on the shore.

This involved complex atmospheric, acoustic and landscape interaction modelling to incorporate directly into the composition the atmospheric conditions and the physics of distance, as well as the timbral reverberation of the landscape. Tracking the position of each horn, the technology allowed us to compensate for the speed of sound, so that each ship positioned at sea functioned as a tuned musical instrument in the score. We hoped that by defying our normal expectations of physics, the experience of hearing sounds from different distances coming together at the same time would be profoundly strange.

Another challenge was how to position fifty ships in positions close to each other, safely, just off Souter Lighthouse, a location of multiple shipwrecks, without any control over the weather conditions on the day. South Shields Marine School helped us to position participating vessels in exact orchestral positions, using a maritime simulation system. This enabled us to test the location and safety of the vessels under different weather impacts and to provide each vessel with a dedicated GPS-based position for the performance.

Foghorn Requiem was developed in close collaboration with coastal communities in the North East over a period of two years, and involved more than twenty-five maritime organisations. Vessels travelled to

Souter Lighthouse from the whole region and anchored on their allocated orchestral positions. There were fishing vessels, rowing boats, yachts, rescue vessels, harbour tugs, research vessels and government fishing inspection vessels, as well as a huge cross-Channel ferry with 300 passengers. The performance had generated considerable anticipation, and audiences from all walks of life came equipped to picnic and, some, to camp overnight. The 50-minute performance took place under a slightly threatening grey summer sky. It was an unusual experience shared by an estimated audience of around 10,000 on land and at sea.

The performance passed as a bit of a blur for us, exhausted from days of preparation. What remains in our memory are impressionistic fragments: the solo cornet prelude from the top of the lighthouse; the moment of the first chord played by the ships' horns; the call and response between the brass band and the ships; and the vast sound space generated as the chords travelled across the sea. Each time the lighthouse foghorn itself sounded to punctuate passages of the music, the sound was so physically penetrating that listeners would jump from the shock.

Although we had planned it carefully, the last passages of the music were so affecting that we watched the performance through tears. At the end, the brass players turned their backs to the audience and played directly to the sea, their music suddenly tiny in comparison to the vast space. The ships answered with an enormous chord, and the foghorn played its final blast: one continuous note, sustained until its air tanks were almost empty. The extraordinary cry lasted for more than a minute before it began to waver and choke as the huge lungs were exhausted, until they could no longer produce a musical tone, and all that remained was the gentle sound of moving air, like a dying creature exhaling its last breath out over the sea. It felt melancholic and timeless, somehow epitomising a sense of the past and the present at the same time. The silence hung for a brief moment and then the call was answered by a sustained chorus from the ships: a farewell and a final raucous salute.

Death of a lighthouse

Caitlin DeSilvey

Peter Greenaway's film *A Zed and Two Noughts* tells the story of two brothers, Oliver and Oswald, who have both recently lost their wives in a car accident involving a fatal collision with a swan. The brothers become obsessed with decay and, at the zoo where they work, Oliver sets up time-lapse cameras in the lab to document the gradual decomposition of, first, an

(continued)

(continued)

apple and a bowl of prawns; later, a juvenile crocodile, the culpable swan, a road-killed dog and a zebra. In one scene, the lab's darkness is punctuated by irregular flashes of light, which illuminate the subjects in polythene enclosures, the progress of putrification and the breakdown of each body measured against a background grid. Oliver comments:

> I sit here for hours. It's like sitting amongst lighthouses. Each lighthouse is giving you a bearing on lost spaces of time. There are tens of thousands of photographs taken here, all taken very patiently. Because decay can be very slow. Nine months for the human body, they say.
> (Greenaway, 1985)

The Orfordness Lighthouse began operating in 1792, having been built to replace other beacons lost to longshore drift on the fragile shingle spit off the Suffolk coast. The 30-metre masonry structure was topped with a lantern lit by fourteen oil lamps, set in silver-plated reflectors. In 2010, Trinity House determined that the lighthouse was no longer required as an aid to navigation. Behind this decision was the inexorable erosion of the bank beneath the lighthouse: by 2012, the span from lighthouse base to beach crest was only 15 metres, and with erosion on the spit estimated at (on average) 3.5 metres per annum, the structure didn't have much time. Trinity House and the National Trust discussed the potential for a transfer of ownership or a lease agreement, given that the Trust owned much of the rest of the Ness. However, the trust made it clear that if it accepted responsibility for the structure it would take no measures to defend it and would follow the guidance set out in the Shoreline Management Plan (2010), which recommended 'no active intervention' on this stretch of coastline. Eventually, the lighthouse would cede its ground to the sea. The Trust decided not to seek acquisition, and when Trinity House decommissioned the light in June 2013, the BBC marked the occasion with a headline reading, 'Orfordness lighthouse gets switched off and left to the sea' (BBC, 2013).

Then there was an unexpected turn of events. A London lawyer with a second home near Orford purchased the structure from Trinity House and promptly formed the Orfordness Lighthouse Company (Fletcher, 2014). Its stated aim was 'preservation so far as possible' of the beleaguered lighthouse, 'until such time as it may fall victim to the sea and waves' (Gold, nd). As autumn storms battered the Suffolk coastline that winter, it seemed that time might be closer than anyone had imagined. Each sea swell and storm event brought the base of the lighthouse closer to the waves, and the newly-formed company devised a hasty plan to stabilise the beach crest with a 50-metre long barrier of geotextile bags filled with beach pebbles (Planning Application, 2014).

The National Trust expressed concerns about the proposal, pointing out that when Trinity House decommissioned the lighthouse they had agreed a position that 'would allow natural forces to dictate the future of the building'. They suggested that sea defences might accelerate erosion elsewhere on the spit (National Trust, 2014a; Natural England, 2014). But they acknowledged that temporary stabilisation measures might be necessary to 'allow time to remove the principal features and fittings from this historically important building' (National Trust, 2014b). Some of those who commented on the planning proposal seemed not to appreciate the temporary nature of the solution. One local resident opined, 'All efforts should be made to *prolong the life* of this historic building' (Underwood, 2014, emphasis added).

Meanwhile, other local residents were making different plans: they wanted to hold a 'wake' for the dying lighthouse. Although the idea of holding a wake for a building may seem strange, the impulse to understand the destruction of built structures by drawing parallels with our own corporeal vulnerability, and eventual mortality, is a very old one. Rose Macaulay diagnosed the 'realization of mortality' as the dominant emotion that is inspired by architectural ruination (Macaulay, 1953: 23). If we accept that our buildings have lives, then we also must accept that they have deaths. '[O]bjects and structures that display the erosions and accretions of age seem conformable with our own transient and ever-changing selves,' observes David Lowenthal (1994: 43).

Michael Shanks goes further to make 'a plea for pathology' (1998: 17). 'Death and decay await us all, people and objects alike,' he writes: 'In common we have our materiality' (ibid: 19). For Shanks, recognition of common life cycles is a precondition for an awareness of the 'symmetry of people and things', which works to 'dissolve the absolute distinction between people and the object world' (ibid: 22). Shanks' insights find common ground in recent work in geography, philosophy and anthropology, which has also sought to question the exceptionalism of human life. We are linked through our 'shared finitude', writes Pepe Romanillos, and when we extend our ethical response to non-human subjects, both organic and inorganic, we find ourselves in a relation of care and compassion for all vulnerable 'mortal' subjects (2011: 2549).

Both the National Trust and the Orfordness Lighthouse Company wished to extend care and compassion to the lighthouse in its final days: they simply had different ideas about how this should be done, and about what constituted appropriate rituals of retreat. The company and its supporters wanted to use artificial means to provide architectural life support. Their temporary defences did not promise a miracle cure but sought to prolong the life of the structure 'so far as possible', which may have meant months or, more optimistically, years. The position held by the National Trust echoed the clarity of a 'do not resuscitate' order, which accepted the loss of the lighthouse as part of a natural process of erosion and landscape change.

(continued)

(continued)

We need to 'think of a world not of finished entities . . . but of processes that are continually carrying on', asserts Tim Ingold, and to 'think of the life of the person, too, as a process without beginning or end, punctuated but not originated or terminated by key events such as birth and death, and the other things that happen in between' (Ingold, 2010: 163–164).

How can we understand the lighthouse as a process, rather than a thing? Our convention is to pinpoint age to the moment of the 'making' of an object or structure, as with the birth of an individual person. But what if we allow the life cycle of the lighthouse to encompass the pre-history of its construction in 1792, and tell the life stories of its constituent materials as well? The iron, brick and concrete that make up most of the structure have biographies of formation, extraction and transformation that vastly precede their assembly in the ostensibly coherent shape of the lighthouse, and a future extending long after the structure loses its current form. We are willing to accept that the integrity of the shingle spit endures, despite its continual reshaping and reassembly, pebble by shifting pebble. Why not extend this dynamic distributed identity to the lighthouse as well?

Reproduced with permission: DeSilvey, C. (2017) *Curated Decay: Heritage Beyond Saving*, University of Minnesota Press, excerpt from chapter 7, 'Palliative Curation: The Death of a Lighthouse'. Copyright 2017 by the Regents of the University of Minnesota.

LIGHT MESSAGES

Tim Edensor

A recurrent theme throughout this book is that lighthouses, the light that they cast, their function and their presence, are highly ambiguous. While they may represent safety and welcome for some, for others, they symbolise surveillance, state power and colonial intrusion. This section explores these contesting and diverse messages. The following essay explores the multiple meanings associated with the light beam itself and the uses to which it has been put, whether for observation, drama, war, intimidation or festivity.

Ambiguous beams

Tim Edensor

With the advent of the smokeless, oil-fuelled Argand lamp and reflector system in the late 18th century, the capacity of European lighthouses to focus light intensely transformed a situated, static glow into a concentrated outward-travelling beam. The early 19th-century Fresnel lens allowed the beam to extend further, reaching up to 20 miles out to sea. This distance also depended on the height of the lighthouse. Because of the curvature of the Earth, a light situated 9 feet above sea level can extend to 9 miles, while one placed at 180 feet can be seen from 25 miles (Rhein, 2001).

Unlike light directed across land, a lighthouse beam rarely confronts material elements that diffuse, reflect and refract it, although its intensity is conditioned by levels of atmospheric water vapour and dust. Radiating across the sea, the beam contrasts sharply with the surrounding darkness and focuses the gaze, whereas in daylight the eye roams across a scene in which multiple elements are illuminated by the Sun (Ingold, 2011). Thus, the more intense lighthouse beam magnified by the Fresnel lens would have been especially dramatic in a world that was sparsely illuminated. Since then, the lighthouse beam has become one among many forms of focused shafts of light: applications with distinctive impacts in different nocturnal spaces.

(continued)

(continued)

The first spotlights, illuminating the Paris Opera in 1846 and using electric carbon arc lights, were superseded by luminaires that dramatised events and characters by focusing light on performance spaces rather than radiating illumination across the stage. Similar techniques were thereafter deployed in theatres of war, where, according to Kittler and Winthrop-Young, 'armed eyes emerge with searchlights that mobilize and mechanize vision itself' (2015: 385). In 1882, the British navy used searchlights to prevent Egyptian forces from staffing artillery batteries at Alexandria, and to land their own troops at night. In the First World War, searchlights created 'artificial moonlight' by reflecting beams off the base of the clouds, and in the Second World War, they were used to dazzle foes, seek enemy planes in the night sky and pinpoint targets. Kittler and Winthrop-Young comment that 'searchlights from Paris to Baghdad write the signature of our century across the skies' (ibid: 387). The powerful affective and sensory effects of light on the contemporary battlefield is explored in Pip Thornton's account of the 2003 invasion of Iraq, in which she served as a soldier in the British Army. The intimidation and disorientation of civilians and military opponents was apparent in the allied strategy to produce 'shock and awe' with a 'nightly firework display of bombing, burning oil wells, strobing tracer fire and industrial strength illumination' (Thornton, 2015: 580).

The searchlight's glare has been used in other repressive ways. The desire of the powerful to survey space and scrutinise citizens is exemplified by Bourdais' unrealised design of a giant *Tour Soleil*, equipped with electric lamps intended to transform the Parisian night into day. Searchlights are shone on political opponents, persecuted groups and criminals who seek refuge in darkness. Though contemporary night vision, motion-detection and thermal imaging technologies use no illumination, a powerful beam of light from a lofty building or helicopter remains a potent instrument in discerning and deterring undercover activity. Such beams are also deployed around the perimeters of high-security prisons, imposing continuously illuminated hyper-surveillance. They also express intimidating manifestations of state control: at Warsaw's Palace of Culture, extensive searchlights formerly turned the building into a beacon of power (Gilbert, 2000).

While the lighthouse projects its beam outwards from a fixed point, the development of other light beams has enabled rapid nocturnal mobility. Sandy Isenstadt details how the automobile headlight revolutionised mobile perception: 'to position oneself at the vertex of a cone of light and propel it across a darkened landscape must count as one of the most startling visual experiences of the twentieth century' (2011: 229). This introduced a nocturnal visual practice wherein drivers 'repeatedly scanned a constantly shifting field of view to classify heterogeneous luminous signals in terms of hindrance, continuance, or irrelevance' (ibid: 214). Even the bicycle, with its lamp cutting a moving tunnel through darkness, can 'sensuously extend human capacities into and across the world' and 'provide various ways of framing impression' (Büscher and Urry, 2009: 102). Its narrower focus, and the slower speed at which its glare allows things to be perceived intensifies an appreciation of their form (Cook and Edensor, 2014).

No malign use of the light beam compares to the notorious arrangement of focused illumination deployed by Albert Speer for the Nazi rallies at Nuremberg from 1933. This *Lichtarchitektur* created cathedrals of light, evoking immense classical columns fashioned by 150 giant searchlights shining upwards at intervals of 12 metres. Housing tens of thousands of participants in a mass choreography of light and sound, the spectacle was tinged with mysticism and produced awe among participants.

Less malign uses of searchlights have been staged in advertising, at fairs and festivals. Initially installed to announce movie premieres, they remain present in the logo of 20th Century Fox. At the pyramid-shaped Luxor Hotel in Las Vegas, curved mirrors collect the light from thirty-nine xenon lamps to produce a giant, intense beam shooting skywards. Equally flamboyantly, the gigantic *Symphony of Lights* that animates Hong Kong's waterfront skyscrapers uses fireworks, lasers, projections and searchlights to produce an illuminated spectacle (Petty, 2015).

Light beams may be used to commemorate people and events. New York's *Tribute in Light* consists of two vertical columns of light produced by eighty-eight searchlights to mark the absence of the World Trade Centre's twin towers. Similarly, artist Yoko Ono's *Peace Column* on Viðey Island off the coast of Reykjavik, Iceland, projected from a white circular stone base, memorialises her late husband, John Lennon.

In August 2014, an ambitious light installation commemorated the centenary of the First World War. Sited in Victoria Tower Gardens, next to the Houses of Parliament, *Spectra*, designed by Ryoji Ikeda, was formed by a 20-metre grid containing forty-nine searchlights that blazed 15 miles into the night sky from dusk to dawn (Edensor, 2015). From a distance, it appeared as a single vivid column of white light, but around the installation, the discrete beams created a carnivalesque frenzy of movement and chatter, as people posed for photographs or lay on the grass, staring upwards. The display highlighted the capacity of illumination to engender conviviality and playfulness, defamiliarising a familiar environment to provoke a heightened sense of affective and sensory engagement.

The beam, then, is a multivalent light phenomenon that can create diverse effects and elicit many responses. It can compose a festive atmosphere but also radiate power and promote fear. It has been used to generate fanatical fascist nationalism but also enabled and augmented the experience of night-time driving. It may express sober commemoration and create playful environments. The beam of the lighthouse similarly evokes multiple meanings and feelings. It may exude a sense of safety, be construed as a surveillant glare, conjure up scientific and mechanical exactitude, enchant a nocturnal marine scene or evoke feelings of nostalgia.

Fokko Jan Dijksterhuis highlights two further aspects of lighthouse beams. First, they are territorial markers that delineate the – sometimes shifting – division between land and sea. Second, he explores how the lighthouse's optical signature supplanted the confusion caused by indistinguishable sources of light and thwarted the aims of the wreckers who might lure ships towards shore by using 'false lights'. Following this, Joanna Puckering shows the evolution of ingenious, occasionally improvised, forms of illumination that have been deployed to guide aeroplanes.

Lights across the sky

Fokko Jan Dijksterhuis

Where I grew up in the Netherlands, about 20 miles from the coast, you could still see far-off beams of light at night, rotating and searching the skies. These were the lighthouses of the islands of the Wadden Sea. This line of islands forms the boundary with the North Sea, but behind them the border between land and sea is blurred. A vast plain gradually descends into the intertidal zone of the Wadden Sea, where tides create ever-changing sandbanks and layers of silt. The islands of Schiermonnikoog and Ameland are mere sand dunes that remain where the North Sea has broken through. In my childhood, if I awoke in the middle of the night, or cycled home from some late-night party as an adolescent, the lights circling the sky delineated the outer shore of my home ground. We could not see the lighthouses, but they reminded us that the sea was out there somewhere, across the flat clay plain.

Today the mainland and the islands have been secured by dikes, sluices and basins. The Wadden Sea is a nature reserve, a gas source and a recreational area. With a guide, it is possible to walk from the dikes on either side over to the islands, carefully picking a path between tidal streams and the high tides.

When this region was settled in the Early Middle Ages the division between water and land was much less clear. Behind the dunes at the North Sea shore lay a vast intertidal zone where the high water would often flood large areas and make major incursions into the mainland. An intricate web of banks and gullies enabled people to build artificial islands for their homesteads. The soil was rich but difficult to stabilise, making both land and water untrustworthy. You had to know your way around.

After the turn of the millennium, monastic orders began to manage the land and water on a larger scale. By building dikes and draining polders, they created relatively secure areas for local inhabitants and more definition between land and sea. Lights guided sailors across the water to safe havens. But some people, including my ancestors, took advantage of this new practice by making fires to mislead sailors, causing them to run their vessels aground in the mud where they were an easy target for looting. These artificial fen-fires have long disappeared, but the lights across the night sky still serve as a reminder of a treacherous shore.

Reading the shore

For sailors across the ages, an ability to recognise coasts and their specific landmarks was of vital importance. To help decode the contours of the shores and the various landmarks, guide books were published. For example, in the *Thresoor der Zeevaert* of 1592, Lucas Jansz. Waghenaer (1534/35–1606) showed how to find Sunderland and Newcastle on the 'North Coasts of England and Scotland'.

As light beacons were established, their positions were indicated in such guide books. Lights were also carried on the stern of a ship and used not only to illuminate the compass, but also to signal the ship's presence to others (and might therefore be doused in times of war). But one pinpoint of light at sea looked much like another, and the world-famous publisher, cartographer and astronomer Willem Jansz. Blaeu (1571–1638) entitled his navigation handbook in 1608 *Light of Navigation*, observing that the captain should not rely upon the uncertain lights on the coasts, but on the light of experience and knowledge.

A major change came when it became feasible to distinguish one light source from another. With the advances in artificial light and optical technologies in the early 19th century, it became possible to create a focused, rotating light beam. By timing and interrupting the beam, a lighthouse or other navigational beacon could be given a unique optical signature. Thus, the North Sea shores became a code book that could be deciphered in order to find one's position.

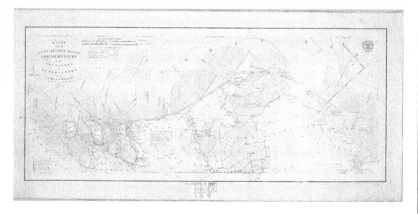

Figure 37 Map of Wadden Sea lighthouses. Credit: Nationaal Archief, Kaartcollectie Binnenland Hingman, nummer archiefinventaris 4.VTHR, inventarisnummer 206, public domain.

Coming in on a wing and a prayer

Joanna Puckering

> Light signals are needed by aircraft in night flying, just as they are required by the mariner.
>
> (*Encyclopaedia Britannica*, 1929)

Just as lighthouses and other navigational aids have been warning and guiding mariners for centuries, land-based lighting is employed to prevent accidents and to offer a sense of security. Rows of reflective cat's eyes improve road safety and visibility, but the use of light technology to guide, caution and constrain is not limited to marine and terrestrial traffic. Almost since the beginning of powered flight, beacons and runway lights have been guiding aircraft, in much the same way that navigational aids control shipping lanes and direct ships safely into port.

An airport beacon, with its highly visible rotating light, fulfils many of the functions of a lighthouse. It acts as a welcoming beam that helps pilots navigate across country at night. Additional lights are then used to guide pilots safely into 'port'. But what about landings that must be made when this type of technology is unavailable? Some short stories illustrate the ingenious solutions deployed to land aircraft in less than ideal circumstances.

In the early days of commercial flight, it was common for pilots to navigate by following roads and railway lines (Millichamp, nd). However, other solutions were required at night, and airfields would often light bonfires to help pilots navigate in the dark (Whealan-George, 2012). By the late 1920s, airports were using rotating lights to enable pilots to find them at night, with 'approach lighting' being introduced in the early 1930s. These landing aids gradually became more sophisticated and by the 1940s, slope-line approach systems used a series of light patterns to guide pilots safely towards the end of the runway, as well as indicating errors in direction or height (Mola, nd).

Radio beams added to the navigational aids provided by light beams, and by the late 1920s, instrument landing systems made use of both approach lighting and radio beacons. A four-course radio range in 1929 guided pilots using different strengths of Morse code signal, and the development of radar in the early 1940s was a further step forward. Since the late 1980s, aviation navigation and landing systems have used more precise and efficient microwave landing and global positioning system (GPS) technologies. However, lights have never lost their practical or symbolic importance.

The following anecdotes illustrate just some of the challenges faced by pilots who have needed to make unusual night landings, and the continuing importance of a guiding light.

During the Second World War, secret squadrons took Allied agents in and out of enemy territory, dropping them by parachute or landing in fields under cover of night. French resistance fighters would often guide them in to land using no more than three torches. Operating out of British RAF stations, these 'special duty' flights were known affectionately as the 'Moonlight' or 'Cloak and Dagger' Squadrons (Possum Line, nd; Verity, 2000). The Westland Lysander was an ideal aircraft for this type of mission, being able to land in an exceptionally short distance: based at RAF Tempsford, the Lysanders – painted matt black to make them harder to see at night – were known as the 'Tempsford Taxis'. Agents were trained to identify suitable landing sites and to create miniature 'flarepaths' using three torches in the shape of an inverted 'L'. A fourth torch would be used to signal the approaching Lysander with a pre-arranged letter in Morse code. In the absence of the correct flashing letter, the mission would be aborted (Royal Aviation Museum, nd; Verity, 2000).

There have been other creative approaches to aid emergency landings in the dark. Founded in 1928, the Royal Flying Doctor Service (RFDS) plays a critical role providing medical support to communities and homesteads in remote areas of Australia. Airstrip owners and RFDS users are expected to take an active role in the preparation and maintenance of landing strips (RFDS, nd). Most now have landing strips with flares available for night landings, but sometimes a less conventional approach is required.

In 2016, an RFDS pilot in North West Queensland, called in to rescue an injured station hand, explained that toilet rolls provide excellent emergency runway lighting for flying doctors. 'Sometimes in the outback, you have to make do', especially in the case of a medical emergency that requires doctors to land in the dark. 'Basically, if we are going to a station that doesn't have flares handy, dunny-roll landings would be the next best option'. This involves lining the runway with diesel-soaked toilet rolls, which are then set alight. Provided the toilet rolls are placed at correct intervals over the length of the landing strip, this is considered a 'regulation landing', unlike the alternative of positioning cars at each corner of the runway, which is considered a landing of 'last resort' (Margolis and Cillekens, 2016; Wahlquist, 2016).

Staying in Australia, an extraordinary night landing took place towards the end of the 1934 London–Melbourne Air Race (Buzacott, 2014). A KLM Royal Dutch Airlines DC2, known as the Uiver, was in second place when it flew into an electrical storm, lost all communication and was forced to make a night landing in Albury, a small town in New South Wales with no landing strip. Albury's Mayor organised a swift response, and the Uiver landed safely on the town's racecourse after being guided down through the storm by an ingenious use of light. The town's lighting grid became a temporary beacon, sending beams of light into the sky and communicating with the aircraft in Morse code, and residents brought their cars to illuminate the improvised landing strip with a line of headlights.

(continued)

(continued)

Sometimes, however, the best emergency beacons are those that do not need to be used. In the late 1980s, scientists from NASA set up a series of giant lights shining upwards near the village of Baafuloto, in Gambia, as an emergency beacon for the space shuttle (Lacey, 2005). After the loss of the *Challenger* in 1986, this became standard practice to guide the shuttle back to earth in the event of a problem during take-off or landing. Baafuloto is situated conveniently close to Banjul International Airport in Gambia which, between 1988 and 2001, was one of NASA's transoceanic abort landing sites, where the shuttles could land if they experienced a problem during launch (NASA, 2010).

Fortunately, on this occasion, the scientists from NASA were able to leave without ever needing to use their improvised aerial lighthouse.

In turning to consider the role of light in manifesting more overt forms of power, Steve Millington traces the evolution of centralised state control over lighthouses in Britain and the USA. He argues that these extensive administrative systems not only render the lighthouse system more effective, but are also a material and symbolic expression of state power. Here, the lighthouse becomes part of a broader network of maritime rule, administered from Trinity House in London, and part of a system that extended beyond the nation into colonial domains. This is followed by Eric Tagliacozzo's examination of the progressive installation of lighthouses as part of the maritime architecture of Dutch and British colonial administration in Southeast Asia. Tagliacozzo shows how greater safety and commercial potential were secured through careful negotiation with local commercial and political interests and in the context of the colonial rivalry between the two European powers.

Trinity House and the formation of the modern British state

Steve Millington

A primary function of the lighthouse has always been to aid navigation and trade. Prior to the invention of the compass it was necessary for ships to hug the coastline, aided by *portlans* or *rutters*, to avoid running aground. Phoenician traders possibly constructed the earliest lighthouse at Cadiz in the 5th century BC, but the lighthouse is later connected to nation- and empire-building projects. A network of lighthouses around the Mediterranean supported the expansion of the Roman Empire, with their earliest lighthouse in the British Isles most likely located at the naval fort of Portus Dubris (Dover).

For powerful elites, maritime trade presented a valuable opportunity to boost the coffers. In Britain, as early as 1261, the collection of tolls or duties from traders was established to provide for the construction and maintenance of new lighthouses (Hague and Christie, 1975). This connection between light and governance is affirmed through the historical development of the lighthouse, particularly within the British context (Otter, 2008).

Medieval British waters were a lawless space, endangered by physical hazards and by wild and chaotic people, smugglers, wreckers, pirates and the vessels of suspicious *foreign sailors*. Lighthouses were often private or voluntary affairs, and their operation was subject to much corruption. Often serving as moneymaking scams, lighthouses became sites of 'tenacious avarice' whereby owners derived income by extracting dues from passing vessels (Hague and Christie, 1975: 36), thus diverting taxes away from the government. An unregulated coast not only jeopardised the safety of mariners, but also posed a threat to trade and potentially national security.

The Brotherhood of Trinity House of Deptford Strond (est. 1514) was the first charitable organisation to be granted a Royal Charter, initially to support the families of men lost at sea and mariners fallen on hard times. In 1536, however, the Brethren at Newcastle-upon-Tyne shouldered the responsibility for building and maintaining lighthouses at North Shields. Its members understood that promoting the safety of ships also served their fiscal interests. The 1566 Seamarks Act extended these powers across the country, granting Trinity House the authority to construct lighthouses and – in effect – establish a state monopoly on the coastal infrastructure designed to aid navigation. Legislation in 1836 abolished private lighthouses, placing all lighthouses and seamarks under state control and the central administration of Trinity House. Funded through a system of *light dues* and *user fees*, Trinity House became an early provider of a public good, creating a free service at point of access to all users (Lindberg, 2009). Thus, lighthouses are integral to a historical narrative describing how the establishment of public administration and taxation aided the transformation of Britain from a feudal system to a modern state.

Under the auspices of Trinity House, lighthouses became part of a nautical network promoting the regulation and standardisation of shipping practices in British and imperial waters through enhanced risk management and the mitigation of excessive insurance claims. As Hannah Conway observes in this book, multiple shipping losses prompted Faraday

(continued)

(continued)

in 1860 to persuade the Royal Institution that the safety and regulation provided by lighthouses were of great societal importance. And it was clear that ensuring consistent finance and maintenance through a standardised system also supported the functional performance of lighthouses, in terms of their durability and reliability.

The export of the pioneering designs of John Smeaton across the British Empire soon established this iconic lighthouse form as a beacon of the imperial centre, imprinting British colonial power across the oceans. Simultaneously, the direction of seaborne traffic into safe channels and routes also represented a broader territorial organisation of Britain's inshore/offshore areas into distinct zones, boundaries and networks, a land and waterscape familiar to many via BBC Radio 4's *Shipping Forecast*. Whereas ships previously had to put to anchor when darkness fell, night-time navigation enabled vessels to sail on, vastly reducing journey times (Otter, 2008). By facilitating greater speed and efficiency of international travel, Jakle (2001) suggests that lighthouses are aligned with a 'new age of travel': part of a pantheon of lighting apparatus produced in Britain, Europe and the USA to facilitate economic and social 'progress'.

The economic consequences of the new technologies and infrastructures that emerged from the Industrial Revolution were clear. With the growing authority of Trinity House, there was an expansion of overseas trade and seaborne industries which underpinned the economic growth of Britain as a trading nation and imperial power. The 1819 Reciprocity Treaty, for example, regulated against excessive lighthouse tolls, removing a key barrier to free trade.

There is also a political dimension connecting lighthouses to the process of nation building. As visible territorial markers, and as technologies of surveillance and control, these structures became symbols of state authority and power. The USA, for example, adopted not only the technological innovations pioneered in Britain, but, following the 1789 Lighthouses Act, American lighthouses came under federal control (Miller, 2010). By 1907, the US government had created its own network of '1495 lighthouses and automated beacons and sixty lightships' (Jakle, 2001: 188), to establish a visible presence of federal government as part of an American nation-building project. Ultimately, the governance and regulation of lighthouses is bound to the formation of modern nation states.

Today, Trinity House is a multi-functional organisation acting as the General Lighthouse Authority (GLA) and Deep Sea Pilotage Authority (DPSA) for England, Wales, the Channel Islands and Gibraltar, as well as continuing to provide charitable welfare and other forms of support for mariners.

The lit archipelago

Eric Tagliacozzo

The role of lighthouses, beacons and buoys in European expansion illustrates the nature of the imperial project, and this is especially true for Southeast Asia. Lighthouses were both symbols and structures of power, playing a crucial role in European colonies, mapping a grid of colonial vision onto a vast maritime domain. This contribution examines patterns of movement, technology and colonialism by examining the contribution of lighthouses, beacons and buoys to British and Dutch programmes of colonial state formation in the second half of the 19th century.

Charting silent seas

Though significant inland sections of the East Indies remained *terra incognita* to Europeans until the end of the 19th century, the region's coasts and seas were extensively charted by the 1870s and 1880s. An active policy, determined by central planners in the Dutch and British Southeast Asian colonial capitals of Batavia and Singapore, this was part of a larger programme that also included research in astronomy and geophysics. Expeditions were sent out in all directions as the Dutch imperium in particular expanded, and many of these were concerned with mapping.

The introduction of steam into Southeast Asia gave added impetus to these developments. The opening of the Suez Canal in 1869 had a momentous effect on ports like Singapore, as shipping distances were reduced and steamships brought the colonies closer to metropolitan markets. Steam also galvanised Dutch expansion in the East Indies, leading to the growth of massive shipyards such as Onrust, near Batavia, and the Surabaya harbour works, both of which serviced generations of steamers trading in the archipelago. Indeed, with limited resources in the outer islands, Batavia eventually established a partnership with steam shipping services in the East Indies, financing (and in turn being financed by) private concerns to the benefit of both business and empire. These were the circumstances in which maritime infrastructure developed, and lighthouses were very much the product of this public–private cooperation.

Lighting a dim archipelago

Few places in the world experienced such explosive growth in shipping traffic as Southeast Asia in the second half of the 19th century. Numerous English-language guides to navigating the intricate waterways of the region

(continued)

(continued)

appeared, describing winds, storms and currents for the merchants of many nations. Shipping insurers from Britain, Hong Kong, the Netherlands and New Zealand advertised their services to eager clients. The result was a highly commercial milieu involving Asians as well as Europeans. Vessels ran west to Suez and the Indian Ocean, north to China and Japan, and south to the expanding ports of Australia and New Zealand.

More traffic created an increase in maritime disasters. On its inaugural run in the Dutch East Indies archipelago, the *Willem I* ran aground off Ambon in 1837, and was attacked by pirates from Mindanao. The crew eventually gained their freedom through a ransom of cash, opium and precious linen. British ships were wrecked on unseen rocks and reefs too. Poorly lit or poorly charted coasts caused many accidents near the large ports, but there were others in more remote locales, particularly on the most peripheral coasts of the region, for example in British Borneo.

Better lighting of these dangerous seas was therefore seen by both the British and Dutch as an imperative imperial act, in the interest of shipping generally and empire specifically. Neither wanted to be seen as deficient; the monetary losses would be substantial, but the loss of face even more damaging. Yet, especially in the early years, resources were scarce and the reach of the colonial powers was limited.

A confluence of key trends – increasing maritime traffic, increasing numbers of shipwrecks and overextension of maritime resources by state programmes of expansion – led to changes in the organisational structure of lighting, beaconing and buoying, especially in the Dutch East Indies. By 1860, Batavia saw lighting the East Indies' dim seas as an imperial priority. In 1861, the Gouvernements Marine was created, and, in 1867, a reorganisation shifted responsibility to the larger Ministerie van Marine. Further reorganisations in the 1880s and 1890s saw the lighting, beaconing and pilotage service alternately located in the Gouvernements Marine and given a separate identity under the Ministerie van Marine.

During this period, the foundations of coastal lighting were laid. Islands and shoals, important waterways, approaches to major ports, and unseen rocks all received attention. Singapore and Batavia competed to attract shipping, and lighting provided an advantage. Lights in British waters in the 1860s included a 95-foot-high tower called the Horsburgh, near Singapore (along with other light sources in this vicinity), as well as installations at Malacca. Dutch lights were fewer at this stage: Batavia had its own lighthouse, as did the Bangka Strait. But the 1870s saw a massive programme of expansion, especially in Dutch waters. Dozens of new lighthouses, lightships and beacons went into operation throughout the western half of the archipelago.

By the 1880s and 1890s, expansion on both sides of the Strait of Malacca was well underway. Major harbours, dangerous geographic anomalies and international waterways had been priorities previously, but now larger maritime areas were also lit, as both states extended their reach. By the 20th century, lights, beacons and buoys had become commonplace, and there was an *afronding*, or rounding off, as Singapore and Batavia tried to light the few spaces that remained opaque. The western archipelago had an abundance of lit passages, channelling trade and movement along routes easily visible to both regimes.

The rise of Chinese trading between Sumatra and Singapore helped give impetus to construction of yet more lights in the Strait of Malacca. Increasing private participation in the prosperity of the vast ocean steamship lines (some of it indigenous) added further coastal lighting, and businesses such as the Labuan Coalfields Company pestered the Colonial Office in London for better lights, buoys and beacons, to protect their investments in notoriously dangerous seas.

Yet the hand of the state determined the pace of lighting and buoying. This is evident in the simultaneous growth of coast lighting and the petroleum industry in Sumatra and Borneo. It can be seen in the appearance of lights along new shipping routes, carrying East Indies agricultural exports via relatively underused sea passages to Australia and Japan. The Dutch even attempted to make lights as uniform as possible throughout the East Indies, enacting a conscious programme of 'seeing like a state' (Scott, 1998).

The politics of lighting

Complicating all of these developments were attempts to retain centralisation and control in London and The Hague, where leaders viewed coastal lighting in the context of empire-wide strategic concerns. Both colonies also contained countervailing political forces, and the construction of imperial lighthouses was often contested, not simply dictated by a monolithic state. Different interests sometimes converged when it came to coastal lighting, but the fragmented nature of British authority in the region made it difficult to coordinate policy, as the Straits Settlements, British North Borneo and Sarawak rarely agreed on who should be responsible for building and maintaining lights. In the early 1870s, the Straits Settlements repeatedly petitioned the Colonial Office to mark harbour channels, even offering to pay part of the costs of acquiring new, high-technology buoys, and paying for new equipment and installations was always a source of friction. This pattern can be seen repeatedly: over lightships on Formosa Bank in 1887, for example, or new lanterns for the Raffles Light in 1904.

The politics of lighting were thus largely focused on the costs of building and maintaining lighthouses. For instance, Labuan, Britain's small island outpost, was seen as a strategic way-station along the China routes in the middle of the 19th century. The dangers of piracy in these waters also made it a Colonial Office priority. By the turn of the 20th century, however, Labuan's importance had diminished, and Whitehall repeatedly refused

(continued)

(continued)

requests for more lighting by the North Borneo Company. The Colonial Office felt that the company should be responsible for coast lighting; the company, trying to stretch its profits, sought to pass the task on to London. By 1907, however, London acknowledged that Borneo's underlit coasts had implications for regional security as well as shipping and funded some lighting developments, but no one seemed fully satisfied with the solution.

Lighting was also contentious between the colonial powers and local elites. Southeast Asians understood that the grafting of coast-lighting technologies onto local seascapes had significant power implications. The Sultan of Johor obtained revenue from Singapore in exchange for permission to build a British lighthouse in Johor. Conversely, across the Strait of Malacca the Acehnese lost their sultanate to Batavia, partly because of the support for Dutch naval navigation provided by the massive lighthouse on Pulau Bras. The introduction of lights as tools of empire, therefore, supported indigenous authority on the one hand and hastened its demise on the other.

Political tensions over lights were also generated between the two colonial powers. Sharing a long maritime frontier imposed certain political realities, and the expense of lighting the archipelago produced both cooperation and competition. In the British view, the waters of the Dutch East Indies were insufficiently lit, which was problematic for Singapore and London as well, with so many English vessels passing through. The English solution was to disparage Dutch ineptitude in private while publicly coaxing Batavia to provide better lighting.

Batavia's calculus was rather different. The Dutch needed the British lights on the other side of the Strait of Malacca to ensure the safety of their own international shipping, so goodwill was an important factor in Dutch planning. Much of the East Indies' exports were carried in British vessels too, which encouraged collaboration. Yet many Dutch people also felt that their own imperial project depended too heavily on English power and technology, and this seems to have been especially true in the maritime realm. Dutch authors periodically aired their grievances on this issue, decrying Batavia's willingness to depend on British lights, beacons and hydrographic surveys. Thus, while each colony relied on the other to light their common maritime frontier, each did so according to different rationales. The British resented the Dutch and their insufficient lighting infrastructure, while the Dutch felt rather overwhelmed by the prowess and demands of their northern neighbour.

Symbols of a new world

The history of lighthouses in maritime Southeast Asia offers some important lessons about evolving imperial control. Lighthouses, like other technologies of colonial governance, appeared in increasing numbers in concert with growing state concerns over maritime safety and navigation.

The darkened maze of islands that confronted the British and Dutch in 1860 had been transformed by 1910 into a lit archipelago that could be watched and policed. The sea had been irrevocably mastered by the British and Dutch, and it was precisely technologies of maritime control that allowed such small numbers of Europeans to rule over one of the world's largest maritime regions.

This is an abridged version of Eric Tagliacozzo's 2005 paper, 'The Lit Archipelago: Coast Lighting and the Imperial Optic in Insular Southeast Asia, 1860–1910', *Technology and Culture*, 46(2): 306–328.

Dini Lallah shows how colonial history is also exemplified in Mauritius, by the installation of Albion Lighthouse on this critically strategic island. Yet following the end of colonial rule and the rise of American power, the lighthouse, and Mauritius itself, has been side-lined as the forcibly depopulated island of Diego Garcia, ostensibly within the sovereignty of Mauritius, has become the site of a significant US military base. The demise of the lighthouse as a key symbol of power testifies to the emergence of an alternative maritime order.

The Albion Lighthouse
From Dutch shipwrecks to British colonialism and US imperialism

Dini Lallah

Two friends walk, scanning the beach. The gentle surf cools their feet under the hot sun. Trees shade this thin stretch of sand, various greens and wild flowers hinting at the tropical forest that once covered this Indian Ocean island of Mauritius. The friends are not seeking shells or coral but smooth pieces of porcelain, bright with blue designs, unblemished by the passing of time. These broken pieces of Chinese Ming cups, bowls, saucers and plates come from three shipwrecks among a fleet of four tall ships belonging to the Dutch East India Company. Four hundred years ago, the *Banda*, *Gelderland* and *Geünieerde Provinciën* were torn apart by a fierce cyclone while the sailors fought for their lives. Only the *Delft* survived to reach Amsterdam with its ceramic cargo intact. Among the men who drowned was the fleet's admiral, Pieter Both. A mountain on the east coast of Mauritius, with a head-like boulder balanced on its summit, bears his name. The shattered pieces of crockery are still carried by the waves from the shipwrecked site to Albion Beach, where beachcombers collect them, sometimes setting them in glass to be used as paperweights or as components in artistic assemblages.

(continued)

(continued)

At the other end of the bay, a white lighthouse ringed with two red horizontal strips ascends 30 metres from the headland. Featuring in picture postcards and in Mauritian literature and painting, the lighthouse and its surroundings have served as a romantic setting for several Bollywood movies. While the island is almost completely encircled by a coral reef, here it is absent, and the open sea breaks into the bay. Exploding swells have moulded the hard, black volcanic rock into an arch and several caves, and rounded the boulders on the beach.

Mauritius was under British colonial rule from 1810 to 1968, and the concrete and masonry lighthouse, with its cast-iron dome, was constructed in 1910 under the government of Sir Charles Cavendish Boyle. Sited in a pivotal location, 10 kilometres south-west of Port Louis, the lighthouse still plays a major role as a navigational guide for the naval vessels, cruise ships, bulk carriers and liners that disrupt the flatness of the horizon on their way into the harbour. From the dome, two white flashes of light illuminate the land and sea every fifteen seconds, extending to a 29-mile radius, while from the second floor, a continuous red light leads ships towards the harbour entrance. The name given to the nearby village, the bay and the lighthouse conjures up its colonial origins, imprinting upon it the oldest literary name given to Great Britain: Albion.

Though the Dutch shipwreck and the building of the lighthouse were separated by 300 years, it is tempting to imagine that if the lighthouse had been present on that day in 1615, it might have prevented the drowning of seventy-five sailors. Following the devastation caused by the cyclone, the Dutch became wary of the perils posed by the coastline: 'the enthusiasm of the first expeditions soon gave way to a certain distrust of the island', revealing that the shipwrecks 'left such a deep mark on people's minds that for many years, Dutch expeditions avoided the now accursed port of call' (Piat, 2011: 33).

Initially this uninhabited island had fulfilled a Dutch requirement for a post at which they could replenish their supplies and repair their ships as they sailed along the Spice Route from the East Indies to Europe. One consequence was the extinction of the Mauritian dodo by 1680, as the dogs, cats, rats and pigs they introduced, destroyed its eggs and habitat. Later, Mauritius acquired an enhanced military significance as a foothold from which the Dutch could fend off their colonial rivals, the French and the British. Yet, in due course, the more powerful French appropriated the island, maintaining a slavery-driven sugar-cane plantation system, thus populating Mauritius with slaves mainly from Africa and Madagascar, and a small percentage from South Asia. In 1810, when the British had achieved global naval supremacy, they replaced the French as the colonial power. Slavery was abolished and Indian indentured labourers replaced them in the fields, though French settlers were permitted to keep the land.

The British were initially less concerned with the economic viability of the island than with its strategic location. 'It remained a link in imperial communications and the control of the sea lanes, part of the eastern group of British colonies that at the end of the Napoleonic Wars also included Ceylon and the Straits Settlement in Malaya' (Jackson, 2001: 8). Yet it became 'an important part of Britain's tropical treasure trove, expanding its export of sugar to Britain . . . By the late nineteenth century it was second only to Ceylon in the colonial import-export league table' (Jackson, 2001: 8).

In all three colonial periods, the strategic positioning of the island in the Indian Ocean was a common denominator. The Albion Lighthouse was central to British colonial administration, ensuring that the thousands of vessels visiting Mauritius did not meet the same fate as Pieter Both's ships. It played an important role as a navigational aid during the 58 years of British rule that followed its construction, and it continues to be a beacon in the sea lanes in and out of Port Louis.

Although the colonial era that created the lighthouse seemed to end with Mauritian independence in 1968, Britain retained control over the Chagos Archipelago. An American military base was established on the largest island, Diego Garcia, to serve US and British economic and military interests, and the local population was expelled to Mauritius and the Seychelles. Thus, Diego Garcia replaced the strategic importance of the main island of Mauritius, becoming integral to the machinations of global superpowers and serving as a launch-pad for American and British military interventions in Afghanistan and Iraq. A growing peace movement continues to oppose this occupation.

The symbolic salience of the lighthouse in colonial history is also evident in Robert Shaw's description of a monument known as 'the Hoad' in Ulverston, Cumbria, England. Taking the exact form of a full-sized lighthouse, with the exception that it does not radiate any light, and situated on a prominent hill overlooking the town, the monument celebrates the life of a locally born colonial administrator and 'explorer', a man deeply involved in the expansion of British colonial rule.

The lighthouse without a light

Lighthouses, exploration and geography

Robert Shaw

In the town of Ulverston on the Furness Peninsula in North West England, there is an unusual lighthouse. Completed in 1851 and known locally as

(continued)

(continued)

Figure 38 The Hoad. Photograph: Tim Edensor.

'the Hoad', its architecture and design are not remarkable. Indeed, the Hoad is exemplary of the lighthouses of this era: it was built as a replica of Smeaton's Tower in the English Channel, itself a major innovation in lighthouse design. Thirty metres high and built from local limestone, the lighthouse reflects the new confidence of engineering in the Victorian era. A prominent local landmark, the Hoad is a symbol of the town and indeed the wider region. What makes it unusual, however, are two key features. First, it has never had any sort of light at its top. Second, it is located on the top of the 133-metre-high Hoad Hill, slightly less than 2 kilometres from the sea. The Hoad was never designed to function as a lighthouse: rather, it is the 'Sir John Barrow Monument', built to commemorate a colonial administrator, cartographer and artist born in Ulverston in 1764.

Barrow served for forty years as Second Secretary to the Admiralty, the most senior civil servant in British shipping. In this role, he supported Arctic exploration, and the Barrow Straits and town of Barrow in Alaska are both named after him. In addition, he spent time in southern Africa, producing the first map of the Cape of Good Hope. In his role as a supporter of cartography and exploration, Barrow was a founding member of the Royal Geographical Society, serving as its fourth president (Barrow, 1849).

As an administrator–explorer equally comfortable in the civil service in London or constructing maps in southern Africa, John Barrow represents the 'empire' era of geography. The choice of a lighthouse as a memorial for Barrow is therefore interesting. Memorials reveal how national cultures imagine their pasts, presents and futures (Johnson, 1995). This memorial suggests that the lighthouse encapsulates geography at this point in the 19th century, when people such as Barrow were connecting the traditions of exploration and travel that defined pre-academic geography, and the more formalised structures of government and empire that helped create geography as a discipline (Martin and Martin, 2005). Like Barrow, then, lighthouses represent a particular relationship between geography, exploration and power. Map-making, transportation and acquiring knowledge of distant lands were all key forms of governmental control, and, as Mackinder (1904) argues, control over the oceans was central. The lighthouse, and particularly the lighthouse-as-memorial in the form of the Hoad, forces both the discipline of geography, and a wider audience, to face up to Britain's uncomfortable imperial heritage, as a nation and discipline of empire (Driver, 2000).

The ambiguous status of lighthouses is particularly salient in more contemporary accounts of the journeys of migrants and refugees escaping by sea. Philip Steinberg discusses how the lighthouse can both symbolise a military safeguard against the intrusion of unwanted migrants and a longed-for beacon to those seeking safety. He shows how this ambiguity extends to undermine the traditional dichotomies of land and sea: for migrants making these perilous journeys, the sea may not represent chaos and danger, and land may not provide security. Uma Kothari also considers the lighthouse as a space of both danger and welcome for contemporary migrants and asylum seekers, discussing how its shifting legal status and the ways in which it has been deployed by rescue volunteers and artists further draw out its symbolic and functional polysemy.

The lighthouse as survival

Philip Steinberg

Europe's recent refugee crisis has often been presented as a battle against the sea. Nations were galvanised by the sobering image of drowned Syrian toddler Aylan Kurdi on a beach in Turkey (Hopkins and Waugh, 2015) and the inspiring image of off-duty soldier Antonis Deligiorgis pulling a terrified Eritrean woman, Wegasi Nebiat, from the surf in Rhodes (Tufft, 2015). Dutch advocates of a humane refugee policy have marched through The Hague dressed as coastal rescue workers and carrying a life buoy (Agence

(continued)

(continued)

France Presse, 2015). EU policy makers have tried to pick up the pieces from their failed *Mare Nostrum* (Our Seas) border protection programme. And British artist Banksy has drawn attention to the refugee crisis with a provocative reinterpretation of the EU flag as a series of floating corpses at sea (Earthly Mission, nd).

In short, across the political spectrum, and in a variety of media, narrations of the refugee crisis and calls for intervention have represented the sea as a space of danger. The right focuses on the dangers that the sea spits up on Europe's shores: migrants, Muslims, terrorists. The left focuses on the sea *itself* as a danger that challenges Europeans to find their inner humanity. According to the right, Europe needs sentinel posts along its coast. According to the left, Europe needs beacons of hope to direct the sea's victims to safe havens. Either way, the lighthouse is enlisted as an illustrative trope, joining the ideals of military guardianship with those of humanitarian assistance that constitute parallel coastal responses to the refugee crisis.

In fact, though, neither the refugee experience nor the lighthouse is rooted in a simple geography where land is the space of life and water is the space of death. Asserting a verticality that rises above both land and sea, the lighthouse offers a geography that transcends facile divisions of space.

Figure 39 Asylum seekers and migrants descend from a large fishing vessel used to transport them from Turkey to the Greek island of Lesbos, 11 October 2015. Credit: © 2015 Zalmaï for Human Rights Watch, CC BY-NC-ND 3.0 US (https://creativecommons.org/licenses/by-nc-nd/3.0/us/).

The lighthouse as survival 181

One should recall that the purpose of many lighthouses is not to facilitate safe passage to a harbour, but to draw attention to a dangerous coast. Sailors who think they are safely at sea but suddenly spot the beam of a lighthouse on a foggy night are likely to respond with fear, not joy. Indeed, if lighthouses could speak, many would be casting out words that sound not like left-wing peaceniks in Stockholm, but right-wing hooligans in Budapest: not 'Follow my light to peace and comfort' but 'If you come any closer you will be drowned'.

Additionally, while refugees are indeed seeking refuge from the sea, water is not the central danger in a refugee's life. It is land. As British-Somali poet Warsan Shire (2013: xi–xii) has written:

> you have to understand,
>
> that no one puts their children in a boat
>
> unless the water is safer than the land
>
> . . .
>
> and no one would leave home
>
> unless home chased you to the shore
>
> unless home told you
>
> to quicken your legs
>
> leave your clothes behind
>
> crawl through the desert
>
> wade through the oceans
>
> drown
>
> save
>
> be hunger
>
> beg
>
> forget pride
>
> your survival is more important

Shire directs her missives at those who would advocate sending refugees back to a 'home' that no longer exists. But her words should also give pause to those whose impulse is to assume that refugees must be saved 'from the sea'. Their problems emanate not from the sea but from the land, and it is on land where changes must be made to protect refugee livelihoods.

Furthermore, the land that awaits the refugee is rarely one of seamless assimilation. As Shire continues:

(continued)

(continued)

> no one chooses refugee camps
>
> or strip searches where your
>
> body is left aching
>
> or prison,
>
> because prison is safer
>
> than a city of fire
>
> and one prison guard
>
> in the night
>
> is better than a truckload
>
> of men who look like your father
>
> no one could take it
>
> no one could stomach it
>
> no one skin would be tough enough

For several years now, scholars from a range of academic disciplines including history (Bentley et al., 2007), anthropology (Hastrup and Hastrup, 2015), literary studies (Klein and Mackenthun, 2004) and geography (Anderson and Peters, 2014), have challenged an assumed binary between land and sea, where land is understood as the space of stasis, home, safety and society, and the sea as its antithesis. Questioning this binary does more than invert the way we think about the sea: it can challenge how we understand our 'place' as landed beings in a world of flows, connections, mobilities and immobilities. While my previous work in this area has highlighted the potential of the maritime region (Steinberg, 2011, 2013), the floating city (Steinberg et al., 2012), the bridged island (Steinberg and Chapman, 2009) and the ocean itself (Peters and Steinberg, 2014; Steinberg and Peters, 2015), the lighthouse is also a provocative object that disrupts terracentric perspectives. It is both of the sea and of the land. It signals both safety and danger, and human successes in managing that danger as well as the ultimate futility of such efforts. It evokes (and, at times, marks) the routes plied by warships, slave ships, cargo ships, and modern-day smugglers of refugees and migrants that have brought fear and hope to residents of distant shores.

The lighthouse is not the only object with an evocative power to challenge simple binaries of land and sea, enabling critical thinking about both the effects and affects of ocean (and trans-ocean) encounters. The sand bar, the island, the archipelago, the ship, the shipwreck, the shipping route, the seabed, sea ice and countless other features all can be put to similar purpose. But perhaps because of its iconic place in Western culture – from the drama of the oil painting to the banality of the tea towel – the lighthouse is a particularly powerful trope for danger and salvation, longing and loss.

In response to the photo of Antonis Deligiorgis rescuing Wegasi Nebiat, it is easy to think of the lighthouse as the embrace at the conclusion of an arduous journey, an end point, a destination. But, as Shire's poem and the experiences of countless refugees, including Nebiat, suggest, the interruption offered by the lighthouse is more ambiguous: a liminal point in a journey where the future may be only a marginal improvement on the past; a node of brief respite in a series of journeys that, in the case of the refugee,

Figure 40 Image of off-duty soldier, Antonis Deligiorgis, pulling Wegasi Nebiat from the surf in Rhodes, 2015. Credit: Associated Press.

(continued)

(continued)

will now proceed on land or which, in the case of the sailor, will involve being cast back out to sea.

If, for Yi-Fu Tuan (1977: 138), a 'place' is a 'pause in movement', the lighthouse is a different kind of place altogether. Like its rotating light, alternately repetitive and absent, resting on a pillar that is invisible when the lighthouse is needed most, the lighthouse's ephemeral materiality is matched by its ambiguous function. The lighthouse generates the hope of a smooth space of mobility, but simultaneously reminds us that such smoothness can never be achieved. A coastline dotted with lighthouses is not a series of destinations, but a limin in a universe of perpetual navigation. No sailor pauses at a lighthouse.

The lighthouse, then, signals neither an end nor a beginning. Nor does it truly offer hope that the dangers of the sea can be beaten back by the security of land, since it reminds us that land, sea and the spaces where they meet are all spaces of mortal danger. But in offering at least a dream of transcending these dangers, the lighthouse does offer hope. And in this sense, the lighthouse echoes the actions of Warsan Shire's refugee, Aylan Kurdi's parents or Wegasi Nebiat, who all made difficult choices out of a combination of desperation and calculation. Like the refugee's journey, the lighthouse signals neither just the dangers of the present nor the hope of a better future. As a beacon that rises above the tumultuous tableau, the lighthouse suggests both, and neither. But by bringing these potentials into stark relief, and by revealing how they may be encountered on the maritime journey, the lighthouse signals how the maritime migrant navigates environments of both safety and danger, impelled by an overriding will to survive.

The lighthouse as a site of refuge and welcome

Uma Kothari

Although, as previous essays have shown, the major function of the lighthouse is to warn those at sea of the dangers on the coastline, for many sea travellers it also represents the safety of the land, of arrival. Materially and symbolically, lighthouses define borders and boundaries. In the late 1800s, for example, Cape Otway Lighthouse signalled the first landfall for emigrants seeking a new home in Australia, its beam a welcome signal that they had reached the end of a long, arduous journey and offering a promise of new beginnings. While acknowledging that the lighthouse can signal physical danger and mark a border that is sometimes restricted, this essay focuses on how lighthouses compose sites of refuge, welcome and solidarity.

The 136-year-old Shoal Lighthouse, 7 miles off the Florida Keys, USA, delineates a territorial border. In June 2016, a group of Cuban migrants attempting to reach the US by boat scaled the structure, instigating a legal controversy over whether or not the lighthouse represented American territory, thereby determining whether the migrants could stay in the US or could legally be returned to Cuba. Lawyers representing the migrants drew on the 'wet foot, dry foot' policy, which allows Cubans who have set foot on American soil the opportunity to remain in the US (Grimm, 2016). They contended that the refugees had 'landed and disembarked on a US federal building that was on US federal property. And that constituted a landing with feet that were literally – and legally – dry' (Grimm, 2016: np). However, the federal government argued that while the lighthouse is US property, it is not US *territory*. Climbing up an offshore lighthouse, it asserted, is not the same as landing in America and reaching dry land. Moreover, they asserted, the migrants jumped into the water and swam to the lighthouse and so literally – and legally – had 'wet feet'.

Fearful of the perils of the sea, the mother of one migrant was reassured by TV footage of him on the lighthouse (Shoichet, 2015). However, in June 2016, a federal judge ruled that the Cubans must return home as the lighthouse is not considered US soil. He wrote: 'No one has resided in the Lighthouse since at least 1963. It has never been connected to dry land', and because the migrants 'would necessarily require transportation from the Lighthouse to the mainland in order to survive, landing on the Lighthouse is essentially no different than having been interdicted at sea' (RT Question More, 2016: np).

Thus, the Shoal Lighthouse was ambiguous, simultaneously expressing control and engendering hopefulness. This ambiguity is also invoked in the work of Stephen Copland, who considers how, as 'architectural forms on the edge of the continent' (Pattenden, 2009: 12), lighthouses frame and mark the Australian coast. His 2009 work, *Border Protection*, featured 147 miniature paintings of every lighthouse in Australia. In this 'map', lighthouses serve as a metaphor for a 'coast that is in a state of flux and change' (Copland, 2013: 50), destabilising the sense of place of this island continent, yet also standing as a symbol of hope and salvation. While offering protection and safety, and resonating surveillance, they also evoke 'the fluid anxiety that needs to fix a clear line of demarcation when faced with issues of difference' (Pattenden, 2009: 12). The sites of inclusion and exclusion that they delineate must be negotiated by those attempting to pass from sea to land, a dimension so powerfully evident in Europe when more than 1 million migrants arrived by sea in 2015, with more than 4,000 dying in attempts to cross the Mediterranean.

In witnessing the current humanitarian catastrophe of millions of refugees compelled to flee violence and persecution, and to embark on traumatic journeys across water, we are further reminded of the lighthouse's material

(continued)

(continued)

and symbolic ambiguity. Lured by the captivating regularity of its beams, refugees are drawn to a dangerous shoreline where the lighthouse symbolises exclusion, restriction and surveillance. While acknowledging Philip Steinberg's repudiation (in this volume) of a simple geographical dualism whereby land represents life and water epitomises death, the lighthouse nevertheless marks both a real and a symbolic border, a point in a journey where land appears to be safer than enduring passage in makeshift, overloaded boats. For example, during September 2015, 50,000 people arrived in Greece from Turkey. As one volunteer observed:

> As darkness falls and the last of the shorefront cafes in Bodrum clear their tables for the night, dozens of migrants pour out of a waiting bus. In the gloam, they charge for the sea, dragging a large rubber dinghy. Their smugglers point them toward the flashing lighthouse on the Greek island of Kos, as little as 25 minutes away in a good boat.
> (Yeginsu and Hartocollis, 2015: np)

Besides the hope offered by their beckoning light, these Greek lighthouses have emerged as sites of welcome, solidarity and conviviality. Despite extensive media coverage vilifying refugees, there has been an outpouring of compassion from volunteers distributing supplies and journalists documenting hazardous journeys. One of the most profound and widespread developments has been a visual language of 'welcome' – friendly banners, handmade placards, shop signs, street art and graffiti – as well as tactile gestures or the provision of blankets, at sites such as Malmo Central Station, Toronto Airport and Copenhagen's Comfort Zone – and at Korakas Lighthouse, on the north shore of Lesvos.

Difficult to access, a remote, windswept site with no electricity or running water, the Korakas Lighthouse stands 6 miles from the Turkish coast, and as with beams from Kos, refugees have used the lighthouse to guide them in their attempt to reach Greece. However, the surrounding cliffs and rocks make it an extremely dangerous place to land. One volunteer wrote, 'you see a lighthouse, you think of safety, but it's actually the opposite . . . the lighthouse will blink its lights and the refugees think, "oh, that's where we have to head to"' (Morrow, 2015: np). Another reported, 'we were manning Korakas lighthouse which was meant to warn of the danger, but it attracted refugees like moths to a flame' (Northern Echo, 2016: np).

During the winter of 2015, over thirty boats arrived on the shores of Lesvos every day, but there were no NGOs to help. Motivated by the thousands of dead and wounded refugees who had attempted the sea crossing, *Lighthouse Relief*, a Swedish NGO, intervened to provide immediate crisis response to those attempting to reach safety along the dangerous shoreline. Their aim? To 'act like a lighthouse – to stand firm in harsh conditions, lighting the way to guide people in need'. Members of *Lighthouse Relief* run down to the rocks on which many had previously perished, to guide boats in safely and pull them ashore. At night a team of six volunteers, including two medical personnel, ensures the safest possible landing (Lighthouse Relief, 2015).

The Korakas shoreline is covered by over 600,000 discarded life jackets and 10,000 punctured rubber dinghies. This material legacy of those who have attempted the journey before makes the landing even more hazardous and difficult. Yet this debris has also provided source material for creative representations of the plight of refugees aiming to raise awareness and motivate public action. In artist Thomas Kilpper's video, *Lighthouse for Lampedusa*, he investigates the migration of refugees from Africa to the small Italian island of Lampedusa. To create a social dialogue with its inhabitants, he created lighthouses made from materials retrieved from boats carrying refugees and remnants of their dinghies. He also plans to create a permanent lighthouse structure that refers to the Alexandria Pharos and the existing Cape Grecale Lighthouse on Lampedusa. With a light to guide boats to safety it will also function as a cultural centre for events that raise awareness about human rights (Kilpper, 2016).

The lighthouse is thus a new space of compassion and solidarity, a symbolic site of encounter and integration. For many refugees, the lighthouse offers protection and real respite in the long process of migration.

The sense that lighthouses are points from which to observe the dispassionate and dangerous expanse of the ocean, in comparison to which they are mere slivers in the landscape, is explored by artist Julie Westerman in her compelling discussion of *Disappearance at Sea* by Tacita Dean. Beyond the beam, there may be no possibility of reprieve, no help at all. Dean's work powerfully conjures the terror and isolation of an individual literally 'all at sea'.

A vigil

Disappearance at Sea, Tacita Dean, 1996

Julie Westerman

Artists have long been drawn to the lighthouse as a place, and as object and symbol. Used as a vehicle to explore the balance of the mind, it has been richly imbued with a sense of the uncanny and the mariner's struggle against the forces of nature. It is replete with binary notions: the beam of light both a projection and a beacon, exclaiming 'stay away' or 'come hither'; the lighthouse a marker on the liminal point between the land and the sea, solid ground and uncertain depths.

(continued)

(continued)

Many artists have used these often-contradictory readings to disrupt our understandings and introduce doubt. A key to the lighthouse's appeal is its impartiality to the disasters that unfold within the scope of its beam, and often at its feet. For J. M. W. Turner, the image of the lighthouse provided a pivotal point in many of his emotive paintings of storms, where water-laden, foreboding skies meet with seething mountainous seas. He filled numerous sketchbooks with such studies, in which the lighthouse provides the still focal point in the animation of a storm: a sturdy human-made endeavour against the glory of the elements.

Tacita Dean made a pair of compelling 16 mm films shot from the lantern rooms of two lighthouses in the North East of England: the 14-minute-long *Disappearance at Sea* (1996), filmed from St Abb's Head Lighthouse and the 4-minute *Disappearance at Sea II* (1997a), shot at the Longstone Lighthouse in Northumberland. From this vantage point, the works capture the sense of being on the edge, both physically and mentally. The crows-nest perspective of the lantern rooms locates the viewer at the last point between the solid land and the vastness of the sea, positioning them between the two states. As the film tracks the transition between light and dark, it embodies a sense of loss of the physical body and of emotional stability.

Disappearance at Sea was projected onto a single screen accompanied by a soundtrack of the mechanical clicking and murmuring of the turning gear. Seven long slow pans alternate between the rotating lenses of the lamp and a static camera angle looking out to sea. The lengthy duration of the shots evokes a sense of longing and a lonely vigil. The film is partly inspired by the strange and desperate story of a man lost at sea.

Figure 41 Wish you were here – Gratiot Light, by Julie Westerman, 2017.
© Julie Westerman. Postcard and watercolour.

Also see Plate 6.

Donald Crowhurst, an amateur yachtsman and failing businessman, entered the 1968 Sunday Times Golden Globe Race, a round-the-world yacht race, woefully unprepared for the challenges. As his lack of skill and experience became inescapable, he slipped out of the race and hid in the South Atlantic, faking his position. His log documented his desperation as he lost his grasp on reality. When it became clear to him that his deception was going to be exposed, he jumped into the sea. His vessel, the *Teignmouth Electron*, was later found deserted.

The film explores not only physical loss at sea but the loss of mental balance exposed in Crowhurst's story. The film situates us close to the revolving lens: the lighthouse's eye is our eye. Time is marked by the rhythmic sounds of the lens mechanism and the gaps between the intense flashes of the light beam that pass across the screen. The atmosphere is melancholic and our position that of the lonely vigil, as the grounded and mesmerising reality conveyed by the mechanical revolutions of the light is set against a sense that time is running out. The beam automatically lights up and scans the horizon as daylight fades from day to dusk to night. The light diminishes almost imperceptibly until all we have is the black sea. Throughout his time adrift, Crowhurst maintained a radio silence, and, at the point when all was lost, he took his chronometer with him into the sea:

> His story is about human failing; about pitching his sanity against the sea, where there is no human presence or support system left on which to hang a tortured psychological state. His was a world of acute solitude, filled with the ramblings of a troubled mind.
>
> (Dean, 1997b: 17)

The final contributions to this section change tack to consider how the lighthouse transmits powerful messages to non-humans, demonstrating that such light messages might be rendered more benign. Tim Edensor explores the fate of birds, moths and other creatures who are fatally lured into the lighthouse beam, and Charles Cockell describes the inventive way in which he deployed illumination while flying above a tropical forest to catch moths for less harmful purposes.

The deadly lighthouse beam

Tim Edensor

Though lighthouses have often enhanced the safety of humans at sea, their impact upon other species that share the marine environment has been less benign. Lighthouses are the first large illuminated structures to have wrought

(continued)

(continued)

significant devastation on passing birds, insects and marine animals. Over the past two centuries, their distinctive beams have been supplemented by increasing illumination from oil rig platforms, windfarms, ships, harbours and navigation devices.

So, although attention to light pollution has focused on land, artificial illumination also exerts malign effects upon marine environments. The capacity of coral species to spawn in accordance with lunar cycles has been damaged, as has the migration of plankton to the sea's surface at nightfall. The ability of sea turtle hatchlings to use natural light cues to navigate towards the sea is impaired, along with the efficacy of the bioluminescence deployed by marine animals to prey or communicate. Recent research also identifies how lighting around British coasts suppresses the colonisation of certain species yet encourages harmful others including the sea squirts and keel worms that foul harbours (Davies et al., 2015). These baleful effects of illumination combine with global warming, pesticides and the loss of environmental bio-diversity in contributing to 'the Great Acceleration' of human-driven environmental change (Hylland Eriksen, 2016).

Awareness about bird death at lighthouses is long-standing. In 1865, R. M. Ballantyne researched his novel, *The Lighthouse* at the Bell Rock Lighthouse off the east coast of Scotland:

> They tell me that thousands of land birds take refuge on the lantern, not so much in stormy as in foggy weather – blackbirds, thrushes, larks, crows, owls, and others. They seem to get lost in the fog, and when night comes on they see the light and flock to it in dozens. The men go out, catch and kill them to eat. Some of the birds made excellent stews. Laidlaw said he caught seventy one night, and might have got more if he had chosen. It seems cruel to treat the birds thus, but what can be done? The lighthouse cannot be converted into an asylum for strayed birds. They usually sit on the sills of the lantern windows and peck at the glass, trying to get in to the cheerful light. Poor little things! It is comforting to know, however, that when morning comes they usually take flight for the shore. Wither says he has seen so many of these little birds of all kinds fly past in foggy weather that the air seemed darkened by them.
>
> (Bell Rock Lighthouse, nd)

More recently, writing about events in late spring, lighthouse keeper Norman McCanch depicts similar scenes of avian decimation:

> Without warning, a small, brilliantly lit shape dances momentarily in the beams of the light and is gone. Gradually another appears, and a couple more, until perhaps twenty or thirty small warblers and chats are

flickering in the dazzling light. Unable to pinpoint any other landmark in the drizzle and mist, they fly towards the light, circling in its beams until exhaustion or daybreak frees them. Some flutter at the glazing, others crash into the glass or aerial wires and are killed, their tiny bodies falling into the yard and guttering.

(1985: 10)

Notoriously, though of limited efficacy as a lighthouse, the Statue of Liberty's lamp, first lit in 1886, killed tens of thousands of birds, with over 1,300 dying in a single night in October 1887. Jones and Francis (2003) record death tolls from Long Point Lighthouse on Lake Erie, Canada, with up to 2,000 birds killed in one night. Especially fatal under overcast or foggy conditions, the circling beam traps birds: they become exhausted, collide with glass or are preyed upon by raptors. Those that migrate by night, including thrushes and warblers, seem particularly susceptible to the beam's fatal lure. While the reasons remain obscure, it is likely that the birds' magnetic orientation is impaired by the light's particular spectral composition, an effect exacerbated when cloud cover is thick and celestial visual cues are absent.

Charles Cockell, below, describes how the deployment of illumination has advanced scientific understanding about moth numbers and diversity in a tropical rainforest. But, less progressively, lighthouses and other beacons continue to cause huge death tolls, as moths become exhausted, burn when they come too close and become vulnerable to predation by birds, bats and spiders. As with birds, their attraction to light remains an enigma. One theory surmises that moths use 'transverse orientation', travelling at a constant angle to moon and stars, and artificial lights confound this navigational practice. Another suggests that certain light sources emit infrared light frequencies akin to those radiated by the moth's sex pheromones, while a third contends that moths actually seek to navigate in the dark but light thwarts this ability (Gandy, 2016). Whatever the cause, light pollution has thoroughly interfered with the moth's day–night cycle, reshaping patterns of feeding and reproduction.

For birds, moths and the numerous other species adversely affected by marine illumination, a range of solutions is emerging. These include the designation of marine dark sky parks in parallel with those being created on land (Davies et al., 2015). More specific measures try to ameliorate the lighthouses' damaging effects. An early strategy was the installation of floodlights around the base of lighthouses allowing birds to orient themselves (Marquenie et al., 2013). Subsequent technologies have transformed the properties of the lighthouse beam. In 1961, Dungeness Lighthouse in Kent, UK, replaced a revolving beam with a strobe light that emitted short pulses of illumination, curtailing bird death while, in 1989, the Long Point

(continued)

(continued)

Lighthouse deployed a far less intense light to similar effect (Jones and Francis, 2003). Changes in the spectral composition of the beam have also helped. In 2014 Bardsey Lighthouse, situated on a small island off the North Wales coast, and an important station for migrating birds, replaced its massive Fresnel lens that projected a sweeping, 89,900-candela white beam 22 miles out to sea with a solar-powered LED light system that produces an intermittent red glow. Once thousands of birds were drawn to their deaths, but they no longer flock towards the only light source for miles around. The lighthouse beam has been rendered bird-friendly.

The phrase 'like a moth to a flame' captures the ubiquitous tendencies of moths to be drawn towards artificial light, a phenomenon that has proved useful to legions of amateur entomologists and lepidopterists armed with killing jars. In a 1993 expedition to Sumatra, this predisposition also helped Charles Cockell and his team to collect moths from a dense rainforest. In the following contribution, he describes how his efforts to entice moths towards the light led to the loss of his own wings.

Moth hunting in Sumatra

Charles Cockell

How do you catch moths over a rainforest in the dead of night? Why do you catch moths over a rainforest in the dead of night? Well the latter question is easy to answer; the former takes a bit more work.

In 1993, I planned an expedition to Sumatra, Indonesia, that was driven by a childhood fascination with moths. These elusive, usually nocturnal creatures are sensitive to changes in their environment. Studying them gives us an early warning that their habitat is changing or under stress. My objective was to contribute to a study being undertaken as part of the preservation of the Kerinci-Seblat National Park, Sumatra, Indonesia. Joined by three fellow PhD students from Oxford University, our work included collecting moths and plants for Kew Gardens. We were joined by a botanical artist.

How do you do this? Moths are attracted to lights, yet previous experience of collecting moths in Mongolia showed that they are difficult to entice from treetop canopies. It was in the steppes of Mongolia that I conceived of a moth-collecting aircraft.

In 1992, I began flying lessons to acquire a microlight pilot's licence and engaged a team of engineers to help build the Moth Machine. After several months' work, we had a modified aircraft. The machine had a butterfly net turned into a scoop to collect the moths. Two 1-million-candlepower lamps pointed downwards to illuminate the top of the trees and ensure one didn't fly too low. A bank of ultraviolet lamps was also installed to help attract moths, along with infrared night vision apparatus borrowed from the Royal Air Force (617 Squadron).

We drove the Moth Machine to the forests of Sumatra in 1993 and test-flew it at the main airport in Bengkulu. Then, onwards to the rainforest of Kerinci, where we spent 3 months implementing the expedition's scientific objectives. Several times the Moth Machine was flown over the forests at dusk, its lighthouse-like beams guiding me in my quest to scoop moths in the canopy while moths were simultaneously collected on the ground. Over 10,000 moths were eventually collected and sent to institutes in Germany for identification and analysis.

However, a month into the expedition, the Moth Machine clipped the top of a tree as I landed. Somersaulting three times, it was completely destroyed, bringing an end to the experiment in aerial moth catching. I walked away with nothing more than a wry grin. For the remainder of the expedition, we expanded our reach into the forests by hiring a herd of elephants. As *The Times* put it, we had switched from microlight to jumbo.

SPACE AND PLACE

Tim Edensor

Lighthouses are profoundly embedded in place as place-signifiers and as parts of larger spatial networks. Their connection to place resonates throughout this book, as signified by distinctive architectural styles, the materialities used in construction, local historical contexts and events, cultural associations and tourism. In developing this theme, the next contribution explores how lighthouses are rhythmically sedimented in place through the distinctive rhythms of light and sound they produce, and how these intersect with contiguous human and non-human rhythms.

The rhythms of place, the rhythms of the lighthouse

Tim Edensor

Henri Lefebvre (2004) asserts that places are ceaselessly (re)constituted by multiple rhythms. Thus, the lighthouse is enfolded in shifting polyrhythmic ensembles to which it contributes several highly distinctive rhythms. Places are made particular by the linear and cyclical rhythms that provide a backdrop to everyday life. Such rhythms signify diverse temporal scales, from epochal and geological time, to life cycles, annual and seasonal events, weekly routines and daily procedures (Edensor, 2010). They are shaped by non-human agencies and regular human practices of commerce, work, leisure, transport and commemoration. The routines of individual people are often rhythmically aligned with those of others, creating collective synchronicities that sediment habitual ways of dwelling in and practising place, producing shared rhythms of eating, watching television and worshipping.

Most obviously, the lighthouse constitutes an enduring element in the material assemblage of place. Other rhythms synchronise and meld with those of the lighthouse, marking everyday schedules: fishermen set out to sea as night falls and the lighthouse beam begins to flash; postal workers deliver mail to the lighthouse; lighthouse keepers are served in local shops.

More distinctively, the lighthouse beam marks the passage of the seasons, illuminating the environs for longer and shorter spells. Moreover, its unique rhythmic light pattern – its *character* – marks its individual identity as delineated in the *Light List*. A lighthouse may display a single flash that is repeated after singular intervals, a regular group of flashes followed by a longer eclipse, or shorter eclipses that momentarily extinguish the light. At Eilean Glas Lighthouse on Scalpay in the Western Isles of Scotland, there are three white flashes every 20 seconds; at Sanda Lighthouse in Argyllshire, an extended white and red flash occurs every 24 seconds (MacPherson, 2009).

Sonic rhythms

Lefebvre (2004: 87) contends that a rhythm analyst is 'capable of listening to a house, street, a town as one listens to a symphony, an opera'. For humans also produce auditory rhythms that are central constituents in local soundscapes. Inhabitants become attuned to regular sonic rhythms, which provide, according to Brandon Labelle (2008), an 'auditory scaffolding' or what Paul Rodaway (1994) calls *soundmarks*: sounds recognised and shared by a community. These sounds signify everyday practices: the throb of morning rush-hour traffic or the nocturnal clamour of club-goers.

So it was with the lighthouse's foghorn. Though not necessarily a regular element of the soundscape, inhabitants would know that as visibility declined in inclement weather, the foghorn would provide a reassuring auditory pulse. Foghorns also possessed their own time signatures with sound emitted in distinctive rhythms. At the aforementioned Eilean Glas Lighthouse, a blast of 4.5 seconds' duration occurred every 45 seconds, whereas at Sanda Lighthouse the foghorn sounded for 7 seconds every 60 seconds (MacPherson, 2009). Such distinctions would have been especially important for large harbours such as San Francisco Bay, which in 1936 featured a soundscape 'alive with a cacophony of 51 diaphones, whistles, bells and sirens all moaning, hooting, screeching and dinging' (Wheeler, nd).

The sonic rhythms of places are shaped by particular historical, social and cultural contexts. Accordingly, while they may contribute to a stable, reliable sense of belonging for a while, they may disappear, as with the foghorn, now largely silenced by a switch to GPS and satellite technology.

Work rhythms

Barbara Adam draws attention to how 'the when, how often, how long, in what order and at what speed' are governed by a host of temporal 'norms, habits and conventions' (1995: 66). While most pre-industrial work and worship rhythms followed diurnal patterns of light and the seasons, and

(continued)

(continued)

regularly scheduled church bells, modern industry enforced the ubiquitous deployment of clock time to organise labour and ensure predictable outputs (Strang, 2015b). Such authoritative schedules also specified the duties of the lighthouse keeper. As Lefebvre observes, power 'knows how to utilize and manipulate time, dates, time-tables' (2004: 68) and often develops disciplinary systems through which the working body is entrained through 'dressage' to (re)produce 'an automatism of repetitions' (ibid: 40).

Such training was undertaken by lighthouse keepers, and they were expected to follow rigorously observed, regular procedures. Thus, Norman McCanch (1985) discusses the 8-hour shifts of three keepers. Daily routines included lighting and extinguishing the lamp according to detailed timetables, refuelling oil supply, cleaning the lens and windows, cleaning the premises, carrying out maintenance and repairs, and maintaining inventories of supplies in good order. English keepers were required to keep a daily logbook of events, surveying weather and tide conditions every three hours, and recording shipping traffic, as well as compiling monthly weather and maintenance reports.

McCanch asserts that it is 'surprising how quickly one's body becomes accustomed to the routine' (1985: 56). Such rhythms became sedimented in bodies, as an interview with Tom, a keeper assigned to a rock lighthouse, exemplifies:

> It does something to you, being cooped up eight weeks there and no exercise; you were like a tired old woman when you came ashore, you couldn't hardly exert yourself for anything. The first day or two on land it hurt you to walk even half a mile on the flat; it was like someone had been kicking at the back of your knees, because all your leg muscles was used to was going up and down stairs.
>
> (Palmer, 1975: 74)

These work schedules were supplemented by timetabled maintenance and supply, without which a lighthouse would become vulnerable (Edensor, 2011), subject to the damaging agencies of water, salt, wind, insects, biofilms and plants. Regular provisions were similarly crucial. The lighthouse was thus an exemplary site at which a host of organised rhythmic activities were deployed to maximise smooth operation, minimise danger and discipline workers.

Non-human rhythms

The rhythms of the non-human agents composing lighthouses' marine environments are similarly omnipresent. The rhythmic patterns of monsoons' heat, drought, ice, snow and wind shape regular maintenance routines and the keepers' temporal relationships with the outside. The surging rhythms of tides, 'forms of lunisolar, *hybrid* temporality ... driven by the interlocking rhythms of day-night (solar rhythm) and tidal rise and fall (lunar rhythm)' (Jones, 2010: 190), are especially profound. While tides generally rise and fall twice daily, there is great rhythmic variation, depending upon the Moon's position, wind force, shape of the coast, and time of year. Tides affect the practices of fisherfolk, determine when ships enter and leave harbours, and influence the activities of recreational sailors, canoeists and birdwatchers. Lighthouse keepers thus require a detailed knowledge of tides to monitor ship movements.

The rhythms of non-human creatures also circulate around lighthouses. At Bell Rock Lighthouse, 11 miles from the east coast of Scotland, keeper John Campbell made copious observations, describing the seasonal migration patterns of birds and butterflies, the winter visitations of sea ducks, the blooming of flowers, and the breeding seasons of fish. He remarks that 'the usual signs which to the landsman's eye chronicle the passing seasons are here unknown; but to us, the fish, shell fish, marine plants, migratory birds etc., constitute an endless calendar' (cited in Love, 2015: 93).

Arrhythmia and new rhythms

Although predictable rhythmic procedures are integral to the lighthouse's functionality, arrhythmia may ensue when procedures are neglected or unexpected events occur. The oft-cited disappearance of three keepers on the Flannan Isles, explored in Chris Watson's contribution, may have been caused by their being engulfed by a freak wave, or by the social and mental strains of dwelling in a remote lighthouse.

Today, many of the rhythms identified above have been replaced. The lighthouse is still an important place-symbol and persists as a material fixture around which everyday rhythms are performed, yet instead of articulating rhythms of work and sound, the lighthouse is more often subject to the rhythms of tourism, synchronised with school holidays and seasonal clemency in the weather.

The spatial contexts of the lighthouse are shaped by its incorporation into networks of varying scale. Lighthouses come to embody and reflect national or regional senses of place in distinctive ways, as exemplified in Phil Wood's account of a Norwegian lighthouse. The design and function of the lighthouse here take a particular form, as do the symbolic meanings attached to it. In considering its national character, Wood draws upon an instructive comparison with British lighthouses.

The watcher at the edge

Phil Wood

One of the many intriguing qualities of a lighthouse is its effortless straddling of the littoral zone, a physical and a figurative borderland. Teresa Costa suggests that:

> The liminal space materialized by the border is normally a site and symbol of power display, at times emphasized by the military paraphernalia that is token to the sovereignty of states. Beyond the material apparatus and ritual of state power, the paramount significance of the border relies on the symbolic, invisible, affective and effective complexity that such spaces entail and generate as lines of division or encounter.
>
> (2012: 87)

The lighthouse does indeed occupy a potent but nevertheless ambiguous position, which can vary from one cultural or political space to another, and I will exemplify this with an account of the Tungenes Fyr in Norway.

There has been a lighthouse (or *fyr*) at the place where the Byfjorden meets the open sea since 1828. It overlooks the narrow channel between the Tungenes headland and the island of Bru, guiding vessels in and out of Stavanger's harbour. It was the first foreign building I encountered beyond British shores in 1975, as the Newcastle to Bergen ferry made landfall in Stavanger. I had a distinctly British conception of what a lighthouse should look like, and this was not it.

My early imaginary of lighthouses was formed by those near my Yorkshire home: at Flamborough Head, Spurn Point and Scarborough. It was shaped by the media, with images of the iconic sea-washed lighthouses such as Eddystone or Skerryvore, which thrust up heroically to almost 50 metres and withstood the worst that the elements could hurl at them. In a decomposing end-of-empire atmosphere, these splendidly isolated, phallic towers still stirred some vestigial symbolism of a plucky island nation.

Tungenes, on the other hand, looked more like a farmhouse with an observation platform appended to the roof. It had a job to do, and had done it well over the years, but it had never felt the need to say 'look at me, and admire'.

Subsequently, I've returned to Norway many times, travelling the length of its dramatic coastline. As the lovingly assembled *Lighthouses of Norway* website (which can be viewed at http://lighthousesofnorway.com) attests, the Norwegians are not averse to erecting the occasional towering sentinel, such as the lighthouses at Sletringen or Lille Færder, but these are rather the exception to the rule governing local lighthouse design. Even on one of the most storm-battered stretches of coastline in Europe at Kråkenes, and on the tiny islet of Saltholmen, the lighthouses are robust but modest in the extreme.

What does the making, the remaking and the iconography of their respective lighthouses tell us about Norwegian and British ideas about ideal architectural design for lighthouses and their purpose? Britain's main historic period of lighthouse construction coincided with its domination of the world stage as maritime policeman and enforcer. Norway at that time – long before the oil wealth came – struggled in an impoverished union with Sweden. Its fishing industry was unable to sustain a population that turned increasingly to overseas emigration. '*Hytter og hus, men ingen borge*' ('Cottages and houses, but no castles') says the national anthem, and this egalitarian view apparently influenced the modest design of lighthouses too.

Another difference may be respective cultural ideas about isolation. Britons, by the 19th century, largely accustomed to urban life, with power, wealth and cultural status corralled in the capital and major urban areas, may not have seen the isolated lot of the lighthouse keeper as a happy or enviable one. Norwegians were by tradition 'egalitarian individualists' (Hylland Eriksen, 1993), raised on isolated farmsteads and expected to be self-reliant. Norwegian discourse has continued to valorise localism, and politicians of all stripes have maintained a policy of *spredtbosetting* or scattered settlement. While the lonely and melancholic lighthouse keeper is a common trope in English-language literature, for his counterparts at Tungenes and elsewhere in Norway, the prospect of escaping the throng and making one's livelihood alone and in isolation may have been seen quite differently.

Returning to Costa's point about liminal borderlands as spaces for architectural demonstrations of state power, this has a rather different slant at Tungenes. The lighthouse was built to protect the herring fleets rather than the State, and Stavanger was never used for military purposes by the small Norwegian navy. Adjacent to the light, however, are remnants of the concrete fortifications that were erected by the Nazis as part of the Atlantic Wall. This suggests that Tungenes retained the status of 'innocent bystander' in a conflict foisted upon it by the Germans and British.

So, while lighthouses might have been seen by more martial states as part of the paraphernalia of defending the realm, for Norway the story was of a dwindling status, rather than an expression of potency. From 1825, for over a century, Stavanger was a major port of embarkation for the emigrants seeking a better life in North America. Tungenes would thus have been a rather doleful sight for many: the last image of their Norwegian homeland.

However, having remained empty for several years after it was decommissioned in 1984, Tungenes Lighthouse has a new focus of activity. The Norwegian Coastal Administration and the local council have restored it to replicate the way it would have been for the keepers and their families in the 1930s. The lodgings have been carefully recreated as an expression of *hyggelig*, that

(continued)

(continued)

special Norwegian concept of huddled 'cosiness' around the hearth, against the mischief of the world outside. So, to this extent, it shares with the martial, upstanding lighthouses across the North Sea an aspiration to create a safe haven.

Reflecting this notion of 'retreat', Tungenes has also been promoted as a place where international artists might stay for creative residencies. The Japanese light artist, Jio Shimizu, spent several weeks there with his family in 2012. This restored the domestic presence of young children to the site, but also thrust this quiet retreat to the fore with a display of cutting-edge art made with laser beams.

In accord with the fundamental purpose of a lighthouse, Shimizu used his residency to explore sound and light, creating works that united art and science by highlighting physical phenomena, such as sound-wave formation. His installation at Tungenes examined principles of space through the perspectives of waves, frequencies and modulations. While complex in scope, the work employed a simple structure that allowed light to pass through and reflect upon a rotating glass vessel (a Claisen flask), which generated alchemical effects and what he described as 'maximum material ecstasy' (Shimizu, 2010).

By passing parallel laser beams through several special lenses, Shimizu was able to generate peculiar waveforms which resonated and radiated wavelengths of light. Only by directly experiencing the work and being in the space could the visitor to Tungenes tell that it was composed of extremely fine filaments of light generated by these refractions and interferences. Shimizu described the intention of his work as an attempt to create a hybrid of art and science that mimicked the production of energy by protobacteria, as a metaphor for the emergence of life (On the Edge, 2012).

While lighthouses in the past may have fulfilled a vital primary function as well as a significant but secondary expression of cultural meaning and identity, what do they have to say to us today? Based upon my experience of Tungenes and, in particular, its collaboration with Jio Shimizu, I would suggest two things. First, they express the continuing bonds that exist between a community and their sentinel, evidenced by the people of Randaberg's striving to imbue their *Fyr* with a new function and sense of purpose. Secondly, it underlines our deep and ongoing fascination with light and what it can say to us about the human condition.

As many of the essays in this volume show, whether constituted at a national, colonial or transnational level, lighthouses are invariably part of larger systems of power, policing and navigation. By identifying the connections through which such systems incorporate individual lighthouses, Robert Shaw reveals them as relational fixtures that undermine parochial understandings of place. The lighthouse exemplifies how places are invariably constituted through changing relationships with elsewhere, facilitating cultural, financial and social transactions between people on a global scale.

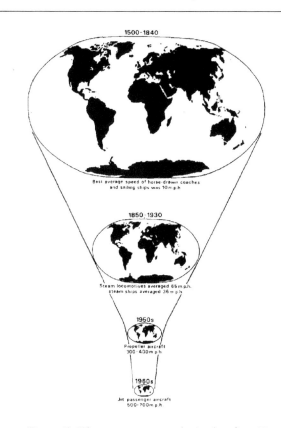

Figure 42 'Time–space compression', taken from Harvey, D. (1989: 241), Plate 3.1 'The shrinking map of the world through innovations in transport which "annihilate space through time"'. *The Condition of Postmodernity: An Enquiry into the Origins of Cultural Change*, John Wiley and Sons Ltd/Blackwell Publishers Ltd. Copyright © David Harvey, 1989.

Relational places

Lighthouses and networks of mobility

Robert Shaw

Harvey's (1989) diagram of 'time–space compression' (Figure 42) has become symbolic of understandings of the changing relationships between places that have occurred alongside exploration and technological development. Lighthouses have been central to the transport and mobility that has

(continued)

(continued)

driven this change, and their role offers a useful challenge to assumptions about 'place' in a globalised world.

In the early modern period, horse travel and sailing ships were the fastest forms of transport: thus, the legend of Dick Turpin turns upon the difficulty of travelling between London and York (just over 200 miles) in under twelve hours. It is now possible to make the same journey in two hours via public transport, and even more quickly by private aircraft. In contrast, in twelve hours from London, it is now possible to reach Bangkok, Johannesburg and Mexico City. An astronaut in the International Space Station will circle the globe 7.7 times in the same period.

This changing mobility has shaped people's understandings of place: places were previously 'finite, centred ... [and] matched time-honoured routines of daily life set in the infinity and unknowability of "enduring time"' (Harvey, 1989: 241). But with the exploration of the globe, the innovation of new transport and communications technology and (critically for Harvey) the constant need for expansion of the capitalist system, places are now understood through their engagement and interaction with other places.

Such narratives connect several contemporary understandings of place. From a phenomenological perspective, place is understood as 'the immediate environment of my lived body – an arena of action that is at once physical, historical, social and cultural' (Casey, 2001: 683). This opposes place to space: where space is thought of as general, universal and abstract, place is presumed to be specific, particular and lived. Places are embodied and practised, tied into local cultures and ways of living. Thus, theories arguing in favour of 'place' have long been considered reactive and conservative, emphasising the parochial over the cosmopolitan and the learned. To be tied to place is, for certain theories of modernity, to be tied to tradition and to reject the global. As Brockelman argues, then, to 'be modern is to give up the "sense of place" associated with the late medieval hierarchical world in favour of a space and time conceived to be populated by infinite numbers of entirely exchangeable loci' (2003: 36–37). I can follow my friends' holidays on other continents via their photographs on Facebook, each of us experiencing our current place in relation to others; while migrants – both elite and poorer – connect to homelands via Skype. Thus, the argument goes, a traditional sense of place has been lost or become outdated.

Through such understandings of place, what are we to make of the lighthouse? Possibly the lighthouse offers something different: evidence that, rather than shifting from inward-looking to outward-looking, there is a longer history of place as relational. Lighthouses form part of an infrastructure of mobility which pre-dates the modern era, yet which also continues to play a core role in the contemporary globalised world. Through the lighthouse, modern shipping routes are connected to the earliest explorers, sailors and navigators.

> In his classic history of seafaring, Fayle argues that 'our theories of life, our fashions in dress and manners and amusements are continually being affected by the ideas and habits of peoples living hundreds and even thousands of miles away from us' (1933: 22–23) and that this has occurred via the sea's fluid 'highway'. Lighthouses have long helped sailors to identify ports and offered hospitality and invitation to the traveller. The interchange of ideas that has led to technological advancement and an increasingly interconnected world has taken place through travel and communication on the seas. As such, we can argue that coastal communities have always been defined by their relationships with the people (and animals, materials and weather) that have travelled to them across the sea: the place of the port has always been relational, and the lighthouse has been central to this exteriority.
>
> From this perspective, then, the lighthouse upholds Crary's argument that the 'contemporary phenomenon of acceleration is not simply a linear succession of innovations in which there is a substitution of a new item for something out of date' (2013: 43). Rather, lighthouses help reveal a longer history of what Massey (1994) calls a 'relational sense of place'. She argues that 'what gives a place its specificity is not some long-internalised history but . . . a particular constellation of social relations, meeting and weaving together at a particular locus' (Massey, 1994: 152). The lighthouse – opening up to the world – is indicative of this relationality.

Shaw (pers. comm.) also considers how the opportunity to see from alternate disciplinary viewpoints changed the conversation and highlighted the value of 'looking at the peripheral':

> Lighthouses are on the edge (literally) of land and sea, but also on the edge of many disciplines: the contributions to the book push the authors to the boundary of what people in their field would consider traditionally. Wood talks of the isolation of the lighthouse keeper as something that can be valorised, and this resonates with the book and the project. In going to the edge of our disciplines, we also go to some unexpected places: children's television, experimental physics, medieval philosophy and so forth. This is a more creative vision of academic thought. I've also been led to consider the power of light; it brings life and death to many in the book, including animals disrupted by light pollution. The relationship between light and knowledge is made clear too, in several chapters, and the attempt to control it is symbolic of wider approaches to developing and using knowledge.

The final contribution to this section resonates with Jennifer Allan's focus on the soundscape of place, here, in sound artist Chris Watson's account of his travels to sites at which lighthouses are a key element of the landscape. The recordings that

Watson makes are not those of the foghorn but of the surrounding sounds that both amplify and assuage the haunting sensations provoked by the dramatic histories of these two locations, the Flannan Isles in North West Scotland and Skellig Michael off the west coast of Ireland. The reassuring and revealing beam of the lighthouse, as well as its stable presence as a base from which to explore these wind-beaten locations, further contribute to the powerful, sensory apprehension of island place.

No keepers

Chris Watson

> A dreadful accident has happened at Flannans. The three Keepers, Ducat, Marshall and the occasional have disappeared from the island. On our arrival there this afternoon no sign of life was to be seen on the Island. Fired a rocket but, as no response was made, managed to land Moore, who went up to the Station but found no Keepers there.

On 26 December 1900, Captain Harvey, Master of the *Hesperus*, sent this telegram while moored off the Flannan Isles, a group of seven islands 18 miles north-west off the island of Lewis in the Outer Hebrides. The relief ship *Hesperus* had been routinely dispatched from Oban, although the light had been reported as missing ten days earlier by a passing vessel. After investigation of the lighthouse and the island no trace of the keepers was found: all three men had vanished, possibly swept off the island by a freak wave which would have caught them at 110 feet above sea level. However, the mystery was never solved (Northern Lighthouse Board, nd).

As a sixteen-year-old, I was introduced to *Flannan Isle*, a poem written in 1912 by Wilfred Gibson, which is a romanticised account of the lighthouse keepers' disappearance. Living in landlocked Sheffield, I found islands and lighthouses magically attractive as remote outposts on the edge of the world. During this period, I was also developing my interests in natural history and sound recording, so the idea of visiting wild and remote locations with my tape recorder was very appealing. A few lines of Gibson's poem struck me as being particularly strange, for as the search party landed:

> We saw three queer, black, ugly birds –
>
> Too big, by far, in my belief,
>
> For guillemot or shag –
>
> Like seamen sitting bolt-upright
>
> Upon a half-tide reef:

But, as we neared, they plunged from sight,

Without a sound, or spurt of white.

(lines 24–30)

Naively thinking at the time that this was part of the actual account, I wondered how this might be possible, as it was completely at odds with the raucous clamour of the only seabird colony I was familiar with in 1969, the Royal Society for the Protection of Birds (RSPB) reserve at Bempton cliffs on the Yorkshire coast.

The sounds of that island and Gibson's melodrama about the lighthouse haunted my imagination for well over a decade. Finally, in 1981, I made it out to Lewis and, after recording the rattle of corncrakes in the iris beds and the shrieks of Arctic skuas overhead, I enquired at the harbour in Miavaig about sailing out to the Flannans, as the main island, Eilean Mor where the Flannan light was built, also has a breeding colony of the rare Leach's petrel. These are tiny black seabirds who return to the islands each spring to nest in rock crevices, and they communicate with strange clockwork-like cackles.

The reluctance I met in asking about a trip out to the islands was explained to me later in the offices of the *Stornoway Gazette*. The accounts of the events almost a century ago on the island still linger with some local fishermen on the west coast of Lewis, and they would not sail out there without a very good cause. The Flannan Isle light was made automatic in 1971, and I finally managed to record Leach's petrel on Hirta in the St Kilda archipelago during June 2002.

As a wildlife sound recordist, I am often drawn to islands in European coastal waters, as they present excellent opportunities for recording seabirds and marine mammals in locations without human disturbance and background noise. Lighthouses can facilitate my work in these locations by offering a base and respite from the elements in what might otherwise be a very hostile environment.

The island of Skellig Michael is almost 8 miles out into the Atlantic Ocean, south and west off the Irish coast of Kerry. As with the Flannan Isle, Skellig Michael was for me a remote outpost of mystery and imagination fuelled by reports and accounts I picked up over many years. The island was described by George Bernard Shaw as an 'incredible, impossible mad place,' as 'part of our dream world' (World Heritage Ireland, nd).

It attracted the attention of Thomas Charles Lethbridge, who was the Keeper of Anglo-Saxon Antiquities at the Archaeology Museum in Cambridge between 1923 and 1957. Regarded as something of a maverick by his fellows, Lethbridge was interested in parapsychology and used dowsing techniques to discover hidden objects and artefacts. In June 1929

(continued)

(continued)

Lethbridge was on an archaeological expedition to Skellig Michael when, he said, he was flung to the ground by an unseen malevolent force.

As well as having a spectacular seabird colony this precipitous, almost conical island is famous for the 'beehive' stone huts perched at over 650 feet above sea level close to its summit. These are monks' cells built during the 6th century by a Celtic community, and one explanation offered for this remote monastic settlement is that the monks' prayers were intended to create a battery of power on the edge of the known world – a buffer against any onslaught of evil that might emerge out of the west. On the western edge of the island is the lighthouse which, at longitude 10 degrees 32 minutes west, is also on the western edge of Europe. Equipped with a beam that blinks 19 nautical miles out into the Atlantic Ocean, the light was established in 1826 in response to the great loss of lives and merchant ships on this fractured coastline.

Lethbridge suggested that the frequent reports and accounts of ghosts and poltergeists at the lighthouse was a result of the powerful shock and trauma of these tragic events being imprinted upon the fabric of the buildings. Local boatman Des Lavelle explained this story in detail as he landed two others and myself on the rock in June 2011, when we arrived to make a documentary on the island and stay in the now unmanned lighthouse (Watson et al., 2011). Thankfully we spent four undisturbed nights in the lighthouse: nevertheless, the three of us left thinking that Skellig Michael seemed to possess an intangible yet powerful sense and spirit of place. This was demonstrated one night when I was recording around the now-abandoned upper lighthouse station a few hundred feet above sea level.

During spring and summer, sea-going birds such as shearwaters and petrels nest on the island in their thousands. These are burrow or cavity-nesting birds who arrive under cover of darkness to avoid predation by the local gulls. On returning, usually around midnight, they communicate with their nest partners through a variety of harsh loud contact calls as each seeks to home in on its particular nesting chamber. During daylight, these birds are not visible and remain underground, so in the 6th century it would have been easy to imagine, in the darkness, that the air around the island was filled with screaming demons, banshee-like wails and cackles which had arrived out of the unknown. During my 21st-century nocturnal recording session, however, the birds and source of the sounds was revealed to me by the reassuring pattern of the Skellig light, flashing three times every 15 seconds.

THE ART OF LIGHTHOUSES

Veronica Strang, Joanna Puckering and Tim Edensor

Inspirational light

To achieve a 360° view of the lighthouse, we began by talking about light as an object. Now we consider how the lighthouse itself becomes both the object and subject of artistic interpretation in literature, art and other media. This aspect of the lighthouse is by no means detached from the other perspectives: on the contrary, it might be said to encompass and be inspired by them implicitly and often explicitly.

Warren Armstrong's collection, *White for Danger* (1963), exemplifies how the lighthouse lends itself to a wealth of metaphorical roles in storytelling and literature, providing a setting for heroism, premonition, tragedy, isolation, endurance, madness, the uncanny and the horrific. Some of the stories are mythical, others supposedly based on true events. They tell of valiant men, eccentric and wild characters, terrible storms, deep antagonisms between keepers, bereft wives, monsters and spectres. The contributions in this section further reveal how representations of the lighthouses across the arts echo the ambiguities explored throughout this book. Thus, poet Linda France imagines the last lighthouse keeper, and literary scholar Patricia Waugh examines Woolf's *To the Lighthouse* (1927), capturing both the homologous notion of the lighthouse as a person and its capacity to express ideas about looking, seeing and perceiving.

'The Last Lighthousekeeper'

Linda France

> A hundred and thirty-seven steps spiral
>
> inside the architecture of a whelk – his knees'
>
> habit to rise and flex; eyes scan
>
> postage-stamp windows for messages in salt,

(continued)

(continued)

> lips humour help in ages past. Up
>
> in the lantern room, time, crucified
>
> by a mewing weathervane, is lost to all
>
> compass points. Diamond-spun glass
>
> caps a trapdoor for cleaning duty twice
>
> a week, the leap year disappearing act.
>
> A life defined by optic apparatus, radio static,
>
> moon and tides leaves him bleached, stranded,
>
> an island to himself. Light, like memories,
>
> can't be kept – mercury, paraffin, electricity, breath.

'There'll be no landing at the lighthouse tomorrow'
Virginia Woolf and the Godrevy Lighthouse
Patricia Waugh

> I meant *nothing* by The Lighthouse. . . . I saw that all kinds of feelings would accrue to this, but I refused to think them out, and trusted that people would make it the deposit for their own emotions – which they have done . . . I can't manage Symbolism except in this vague, generalized kind of way.
>
> (Woolf, 1977: 385)

So wrote Virginia Woolf to her friend, the art critic Roger Fry, on 27 May, 1927. But this lighthouse also had an existence beyond fiction. Woolf revisited St Ives, Cornwall and the Godrevy Lighthouse (built 1859), just off its coast, with its 'great plateful of water' and 'the hoary Lighthouse, distant, austere, in the midst' (Woolf, 2004: 14), as she was revising final drafts of her fifth novel, *To the Lighthouse*, in 1926. But she had revisited the lighthouse in imagination all her life: for this was her *temps perdu*, the place of the wild joys and freedoms of childhood summers spent at Talland House, the Stephen family summer retreat, acquired by her father when Virginia was just six months old, until her mother's death in 1895, when Leslie Stephen abruptly cancelled the lease. For the thirteen-year-old Virginia, summer, childhood, was over; henceforth, only the long vanishing avenue of memory leading to that mysterious light still winking across the bay. No rite of passage could have been sharper.

In a letter written on Christmas Day 1926, on Woolf's visit to the real, the Godrevy, lighthouse, she reflects wryly how 'all my facts about Lighthouses are simply wrong' (Woolf, 1977: 310). Similarly, in the novel, as Lily Briscoe returns, ten years after Mrs Ramsay's death, the first sight of the lighthouse across the bay, an 'immense distance' now, 'opened doors in one's mind that went banging and swinging to and fro', so that, 'like everything else this strange morning, the words became symbols' (Woolf, 2004: 122). What is the relation of imaginary and fictional objects to 'real' things? Why are we interested in the factual or experiential sources of art, fascinated with biographies of writers and artists? How do objects in art take on symbolic values and what do we mean by aesthetic value? These are questions that the lighthouse poses.

Certainly, this lighthouse defies ontological containment and material placement: it seems to have its source in an actual lighthouse which is a real place of pilgrimage and sanctuary, but also a place in and of memory, reconsolidated time and again. It is the location for her most intense childhood experiences and sensations, feelings on which she would draw all her life and which endowed those memories with a vivid quality, more intense even than ordinary external perception: for 'if life has base that it stands upon, if it is a bowl that one fills and fills and fills – then my bowl without doubt stands upon this memory . . . in bed in the nursery at St Ives . . . hearing this splash and seeing this light . . . and feeling the purest ecstasy I can conceive' (Woolf, 1985: 65). So, this is an actual lighthouse; a lighthouse seen with the inner or mind's eye of memory; a lighthouse that is a fictional construct rendered through the multiple spatial perspectives of the characters in the novel for whom it is a shimmering object of desire, the inspiration for and place of termination of their various journeys. No wonder it has become a powerful receptacle for readerly emotion and imaginative projection. If the lighthouse is a symbol, it would seem to be a symbol of a symbol: that is to say, of the essential indeterminacy but ironic inclusivity of art, its complex and ongoing and unpredictable emergence as meaning; its reminder of the complexity of the world, the many ways in which that world might be modelled and the way that entanglement with the model or the knower provides the steady and constant and dynamic generation of ever-new worlds. Viewed thus, the lighthouse of Woolf's novel might already be seen to propel plot, position characters and articulate its aesthetic of multitude: the capacity of art to communicate the singularity of experience even as it facilitates the expression and recognition of emotions that encourage or cement commonality.

'There'll be no landing at the lighthouse tomorrow' (Woolf, 2004: 10), Charles Tansley insists. Indeed, since its publication in 1927, generations of critics and 'common' readers have tried to 'land there', to

(continued)

(continued)

make the work their own; the novel has been read through feminist, Marxist, biographical, formalist, Symbolist, existentialist, phenomenological, quantum theoretical, psycho-historical, anthropological and a variety of psychological and psychoanalytical perspectives (Jamesian, Kleinian, Freudian, Winnicottian). It has been read as an exploration of the New (Cambridge) Realism of Russell and Moore, an affirmation of the German Idealism of Hegel's Beautiful Soul, an articulation of the Uncertainty Principle of Werner Heisenberg's New Physics, an exploration of the Post-Impressionist aesthetics of Fry.

With its steady beam, its rhythmical 'stroke' that illuminates a common but variegated world, or meets the multiple gazes of various onlookers, Woolf's lighthouse might be regarded as the modernist equivalent of George Eliot's famous 19th-century image of the pier glass in *Middlemarch* (1871). The pier glass, with its haphazardly scratched surface, is magically shaped into multiple patterns under the penumbra of a moving light. Woolf's lighthouse, beaming steadily through the distances of space, but also in memory through those of time, is presented, however, as both a material object that is the source of illumination and as an object in the inner eye, the mind's eye, lit up by its beam, as experience is recreated and reconsolidated into new shapes in imagination. The lighthouse is a figure for the art object itself, emerging in a place mysteriously between the material and the imaginary, a covert category that changes and redefines the relations and perspectives of everything around it. James Ramsay sees in the distance its 'misty eye' and thinks of his long dead mother. But as the boat finally arrives at the lighthouse after all these years, he now sees a solid and somewhat mundane structure, 'the tower stark and straight', firmly planted on its foundation of rock; for the lighthouse is also the home and place of work, of sustenance for the lighthouse keeper and his son, projecting the steady beam to safeguard storm-tossed vessels that might otherwise founder against the treacherous rocks. James (and the reader) are reminded that the lighthouse, a figure of complementarity, is above all, perhaps, an image of survival, of the many and often seemingly contradictory ways in which humans have fashioned techniques, arts and sciences, to provide meaning and shelter in a world of nature indifferent to its ends. 'For nothing was simply one thing. The other was the Lighthouse too' (Woolf, 2004: 152), James finally thinks.

In the letter to Fry, Woolf questions the authority of the artist's statement of intentionality because she knows that as art emerges from life as a problem to be solved, so it re-enters life as a newly discovered proposition to the world that will resonate with and change existence. The novel, which she claimed later, 'bubbled up', 'syllabing' itself into existence as she walked round Tavistock Square, brought her near to suicide as she revisited, in prolonged acts of memory, her relations with Leslie and Julia Stephen, her parents and with her siblings and half-siblings from their earlier marriages (Woolf, 1985: 81). Refashioning them in the guise of Mr and Mrs Ramsay, and fashioning a kind of composite of herself and her sister Vanessa Bell, the painter, she worked through her own profound and heretofore largely unacknowledged ambivalences towards them, and towards the straightened Victorian social world which had borne her, and Vanessa, as female children and therefore second-class citizens.

In this process, she consolidated her modernist aesthetic: that the creation of art is not a process where a coherent intentionality (vision) is realised externally through purposeful embodiment in a formal design, but is an ever-open and entangled process of the emergence of the new in every reading. She found this idea of emergence in the newest sciences of her time, in quantum theory, in the phenomenology of Husserl and Heidegger, the process philosophy of Whitehead, and in the perceptual horizons and fringes of becoming, the distributed idea of consciousness in William James. While Mr Ramsay's eidetic table suggests a Platonic or Romantic conjuring of an image or proposition in the mind's eye and its material realisation as design through artistic labour within a given medium, Woolf's 'I meant nothing' suggests an entangled and emergent understanding of the process of creativity that challenges the idea of art's autonomy and makes it fully part of the entanglement of subjects and objects in life as they enter each other's force fields.

The intensive, rhythmic and corporeally absorbed execution of Lily's painting models this process, as it shifts and loops and emerges like the sound of the waves into the vision that finally prompts her to lay down her brush exhausted. Lacking formal training in her discipline, unmarried and childless, Lily is patronised by both adult Ramsays for gender arrogance in her creative ambition and for gender inadequacy in her incapacity to make her life's work the sympathetic aggrandising of the male ego. Lily thinks to herself: 'It was an odd kind of road to be walking, this of painting. Out and out one went, further and further, until at last one seemed to be on a narrow plank, perfectly alone, over the sea' (Woolf, 2004: 265). The path is a precarious one, but for Woolf too, for whom every novel was an existential as well as formal experiment, only a recognition of the unpredictability of things, the complexity of the world, the need to fling oneself forward on the back of risk, might allow the generation of some agential force that might actually change the present and begin to shape an as yet unknown but better future.

Mr Ramsay's thinking is also walking, but over trails always already laid down by former thoughts, deepening the same furrows in field and brow, terrified of posthumous demise, of future eradication from his disciplinary canon. His 'extraordinary' and highly trained mind tramps

(continued)

(continued)

through the familiar paths of logic and metaphysics, hoping for a breakthrough, obsessed with his legacy, intent on getting to a pre-destined letter R in a line as straight as that with which he predicts the weather at the opening of the novel: it will rain; there will be no going to the lighthouse tomorrow; only an impossibly vague, a woman's mind, could tamper with those facts. He knows that, looking back, he will have been proved right. But his wife, Mrs Ramsay, dying in parentheses in 'Time Passes', the middle section of the novel also, characteristically, looks backward; she is already a ghost haunting a dying world. They are the last Victorians, struggling to come to terms with their broken faiths and the carnage and ruptures of the First World War. Unable to imagine a future, she consoles James, her youngest son, thereby enraging her husband, by insisting, without a scrap of evidence, that tomorrow it will be fine; they will go to the lighthouse.

James' mood is transfigured: in imagination he is already at the lighthouse, looking back. But this motif of future anteriority, this 'archive fever', projecting a future in order to preserve the present as past, is also Woolf's evocation of a world that cannot really look forward: that cannot change because it is blind to the way that war is mostly the outcome of a social system that sacrifices women to domestic slavery in order to render the male fit to shoulder the burdens of nation and empire and territorial control. Lily, like Woolf, struggling to become a modern woman, independent if hardly 'liberated', is at least free to make her own artistic conventions, to invent with absolute precision her own forms, to produce symbolic resonance in the 'vague, generalized' way that Woolf defends in her letter to Fry. Sitting at Mrs Ramsay's dining table, avoiding the gaze that demands she use her female charms to rescue Mr Tansley from social embarrassment, she moves the salt cellar across the tablecloth, realises she needs to find balance and perspective, to move the tree to the centre of the canvas, when suddenly, in a flash of insight, she recognises that 'she need not marry'.

Mr and Mrs Ramsay loom throughout as larger-than-life figures, icons of a vanished world, the Imago-like view of the parents through the small child's eyes. For the lighthouse that illuminates these stately moving figures from the past is the symbol and object of quest and recovery, a figure for those mysterious processes of memory and of its complex remodelling into art. Like the Godrevy Lighthouse at St Ives, they had remained at the centre of that 'great Cathedral space' of memory from which Woolf drew her art (Woolf, 1985: 81). The mood associated with these family summers suffuses the first long section of the novel: washed with the light of the coastal sky, the night-time candles illuminating the house without electricity, the sonorous rhythms of the sea, the echoing laughter and excited voices of children. At its centre was and is the lighthouse, with its steady and comforting beam, its perpetual pulse, like the consolatory rhythm of a nursery song, beating through and across the windows and doors of the slowly decaying house, and into the consciousness of the adult writer, Virginia Woolf. Entangled with the childhood annual rhythm of escape and adventure, the beam of light and the steady wash of water, life opening up to wider and freer horizons, the lighthouse on its steady rock, with its rhythmical beam, comes to stand too as a symbol of the capacity of the imagination, working on memory, to conjure up alternative and even utopian worlds. The moment that Woolf lost her beloved Godrevy Lighthouse was the beginning of a restless, lifelong, search for a place in the imagination, an inner world, where she might recover all those powerful feelings and sensations of childhood. The final 'message' of the lighthouse? That the truest paradises, forever lost, are those perpetually calling us to rebuild them.

Another major light in the literary canon is provided by Robert Louis Stevenson (1850–1894). He was better placed than most writers to draw inspiration from lighthouses, being practically the only member of the famous Stevenson dynasty of civil engineers not to make his living directly from their construction, which included his grandfather's involvement in the building of the Bell Rock Lighthouse. Stevenson is believed to have been inspired by the rocky island of Fidra in the Firth of Forth when writing *Treasure Island*, and he was also very familiar with the island of Erraid, off Mull (where David Balfour, the hero of his novel *Kidnapped*, is shipwrecked), having spent a number of weeks on the island while his family was working on the Dubh Artach Lighthouse, which was completed in 1872.

The lighthouse's use as a location for dramatic intrigue becomes apparent in crime-writer P. D. James' 2006 detective thriller, *The Lighthouse*, in which a Cornish offshore lighthouse, a luxury haven for the wealthy, is the setting for a series of murders. More recently, Alison Moore's hugely popular, award-winning novel, *The Lighthouse* (2012), uses as its epigraph a quotation from a short story by Muriel Spark that hints homologously at the problems experienced by the novel's protagonist, Futh, in being both lured and betrayed by women: 'She became a tall lighthouse sending out kindly beams which some took for welcome instead of warning against the rocks' (Spark, 2011: 63). In spite of the troubled history with his mother, Futh carries with him, 'as if it were his Saint Christopher' (Moore, 2012: 80), a small silver lighthouse which, as a perfume bottle with the traces of his mother's scent, is also a container of history and memory.

History and memory also play an important part in Ysanne Holt's comparison, below, of the fluid and diverse appropriations in which the figure of Grace Darling is represented in popular culture.

The centenary celebrations of Grace Darling and the Longstone Lighthouse

Ysanne Holt

The Longstone Lighthouse stands on one of the small, treeless Farne Islands 5 kilometres off the coast of Northumberland. Like many islands off the northern UK coastline, the windswept Farnes appear isolated and marginal. Cut off from the mainland and often difficult to reach, they seem far from modern existence and material concerns.

Such islands are often laden with accumulated myths and narratives. Yet, as the presence of the lighthouse asserts, they are also sites of everyday life and work. Far from being peripheral, they can be seen as unique centres of modernity. Island lighthouses such as the Longstone, first lit in 1826, are complex structures at the forefront of the technological knowledge of their day. Lighthouse islands therefore have a range of meanings and identities in relation to shifting historical circumstances.

Accounts of Grace Darling, the 1838 heroine of Longstone, describe the disaster on 7 September 1838 when, during a violent storm, the SS *Forfarshire*, sailing from Hull to Dundee, struck Big Harcar Rock in the Farnes and sank with forty-eight people on board. Courageously, Grace and her father rowed out in a coble, an open rowing boat, from Longstone, rescued nine survivors found clinging to the rock, including one woman still holding her two dead children, and rowed them back to the lighthouse to await lifeboats from Seahouses.

Artists soon produced popular, romantic impressions of the terrifying night-time rescue, the struggle to manage the coble amid turbulent seas, the half-drowned survivors and the lighthouse itself, a symbol of ultimate safety in the distance. Widely circulated, these images, accompanying press reports, poems and biographies, all contributed to the legend of Grace, her bravery and her modesty. A stream of visitors to the island included artist Henry Perlee Parker who, aided by the Darling family, reconstructed the scene within the lighthouse after the safe landing. In his painting, bedraggled victims are tended to by the family at their warm fireside in surroundings of respectable domesticity. The Darling family emerge as a model of simple virtue and dependability. In the late 1830s and 40s, a period of widespread political unrest, with calls for reform at home and revolution overseas, this was an aspiring ideal for a nation.

The 1930s centenary of Grace's heroism was a similarly conflicted era, with social inequality at home, and international tension and insecurity. The celebratory accounts of the rescue speak of the broader anxieties of that era. These social and political concerns found expression by focusing on Grace herself. Women in particular celebrated her life, with

Figure 43 The interior of Longstone Lighthouse, Fern Islands. Grace Darling and her parents administering to the unfortunate survivors saved from the wreck of the Forfarshire steam packet on the 7th September 1838. Engraving by A. J. Isaacs, from a painting by Henry Perlee Parker, 1866. © The Trustees of the British Museum.

the Birmingham-born journalist, playwright and feminist campaigner Constance Smedley perhaps the best known of these. Smedley founded the Grace Darling League in 1933, with plans to set up the first memorial museum. With its relics of the sea-heroine, pictures and artefacts from the lighthouse, the museum was opened in 1938 in Bamburgh, Grace's birthplace, on a site donated by local landowner and armaments manufacturer Lord Armstrong.

The 1932 study *Grace Darling and her Times* originated from Smedley's fascination with her subject's life on the Farne Islands and her place in a roll call of humanitarian Victorian women, including Florence Nightingale and Josephine Butler. Grace's character is seen as being formed by her isolated environment. Her moral strength mirrors the structure of the lighthouse itself. To Grace the lighthouse was 'a rock and a fortress . . . whereon and wherein the weakest might feel completely safe' (Smedley, 1932: 42). Her sense of duty is instilled through the 'light-keeper's calling', which bred individualism and compassion. In this, the Darling family possessed characteristics as 'pronounced as any of the great families in their part of the world': a reference to the

(continued)

(continued)

Dukes of Northumberland. The moral virtue of the family is thus viewed in relation to left-leaning 1930s perceptions of the stoical worker as a dying breed, cast aside in 'distressed areas' of the industrial and coastal north by the greed and moral bankruptcy of modern capitalism (here represented by local landowners).

Smedley's account of the lighthouse evokes the orderliness in Perlee Parker's painting, describing a well-furnished dwelling and circular bedrooms up the spiral staircase above the kitchen/living room, with neat bunks built into the walls. Moral propriety is recognised by bookshelves well-stocked with poetry and natural history, and self-discipline implied through daylight hours spent polishing the oil lamps and the metal reflectors and the common responsibility of the Light, keeping watch through the night.

Citing Alan Stevenson's 'Regulations', Smedley presents light-keeping as a matter of sober and industrious lighthouse keepers cleaning their lamps, 'remaining cleanly in their persons and linens, and orderly in their families' (1932: 61). But these were also people hardy enough to withstand northern gales: those nights 'when the furies around the Farnes were howling loud!' The sensory experience of an island storm is vividly described and surely witnessed personally:

> When one stepped into the lantern, one entered a dome of noise, resounding with the screaming of the wind, the clash and crepitation of the waves, the drumming of the rain upon the panes, a clanging uproar, booming, blaring, with perpetual salvos, wild alarums, reverberating until the ear was deafened and the senses stunned.
>
> (Smedley, 1932: 75)

Smedley's particular representation echoed popular visual and literary forms throughout the decade, including radio and television, with their mission to educate and unite the nation, to instil moral and cultural values, and to influence and shape regional cultures. Amid this democratising zeal, at least two radio and television plays about Grace were produced, both written by women.

One of these, Yvette Pienne's *The Fame of Grace Darling*, was broadcast on a Sunday evening in 1939, shortly before television was closed down for the duration of the war (9 July, 21.05). In her television debut, the actress Wendy Hiller played Grace, and though no attempt was made to provide an authentic regional accent, for fear of unintelligibility, the main setting of the play, the lighthouse kitchen/living room, was painstakingly modelled on Perlee Parker's painting. But Grace Wyndham Goldie, the reviewer for *The Listener*, was far from complimentary: 'The writing was banal; the characters stereotyped; the plot non-existent; the whole thing an essay in outmoded sentimentality which came near to burlesquing itself'

(Goldie, 1939: 151). Goldie lived in Liverpool in the early 1930s, where she delivered Workers Educational Association lectures to unemployed miners in Lancashire villages – an experience rendering her especially critical of crass sentimentality.

A reformist agenda from another northern professional, Mary D. or Dorothy Sheridan, underpinned a radio play performed in the previous year, on the exact centenary of the rescue. *Longstone Light*, broadcast by the 'Regional Programme Northern', was introduced by the new Bamburgh museum's honorary curator, and produced by Cecil McGivern (5 September 1938, 20.15). McGivern was from Tyneside, a member of Newcastle's People's Theatre in the early 1930s, and a graduate of Durham University (Vall, 2007: 184–185), and he supported the use of dialect in regional broadcasting and the celebration of local history and popular culture.

Like Goldie, Sheridan was also connected with the northern working class. One of the first women medical students to graduate from Liverpool University, she worked in paediatrics, observing the effects of deprivation on children in the poorer areas of Manchester. Sheridan was also, however, descended from her namesake, the 18th-century playwright. Through involvement with Liverpool Repertory Theatre, she wrote plays on the subject of women, including *The Brontës at Haworth*, and *The Courageous Sex*, on women doctors and feminism. A strong social conscience, and an identification with northern women in particular, made Grace Darling an inevitable subject.

Sheridan's professional focus in the pre-NHS years of the 1930s underlines another dimension of the wider interest in Grace: her death from tuberculosis at the age of 26. A 1938 issue of *The Children's Newspaper* devoted to 'The Heroine of the Longstone Lighthouse', blamed the unopenable lighthouse window for the fact that Grace, her constitution weakened by the long-term effects of her heroic rescue, lay suffocating in an airless room for too long before she was taken to Bamburgh, where she died, in 1843. The article's author observed reassuringly that tuberculosis had been largely conquered in the hundred years since Grace's death: 'no more rooms in the land are built with no window that will open' (*The Children's Newspaper*, 1938: 7).

To ensure remembrance for her 'golden deed', the same paper noted that the league planned to plant Grace Darling trees in London and at British ports throughout the empire. This was a slightly odd tribute, given the treelessness of the Farnes, but it was clearly intended to link a Northumberland island, its lighthouse, and its famous inhabitant with national and imperial ideals of duty, security and self-sacrifice in the decade between two world wars. To make that symbolism even clearer, Grace herself was pictured (by artist Maxwell Armfield, Constance Smedley's husband), in statuesque pose upon the rocky shore of Longstone just in front of (and supplanting) its lighthouse.

(continued)

> *(continued)*
>
> Both in the 1800s and the 1930s then, a range of narratives and visual representations of Grace address ideal national, regional, class and gender identities, and use the meanings of the lighthouse, as a bastion of stability and security, to promote social and cultural ideals and to affirm the strength of the nation state.

Complex gender issues, and fluid visions of the lighthouse as a place of both safety and danger, also run through a recent novel (and film), *The Light Between Oceans* by M. L. Stedman (2012). This tells the story of Tom, an Australian serviceman, returning from the First World War to take up a post on the island of Janus as a lighthouse keeper. Such postings were commonly reserved for veterans, with the recognition that they provided a safe and peaceful haven:

> Janus Light was the last sign of Australia he had seen as his troopship steamed for Egypt in 1915. The smell of the eucalyptus had wafted offshore from Albany, and when the scent faded away he was suddenly sick at the loss of something he didn't know he could miss. Then, hours later, true and steady, the light, with its five second flash, came into view – his homeland's furthest reach – and its memory stayed with him through the years of hell that followed, like a farewell kiss.
>
> (Stedman, 2012: 24)

But the story is more concerned with the way that the liminal, isolated space creates an ambiguous world in which reality can slip away. On leave, Tom meets Isabel, 'who lit the way for him back into life, after all the years of death' (ibid: 414). But after three miscarriages the couple's hopes of making a family on Janus founder until a baby is miraculously washed ashore, to become 'the light' in their lives. They call her Lucy ('Lucy means "light", so it's perfect, isn't it?' (ibid: 137)). But when the situation goes awry, Tom's omission of this information from the lighthouse logbook is shocking, confounding an expectation that like the lighthouse itself, he will be a reliable, upstanding citizen: 'Being a lighthouse keeper's a position of trust, you know. Our whole country – the whole world, if you want to look at it that way – depends on them being men of good character: honest, decent' (ibid: 347). Isabel also learns that the lighthouse on Janus is itself two-faced: 'A lighthouse warns of danger – tells people to keep their distance. She had mistaken it for a place of safety' (ibid: 308).

The well-worn associations of the lighthouses in literature also feature in numerous films and television programmes. In the Jean-Jacques Beineix's cult movie *Diva* (1981), the ingénue Jules, pursued by lethal gangsters, is taken to the safe refuge of the Phare de Gattevill by the enigmatic Gorodish and Alba. In Woody Allen's *Vicky Cristina Barcelona* (2008), the lighthouse at Avilés, Asturias, Spain serves as a metaphor for the liminal identities and relationships of the film's protagonists (Costa, 2012). And in John Carpenter's horror movie,

Figure 44 Cape Bruny Lighthouse interior. Photograph: Tim Edensor.

The Fog (1980), the revenants of drowned passengers and crew on a ship deliberately sunk arrive to seek revenge, and gravitate to the Point Reyes Lighthouse in California – ghostly associations that are further investigated in another form of media, namely on the website *Angels and Ghosts: Exploring Ghost and Spirit Phenomena* (nd), which has a special section devoted to haunted lighthouses.

In other cinematic and televisual representations, the ambiguity of the lighthouse is expressed by its interior space. With its helter-skelter staircase and circular, vertically stacked rooms, it offers an idiosyncratic home, which readily becomes, as geographer Peter Adey observes, a joyfully anarchic environment in a children's television programme. This *unheimlich* interior is further explored in Peter Hutchings' examination of the lighthouses that have been utilised as locations for various British horror movies.

Going round the twist

Peter Adey

We are used to thinking about lighthouses as highlights, designed to be seen from a distance. Lighthouses are by implication vertical and prominent.

(continued)

(continued)

They sit on outcrops jutting into the sea; they project light into space and into the dark. But in their assertions upwards and outwards, they are not at all straightforward. The social and cultural gestures of lighthouses are, in fact, anything but linear. A ribbon of paint often climbs these structures. They twist and turn, helter-skelter-like.

We can, therefore, explore the lighthouse as a perceptibly odd space where odd things tend to happen. I do not mean oddness in the sense of what is not normal or what might be judged morally or ethically, but odd in the sense that the lighthouse reveals, animates and embraces difference. Indeed, the lighthouse is architecturally convoluted: it comprises a mixture of settings. It is a household – a domestic interior for solitude or family life. It is simultaneously a space of work and maintenance. A lighthouse is tended to, or kept; the light is cared for. As nodes in the communication networks of maritime, marital and non-marital relations, and perched on the threshold of land and sea, the lighthouse provides a place of betweenness.

Many lighthouses go down into rock, and some, simultaneously, into other worlds. Children's television has looked underneath the lighthouse to express this. The most well-known example is *Fraggle Rock*, Jim Henson's live action puppet series from the 1980s. The series was set underneath a lighthouse in a miniature subterranean world of 'fraggles': fun loving creatures who live in a network of caves under the lighthouse. They stick to a 30-minute working week and live with 'doozers', a smaller species of creatures more dedicated to work and construction. The humans living and working above them are known as 'gargs'.

The show begins with the camera hovering above a lighthouse in Cornwall, before spiralling slowly down to peer in through the skylight of the lighthouse keeper's cottage. A bearded lighthouse keeper sits playing chess on his own in a nautically adorned room, while his shaggy dog looks on. The camera drops into a hole in the bottom of the room, behind a stove and under a plastic plumbing fixture, where it follows the back of a purple fraggle hopping and dancing its way through a tunnel into a vast cave of singing fraggles.

There is maybe more to this world than meets the eye. The fraggles regularly connect to the outside – 'our world' – which they call 'outerspace', and seem to live in symbiosis with other creatures. In many respects, just as the lighthouse sits on the seam between land and sea, the terrestrial and maritime, the fraggles' lighthouse is a conduit to, or a rip in the fabric that separates different worlds.

Broadcasting *Fraggle Rock* to other domestic markets demonstrated some clever transposition of worlds too. The international nature of the programme meant that the original location of the programme in a lighthouse (St Anthony's Lighthouse near Falmouth in Cornwall) underwent some translation. In Germany, as in the United States, *Fraggle Rock* could be found beneath a workshop. In these non-UK series, the visual movement into the other world starts by looking through the workshop window, before making a similar subterranean plunge.

While *Fraggle Rock* illuminates the relationship between the lighthouse and the fantastical through other realms and regions, other portrayals of the lighthouse also spin out from its vortical, helter-skelter form. Lighthouses go up, certainly, but like the stairs that spiral through the internal structure, the stories winding around the lighthouse's form highlight the strange and the topsy-turvy.

'Have you ever, ever felt like this, when strange things happen? Are you going round the twist?' These are the opening lines of the syndicated Australian children's television programme, *Round the Twist* (Edgar, 1989–2001). The programme, first broadcast by the BBC in 1989, featured a family headed by a widower, Tony Twist, who took his children to live in a lighthouse in Port Niranda (the lighthouse was actually at Split End Point, located in Aireys Inlet, on the Great Ocean Road in Victoria). The series was based on stories written by author Paul Jennings, who also wrote the first two series' screenplays. Strange things do happen inside and outside the lighthouse, which appeared to be haunted by multiple spectral presences and happenings.

Round the Twist, however, is probably more suggestive of the liminal and surreal in adolescent fantasy than of more traditional forms of ghostly hauntings. In most episodes, strange powers are given to everyday objects. Lipstick passed on by a gypsy woman empowers whoever wears it with irresistible attraction. There is a remote control that can control living things. There are magical under(wonder)pants. The series is a celebration of the carnivalesque in all of its excesses. Things often go too far, and wrong, and teenage embarrassment is a common theme. There are even hints of grotesque bodily deformations in the opening sequences, which warp the children's images like a fairground mirror.

But while the lighthouse provides a helical space describing warped and twisted attachments, some connections are more regular, tethering the lighthouse to more familiar stories of gendered domesticity. When I think about lighthouses, I often recall a book from my own childhood, *The Lighthouse Keeper's Lunch* (1977), written and illustrated by Ronda and David Armitage.

In a series of books about the lighthouse keeper Mr Grinling and his family, the story goes a bit like this. The lighthouse keeper lives in a cottage on the mainland, disconnected from the lighthouse. When he rows out each day to tend to the light, his wife, Mrs Grinling, sends his lunchtime sandwiches from their cottage to the lighthouse. They have rigged a clever

(continued)

(continued)

contraption: a washing line is strung between the two buildings, and his wife winches his lunch hamper out over the frothing sea and the sharp rocks below. Unfortunately for the lighthouse keeper, each day seagulls steal his lunch as it slips by on the line. His wife experiments with different sandwiches to see if any will prove unattractive to them. Mustard does not work. Eventually she puts his cat in the basket, which does little to scare the seagulls, but it does scare the cat, jittery from being floated so high over the rough sea.

This delightful story of a lighthouse keeper's rumbling stomach is also representative of traditional notions of the family, and familial labour relations and practices. Presumably the lighthouse keeper insists that his sandwiches are made fresh and dry, otherwise he could have rowed with them in the morning, instead of expecting his wife to keep to the temporal regularities of his work-time. Yet this apparent straightforwardness is somewhat at odds with the lighthouse's resistance to the domestic tether.

The capacity of the liminal, spiralling space of the lighthouse to challenge conventions rather than conform to them, is perhaps not at first obvious given the orthodoxy of *The Lighthouse Keeper's Lunch*. But as seen above, lighthouses have inspired many imaginative leaps. Some analysts have asserted that disruptions to hetero-normativity can be found in the twisting narrative of Virginia Woolf's (1927) *To the Lighthouse*, previously discussed by Patricia Waugh. Within the novel, we see the erosion and undermining of traditional heterosexual marriage and the portrayal of implicit homosexual passions and relations. Woolf displays what other scholars have called 'queer time' (Kavaloski, 2014) by refusing to hold the narration of the story and its characters to traditional and hetero-normative conventions, or other linear and singular perspectives. The narrative especially questions romance and marriage as a source of female fulfilment (Kavaloski, 2014). Thus, while *The Lighthouse Keeper's Lunch* presents the lighthouse, and the labour it requires, as reflecting the rhythm and regularity of the gendered dynamics of heterosexual family life, Woolf allows the lighthouse to express difference.

These works invite us to consider a different view of the lighthouse. The lighthouse might be most obviously read through its external phallic and vertical prominence, jutting upwards and spraying light outwards to mark territory and steer and regulate maritime mobilities. But it also has inner, interior worlds, representations of fantastic societies, expressions of adolescent desire, and alternative gendered and sexual relations. Lighthouses are not straight at all: they twist and corkscrew, turning and subverting normative conceptions of time, space and gender.

The haunted lighthouses of death

Peter Hutchings

It appears to be in the nature of lighthouse keepers to go mad, or to disappear in mysterious circumstances. At least, this is what an array of British films and television programmes featuring lighthouses would have us believe. To be fair, there are some real-life historical precedents for both possibilities. In 1801, one of the two keepers servicing the Smalls Lighthouse off the Welsh coast died of natural causes. His fellow keeper, fearful that he might be accused of murder if he pitched the corpse into the sea, kept the body close at hand for an extended period while awaiting a relief ship. By the time it arrived, he was by all accounts in a sorry mental state and unrecognisable to his acquaintances. A more gothic-tinged (and possibly less reliable) version of the story has him boxing up the corpse and placing it outside the lighthouse, only for the action of the severe weather to free the corpse's arm, which then proceeded to beckon to the increasingly disturbed survivor.

As for lighthouse keepers being spirited away, as Chris Watson observes above, one needs look no further than the Flannan Isles Lighthouse in the Outer Hebrides from which, in 1900, all three of its keepers disappeared. Subsequent speculation has generated scenarios involving murder and suicide, sea monsters and, more recently, alien abduction. Wilfrid Wilson Gibson's 1912 poem, *Flannan Isle*, told from the viewpoint of a rescue party, features a Mary Celeste-like scene of abrupt and mysterious abandonment:

> Aye: though we hunted high and low,
>
> And hunted everywhere,
>
> Of the three men's fate we found no trace
>
> Of any kind in any place,
>
> But a door ajar, and an untouched meal,
>
> And an overtoppled chair.
>
> (lines 83–88)

So resonant are these lines that they ended up being quoted in 'Horror of Fang Rock', a 1977 *Doctor Who* story (Dicks, 1977) set on a lighthouse besieged by an extraterrestrial. However, it seems that no such scene of domestic eeriness was actually found in the Flannan Isles Lighthouse. Gibson's poem turned out to be an early example of someone talking up the mysteriousness of

(continued)

(continued)

lighthouses (and, for the record, the quotation fails to capture the events in 'Horror of Fang Rock' as well).

The first significant British lighthouse film was *The Phantom Light*, directed by Michael Powell in 1935. This established a template for creepy lighthouse movies, in both narrative and style. Reviewing the film, novelist Graham Greene (1935) connected it to Gibson's poem, and one can see why since, in the form of a supernatural-themed comedy thriller, *The Phantom Light* manages to combine disappearing lighthouse keepers with a mad one (Parkinson, 1995: 9). In the first volume of his autobiography, Powell admits 'I am a sucker for lighthouses. The lonelier and more inaccessible the better' (Powell, 1986: 236).

In this case, the inaccessible lighthouse, like the Smalls Lighthouse, is located off the Welsh coast. A new chief lighthouse keeper arrives to find that two of his predecessors have vanished in possibly supernatural circumstances, while a third has apparently lost his mind. To make matters worse, the local community believes that the lighthouse is haunted and that a phantom light periodically appears to lure passing ships onto the rocks. The insane keeper is prone to wandering around the lighthouse and attacking anyone he encounters. However, after various plot shenanigans, a rational explanation finally emerges: wreckers are at work, intent on claiming the insurance on the boats lost to the phantom light, and the mad keeper is not really mad but one of the conspirators.

Alongside its narrative evocation of madness and mystery, *The Phantom Light* offers a visual exploration of the lighthouse and its exterior and interior spaces. The emphasis throughout is on awkwardness and unfriendliness. Not only is this building difficult to reach, located on a storm-swept island; once there, it is difficult to get into, with the sole entrance achieved via a perilous-looking rope ladder. Once inside, it is difficult to move around the claustrophobic interior, or even to be able to perceive or understand it as a coherent spatial whole.

Central to the spatial discomfort is the lighthouse's verticality and the way in which its various rooms – domestic and work-related – are dispersed across different levels in a manner that is neither rational nor predictable. This is not a comfortable, integrated location, but one that is disarranged and uneasy, with a madman in one room, technology in others, and domesticated living quarters elsewhere. The spiral staircase that links these spaces has long been used in cinema as an image of mental instability, particularly when filmed from above, but in *The Phantom Light* (and in later lighthouse movies) it also provides a confined setting in which conflicts and tensions emanating from the various discrete spaces within the lighthouse are enacted. Suspense is also generated on the staircase, for who knows what awaits you around the next bend? This necessarily entails a series of up-down movements which can involve fighting one's way upwards through the lighthouse, defending the light from below, or bodies falling downwards. In the case of *The Phantom Light*, the final downward movement is provided by the villain, as he jumps to his death from the top of the lighthouse.

Inaccessibility, discomfort, inexplicability – these qualities prevail in later lighthouse movies along with an emphasis on ghosts and on madness. The more distant the lighthouse from the shore, and from the rationality and social integration that the mainland represents, the more extreme its dysfunction. For example, in the wartime comedy thriller *Back Room Boy* (Mason, 1942), the lighthouse is located on an uninhabited isle on the far edge of the remote (and fictional) Orrey Islands off the north-east coast of Scotland, which are described in the film as 'the bleakest collection of desolate rocks in the whole of the United Kingdom'. Here the lighthouse has been turned into a meteorological station, and when the new meteorologist (played by Arthur Askey) arrives from London, the locals inform him, in the manner of *The Phantom Light*, that the lighthouse island is haunted by a water kelpie or spirit. 'You'll go mad,' says one of the locals matter-of-factly, 'They all do.'

This time, the alleged hauntings turn out to be the work of a Nazi fifth columnist (something of a convention in British cinema of this period, with Nazified ghosts featuring in *The Ghost of St Michael's* (Varnel, 1941) and *The Ghost Train* (Forde, 1941) as well). Alongside this story, *Back Room Boy* accentuates the masculine qualities of the rough-hewn working and living spaces within the lighthouse: this is not a location suited for women. Indeed, the main reason that the Askey character has travelled there is to escape from females after an unhappy love life. The sole female who gets into the lighthouse in *The Phantom Light* is a distracting and unwanted presence, but *Back Room Boy* takes this to another level when a veritable host of women, models escaping from a torpedoed ship, invade the lighthouse. The result is a progressive deterioration in Askey's control of the interior space, with objects mysteriously moving from one room to another and then people also disappearing from rooms in a manner that should not be possible. 'Who built this lighthouse?' asks Askey in exasperation. 'Jaspar Maskelyne?' Maskelyne was a famous stage illusionist of the day, and this reference to him underlines the extent to which the lighthouse has by this stage become a truly uncanny location.

Offering something similar, albeit in more sombre hues, is *Tower of Terror* (Huntington, 1941), a German-set thriller in which the lighthouse keeper, played by British actor Wilfrid Lawson, is a genuinely disturbed creature who, it turns out, murdered his wife many years before and buried her beneath the lighthouse. When a female refugee shows up looking for sanctuary, he insanely believes her to be his wife returned from the dead. Critics were not kind to what, at the time, *The New York Times* described as

(continued)

(continued)

a 'dire little melodrama' in which Lawson 'gives a ludicrously overwrought portrait of insanity' (T. S., 1942: 11). Be this as it may, *Tower of Terror* effectively makes a connection between the isolation of the lighthouse itself and the social disengagement of its keeper, and further maps the internal geography of the building onto the keeper's disturbed psyche. In true gothic fashion, the psychologically repressed secret of his wife's death is finally discovered beneath the lighthouse's floor.

More male isolation in a lighthouse, of a considerably more upmarket kind, appears in the Boulting Brothers' *Thunder Rock* (1942), set on Lake Michigan but filmed in Britain. Here the keeper, played by Michael Redgrave, has isolated himself in despair at the state of the world. He is visited by a series of ghosts – which, in the film's general eschewal of gothic and melodramatic elements, might or might not be psychological projections – who challenge him, ultimately successfully, to re-engage with society in a clear, propagandistic warning against the dangers of political and military isolationism.

Even after the war, lighthouses retained their association with madness. Beachy Head Lighthouse in East Sussex forged a surprising connection with megalomania twice in this period, first in *Dick Barton at Bay* (Grayson, 1950), in which it is the base from which the dastardly supervillain operates his Death Ray, and second in 'The Girl Who was Death' episode of the cult television series *The Prisoner* (Tomblin, 1967). In this episode, another megalomaniac, one in the habit of dressing up as Napoleon, has transformed the lighthouse itself into a missile with which he plans to destroy London.

When the horror genre finally appropriated the lighthouse setting in the 1970s, things became considerably darker and nastier. The aforementioned *Doctor Who* lighthouse story 'Horror of Fang Rock' arrived during a period when the series was at its most gothic and is now seen as one of the bleakest of all *Doctor Who* stories, for this is where the Doctor fails to save anyone other than himself and his companion Leela: everyone else dies. All the visual conventions of lighthouse drama are present: conflicts staged on the vertical, interactions on the stairs, characters moving in and out of different kinds of spaces at different levels. But the emphasis is much more now on attack and counter-attack, and on death or survival. With the alien controlling the staircase, every room becomes a fatal trap (with the Doctor surviving only by climbing out of the lighthouse), and the alien's inexorable movement upwards through the building threatens universal extinction.

The more adult-centred British horror films, *Tower of Evil* (O'Connolly, 1972) and *Lighthouse* (Hunter, 1999), offer lighthouses that are already – or soon will be – decommissioned. In each case, psychopathic killers move in, and the lighthouse is presented as an appropriate setting for their madness. The survivalist horror purveyed here requires constant spatial entrapment, and the lighthouses in both films exploit their settings to this end. In the case of *Lighthouse* in particular, the film is largely structured around a gradual movement up through the building as opportunities to hide from an apparently unstoppable killer gradually run out and a final stand has to be taken at the top of the tower. In contrast, the general movement in *Tower of Evil* is downwards, into caves beneath the lighthouse, although there is also a memorable scene in which a severed human head bounces down the lighthouse's stairs. Both films end explosively. The lighthouse in *Tower of Evil* is completely destroyed as the result of a fire caused by the struggle for survival, while the building in *Lighthouse* is destroyed in order to defeat the killer.

We seem to have come a long way here from the more innocent stories of *The Phantom Light* and *Back Room Boy* and their gentler invocation of uncanny feelings in relation to lighthouses. Yet for all the blood and thunder exhibited by horror's lighthouses, many of the themes and stylistic conventions exhibited by earlier films carry over into the more contemporary work. In this respect, it is worth considering what might seem like a throwback to an older type of cinema, and that is the Demi Moore vehicle *Half Light* (Rosenberg, 2006).

In this film, the character played by Moore travels to a remote Scottish lighthouse, where she falls in love with the keeper, only to find that he had committed suicide some years before, after killing his wife and her lover. It is, therefore, a haunted lighthouse narrative. But then we discover that there is no ghost: instead, this is a conspiracy led by Moore's husband to drive his wife mad. So we are sent back to the false ghosts of *The Phantom Light* and *Back Room Boy*. Finally, however, the real ghost of the lighthouse keeper shows up to defeat the conspiracy. Thus, for the first time, we are presented with an unambiguously haunted lighthouse (as opposed to the very ambiguous ghosts found in *Thunder Rock*).

Previous film and television lighthouses, for all their apparently haunted qualities, were fashioned in relation to psychological premises rather than supernatural ones. What we are left with at the end of *Half Light* is a sense of this particular lighthouse as uninhabitable, with the living characters either dying in the lighthouse – one of the conspirators throwing himself from the top of the building – or retreating from it. It is this difference in *Half Light*, its ostensible exceptionality, which underlines what has been going on elsewhere, notably the presentation of lighthouses as spaces that challenge human perceptions and which, for all the clarity and value of the lighthouse's function, are dangerous places to be. *Half Light*'s final message – leave the lighthouse to the dead – might not be very practical, but it certainly works for the films and television programmes discussed here.

These filmic uses of the lighthouse also extend to the use of video and film by artists. Julie Westerman shows how a sense of disorientation is produced by the multi-perspectival, swooping camera work in Catherine Yass' film of the extraordinary Royal Sovereign Lighthouse, a work that honours the dynamic elements surrounding the structure.

228 Lighthouse, *Catherine Yass, 2011*

Figure 45 Wish you were here – Douglas Head, by Julie Westerman, 2017
  © Julie Westerman. Postcard and watercolour.

Also see Plate 7.

Uncanny architecture

Lighthouse, Catherine Yass, 2011

Julie Westerman

The Royal Sovereign Lighthouse, built in the 1970s, is a distinctive and curious structure. Its striking form is best considered in sculptural terms, as a stack of geometric shapes appearing both monumental and unbalanced. A single vertical central pillar rises direct from the seabed to 28 metres above the surface of the ocean, and is crossed with a heavy rectangular slab of a platform, finished with a circular tower and topped with the delicate tracery of the lantern house windows.

Standing 5 miles out from the coast from Bexhill on Sea, the lighthouse appears remote, often lost in the sea mist; on a good day, it is just within the field of vision. As such it has always been an object of fascination and attraction. Concerned with capturing the psychological and affective qualities of architecture, artist Catherine Yass focused on it in her film *Lighthouse* (2011).

This single-screen projection flows between three viewpoints: from a boat, from the air and from beneath the water. Beginning at sea level with the journey to the lighthouse, the horizon splits the screen, depicting

Figure 46 Lighthouse (East), by Catherine Yass, 2011. © Catherine Yass. All Rights Reserved, DACS 2017.

Also see Plate 8.

only sea and sky. In spite of the greyness, there is a silvery allure from the light reflecting on the water. Our encounter with the lighthouse itself begins in the air with a dizzying, circling shot dive-bombing or mobbing the structure. Our view then shifts to the perspective of the bobbing boat, before diving beneath the waves. At times, the film is rotated through 180 degrees and the structure emerges upside down. Air replaces water,

(continued)

(continued)

and the lighthouse emerges framed against the sky, appearing untethered, floating, more like a space station than a lighthouse. We are returned to the sea twisting and diving, perhaps drowning, challenging our certainty that the lighthouse is a fixed point in the storm. The boundaries between the elements become blurred, engendering a heightening sense of awe and isolation, as well as soliciting an appreciation for the construction of the lighthouse in this raging environment, and its strangeness and precariousness. The whole experience leaves us disorientated and displaced.

The beam's perspective: *Phare*, Ron Haselden, 2008

Ron Haselden's work *Phare* was sparked by an image on a box of matches, showing a simplistic representation of a lighthouse and a beam of light. Haselden's resulting sculpture in Plouër-sur-Rance, France, is a three-dimensional representation of this diagram. *Phare* stretches across an undulating field with dense, dark chestnut trees merging into the lush, green grass. Two converging lines of black, metal poles march up the rise of the field, spaced at decreasing intervals. Tensioned between the poles, three parallel strands of zingy yellow twine zigzag above the line of sight. The vibrant yellow lines radiate against the background of verdant green,

Figure 47 Phare, by Ron Haselden, 2008. A 60-metre-long sculpture constructed in fisherman's cord and steel rods. Au Pont Mévault. Plouër-sur-Rance, France.

Also see Plate 9.

> describing a level beam of light that resonates with historic artistic renderings of perspective. Visitors approach the sculpture from the broad open end of the triangle, with the twine crossing above head height, and the narrowing beam increasing in intensity overhead to the point of origin, where forward movement must stop. Along the way, the undulations of the field mean that the eyes meet the twine beam; and so, the linear geometric imposition confronts the irregular materiality of the world with which it coexists.

In an earlier contribution, James Purdon explored how the ultimate 'painter of light', J. M. W. Turner, celebrated the modern technological utility of the lighthouse while also rendering the surrounding seascapes as dynamic and atmospheric. The lighthouse has also been a popular subject for modernist painters, including John Piper, Eric Ravilious and Edward Hopper, as well as legions of professional and amateur photographers. In his illustrative volume of vintage postcards, Christopher Nicholson (2010) traces the history of lighthouses as popular romantic icons, whether sepia, black and white, or hand-tinted with colour. Such popular photographic representations persist as lighthouses become

Figure 48 Harbour Scene, Newhaven, by John Piper, c.1937 (watercolour, body colour, gouache, collage, pen, brush and black). Credit: Private Collection / Bridgeman Images. © The Piper Estate / DACS 2017.

Also see Plate 10.

'The Weather is Lovely'

Julie Westerman

Figure 49 The Weather is Lovely – George Olson aground at Cape Disappointment Lighthouse, by Julie Westerman, 2017 © Julie Westerman. Watercolour.

Also see Plate 11.

Figure 50 The Weather is Lovely – Shipwreck by Lighthouse, by Julie Westerman, 2017 © Julie Westerman. Watercolour.

Also see Plate 12.

venerated objects of cultural heritage and nostalgia. Yet artist Julie Westerman subverts the romance attached to these postcards in her series 'The Weather is Lovely', revealing the ambiguity of the lighthouse's location and its location in a liminal space of danger.

Earlier discussions from Douglas Davies, David Wilkinson and Tom Mole highlighted the metaphorical power of the lighthouse as emblematic of the illumination bestowed by God or by the Enlightenment and scientific progress, offering a beacon of light to guide us to safety. Such visions of light speak of its elemental power amid the storm, but also the possibility that disaster may strike and that it will be replaced by an all-encompassing, primeval darkness. These themes are explored in Rona Lee's powerful installation, and are supplemented by stories of shipwreck that highlight the experience of the women who wait and grieve.

Figure 51 the encircling of a shadow, by Rona Lee, 2001. Credit: Steve Tanner.

the encircling of a shadow
The house of light made dark
Rona Lee

Wednesday 4 December 2016, four days before the solstice, the darkest time of the year. As I write, the Christmas lights of Mousehole Harbour, Cornwall – transforming boats into whales, serpents and galleons – are dimmed to mark the anniversary of the Penlee lifeboat disaster, the date in

(continued)

(continued)

1981 when the *Solomon Browne*, all eight of its volunteer Mousehole crew and eight other lives were lost at sea in 15-metre-high waves.

Situated at physical and symbolic peripheries, coastal locations are places of transition where the lines between liquid and solid, harbour and high sea, domestic and alien, moored and mobile are both apparent and made mutable. In 2001, I was invited by Newlyn Art Gallery, Cornwall, a publicly funded contemporary art space, to make a new body of context-responsive artwork. Like a detective assembling a body of evidence, I wove a range of 'finds' together in a meditation on the littoral as a space of difference.

My first action was to return to the gallery a painting, *The Departure of the Fleet for the North* by Walter Langley, a member of a colony of '*plein air*' painters active in the area c.1880–1940, whose work the gallery was originally built to house. It is striking how many of the Newlyn School works depict women in doorways, at windows or on the shoreline. Rooted in the historical division of coastal communities along gender lines – women at home, men at sea – they belong to a plethora of representations of women as those who wait. Opposite the painting, I installed a graphic that listed ninety women's names, each the name of a local fishing boat, taken from a computer print-out of the contemporary register of shipping: Ann, Anna, Amy, Alisha, Carol, Catherine, Charlotte, Clair, Daisy; traditional associations of women and home continue to run deep.

Upstairs, video footage of a local lighthouse, its rays made black by reversing the black and white spectrum, filled the end wall of the gallery. As the rotating smear of darkness that replaced its beam reached its zenith, a silhouette of a woman appeared and vanished in tandem on the adjacent wall; her ghostly figure intermittently overlaid by the shadow of visitors caught in the actual beam of the projector.

The origins of this work lay partly in the experience of visiting Lamorna Cove, the nearest point to where the *Solomon Brown* went down. Walking along the coastal path as the light was fading, I reached the nearby Tater Du (or Black Rock) Lighthouse: 1965 optic 4th order (250 mm) rotating, character Fl (3) 15 seconds, intensity 96,900 candela, range of light 20 nautical miles. As I stood looking towards it, the light, which had until that moment been directed out to sea, swung round – catching me in its beam and casting my shadow onto the surrounding landscape.

Historically, the Cornish coast was infamous (perhaps erroneously) for the practice of shining 'false' lights to lure ships carrying plunder on to the rocks – the stuff of gothic fiction and contemporary tourism. How much more preternatural still to transform a lighthouse, symbol of guidance and instrument of safe return, into an active source of Cimmerian blackness? Light and house: how seamlessly one marries with the other. The simple act of reversing black and white, light and dark, generates the literally and existentially *unheimlich* (the unhomely, the familiar made strange) – a beam of dystopian darkness, which, in its confusion of homecoming and horror, might sear the imagination.

How too might darkness generate a shadow? What of the figure caught in its uncanny sweep, loyal vigil keeper or 'witch of the place', siren or patience personified? The elision of women and home plays an axiomatic role within patriarchal narratives of seafaring and exploration but, as shipwreck maps reveal, the waters closest to shore are the most hazardous, a circumstance which might be said to chime with Freud's analysis of the uncanny disquiet evoked by the female body itself – simultaneously symptom and sentinel, the wanderer's abject other.

Mine was a project in which inversions of function and form, a tangling of the symbolic and the material, active and passive, benign and malign, were central, generating a critical and affective confusion between warning and welcome, watchtower and watchkeeper. The house from which darkness blooms is a place of excess and absence, a space of double dealing and a harbinger of the repressed.

the encircling of a shadow was a body of performance, video and installation work (discussed here in part) exhibited at three locations – Penlee House, Penzance; the foreshore Newlyn; and Newlyn Art Gallery 12 May–9 June 2001.

Besides such installations, the lighthouse itself has become a venue for artistic works referring to its previous function and location. We have read of the complex light waves produced by Jio Shimizu at Tungenes Fyr in Norway. The lighthouse at Rubjerg Knude in northern Denmark currently transforms the tower's interior into a giant kaleidoscope that casts a dancing sea of light as it reflects the Sun's rays. An LED was placed in Perch Rock Lighthouse in New Brighton to send Morse code messages naming those lost at sea, including the souls who perished on the *Titanic*. Thus, beyond the abundance of historic representations, lighthouses continue to inspire new creative responses.

360°

Veronica Strang

One of the key things that an interdisciplinary endeavour brings to our understanding of light is that the perceptual separation between academic 'expertise' and human experience is illusory. Alternate disciplinary reflections on light, from the arts and humanities and from the social sciences, demonstrate that the analytic thought through which science 'deconstructs' light is not separate from – indeed it is intimately entangled with – the totality of a much more complex human engagement with light, in which phenomenological experience, culture, knowledge and imagination are equally important, and which includes, for some, a spiritual search for meaning.

This point is trenchantly made by Tom McLeish, who provides a parable about the capacity of music to reconnect science with the wholeness of human experience. His piece reminds us that, while we may look at the lighthouse through focused disciplinary lenses, our eyes, our bodies, our minds and our memories situate this specific gaze within a larger, much messier and more complex engagement with an object that retains multiple meanings and purposes. As philosopher H. Martyn Evans observes, the lighthouse's material, spatial and symbolic qualities inspire 'wonder' both in daylight and at night. Thus our 360° journey around the lighthouse brings us back to the original point of our interdisciplinary experiment: that bringing together disciplinary ways of seeing from all points of the compass allows us to reconnect and synthesise different understandings and to provide a deeper and more holistic view that is genuinely 'more than the sum of its parts'.

The metaphor, metaphysics and music of light in medieval and modern thought

Tom McLeish

I would like to explore a question that, at first, seems to bear in no way on the metaphor or reality of lighthouses, but one that worries me whenever I hear science talked about publicly. The illumination of and by light will emerge. I am increasingly troubled that science is not more like music. The sense of comparison is their cultural settings – music is universally 'possessed' in a way that science is not. Why, in this sense, is science songless? And how can it become symphonic?

Music delivers one of the most satisfyingly creative and life-interpreting genres of all art. It stirs our deepest longings, echoes our pains and trumpets our joys. It has sung the story of hope and despair, of worship and celebration throughout human history. It establishes a timeless canon of forms that can be called to mind in musical memory, yet in performance it stitches the same form into diachronic experience. It takes the material stuff of the world, its string, horn, skin, wood and metal – and charges them with the resonances of art under craftsmen and musicians' skill.

But music is not confined to the domain of experts: it is culturally and communally possessed. Those making their first tentative whistles and scrapes are in continuity with the finest exponents of the concerto and sonata. Furthermore, music is performative. Without an audience, even the greatest musician is without an earth for their electricity, has no interior worlds to illuminate and receives no reflection of, no response to, her interpretations. To be an audience does not require the ability to perform, but is integral to the community and process within which art is generated and received.

It is not so with science, which, in the telling words of Jaques Barzun (1964), 'is not with us an object of contemplation'. Humanity has severed an ancient link between itself and one of its greatest creations. The activity we now know as 'science', abstracted as it is into the culture and privilege of 'expertise', is in historical continuity with a long tradition of contemplative observation and re-creation of nature (McLeish, 2014). Natural Philosophy of the early modern era is its immediate predecessor, drawing on a tradition that in ancient cultures was called 'Wisdom'. Wisdom, according to philosopher and theologian Paul Fiddes (2014), responds to a strange aspect of the human predicament, namely the distance that opens up for humans alone among animals, between material nature and ourselves. Arendt (1958), Heidegger (2002) and Steiner (1989) have all given voice to this 'broken contract' in the late modern world. In ancient times Koheleth complains:

> I turned my mind to know and to search out and to seek wisdom and the sum of things . . . See, this is what I found, says the Teacher, adding one thing to another to find the sum, which my mind sought repeatedly, but I have not found.
>
> (Ecclesiastes 7:25, 27–28)

His desire to see – and the deep subficial perception of 'seeing' with the engaged mind was known well to the ancient world – resonates with the motivation and experience of science today. A universal reengagement with disciplines that inherit the tradition of Wisdom, albeit distantly, must change the way that education and the media engage with science itself. It will not do to make better science documentaries – at least not of the kind that enshrine the experts in mystical auras of hidden (and certain)

(continued)

(continued)

knowledge of which we are given at best superficial grasp and none at all of the groping uncertainty of the scientific process. Science engagement needs to move from the presentational to the performative, from the final to the processive.

In an essay to make this concrete, we turn to light itself as a field in the material world, as a multivalent idea in the mind and the great metaphor of understanding itself. Light plays a pivotal role in the history of natural philosophy, also sitting at the nexus of our comparative juxtaposition of science and music. Perhaps the most important text in the intellectual history of light is Robert Grosseteste's treatise of c.1220 *De luce* (Panti, 2013). At the focal point at which the reassessment of Aristotelian texts and Islamic commentaries on them meets Christian scholarship in the High Medieval Renaissance, Grosseteste makes use of these antecedents to look to the future. In this sense, he is an early adopter of the current theological metaphorical power of light discussed by Puckering and Wilkinson in this volume. He takes Avicenna's development of Aristotelian 'first form' in one hand, and the biblical priority of created light in the other – and for the first time identifies them. In an astonishing 'Newtonian leap', this provides him at one stroke with a theory of the extension of matter and with a cosmogony of the Universe as a whole. He knows, and explains mathematically, why no number, however big, of infinitesimal atoms could ever fill the tiniest finite volume. So, he conjectures that light, 'or something with the same properties as light' indwells all solid matter endowing it with extension. Without a particle of presentist retro-projection, his insight deserves the remark that, 700 years later, it was the wave theory of matter that first explained the extensive stability of ordinary matter.

That which can fill out a table can fill out the cosmos – so Grosseteste invokes his extraordinary 'Medieval Big Bang' (Bower et al., 2014) in which light (*lux*) forms and shapes matter, first expanding the primordial sphere of the cosmos. The reradiated light from the firmament (*lumen*) converges inwards, concentrating matter before it and crystallising out the nine other celestial spheres. It is a monumental and masterful vision, and a consummate exercise in early theoretical physics. But it also takes the 'metaphysics of light' to its highest peak, at which the new chapter, the 'physics of light', can be truly begun. It can surely be no coincidence that, in the wake of *De luce* and Grosseteste's other optical works, the pace of a deepening understanding of optics quickened: Roger Bacon's *Optics*, Theodoric of Freiburg's solution of the rainbow, Newton's *Optics*.

Grosseteste's later work on sound, equally perceptive in its identification of transmitted vibration as the source of auditory sensation, continued to invoke the underpinning form of light as its generative energy. So, it seems fitting to experiment, as a first step, with the still misty vision of a 'performative science' by taking inspiration from the science of light and by yoking it to a performance of music similarly inspired by the idea of light.

In 2015, during the international *Lumière* festival in Durham, the Institute of Advanced Study collaborated with the Durham Singers, the university's Physics Department and Trevelyan College to organise a short concert, linked intimately with an afternoon of public experimenting with colour, refraction and reflection. The music encompassed four centuries, from early Renaissance to a première of a new work. It explored our opening question, with the insight that, if science and music can be like each other, this might be most evident when they are in each other's company. So the pieces not only echoed the metaphorical power of light as inner illumination (Handel's *Eternal Source of Light Divine*), of dawning hope (Pärt's *Morgenstern*), of luminous love (Byrd's *O Lux Beata Trinitas*), but also explored further and more structurally the properties of light that require observation, thought, even theorising, to grasp.

Thus, the concert engaged with light as a rich composite of different wavelengths. Light of different frequencies (visible and invisible) creates different hues and saturations, maps onto harmonies and dissonances and builds from sounds of different pitches (audible and inaudible). *The Skies in Their Magnificence* by contemporary British composer Cecilia McDowall is set to a text by Thomas Traherne about colour and the lights of the skies. The performance included two pieces about light – one Renaissance (Victoria), one late 20th-century (Pärt), in which one seems to hear colours unfolding in the music.

The concert also explored in both experience and music the concept of light as carrier of information or of 'Words'. We understand the velocities and chemistries of distant stars by the information carried on their light – the missing wavelengths and their delicate shifts. In the same way that sound conveys information, light-inspired music often picks up the resonance of the theological 'logos', of conveyed ordering principle. In contemporary physics, the 'field theory' of light orders and collates charged matter. Similarly, three settings of *Oh Gladsome Light* from Renaissance to contemporary (Tallis, Rachmaninov and Burrell) reflected on the structured bringing-into-being that light carries into the material world.

Finally, the music moved into engagement with light's creative force. In the Big Bang itself, through cosmic structures shaped by radiation, and through the photosynthesis sustaining life on Earth today, light shapes and orders the Universe. The lived experience of humans is often articulated in terms of a search for light. Thus, the concert centred on a premier performance of *The Light*, a work by a contemporary British composer Janet Graham. The original poem reflected many of the previous musical themes but points more particularly towards life as a reflection on light and as a search for it. Brahms' dark motet *Warum ist das Licht* picks up that theme too, and Harris answers those questions in *Holy is the True Light*, reflecting on the life of the Saints inspired by the Light. The concert concluded with

(continued)

(continued)

that most complex, mathematical and conceptually perfect of composers, using J. S. Bach's motet *O Jesus Christ, Mein Leben's Licht* to complete the parallel musical and scientific reflections on light as structure, energy and metaphor.

Light is both that which gives understanding, and a puzzle itself to be understood. The musical exploration does not leave listeners where they began: something is understood about light, materiality and nature. Music allows us to connect the affective and the cerebral in a way that needs to be breathed again into our possession of science. And it allows us to live with the unanswered questions as well.

Wonder and the lighthouse

H. Martyn Evans

To begin with, it seems, perspective is all. We invariably view lighthouses from sea level (when afloat) or from ground level (when ashore). As we approach them, we are likely to be looking upwards. Images from aloft do exist – typically photographs or film shot from helicopters – but they are generally in daylight. We rarely look down on a lighthouse at night. If we did, what would we see?

We must resist the initial temptation to suppose a bright source of illumination, a jewel in the darkened landscape: the top of the lantern is the lighthouse's opaque roof. Viewed from above on a clear night, the lighthouse is in effect perfectly eclipsed by a tethered moon – its own dome. However, since air is rarely perfectly clear, diffusion would reveal some glowing around the lantern, perhaps reflected from the ground. This glow would appear in concert with the revolving of the lantern's shutters – each gap in the shuttering permitting the regular escape of a flash, visible at sea level to anyone looking horizontally at the lighthouse but, from a bird's eye view, a slowly spinning part-halo.

There must be a sufficient altitude from which the network of lighthouses can be seen spread out, as on a navigation chart. The lighthouses themselves are both figuratively and substantively 'pins' dropped upon the map – an intersection between cartography and reality. This is their purpose after all: to *express* the lay of the land and sea. However, the lighthouse transmits only: it is blind and deaf. Only the eyes of mariners pick out and connect the nodes in this net of lights, making it possible to travel safely to their destinations. But the net is shrouded from all except those at sea level. We are used to aerial images of the Earth at night – the spangled light traces of concentrated human presence scattered liberally across a darkened world – making it a surprising irony that lighthouses themselves may be the least visible of these.

There is a general tendency, in Western societies, to privilege vision above other senses – and this prioritisation of the seen over the heard or felt, and even the unseen – has spilled over into conceptions of wonder and its sources. There is even a notion that 'wonders' can be only visual, because vision's (supposed) all-at-once-ness, its instantaneity, must be a feature of the experience of wonder – bizarrely ruling out the possibility that, for example, wonder might arise from listening to music. As a day-lit monolith, the lighthouse is present to us in an all-at-once experience, but, as a coded pulsing light (or sound) in the darkness, it is present to us in sequence and time. As either presence could in the right circumstances be a source of wonder, the lighthouse resists the domination of wonder by the immediate.

In wonder, the world is made *newly-present*. Having diurnally distinct kinds of presences, the one material and the other functional, semantic and even ethical, the lighthouse can make the world 'newly-present' in two distinct ways. The first presence is material: the physical structure, seen in broad daylight, either from afar or close up. There are doubtless exceptions, but in general we expect our lighthouses to be tall, tapering, slightly waisted columns surmounted by a glazed lamp-house – a helmet with an all-round visor. We expect to find them projecting themselves out of the ground, atop plinths whose masonry brings a kind of fused order to the scrambled rock of whatever outcrop they occupy.

The lighthouse imposes its physical presence upon the viewer as much as upon its footing. As a piece of bravura engineering and as a statement of capability and intent, a good lighthouse will always trump a monument, civic statuary, a commemorative obelisk. Lacking (if not spurning) their extrinsic aesthetics, the lighthouse has grandeur and authority that flows from being something this big, and this simple. It stands in need of no justification for its size or simplicity, no back-story of ideology or symbolism: where else would you put a penetrating, elevated light source other than atop a big tower?

The simplicity of the shape is also a functional necessity. As discussed earlier in this volume, the basic profile and section shape of virtually all subsequent lighthouses was established by John Smeaton's replacement Eddystone Lighthouse (completed 1759 and apparently modelled on an oak tree), designed to dissipate the energy of wave impacts and offer least resistance to wind from all directions. In form, any given lighthouse stands as an archetype of all lighthouses – a symbol as well as an instance of the lighthouse 'brand' that is instantly recognisable.

The lighthouse is not an addition to the landscape so much as a revision of the landscape, rather like a tunnel or a bridge or, in its way, a hedge: an act of terra-forming, a contrived alteration to the world's prior topography to achieve some purpose. The lighthouse makes its own corner of the world present to us in an extended way. By day, the tower draws attention to itself by virtue of its grandeur and authority and, in the process, draws attention to its own footing, its situation and the land whose presence it expressly advertises. But unlike an ordinary signpost, whose meaning is explicit, the lighthouse

(continued)

(continued)

is an *intrinsic* sign, an extruded part of what it – literally – highlights. When we reflect on this relation between the lighthouse and its situation, the land on which the lighthouse stands is also made newly-present.

Scale and simplicity are obvious enough. Stand anywhere within sight of an averagely large lighthouse by day, and you cannot fail to be struck by it. But why also authority and a revisionary 'act' of landscaping? The role of the imagination in the sense of wonder is under-recognised: you have to look at the lighthouse with imagination to see these aspects and, once they are seen, to be struck by them. At that point, the lighthouse is made newly- and dizzyingly present to you – and so, too, is the land on which it sits, and which it proclaims. THIS is the westernmost point of . . . THIS is the skerry . . . THIS is the outer arm of the harbour. The land's *ipseity*, its 'THIS-ness', is just as implacable as the 'this-presence' of the lighthouse. For viewer and navigator alike, there is no getting round either the lighthouse or whatever underpins it. In engineering terms, it may be a triumph of human purpose, but (unlike a bridge or a tunnel) it is still only a negotiated settlement with the landscape. We couldn't do anything about this headland and its obduracy, so we extrude it into a radiant label or, in fog, a warning cry.

The lighthouse's alternative presence comes at night, when it becomes a wholly different object. What we see is no longer the material body but rather its product, its function, its spinning trace. The scanning beam falls momentarily on multiple degrees of the compass in turn, and from any given point is intermittent, emergent, a pulsing coded sequence of light. At extreme range, possibly through rain or murk, even eyes straining in the right direction may glimpse it without recognition, then with dawning realisation and confirmation (and perhaps much relief, for an anxious mariner), then with steady comprehension and fixation.

So it seems that context is all. By day, and close up, the lighthouse's wonder comes in a detached, contemplative, other-regarding experience. By night, from afar, and when it counts – when the lighthouse is doing what it is there for – its wonder is personal, a guide to individual safety, a token that the community of seafarers has taken care that all should be well. Indeed, it might be that a whispered reminder of this shared enterprise forms part of the wonder. Perhaps wonder is here an 'accessory' experience, over and above the relief and security and promise. There is the lighthouse, and there is the *light*. We might just gaze on it, rapt, long after registering it and making the practical arrangements that it indicates. But at all events, the incursion of the lighthouse's trace into a prior blackness that may have been uncertain, terrifying or merely dreary re-orders the world and makes it newly-present. For which graces – aesthetic, spiritual and existential, as well as purely practical – may we – mariners all, at some level – be profoundly and wonderingly thankful.

CONCLUDING COMMENTS

The shifting multiplicity of the lighthouse

Tim Edensor

As we have seen throughout this volume, the lighthouse is a long-lasting fixture; in most cases, it remains in place for a considerable time and extensive efforts are made to ensure that it stays there. The lighthouse also remains saturated with meaning: it persists as a key attribute of place-identity, attracts tourists, and continues to be deployed as metaphorical figure in fiction and poetry, also often serving as a dramatic cinematic and televisual setting. Perhaps this entrenched salience is because the lighthouse was the first and, certainly, the most powerful structure that shone light upon and across a previously dark world, a point underlined by the enduring mythic resonance of the ancient Pharos at Alexandria. As the early sections of this book discuss, light has been central to life on Earth, integral to vision and plant growth, and a key element in the ways in which humans have made sense of the world, interpreting the Sun, Moon and stars as sources of divine power and knowledge, in contrast to its ostensible opposite, darkness.

The contributions to this volume make abundantly clear that there is no dominant viewpoint from which the lighthouse can be clearly perceived, no definitive lighthouse that can be identified once and for all. Rather, the lighthouse serves as a captivating and unstable object that can be interpreted and conceived from multiple perspectives. Though we feature a diverse range of accounts, we are well aware that numerous other lighthouse stories could and will be told.

In this book, this multiplicity is underlined by narratives that reveal how the materiality, function, operation and meaning of the lighthouse has shifted continuously. Though usually a relatively durable structure, the swirling non-human agencies that assail the lighthouse ensure that its composition is endlessly transformed, and it requires ongoing maintenance to survive. Yet neglect may occur, repairs may actually prove to be damaging and strategies to merely manage decay may be adopted as the most realistic option. On occasion, as the fate of the infamous Eddystone lighthouses discloses, the lighthouse may be obliterated.

The rocks and shorelines at which it is located also shift, sometimes dramatically, and accelerating climate change and a corresponding rise in sea levels threaten to bring further challenges to its physical integrity.

The chapters in this book also relate how the function of the lighthouse has changed dramatically over recent decades, with the widespread loss of keepers in unmanned structures. Though lighthouses retain a critical purpose in beaming light out to sea, many have also become tourist attractions, art galleries and dwellings. And, well before this, they have been incorporated into multiple systems of political and economic control. Once private and independent enterprises, lighthouses have largely been absorbed into larger national and institutional networks, serving wider, national strategic functions and extending colonial powers.

Our contributors identify many of the key technological developments that have expanded the efficacy of lighthouses, through the development of optical devices, notably with the introduction of the Fresnel lens, and through building technologies that have produced taller, stronger and more stable structures, from the ancient to the modern(ist), as well as more mobile applications such as lightships. Such innovations have frequently been contested, as with the development of enhanced brilliance in luminosity and the introduction of the foghorn. Geographically and historically, lighthouses have acquired a variety of forms, architectural styles and techniques to secure them in place, yet newer technological developments in marine illumination and GPS locational systems have rendered them less integral to maintaining safety and facilitating navigation at sea. As many contributors show, this stylistic diversity also resonates in the numerous ways in which the lighthouse has spawned homological forms, including modernist towers, airport control towers and minarets, as well as conjuring up echoes of the astronomical rhythms of the pulsars of deep space, and light signals generated by land and marine animals.

And as we have seen, in referring to numerous paintings, films, myths and literary tales, the fluidity that surrounds the lighthouse's metaphorical values and meanings is extraordinary, underpinning its essential ambiguity across space and time. Thus, lighthouses diversely symbolise enlightenment, religious salvation and divine power, refuge, surveillance, isolation, romantic heritage, scientific ingenuity, a common good, phallic authority, colonial and state power, quirkiness, malign horror, the uncanny, and functional modernism, while continuing to serve as a site of wonder. The key figure of the lighthouse keeper is similarly polysemic, alternately conceived as lonesome, heroic and prone to insanity. We envisage that such diversity will continue to persist across popular cultural and academic accounts and representations of the lighthouse.

Interdisciplinary reflections

Veronica Strang

Though it is now widely accepted that many complex problems require collaboration between diverse forms of expertise, traditional institutional structures at all levels – universities, national funding bodies, the international academy – continue to discourage transgression across disciplinary boundaries. Even within institutes or research projects designed to bring specialist knowledges together, the process is far from easy. Achieving genuinely interdisciplinary outcomes demands enthusiasm for collaboration, consistent support and adherence to strong underlying principles of openness, trust and equality.

By initiating a series of interdisciplinary conversations about light and lighthouses, Durham University's Institute of Advanced Study hoped to show that, guided by such principles, it is possible to bring multiple disciplinary perspectives into productive and – in this instance – highly enjoyable engagement with each other. The endeavour involved some risk: a leap of faith that important connections between diverse forms of knowledge would be revealed and that the conversation would generate new ways of understanding the topic. This faith seems to have been well founded: as Tim Edensor's comments above illustrate, there are many discernible thematic continuities running through the different ways that the lighthouse and light itself are imagined and understood. Reflecting on the lighthouse, each contribution illuminates it in a particular way, and yet, as these beams meet each other across the subject, it is clear that there are multiple reflections and that diverse ways of seeing have far more in common than is visible from any single disciplinary perspective. Thus, David Cooper notes how the homologous nature of the lighthouse 'crops up at various points across the book', and describes how the contributions exploring its materiality shifted his own perspective, making him 'more alert to the matter of matter':

> As a teacher and literary critic, I invariably spend my days drifting through worlds of signification and – to a certain degree at least – I feel at home thinking about the lighthouse as symbol . . . *From the Lighthouse*, though, has opened up my thinking about the 'thingyness' of the lighthouse . . . Cumulatively, the contributions reveal the rich complexity of the lighthouse.
> (pers. comm.)

No doubt every reader will discern, in their own way, interdisciplinary connections and patterns that speak to their individual interests. Many will add mentally to the conversation, perhaps introducing new and equally illuminating ways of seeing the lighthouse. But for me, two key outcomes of this interdisciplinary experiment produced the most intriguing revelations.

The first was how the inclusion of perspectives from across the disciplinary spectrum highlighted the relational flows between material and social worlds. In multiple instances it became possible to see how the material properties and behaviours of things – of light itself; of biological organisms; of the surrounding environment; and of lighthouses – are involved dynamically in a recursive relationship with social ideas and practices: the recurrence of rituals expressing spiritual and aesthetic valorisations of light; the development of technologies extending the safety of daylight into dark nights and across dark seas; the metaphorical uses of light, and lighthouses, in art and literature. Thus, the conversation created a bridge across a chasm that typically divides the physical sciences from the social sciences, arts and humanities.

Second, the experiment demonstrated the advantages of having multiple disciplinary scales to 'think with'. Understanding the universal material properties of light, and placing the lighthouse within an evolutionary scale, provided a long view of humankind's biophysical relationship with light. Exploring the need for light from the tiniest micro-organisms to whole ecosystems threw into relief the way that it acts upon all organic life, producing specific adaptations and behaviours. In this way, situating humans alongside other light-dependent species revealed shared and different responses to light and dark, and to the opportunities and dangers that each afford. It showed how, aided by increasingly sophisticated tools, *Homo sapiens* has learned to engage with and make use of light to move safely through marine and terrestrial environments, and (now) through the air too. And, examined in company with marine organisms and fireflies, humankind can be seen as a 'light-signalling species' which has developed myriad languages of light that are communicated not just through lighthouses but also via their historical and contemporary material relatives.

Locating the lighthouse within evolutionary adaptations and phenomenological engagements with light also reveals why and how it has been consistently valorised in religious and secular worldviews. It offers insights into the dualism that tends to shape social thinking about light so that, in many artistic works, it appears as a force for transparent moral good versus the covert evil of darkness; as intellectual clarity versus the blindness of ignorance; as life, form and consciousness versus death and the chaotic formlessness of the sea. It shows how human experiences of light – sensory, emotional and intellectual – engender individual affective responses as well as cross-cutting values about its aesthetic and spiritual meanings so that we are drawn, like moths, to images and objects that shine, shimmer, glitter and gleam.

With a deeper understanding of material and social engagements with light, the cultural evolution of lighthouses – and its multiple geographic and historical manifestations – can be seen as a consistent effort to create and maintain order in the world. Lighthouses enable the movement of people and goods; they mark and, if necessary, defend territories, standing as guardians and/or mediators between local or national selves and others. The shifts in scale are useful here too: we can see how lighthouses compose and represent cultural heritage, both in the ambitious casting of national power and identity over far-flung colonies, pinned down by lighthouses along the shore, and in local communities, where mini-souvenirs condense and make portable each lighthouse's statement of place and belonging.

The commonalities across different disciplinary scales offer insights into human cognition and the way in which models and values are transposed from one domain to another. Echoing the tiny flash of the firefly, the lighthouse sends encoded light messages out into the dark. Its searching beam extends the capacities of the human eye and the human mind. Its form expresses phallic life-generation, as well as the whole human body with a seeing eye; while at a vastly larger scale the shining beam represents the Sun itself. Similarly, in metaphorical terms, the smallest candle is a symbol of light and hope; 'leading lights' offer wisdom, knowledge and enlightenment, while, at a larger scale, sun gods and 'light of the world' deities are believed to illuminate, understand and communicate universally.

We are, on every scale, surrounded and formed by light: it shapes every experience of being in the world; it reaches into all but the darkest corners of our imaginations. We can only understand light fully, therefore, when we reach across the breadth and depth of human knowledge. By synchronising multiple disciplinary flashes of illumination, we are rewarded with glimpses of the whole picture. The view 'from the lighthouse' suggests that if we do this more, if we do this better, we will see more clearly.

References

Abrams, M. (1953) *The Mirror and the Lamp: Romantic Theory and the Critical Tradition*, Oxford: Oxford University Press.
Ackermann, K. (1991) *Building for Industry*, Pewsey: Watermark Publications.
Adam, B. (1995) *Timewatch: The Social Analysis of Time*, Cambridge: Polity.
Adey, P. (2006) 'Airports and Air-Mindedness: Spacing, timing and using the Liverpool airport, 1929–1939', *Social and Cultural Geography*, 7(3): 343–363.
Aeschylus (2009) 'Agamemnon', in Eliot, C. W. (ed.), Morshead, E. D. A., Plumptre, E. H., Murray, G. and Rogers, B. B. (trans) *Nine Greek Dramas by Aeschylus, Sophocles, Euripides, and Aristophanes*, Vol. VIII, New York: Cosimo Classics, pp. 5–70.
Agence France Presse (2015) 'European Migrant Crisis: Thousands rally in solidarity with asylum seekers; Hungary says EU "has no clue" about dangers of influx', *ABC News*, www.abc.net.au/news/2015-09-13/pro-migrant-rallies-in-europe-as-hungary-says-eu-dreaming/6771256 (Accessed 24/1/2018).
Allen, W. (Director) (2008) *Vicky Cristina Barcelona* [Film], The Weinstein Company.
AlSulaiti, F. (2013) 'Minaret', *Ancient History Encyclopaedia*, 6 February 2013, www.ancient.eu/Minaret/ (Accessed 13/9/2016).
Anderson, B. (2006) *Imagined Communities: Reflections on the Origin and Spread of Nationalism*, revised edition, London and New York: Verso.
Anderson, J. and Peters, K. (eds) (2014) *Water Worlds: Human Geographies of the Ocean*, Farnham: Ashgate.
Angels and Ghosts (nd) 'Haunted Lighthouses', *Angels and Ghosts: Exploring Ghost and Spirit Phenomena*, www.angelsghosts.com/haunted_light_houses (Accessed 18/7/2016).
Anon (1876) *The Story of John Smeaton and the Eddystone Lighthouse*, London: T. Nelson and Sons.
Arendt, H. (1958) *The Human Condition*, Chicago: University of Chicago Press.
Aristophanes (1888 [423 BC]) *The Clouds*, Hailstone, H. (trans), Cambridge: E. Johnson.
Armitage, R. (1977) *The Lighthouse Keeper's Lunch*, London: Andre Deutsch.
Armstrong, J. and Bagwell, P. S. (1983) 'Coastal Shipping', in Aldcroft, D. H. and Freeman, M. J. (eds) *Transport in the Industrial Revolution*, Manchester: Manchester University Press, pp. 142–176.
Armstrong, W. (1963) *White for Danger*, London: Elk Books.
Arnold, M. (1932 [1869]) *Culture and Anarchy*, Wilson, D. (ed.), Cambridge: Cambridge University Press.
Arrowsmith, W. (1982) 'Ruskin's Fireflies', in Hunt, J. D. and Holland, F. M. (eds) *The Ruskin Polygon: Essays on the Imagination of John Ruskin*, Manchester: Manchester University Press, pp. 198–235.

References

Asciuto, N. (2015) *T. S. Eliot: Turning Darkness into Light*, doctoral thesis, Durham University.
Atamian, H., Creux, N., Brown, E., Garner, A., Blackman, B. and Harmer, S. (2016) 'Circadian Regulation of Sunflower Heliotropism, Floral Orientation, and Pollinator Visits', *Science*, 353(6299): 587–690.
Attenborough, D. (2016a) *Light on Earth* [Film], Loncraine, J. (Director), Dohrn, M., Loncraine, J. and Reddish, P. (Writers), Ammonite Films.
Attenborough, D. (2016b) *Attenborough's Life that Glows* [TV], BBC2, 9 May 2016, www.bbc.co.uk/programmes/b07bgpft (Accessed 28/7/2016).
Austen, J. (1995 [1811]) 'Sense and Sensibility', in *Jane Austen: The Complete Novels*, London, New York, Sydney and Toronto: BCA, pp. 1–175.
Bachelard, G. (1983) *Water and Dreams: An Essay on the Imagination of Matter*, Farrell, E. (trans), Dallas: Pegasus Foundation.
Bagwell, P. S. and Armstrong, J. (1988) 'Coastal Shipping', in Freeman, M. J. and Aldcroft, D. H. (eds) *Transport in Victorian Britain*, Manchester: Manchester University Press, pp. 171–173.
Baker, J. and Brookes, S. (2014) 'Overseeing the Sea: Some West Saxon responses to waterborne threats in the South-East', in Klein, S., Schipper, W. and Lewis-Simpson, S. (eds) *The Maritime World of the Anglo-Saxons*, Essays in Anglo-Saxon Studies 5, Tempe, AZ: ACMRS, pp. 37–58.
Ball, H. (2016) Interview with Professor Helen Ball, Durham University, conducted on 5 July 2016 by J. Puckering, Durham University.
Ballantyne, R. M. (1865) *The Lighthouse*, London: J. Nisbet and Co.
Banham, R. (1960) *Design in the First Machine Age*, Boston: MIT University Press.
Barrett, J., Locker, A. and Roberts, C. (2004) 'The Origin of Intensive Marine Fishing in Medieval Europe: The English evidence', *Proceedings of the Royal Society of London B*, 271: 2417–2421.
Barrett, J., Orton, D., Johnstone, C., Harland, J., van Neer, W., Ervynck, A., Roberts, C., Locker, A., Amundsen, C. and Enghoff, I. (2011) 'Interpreting the Expansion of Sea Fishing in Medieval Europe Using Stable Isotope Analysis of Archaeological Cod Bones', *Journal of Archaeological Science*, 38(7): 1516–1524.
Barrington, R. M. (1900) *The migration of birds, as observed at Irish lighthouses and lightships including the original reports from 1888–97, now published for the first time, and an analysis of these and of the previously published reports from 1881–87: together with an appendix giving the measurements of about 160 wings*, London: R. H. Potter, https://archive.org/details/migrationofbirds00barr (Accessed 23/3/2017).
Barrow, G. (1687) 'To his learned and ingenious Friend Mr. John Taylor, in the deserved Praise of his Excellent Book intituled Thesaurarium Mathematicae', in Taylor, J., *Thesaurarium Mathematicæ, or the Treasury of Mathematicks*, London: Printed by J. H. for W. Freeman, https://quod.lib.umich.edu/e/eebo/A64224.0001.001?view=toc (Accessed 24/1/2018).
Barrow, J. (1849) *An Auto-Biographical Memoir of Sir John Barrow, Bart, Including Reflections, Observations and Reminiscences at Home and Abroad, from Early Life to Advanced Age*, London: John Murray.
Barzun, J. (1964) *Science: The Glorious Entertainment*, New York: Harper and Row.
Bathurst, B. (2005) *The Wreckers: A Story of Killing Seas, False Lights and Plundered Ships*, London: HarperCollins.
Bathurst, B. (2010) *The Lighthouse Stevensons: The Extraordinary Story of the Building of the Scottish Lighthouses by the Ancestors of Robert Louis Stevenson*, New York: Harper Perennial.

250 References

BBC (2013) 'Orfordness Lighthouse Gets Switched Off and Left to the Sea', *BBC News*, 28 June 2013, www.bbc.co.uk/news/uk-england-suffolk-23091214 (Accessed 16/7/2015).

Beaglehole, H. (2006) *Lighting the Coast: A History of New Zealand's Coastal Lighthouse System*, Christchurch: Canterbury University Press.

Becker, W., Bernhardt, G. and Jessner, A. (2015) 'Interplanetary GPS using pulsar signals', *Astronomical Notes*, 336(8/9): 749–761. Article first published online: 13 November 2015, DOI: 10.1002/asna.201512251.

Bede (1907) *Ecclesiastical History of England*, Colgrave, B. and Mynors, R. (eds and trans), Oxford: Clarendon Press.

Bede (1969) 'Vita Sancti Cuthberti Auctore Beda', in Colgrave, B. (ed. and trans) *Two Lives of Saint Cuthbert*, Cambridge: Cambridge University Press, pp. 141–310.

Behrens-Abouseif, D. (2006) 'The Islamic History of the Lighthouse of Alexandria', *Muqarnas*, 23: 1–14.

Beineix, J-J. (Director) (1981) *Diva* [Film], Les Filmes Galaxie, Greenwich Film Productions, France 2 (FR2).

Bell, T. (1998) 'A Roman Signal Station at Whitby', *Archaeological Journal*, 155: 303–321.

Bell Burnell, J. (2011) 'Dame Jocelyn Bell Burnell', *The Life Scientific* [Radio interview], BBC Radio 2, presented by Jim Al-Khalili, 25 October 2011, www.bbc.co.uk/programmes/b016812j (Accessed 31/10/2015).

Bell Rock Lighthouse (nd) 'Life in the Bell-Rock Lighthouse: Being my journal kept there during a residence for sixteen days' by R. M. Ballantyne, *Bell Rock Lighthouse*, www.bellrock.org.uk/misc/misc_ballantyne.htm (Accessed 17/8/2016).

Bentley, J., Bridenthal, R. and Wigen, K. (eds) (2007) *Seascapes: Maritime Histories, Littoral Cultures, and Transoceanic Exchanges*, Honolulu: University of Hawai'i Press.

Benyus, J. (1997) *Biomimicry: Innovation Inspired by Nature*, New York: HarperCollins.

Betjeman, J. (1977) *Archie and the Strict Baptists*, first edition, London: John Murray.

Bille, M. and Sørensen, T. (2007) 'An Anthropology of Luminosity: The agency of light', *Journal of Material Culture*, 12(3): 263–284.

Bisaccioni, M. (1644) *Apparati scenici per lo teatro novissimo di Venetia nell'anno 1644, d'inventione e cura di Jacomo Torelli da Fano . . . (Descrittione del signor conte M. Bisaccioni.)*, Venice: G. Vecellio et M. Leni.

Bjurström, P. (1962) *Giacomo Torelli and Baroque Stage Design*, Stockholm: National Museum.

Blake, K. (2007) 'Lighthouse Symbolism in the American Landscape', *FOCUS in Geography*, 50(1): 9–15.

Blake, W. (1988a) 'A Vision of the Last Judgement' (1810), in Erdmann, D. (ed.) *The Complete Poetry and Prose of William Blake*, with commentary by Bloom, H., New York: Anchor Books, pp. 554–566.

Blake, W. (1988b) 'Auguries of Innocence', in Erdmann, D. (ed.) *The Complete Poetry and Prose of William Blake*, with commentary by Bloom, H., New York: Anchor Books, pp. 490–493.

Blake, W. (2011) 'Ah! Sun-flower', in Willmott, R. (ed.) *Songs of Innocence and Experience*, Oxford: Oxford University Press, p. 60.

Blankenship, R. (2010) 'Early Evolution of Photosynthesis', *Plant Physiology*, 154(2): 434–438.

Bliss, P. (1871) 'Let the Lower Lights be Burning', in *The Charm: A Collection of Sunday School Music*, Chicago, IL: Root and Cady.

Bloom, J. (1991) 'Creswell and the Origins of the Minaret', *Muqarnas*, 8: 55–58.

Bloom, J. (2013) *The Minaret*, Edinburgh Studies on Islamic Art, Edinburgh: Edinburgh University Press.

Bloom, J. and Blair, S. (eds) (2009) *The Grove Encyclopaedia of Islamic Art and Architecture*, Vols I, II and III, Oxford: Oxford University Press.

Booth, K. (2007) 'The Roman *Pharos* at Dover Castle', *English Heritage Historical Review*, 2: 9–22.

Bosworth, C., van Donzel, E., Lewis, B. and Pellat, Ch. (eds) (1987) *The Encyclopaedia of Islam*, Vol. VI, second edition, Leiden: E. J. Brill.

Boulting, R. (Director) (1942) *Thunder Rock* [Film], Charter Film Productions.

Bourdieu, P. (1977) *Outline of a Theory of Practice*, Nice, R. (trans), Cambridge: Cambridge University Press.

Bower, R., McLeish, T., Tanner, B., Smithson, H., Panti, C., Lewis, N. and Gasper, G. (2014) 'A Medieval Multiverse? Mathematical modelling of the thirteenth century universe of Robert Grosseteste', *Proceedings of the Royal Society A*, 470, 20140025.

Bowers, B. (1998) *Lengthening the Day – A History of Lighting Technology*, Oxford: Oxford University Press.

Bradbury, R. (2001) 'The Fog Horn', in *The Golden Apples of the Sun*, London: Perennial (HarperCollins), pp. 1–9.

Bradley, I. (2005) *The Daily Telegraph Book of Hymns*, London: Continuum.

Brewster, D. (1833) 'On the British Lighthouse System', *The Edinburgh Review*, 57(115): 169–193.

Brewster, D. (1835) 'Review of the Parliamentary Report on Lighthouses', *The Edinburgh Review*, 61(123): 221–241.

Brockelman, T. (2003) 'Lost in Place? On the virtues and vices of Edward Casey's anti-modernism', *Humanitas*, 16: 36–55.

Brox, J. (2010) *Brilliant: The Evolution of Artificial Light*, New York: Houghton Mifflin Harcourt.

Buck-Morss, S. (1991) *The Dialectics of Seeing: Walter Benjamin and the Arcades Project*, Cambridge, MA: MIT Press.

Burkett, A. (2015) 'Photographing Byron's Hand', *European Romantic Review*, 26(2): 129–148.

Büscher, M. and Urry, J. (2009) 'Mobile Methods and the Empirical', *European Journal of Social Theory*, 12(1): 99–116.

Butler, P. (2004) *Liverpool Airport: An Illustrated History*, London: Tempus.

Buzacott, M. (2014) 'Albury and the Uiver Emergency', *Hindsight*, ABC Radio National, 5 November 2014, www.abc.net.au/radionational/programs/hindsight/albury-and-the-uiver-emergency/5867614 (Accessed 20/9/2016).

Byron, G. G., Lord (1986) 'Darkness', in McGann, J. J. (ed.) *Complete Poetical Works*, Vol. IV, Oxford: Clarendon Press, pp. 40–43.

Carpenter, J. (Director) (1980) *The Fog* [Film], Embassy Pictures, EDI, Debra Hill Productions.

Casey, E. (2001) 'Between Geography and Philosophy: What does it mean to be in the place-world?' *Annals of the Association of American Geographers*, 91: 683–693.

Cats, J. (1627) *Proteus ofte Minne-Beelden verandert in Sinne-Beelden*, Rotterdam: Pieter van Waesberge.

252 References

Chamovitz, D. (2012) 'Researcher Argues that Plants See', interview with *Scientific American*, podcast presented by Steve Mirsky, 26 June 2012, www.scientificamerican.com/podcast/episode/researcher-argues-that-plants-see-12-06-26/ (Accessed 7/6/2017).

Chance, J. (1902) *The Lighthouse Work of Sir James Chance, Baronet*, London: Smith, Elder, and Co.

Chornenky, D. (nd) *Initiation, Mystery and Salvation: The Way of Rebirth*, St Paul Lodge #3, Grand Lodge of Minnesota, USA, www.freemasons-freemasonry.com/chornenky.html (Accessed 14/3/2017).

Chubbs, H. and Kearley, W. (2013) *Facing the Sea: Lightkeepers and Their Families*, Canada: Flanker Press.

Clark, A. (2010) *Supersizing the Mind: Embodiment, Action, and Cognitive Extension*, Oxford: Oxford University Press.

Clarke, J. (1999) 'Illuminating the Guénégaud Stage: Some seventeenth-century lighting effects', *French Studies*, 53: 1–15.

Clarke, J. (2007) 'La Lumière comme effet spectaculaire', in Zaiser, R. (ed.) *L'Âge de la Représentation: L'art du spectacle au XVIIe siècle*, Tübingen: Gunter Narr, pp. 89–102.

Clarke, J. (2011a) 'L'Éclairage', in Pasquier, P. and Surgers, A. (eds) *La Représentation théâtrale en France au XVIIe siècle*, Paris: Armand Colin, pp. 119–140.

Clarke, J. (2011b) 'La Représentation de la paix et du pouvoir politique dans les prologues d'opéras et de pièces à machines, 1658–78', in Mazouer, C. (ed.) *Spectacle et Pouvoir Politique*, Tübingen: Gunter Narr, pp. 265–282.

Clarke, J. (2011c) 'The Representation of Peace in Opera and Machine Play Prologues (1660–1680)', in Boussier, P. G. and Banks, K. (eds) *Commonplace Culture in Western Europe in the Early Modern Period: Consolidation of God-given Power*, Leuven-Paris-Walpole, MA: Peeters, pp. 41–64.

Clayton, M. (2016) Interview with Professor Martin Clayton, Durham University, conducted on 26 July 2016 by J. Puckering, Durham University.

Clayton, M., Dueck, B. and Leante, L. (2013) *Experience and Meaning in Music Performance*, Oxford: Oxford University Press.

Clayton, P. and Price, M. (eds) (1988) *The Seven Wonders of the Ancient World*, London and New York: Routledge.

Cloch Foghorn papers and cuttings (1897) T-CN 41.40, Clyde Lighthouse Trust Archive, Glasgow.

Coase, R. (1974) 'The Lighthouse in Economics', *Journal of Law and Economics*, 17(2): 357–376.

Cohn-Sherbok, D. (2003) *Judaism: History, Belief and Practice*, London and New York: Routledge.

Collector's World (nd), www.collectorsworldcapecod.com/harbour/hretired.html (Accessed 17/3/2017).

Collingwood, R. and Wright, R. (1965) *The Roman Inscriptions of Britain*, Oxford: Clarendon Press.

Collins, J. and Jervis, J. (2008) 'Introduction', in Collins, J. and Jervis, J. (eds) *Uncanny Modernity: Cultural Theories, Modern Anxieties*, London: Palgrave, pp. 1–9.

Collins, P. (2009) 'On Resistance: The case of 17th century Quakers', *Durham Anthropology Journal*, 16(2): 8–22.

Cong, P., Ma, X., Hou, X., Edgecombe, G. D. and Strausfeld, N. J. (2014) 'Brain Structure Resolves the Segmental Affinity of Anomalocaridid Appendages', *Nature*, 513: 538–542.

Connor, S. (2010) *The Matter of Air: Science and Art of the Ethereal*, London: Reaktion.

Conzelmann, H. (1995) 'Light', in Kittel, G. and Friedrich, G. (eds) *Theological Dictionary of the New Testament*, Bromiley, G. W. (trans), Vol. IX, Grand Rapids, Michigan: W. B. Eerdmans Publishing Company, pp. 310–358.
Cook, M. and Edensor, T. (2014) 'Cycling through Dark Space: Apprehending the landscape otherwise', *Mobilities*, DOI: 10.1080/17450101.2014.956417.
Copland, S. (2013) 'Border Protection', *Coolabah*, 11, Observatori: Centre d'Estudis Australians, Australian Studies Centre, Universitat de Barcelona.
Corbin, A. (1999) *Village Bells: Sound and Meaning in the 19th Century French Countryside*, London: Macmillan.
Corneille, T. (1708) *Dictionnaire Universel Géographique et Historique*, 3 Vols, Paris: J.-B. Coignard.
Costa, T. (2012) 'To the Lighthouse: Sentinels at the water's edge', in Cusack, T. (ed.) *Art and Identity at the Water's Edge*, Aldershot: Ashgate, pp. 87–106.
Cowall District Committee (1897) Petition by Cowall District Committee to Clyde Lighthouse Trust, 1897. T-CN 41.42, Clyde Lighthouse Trust Archive, Glasgow.
Crary, J. (2013) *24/7*, Los Angeles, CA: Verso.
Creswell, K. (1926) 'The Evolution of the Minaret, with Special Reference to Egypt – II', *The Burlington Magazine for Connoisseurs*, 48(278): 252–259.
Cubitt, S. (2013) 'Electric Light and Electricity', *Theory, Culture and Society*, 30(7/8): 309–323.
Cunliffe, B. (1975) *Excavations at Portchester Castle*, London: Society of Antiquaries of London.
Curran, A. (2004) *Maritime Rites* [2xCD], US: New World Records.
Damon, P. and Kulp, L. (1958) 'Excess Helium and Argon in Beryl and Other Minerals', *American Mineralogist*, 43: 433–459.
Davenport Adams, W. (1891) *Lighthouses and Lightships: Descriptive and Historical*, London: Thomas Nelson and Sons.
Davies, D. (1984) *Meaning and Salvation in Religious Studies* (Studies in the History of Religions, Vol. XLVI), Leiden: E. J. Brill.
Davies, D. (2003) *An Introduction to Mormonism*, Cambridge: Cambridge University Press.
Davies, D. (2005) 'Fire', in Davies, D. J. and Mates, L. H. (eds) *Encyclopedia of Cremation*, Aldershot: Ashgate, pp. 186–195.
Davies, D. (2008) *The Theology of Death*, London: T&T Clark.
Davies, T., Duffy, J., Bennie, J. and Gaston, K. (2015) 'Stemming the Tide of Light Pollution Encroaching into Marine Protected Areas', *Conservation Letters*, 9(3): 151–236.
Dean, T. (1996) *Disappearance at Sea*, [16 mm film projection, colour and sound].
Dean, T. (1997a) *Disappearance at Sea II*, [16 mm anamorphic colour film, optical sound].
Dean, T. (1997b) *Missing Narratives*, exhibition catalogue, Frith Street Gallery, London, pp. 14–18, reproduced pp. 19–21.
de Certeau, M. (1984) *The Practice of Everyday Life*, Berkeley: University of California Press.
de Mare, E. (1973) *The Nautical Style: An Aspect of the Functional Tradition*, London: Architectural Press.
Denny, W. (1653) 'To the Discontented', in *Pelecanicidium, or, The Christian adviser against self-murder together with a guide and the pilgrims passe to the land of the living*, London: Printed for Thomas Hucklescott, https://quod.lib.umich.edu/e/eebo/A356 84.0001.001/1:6?rgn=div1;view=fulltext (Accessed 24/1/2018).

Dettingmeijer, R. (1996) 'The Emergence of the Bathing Culture Marks the End of the North Sea as a Common Cultural Ground', in Roding, J. and Heerma van Voss, L. (eds) *The North Sea and Culture, 1550–1800*, Hilversum: Verloren, pp. 482–491.

De Wire, E. and Reyes-Pergioudakis, D. (2010) *The Lighthouses of Greece*, Sarasota, FL: Pineapple Press.

DeYoung, U. (2011) 'Tyndall's Work as a Scientist: Practice and reception', in *A Vision of Modern Science: John Tyndall and the Role of the Scientist in Victorian Culture*, New York: Palgrave Macmillan, pp. 19–58.

Dickie, M. (1991) 'Heliodorus and Plutarch on the Evil Eye', *Classical Philology*, 86(1): 17–29.

Dicks, T. (Writer) (1977) 'Horror of Fang Rock' [TV], *Doctor Who*, Russell, P. (Director), British Broadcasting Corporation.

Dinkova-Bruun, G., Gasper, G., Huxtable, M., McLeish, T., Panti, C. and Smithson, H. (eds and trans) (2013) *Dimensions of Colour: Robert Grosseteste's De colore*, Durham Medieval and Renaissance Texts, Toronto: Pontifical Institute of Medieval Studies.

Doe, H. (2010) 'Waiting For Her Ship to Come In? The female investor in nineteenth-century sailing vessels', *The Economic History Review*, New Series, 63(1): 85–106.

Dolin, E. J. (2016) *Brilliant Beacons: A History of the American Lighthouse*, New York and London: Liveright Publishing Corporation.

Douglas, D. and Greenaway, G. (eds) (1981) *English Historical Documents, 1042–1189*, Vol. II, second edition, London and New York: Routledge.

Drever, J. (2007) 'Topophonophilia: A study on the relationship between the sounds of Dartmoor and its inhabitants', in Carlyle, A. (ed.) *Autumn Leaves: Sound and the Environment in Artistic Practice*, Paris: Double Entendre, pp. 98–100.

Driver, F. (2000) *Geography Militant: Cultures of Exploration in an Age of Empire*, Oxford: Wiley Blackwell.

Drummond, T. (1830) 'On the Illumination of Light-Houses', *Philosophical Transactions of the Royal Society of London*, 120: 383–397.

Dryden, J. (1779) 'From the Thirteenth Book of Ovid's Metamorphoses (Translations)', in *The Works of the English Poets, Vol. 16: The Poems of Dryden*, London: Printed by R. Hett, pp. 124–132.

Durkheim, E. (2001 [1912]) *The Elementary Forms of Religious Life*, Cosman, C. (trans), Oxford: Oxford University Press.

Earthly Mission (nd) 'Banksy on EU refugee crisis', *Earthly Mission*, www.earthlymission.com/banksy-on-eu-refugee-crisis/ (Accessed 24/1/2018).

Edensor, T. (ed.) (2010) *Geographies of Rhythm: Nature, Place, Mobilities and Bodies*, Farnham: Ashgate.

Edensor, T. (2011) 'Entangled Agencies, Material Networks and Repair in a Building Assemblage: The mutable stone of St Ann's Church, Manchester', *Transactions of the Institute of British Geographers*, 36(2): 238–252.

Edensor, T. (2013) 'Reconnecting with Darkness: Gloomy landscapes, lightless places', *Social and Cultural Geography*, 14(4): 446–465.

Edensor, T. (2015) 'Light Design and Atmosphere', *Journal of Visual Communication*, 14(3): 331–350.

Edensor, T. (2017) *From Light to Dark: Daylight, Illumination and Gloom*, Minneapolis: Minnesota University Press.

Edgar, P. (Executive Producer) (1989–2001) *Round the Twist* [TV], Australian Children's Television Foundation.

Edgerton, D. (2008) *The Shock of the Old: Technology and Global History Since 1900*, London: Profile Books.
Ekirch, R. (2005) *At Day's Close: Night in Times Past*, London: W. W. Norton and Company.
Eliot, G. (2015 [1871]) *Middlemarch, a Study of Provincial Life*, New York: Diversion Classics.
Ellingham, M., Jacobs, D., Brown, H. and McVeigh, S. (2010) *The Rough Guide to Morocco*, Rough Guides.
Engineer's Department letter book (Number 22), 1897–1899. NLC11/1/22, Northern Lighthouse Board Archive, Edinburgh.
Faraday, M. (2008) *The Correspondence of Michael Faraday, Volume 5: 1855–1860*, James, F. A. J. L. (ed.), London: The Institute of Engineering and Technology.
Fayle, C. (1933) *A Short History of the World's Shipping Industry*, London: Allen and Unwin, London.
Fiddes, P. (2014) *Seeing the World and Knowing God*, Oxford: Oxford University Press.
Fitzgerald, S. and Woods, A. (2008) 'The Influence of Stacks on Flow Patterns and Stratification Associated with Natural Ventilation', *Building and Environment*, 43: 1719–1733.
Fletcher, M. (2014) 'Slipping Away: Row threatens centuries-old lighthouse', *The Telegraph*, 12 January 2014.
Flynn, K. and Raven, J. (2016) 'What is the Limit for Photoautotrophic Plankton Growth Rates?' *Journal of Plankton Research*, DOI:10.1093/plankt/fbw067.
Forde, W. (Director) (1941) *The Ghost Train* [Film], Gainsborough Pictures.
Fox Talbot, W. H. (1845) *Sun Pictures in Scotland*, London.
Foxhall, K. (2014) 'Making Modern Migraine Medieval: Men of science, Hildegard of Bingen and the life of a retrospective diagnosis', *Medical History*, 58(3): 354–374.
Freeberg, E. (2013) *The Age of Edison: Electric Light and the Invention of Modern America*, London: Penguin.
Freeman, M. J. (1983) 'Introduction', in Aldcroft, D. H. and Freeman, M. J. (eds) *Transport in the Industrial Revolution*, Manchester: Manchester University Press, pp. 13–14.
Freitag, S. (2005) 'Using Light and Sound Technology with Hypnosis', *Subconsciously Speaking*, 20(5): 10.
Gandy, M. (2016) *Moth*, London: Reaktion.
Garey, W. (1869) *Reflected Rays of Light upon Freemasonry; or, the Freemason's pocket compendium*, Stevenson, J. (ed.), Aberdeen: W. Garey.
Gay, J. (2007 [1716]) 'Trivia, or the art of walking the streets of London', III, in Brant, C. and Whyman, S. E. (eds) *Walking the Streets of Eighteenth-Century London: John Gay's Trivia (1716)*, Oxford: Oxford University Press, pp. 169–218.
Geertz, C. (1973) *The Interpretation of Cultures: Selected Essays*, New York: Basic Books.
Gell, A. (1992) 'The Technology of Enchantment and the Enchantment of Technology', in Coote, J. and Shelton, A. (eds) *Anthropology, Art and Aesthetics*, Oxford: Clarendon Press, pp. 40–63.
Gell, A. (1998) *Art and Agency: An Anthropological Theory*, Oxford: Clarendon Press.
George, R. (2013) *Ninety Percent of Everything: Inside Shipping, the Invisible Industry that Puts Clothes on Your Back, Gas in Your Car, and Food on Your Plate*, Macmillan: London.

256 References

Gibson, W. W. (1912) 'Flannan Isle', in *Fires*, Book 2, New York: Macmillan.

Gilbert, D. (2000) 'Floodlights', in Pile, S. and Thrift, N. (eds) *City a–z: Urban Fragments*, London: Routledge, pp. 76–77.

Gold, N. (nd) quoted in 'Orfordness Lighthouse', *Orford and Orfordness: The Suffolk Heritage Coast*, www.orford.org.uk/community/orfordness-lighthouse-company-2/ (Accessed 25/11/2014).

Goldie, G. Wyndham (1939) 'Critic on the Hearth', *The Listener*, 20 July 1939.

Gordon, A. (2008) *Naked Airport: A Cultural History of the World's Most Revolutionary Structure*, Chicago: University of Chicago Press.

Goudie, A. S. and Viles, H. A. (1997) *Salt Weathering Hazards*, Chichester: J. Wiley and Sons.

Gower, G. (2002) 'A Suggested Anglo-Saxon Signalling System between Chichester and London', *London Archaeologist*, 10(3): 59–63.

Grayson, G. (Director) (1950) *Dick Barton at Bay* [Film], Hammer Films.

Greenaway, P. (1985) *A Zed and Two Noughts* [Film], UK: Artificial Eye.

Greene, G. (1935) 'Reviews of *St Petersburg, Paris Love Song, The Phantom Light*', *The Spectator*, 12 July 1935.

Greenwell, C. (2016) Interview with Professor Chris Greenwell, Durham University, conducted on 22 June 2016 by J. Puckering, Durham University.

Griffin, E. (ed.) (2005) *Hildegard of Bingen: Selections from Her Writings*, Hart, C. and Bishop, J. (trans), San Franciso, CA: Harper.

Grimm, F. (2016) 'Should Cuban Migrants Who Occupied Offshore Lighthouse be Allowed to Stay?' *Miami Herald*, 27 May 2016, www.miamiherald.com/news/local/news-columns-blogs/fred-grimm/article80178737.html (Accessed 15/1/2017).

Gruenberg, C. and Knifton, R. (2007) 'The Crater of the Volcano: Liverpool and the avant-garde', in Gruenberg, C. and Knifton, R. (eds) *Centre of the Creative Universe: Liverpool and the Avant-Garde*, Liverpool: Liverpool University Press, pp. 18–37.

Guichard, J. and Trethewey, K. (2002) *North Atlantic Lighthouses*, Paris: Flammarion.

Guldi, J. (2012) *Roads to Power: Britain Invents the Infrastructure State*, Cambridge: Harvard University Press.

Hague, D. and Christie, R. (1975) *Lighthouses: Their Architecture, History and Archaeology*, Llandysul, Dyfed: Gomer Press.

Harrison, P. (2004) *Castles of God: Fortified Religious Buildings of the World*, Rochester, NY: Boydell Press.

Harrison, T. (2006) 'Lighthouse Depot Acquires Harbour Lights', *Lighthouse Digest*, March 2006, www.lighthousedigest.com/Digest/StoryPage.cfm?StoryKey=2412 (Accessed 17/3/2017).

Harvey, D. (1989) *The Condition of Postmodernity: An Enquiry into the Origins of Cultural Change*, Oxford: John Wiley/Blackwell.

Harvey, P. and Knox, H. (2010) 'Abstraction, Materiality and the "Science of the Concrete" in Engineering Practice', in Bennett, T. and Joyce, P. (eds) *Material Powers: Cultural Studies, History and the Material Turn*, London: Routledge, pp. 124–141.

Harvey, P. and Knox, H. (2012) 'The Enchantments of Infrastructure', *Mobilities*, 7(4): 521–536.

Hastrup, K. and Hastrup, F. (eds) (2015) *Waterworlds: Anthropology in Fluid Environments*, New York: Berghahn.

Hearne, R. (1640) *Ros Cœli. Or, A Miscellany of Ejaculations, Divine, Morall, &c.*, London: Printed by Richard Hearne.

Hegel, G. (1979) *The Phenomenology of Spirit*, Miller, A. V. (trans), Oxford: Oxford University Press.

Heidegger, M. (2002) *On Time and Being*, Stambaugh, J. (trans), Chicago: University of Chicago Press.
Henson, J. (Creator) (1983–1987) *Fraggle Rock* [TV], HBO and The Jim Henson Company.
Hill, R. and Barton, R. (2005) 'Red Enhances Human Performance in Contests', *Nature*, 435: 293.
Hind, C. Lewis (1910) *Turner's Golden Visions*, London: T. C. and E. C. Jack.
Hind, J. G. (2005) 'The Watchtowers and Fortlets on the North Yorkshire Coast: (*turresetcastra*)', *Yorkshire Archaeological Journal*, 77: 17–24.
Holmes, R. (1990) *Coleridge: Early Visions*, London: Penguin Books.
Hooper, M. and Liversedge, E. (2016) *Last Station 2016*, http://eliseandmary.co.uk/last-station/last-station-2016/ (Accessed 21/3/2017).
Hopkins, S. and Waugh, P. (2015) 'Haunting Image of Drowned Boy Sums Up Consequences of "The Syrian War in One Photo"', *The Huffington Post UK*, www.huffingtonpost.co.uk/2015/09/02/haunting-picture-of-drowned-syrian-boy-in-bodrum-prompts-debate_n_8077012.html (Accessed 24/1/2018).
Hunter, S. (Director) (1999) *Lighthouse* [Film], British Screen Productions, Arts Council of England.
Hunter Blair, P. (1985) 'Whitby as a Centre of Learning in the Seventh Century', in Lapidge, M. and Gneuss, H. (eds) *Learning and Literature in Anglo-Saxon England*, Cambridge: Cambridge University Press, pp. 3–33.
Huntington, L. (Director) (1941) *Tower of Terror* [Film], Associated British Picture Corporation.
Hutchison, M. (1990) 'Time Flashes: A short history of sound and light technology', *Megabrain Report: Special Issue on Sound/Light*, 1(2): 2–5.
Huygens, C. (1690) *Traité de la Lumière*, Leiden: Pierre Van der Aa marchand libraire.
Hylland Eriksen, T. (1993) 'Being Norwegian in a Shrinking World: Reflections on Norwegian identity', in Kiel, A. (ed.) *Continuity and Change: Aspects of Modern Norway*, Oslo: Scandinavian University Press, pp. 5–37.
Hylland Eriksen, T. (2016) *Overheating: An Anthropology of Accelerated Change*, Chicago: Pluto Press.
Ingold, T. (2010) 'No More Ancient, No More Human: The future past of archaeology and anthropology', in Garrow, D. and Yarrow, T. (eds) *Archaeology and Anthropology: Understanding Similarities, Exploring Differences*, Oxford: Oxbow Books, pp. 160–170.
Ingold, T. (2011) *Being Alive: Essays on Movement, Knowledge and Description*, London: Routledge.
Isenstadt, S. (2011) 'Auto-specularity: Driving through the American night', *Modernism/Modernity*, 18(2): 213–231.
Jackson, A. (2001) War and Empire in Mauritius and the Indian Ocean, London: MacMillan.
Jacobs, J. and Merriman, P. (2011) 'Practising Architectures', *Social and Cultural Geography*, 12(3): 211–222.
Jakle, J. (2001) *City Lights: Illuminating the American Night (Landscapes of the Night)*, Baltimore, MD: Johns Hopkins University Press.
James, P. D. (2006) *The Lighthouse*, London: Vintage.
Jamie, K. (2003) 'Into the Dark', *London Review of Books*, 25(24): 29–33.
Johnson, N. (1995) 'Cast in Stone: Monuments, geography, and nationalism', *Environment and Planning D*, 13(1): 51–65.
Jones, J. and Francis, C. (2003) 'The Effects of Light Characteristics on Avian Mortality at Lighthouses', *Journal of Avian Biology*, 34(4): 328–333.

Jones, O. (2010) '"The Breath of the Moon": The rhythmic and affective time-spaces of UK tides', in Edensor, T. (ed.) *Geographies of Rhythm*, Aldershot: Ashgate.
Jordan, H. H. (1979) 'A Photograph of Thomas Moore', *Keats-Shelley Journal*, 28: 24–25.
Jordan, P. (2014) *Seven Wonders of the Ancient World*, London: Routledge.
Karlgren, B. (1950) *The Book of Odes*, Stockholm: The Museum of Far Eastern Antiquities.
Kavaloski, J. (2014) *High Modernism: Aestheticism and Performativity in Literature of the 1920s*, New York: Camden House.
Kelly, R. (2008) *Bard of Erin: The Life of Thomas Moore*, London: Penguin.
Kenny, P. and Flynn, K. J. (2015) 'In Silico Optimization for Production of Biomass and Biofuel Feedstocks from Microalgae', *Journal of Applied Phycology*, 27(1): 33–48.
Kenny, P. and Flynn, K. J. (2016) 'Coupling a Simple Irradiance Description to a Mechanistic Growth Model to Predict Algal Production in Industrial-Scale Solar-Powered Photobioreactors', *Journal of Applied Phycology*, 28(6): 3203–3212.
Kepler, J. (1604) *Ad Vitellionem paralipomena: quibus astronomiae pars optica traditur*. Frankfurt: Claudium Marnium & heirs of Joannis Aubrius.
Kepler, J. (2000) *Optics: Paralipomena to Witelo and Optical Part of Astronomy*, Donahue, W. H. (trans), Santa Fe, NM: Green Lion Press.
Kilpper, T. (2016) 'A Lighthouse for Lampedusa! at Bozar, Bruxelles', *Kilpper Projects (Blog)*, http://kilpper-projects.de/blog/?cat=3 (Accessed 15/1/2017).
Kittler, F. and Winthrop-Young, G. (2015) 'A Short History of the Searchlight', *Cultural Politics*, 11(3): 384–390.
Klein, B. and Mackenthun, G. (eds) (2004) *Sea Changes: Historicizing the Ocean*, London: Routledge.
Koenderink, J. (2014) 'The All-Seeing Eye?', *Perception*, 43(1): 1–6.
Koslofsky, C. (2011) *Evening's Empire: A History of Night in Early Modern Europe*, Cambridge: Cambridge University Press.
Krige, J. and Guzzetti, L. (1997) *History of European Scientific and Technological Collaboration*, Brussels: European Commission.
Kutschera, U. and Briggs, W. R. (2016) 'Phototropic Solar Tracking in Sunflower Plants: An integrative perspective', *Annals of Botany*, 117(1): 1–8.
Labelle, B. (2008) 'Pump up the Bass: Rhythm, cars and auditory scaffolding', *The Senses and Society*, 3(2): 187–204.
Lacey, M. (2005) 'Memories Linger Where NASA Lights Shone in Gambia', *The New York Times*, 4 September 2005, www.nytimes.com/2005/09/04/world/africa/memories-linger-where-nasa-lights-shone-in-gambia.html?_r=0 (Accessed 18/9/2016).
Lai, L. W. C., Davies, S. N. G. and Lorne, F. (2008) 'The Political Economy of Coase's Lighthouse in History (Part I): A Review of the Theories and Models of the Provision of a Public Good', *The Town Planning Review*, 79(4): 395–425.
Lambert, M. (1993) 'New Light on Limelight', *Theatre Notebook*, 47(3): 157–163.
Langewiesche, W. (2004) *The Outlaw Sea: A World of Freedom, Chaos, and Crime*, Granta: London.
Lapidge, M. and Rosier, J. (trans) (1985) *Aldhelm: The Poetic Works*, Woodbridge: Brewer.
Lash, N. (1996) *The Beginning and End of Religion*, Cambridge: Cambridge University Press.
Latour, B. (1987) *Science in Action: How to Follow Scientists and Engineers Through Society*, Cambridge, MA: Harvard University Press.
Lavery, B. (2005) *Ship: 5000 Years of Maritime Adventure*, UK: Dorling Kindersley.
Lefebvre, H. (2004) *Rhythmanalysis: Space, Time and Everyday Life*, Elden, S. and Moore, G. (trans), London: Continuum.

Lepard, G. and Barker, K. (2004) 'St Aldhelm and the Chapel at Worth Matravers: Sea-mark, lighthouse or bell tower', *Proceedings of the Dorset Natural History and Archaeological Society*, 124: 148–156.

Levine, M. and Taylor, W. (2016) 'No Lighthouse, No Light', *work in progress*.

Levitt, T. (2013) *A Short Bright Flash: Augustin Fresnel and the Birth of the Modern Lighthouse*, New York: W. W. Norton.

Lighthouse Relief (2015) *Lighthouse Relief*, www.lighthouserelief.org/ (Accessed 10/12/2016).

Lindberg, E. (2009) *The Market and the Lighthouse: Public Goods in Historical Perspective*. Paper presented to the Economic History and Society Conference, 3–5 April, University of Warwick.

Lindberg, E. (2015) 'The Swedish Lighthouse System 1650–1890: Private versus public provision of public goods', *European Review of Economic History*, 19(4): 454–468.

Literature Online (nd) *Proquest Literature Online*, https://literature.proquest.com (Accessed 3/1/2017).

Liverpool Daily Post (1946) 'Nerve Centre of Speke', *Liverpool Daily Post*, 6 August, Liverpool Record Office.

Longfellow, H. W. (1855) *The Song of Hiawatha*, London: David Bogue, Fleet Street.

Longfellow, H. W. (2000) 'The Lighthouse', in McClatchy, J. D. (ed.) *Poems and Other Writings*, New York: Library of America, pp. 131–133.

Love, J. (2015) *A Natural History of Lighthouses*, Dunbeath: Whittles Publishing.

Lowenthal, D. (1994) 'The Value of Age and Decay', in Krumbein, W., Brimblecombe, P., Cosgrove, D. and Staniforth, S. (eds) *Durability and Change: The Science, Responsibility, and Cost of Sustaining Cultural Heritage*, Chichester: Wiley and Sons.

Ma, X., Hou, X., Edgecombe, G. and Strausfeld, N. (2012) 'Complex Brain and Optic Lobes in an Early Cambrian Arthropod', *Nature*, 490: 258–261.

McCall Howard, P. (2013) 'Feeling the Ground', in Carlyle, A. and Lane, C. (eds) *On Listening*, Devon: Uniformbooks, pp. 61–66.

McCanch, N. (1985) *A Lighthouse Notebook*, London: Michael Joseph.

Macaulay, R. (1953) *The Pleasure of Ruins*, London: Thames and Hudson.

McGreevy, J. (1985) 'A Preliminary Scanning Electron Microscope Study of Honeycomb Weathering of Sandstone in a Coastal Environment', *Earth Surface Processes and Landforms*, 10: 509–518.

McKenzie, J. (2007) *Architecture of Alexandria and Egypt: 300 B.C.–A.D. 700*, New Haven and London: Yale University Press.

Mackinder, H. (1904) 'The Geographical Pivot of History', *Geographical Journal*, 23(4): 421–437.

McLeish, T. (2014) *Faith and Wisdom in Science*, Oxford: Oxford University Press.

McLeish, T. and Strang, V. (2014) *Leading Interdisciplinary Research: Transforming the Academic Landscape*, Stimulus Paper, The Leadership Foundation for Higher Education, London, http://dro.dur.ac.uk/19474/1/19474.pdf?DDD5+dng4aeb+d700tmt+dul4eg (Accessed 29/1/2018).

MacLeod, R. (1965) 'The Alkali Acts Administration, 1963–84: The Emergence of the Civil Scientist', *Victorian Studies*, 9(2): 85–112.

MacLeod, R. (1969) 'Science and Government in Victorian England: Lighthouse Illumination and the Board of Trade, 1866–1886', *Isis*, 60(1): 4–38.

MacPherson, M. (2009) *Keepers of the Light*, Glasgow: Brown, Son and Ferguson.

McQuire, S. (2008) *The Media City: Media, Architecture and Urban Spaces*, London: Sage.

Margolis, Z. and Cillekens, E. (2016) 'Flaming Toilet Rolls Guide Royal Flying Doctor Service Aircraft to Remote Airstrip', *ABC News*, 12 August 2016, www.abc.net.au/news/2016-08-12/rfds-use-flaming-toilet-rolls-to-light-up-remote-airstrip/7722858 (Accessed 6/10/2016).

Maritime Coastguard Agency (2014) *Dover Strait Crossings*, www.gov.uk/government/publications/dover-strait-crossings-channel-navigation-information-service/dover-strait-crossings-channel-navigation-information-service-cnis (Accessed 15/08/2014).

Marquenie, J., Donners, M., Poot, H. and de Wit, B. (2013) 'Bird-friendly Light Sources: Adapting the spectral composition of artificial lighting', *IEEE Industry Applications Magazine*, 19(2): 56–62.

Marshall, I. (1984) 'Fog Tropes', *Fog Tropes / Gradual Requiem* [Vinyl LP], New Albion Records.

Martin, G. and Martin, T. (2005) *All Possible Worlds: A History of Geographical Ideas*, Oxford: Oxford University Press.

Mason, H. (Director) (1942) *Back Room Boy* [Film], Gainsborough Pictures.

Masonic Dictionary (nd) 'Light', *Masonic Dictionary*, www.masonicdictionary.com/light.html (Accessed 22/9/2016).

Massey, D. (1994) *Space, Place and Gender*, Minneapolis: University of Minnesota Press.

Mawer, A., Stenton, F. and Gover, J. (1929) *The Place-Names of Sussex*, 2 Vols, English Place-Name Society, 6/7, Cambridge: Cambridge University Press.

Melbin, M. (1978) 'Night as Frontier', *American Sociological Review*, 43(1): 3–22.

Metge, J. (2004 [1967]) *Rautahi: The Maori of New Zealand*, London: Routledge, Taylor and Francis.

Micheletti, L. (1999) *The Use of Auditory and Visual Stimulation for the Treatment of Attention Deficit Hyperactivity Disorder in Children*, Doctoral thesis, University of Houston, Texas.

Mill, J. S. (1848) *Principles of Political Economy with Some of their Applications to Social Philosophy*, Ashley, W. J. (ed.), London: Longmans Green.

Mill, J. S. (1998) *Principles of Political Economy*, Riley, J. (ed.), Oxford: Oxford University Press.

Miller, A. (2010) 'The Lighthouse Top I See: Lighthouses as instruments and manifestations of state building in the early republic', *Buildings and Landscapes: Journal of Vernacular Architecture Forum*, 17(11): 13–14.

Millichamp, M. (nd) 'Aerial Lighthouses', *Lighthouse Compendium*, www.mycetes.co.uk/a/page16.html (Accessed 5/10/2016).

Mitra, A., Flynn, K., Tillmann, U., Raven, J., Caron, D., Stoecker, D. et al. (2016) 'Defining Planktonic Protist Functional Groups on Mechanisms for Energy and Nutrient Acquisition; Incorporation of Diverse Mixotrophic Strategies', *Protist*, 167: 106–120.

Mola, R. (nd) 'History of Aircraft Landing Aids', *U.S. Centennial of Flight Commission*, www.centennialofflight.net/essay/Government_Role/landing_nav/POL14.htm (Accessed 22/9/2016).

Mole, T. (2007) *Byron's Romantic Celebrity: Industrial Culture and the Hermeneutic of Intimacy*, Basingstoke: Palgrave.

Mole, T. (ed.) (2009) *Romanticism and Celebrity Culture*, Cambridge: Cambridge University Press.

Moore, A. (2012) *The Lighthouse*, Cromer: Salt Publishing.

Morel, C. (1675) *A description of the funeral solemnities, performed in the church of Nostre-Dame, at Paris: to honour the memory of his excellency [. . .] Vicount Turenne*, London.

Morphy, H. (1992) 'From Dull to Brilliant: The aesthetics of spiritual power among the Yolngu', in Coote, J. and Shelton, A. (eds) *Anthropology, Art and Aesthetics*, Oxford: Clarendon Press, pp. 181–208.

Morphy, H. (1994) *Aesthetics is a Cross-cultural Category: A Debate Held in the Muriel Stott Centre, John Rylands University Library of Manchester, on 30th October 1993*, Weiner, J. (ed.), Manchester: Group for Debates in Anthropological Theory.

Morrison, R. (2004) 'Lightpole', on *Stop Scratching It* (CD, released 2007), The Spooky Men's Chorale, https://spookymen.com/discography/stop-scratching-it-2007/ (Accessed 29/1/2018).

Morrow, C. (2015) *The Dangerous Lighthouse – Lesbos Greece – Refugee Crisis* [Interview], 3 December 2015, www.youtube.com/watch?v=LgC2PpvzDpw (Accessed 15/1/2017).

Murden, J. (2006) '"City of Change and Challenge": Liverpool since 1945', in Belchem, J. (ed.) *Liverpool 800: Culture, Character and History*, Liverpool: Liverpool University Press, pp. 393–485.

Murphy, J., Sexton, D., Jenkins, G., Boorman, P., Booth, B., Brown, C. et al. (2009) *UK Climate Projections Science Report: Climate Change Projections*, Met Office, Exeter: Hadley Centre.

Murray, P., Murray, L. and Devonshire Jones, T. (eds) (2013) 'The Eye of God', in *The Oxford Dictionary of Christian Art and Architecture*, second edition, Oxford: Oxford University Press.

Murray Schafer, R. (1994 [1977]) *Soundscape: Our Sonic Environment and the Tuning of the World*, original edition, Rochester, VT: Destiny Books.

NASA (2008) 'Finding Fireflies Next to a Lighthouse: Goddard's new technology to study alien worlds', *Goddard Space Flight Centre/News*, 12 September 2008, www.nasa.gov/centers/goddard/news/topstory/2008/planet_search.html (Accessed 28/7/2016).

NASA (2010) 'Roster of Runways Ready to Bring a Shuttle Home', *Space Shuttle Era*, NASA, www.nasa.gov/mission_pages/shuttle/flyout/landing_sites.html (Accessed 26/9/2016).

NASA (2016) 'NASA's Kepler Mission Announces Largest Collection of Planets Ever Discovered', *NASA Press Release*, 10 May 2016, www.nasa.gov/press-release/nasas-kepler-mission-announces-largest-collection-of-planets-ever-discovered (Accessed 7/10/2016).

Nasaw, D. (1999) *Going Out: The Rise and Fall of Public Amusements*, Boston, MA: Harvard University Press.

National Trust (2014a) 'The National Trust's Position on the Orford Ness Lighthouse', *National Trust*, 12 January 2014, http://ntpressoffice.wordpress.com/2014/01/12/national-trusts-position-on-the-orford-ness-lighthouse/ (Accessed 25/11/2014).

National Trust (2014b) *East of England Blog*, 3 February 2014, https://eastofenglandnt.wordpress.com/2014/02/03/orford-ness-lighthouse/ (Accessed 25/11/2014).

Natural England (2014) *Comments on planning application DC/14/0206/FUL*, 14 February 2014, www.eastsuffolk.gov.uk/planning/planning-applications/publicaccess/ (Accessed 25/11/2014).

Neumann, D. (ed.) (2002) *Architecture of the Night: The Illuminated Building*, New York: Prestel.

Nicholson, C. (2010) *Postcards from the Edge: Remote British Lighthouses in Vintage Postcards*, Dunbeath: Whittles.

Northern Echo (2016) 'Durham Man Describes Dramatic Rescue of Lifeless Baby Found Face Down in Sea', *The Northern Echo*, 21 January 2016, www.thenorthernecho.co.uk/news/14218854.Durham_man_describes_dramatic_rescue_of_lifeless_refugee_baby_found_face_down_in_sea/ (Accessed 8/12/2015).

Northern Lighthouse Board (nd) 'The Mystery of Flannan Isle', *NLB/History*, www.nlb.org.uk/HistoricalInformation/FlannanIsles/Main/ (Accessed 13/3/2017).
O'Connolly, J. (Director) (1972) *Tower of Evil* [Film], Grenadier Films.
O'Neill, E. (1922) *Hairy Ape*, www.eoneill.com/texts/ha/contents.htm (Accessed 1/6/2016).
O'Shaughnessy, B. (1984) 'Seeing the Light', *Proceedings of the Aristotelian Society*, 85: 193–218.
Olmstead, R. (2005) 'Use of Auditory and Visual Stimulation to Improve Cognitive Abilities in Learning-Disabled Children', *Journal of Neurotherapy*, 9(2): 49–61.
On the Edge (2012) 'On the Edge 2012: A Chain of Lighthouses', *Lighthouses of Norway*, http://lighthousesofnorway.com/art-on-the-edge-a-chain-of-lighthouses (Accessed 9/2/2017).
Oreskes, N. (forthcoming 2018) 'The Need for Expert Judgement', in Oppenheimer, M., Oreskes, N., Jamieson, D., Brysse, K., O'Reilly, J. and Shindell, M. (eds) *Assessing Assessments: Scientific Knowledge for Public Policy*, Chicago: University of Chicago Press.
Oreskes, N. and Krige, J. (eds) (2014) *Science and Technology in the Global Cold War*, Cambridge, MA: MIT Press.
Ostdiek, V. and Bord, D. (2013) 'Fresnel, Pharos, and Physics', in *Inquiry into Physics*, Boston, MA: Brooks/Cole, pp. 360–361.
Otter, C. (2008) *The Victorian Eye: A Political History of Light and Vision in Britain, 1800–1910*, Chicago: University of Chicago Press.
Owen, J. R. (2013) '"Give Me a Light": The development and regulation of ships' navigation lights up to the mid-1860s', *International Journal of Maritime History*, 25(1): 173–203.
Packer, B. (2005) *The Light of Christ*, The Church of Jesus Christ of Latter-Day Saints. Remarks delivered on 22 June 2004, at the Missionary Training Center, Provo, Utah, www.lds.org/ensign/2005/04/the-light-of-christ?lang=eng (Accessed 14/7/2016).
Palmer, T. (1975) *Lighthouse*, London: Hutchinson.
Panti, C. (2013) 'Robert Grosseteste's *De luce*. A critical edition', in Flood, J., Ginther, J. R. and Goering, J. W. (eds) *Robert Grosseteste and his intellectual milieu, new editions and studies*, Papers in Medieval Studies, Vol. 24, Toronto, Canada: Pontifical Institute of Mediaeval Studies, pp. 191–238.
Parker, A. (2011) 'On the Origin of Optics', *Optics and Laser Technology*, 43: 323–329.
Parkinson, D. (ed.) (1995) *Mornings in the Dark: The Graham Greene Film Reader*, Penguin: Harmondsworth.
Paterson, J., García-Bellido, D., Lee, M., Brock, G., Jago, J. and Edgecombe, G. (2011) 'Acute Vision in the Giant Cambrian Predator *Anomalocaris* and the Origin of Compound Eyes', *Nature*, 480: 237–240.
Pattenden, R. (2009) *Raft – the Drifting Border*, Macquarie University Art Gallery, Catalogue 12.
Peters, K. (2012) 'Manipulating Material Hydro-worlds: Rethinking human and more-than-human relationality through offshore radio piracy', *Environment and Planning A*, 44(5): 1241–1254.
Peters, K. and Steinberg, P. (2014) 'Volume and Vision: Toward a wet ontology', *Harvard Design Magazine*, 39: 124–129.
Pett, P. (1688) *The Happy Future State of England*, London.
Petty, M. (2015) 'Hong Kong: Symphony of lights', in Isenstadt, S., Petty, M. and Neumann, D. (eds) *Cities of Light: Two Centuries of Urban Illumination*, London: Routledge, pp. 164–168.

Piat, D. (2011) *Mauritius: On the Spice Route 1598–1810*, Singapore: Ed Didier Millet.
Pienne, Y. (1939) *The Fame of Grace Darling* [TV], 9 July 1939, British Broadcasting Corporation.
Piper, J. (1938) 'The Nautical Style', *Architectural Review*, 83: 1–14.
Planning Application (2014) *Planning Application DC/14/0206/FUL*, Suffolk Coastal District Council, www.eastsuffolk.gov.uk/planning/planning-applications/publicaccess/ (Accessed 25/11/2014).
Plato (2008) *Laws*, Book 6, Jowett, B. (trans), New York: Cosimo Classics.
Plato (2012) *The Republic*, Book I, Ferrari, G. R. F. (ed.), Griffith, T. (trans), Cambridge: Cambridge University Press.
Plato (2015) *Timaeus*, Jowett, B. (trans), London: Aeterna Press.
Pliny the Elder, *Natural History*, xxxiv.18, Rackham, H. (trans), Cambridge, MA: Harvard University Press.
Porter, D. (1998) *The Life and Times of Sir Goldworthy Gurney, Gentleman Scientist and Inventor, 1793–1875*, London: Associated University Presses.
Porter, R. (2000) *Enlightenment: Britain and the Creation of the Modern World*, London: Allen Lane.
Possum Line (nd) 'The Tempsford Special Duties Squadrons', *The Possum Escape Line*, www.possumline.net/index.htm (Accessed 20/9/2016).
Powell, M. (Director) (1935) *The Phantom Light* [Film], Gainsborough Pictures.
Powell, M. (1986) *A Life in Movies*, Heinemann: London.
Price Edwards, E. (1884) *Our Seamarks; a plain account of the lighthouses, lightships, beacons, buoys, and fog-signals maintained on our coasts for the guidance of mariners*, London: Longmans, Green and Co., available at https://insatiablecollector.files.wordpress.com/2012/10/our-seamarks.jpg (Accessed 21/3/2017).
Qantara (nd) 'Minaret of the Great Mosque of Kairouan', *Qantara: Mediterranean Heritage*, https://web.archive.org/web/20141017222326/http://www.qantara-med.org/qantara4/public/show_document.php?do_id=1287&lang=en (Accessed 29/1/2018).
Quakers in Britain (nd) 'Our History', *Quakers in Britain*, www.quaker.org.uk/about-quakers/our-history (Accessed 12/7/2016).
Quarles, F. (1635) *Emblemes*, London: G[eorge] M[iller] for John Marriot.
Raban, J. (1999) *Passage to Juneau: A Sea and Its Meanings*, Basingstoke and Oxford: Picador.
Raven, J. (2013) 'Rubisco: Still the Most Abundant Protein in Earth?' *New Phytologist*, 198(3): 1–3.
Rayleigh, Lord (1933) 'Beryllium and Helium', *Nature*, 131, 724–724.
Reekie, S. (nd) *Scottish Heritage: The Elie Lighthouse*, www.scottishheritage.net/elielighthouse.htm (Accessed 2/8/2016).
'Report from the Select Committee on Lighthouses 1834', *Parliamentary Papers, Session 1834*, Vol. XII, London: House of Commons.
'Report from the Select Committee on Lighthouses 1845', *Parliamentary Papers, Session 1845*, Vol. IX, London: House of Commons.
'Report of the Commissioners appointed to Inquire into the Condition and Management of Lights, Buoys, and Beacons', London: George Edward Eyre and William Spottiswoode, Vol. I and II, 1861.
RFDS (nd) 'Preparing an Airstrip - Care and Maintenance', *Royal Flying Doctor Service*, www.flyingdoctor.org.au/preparing-airstrip/ (Accessed 26/1/2018).
RFS (1874) 'Report by Professor Tyndall to Trinity House on experiments with regard to fog signals; Letter to Board of Trade by Trinity House on fog signal at Cape Race'.

House of Commons Papers, http://parlipapers.proquest.com/parlipapers/docview/t70.d75.1874-050571?accountid=10342 (Accessed 30/5/2016).

Rhein, M. (2001) *Anatomy of the Lighthouse*, Glasgow: Saraband.

Rocco, C. (1997) 'Democracy and Discipline in Aeschylus's Oresteia', in *Tragedy and Enlightenment: Athenian Political Thought and the Dilemmas of Modernity*, Berkeley: University of California Press, pp. 136–170.

Rodaway, P. (1994) *Sensuous Geographies*, London: Routledge.

Rodner, W. (1986) 'Humanity and Nature in the Steamboat Paintings of J. M. W. Turner', *Albion*, 18(3): 455–474.

Rojek, N. (2001) 'Biological Rationale for Artificial Night-Lighting Concerns in the Channel Island', Unpublished Report, California Department of Fish and Game, Marine Region, Monterey, California, pp. 1–21.

Romanillos, P. (2011) 'Geography, Death and Finitude', *Environment and Planning A*, 43: 2549.

Rosand, E. (1990) *Opera in Seventeenth-Century Venice: The Creation of a Genre*, Berkeley, Los Angeles and Oxford: University of California Press.

Rosenberg, C. (Director) (2006) *Half Light* [Film], Lakeshore Entertainment.

Royal Aviation Museum (nd) *Lysander: By the Light of the Silvery Moon*, Royal Aviation Museum of Western Canada, www.royalaviationmuseum.com/533/war-plane-sample/ (Accessed 20/9/2016).

RT Question More (2016) 'Cuban Migrants Found Clinging to Offshore Lighthouse to be Sent Home', *RT Question More*, 29 June 2016, www.rt.com/usa/348921-cuba-migrants-lighthouse-wet-foot/ (Accessed 10/12/2016).

Ruskin, J. (1843) *Modern Painters*, Vol. I, London: Smith, Elder & Co.

Ruskin, J. (1856) *Modern Painters*, Vol. IV, London: Smith, Elder & Co.

Ruskin, J. (1870) 'Lectures on art and *Aratra Pentelici* with lectures and notes on Greek art and mythology', in Cook, E. T. and Wedderburn, A. (eds) *The Works of John Ruskin: Library Edition*, Vol. XX, London and New York: George Allen.

Ruskin, J. (1908) 'Letter to John James Ruskin (May 28, 1845)', in Cook, E. T. and Wedderburn, A. (eds) *The Works of John Ruskin: Library Edition*, Vol. XXXV (*Praeterita and Dilecta*), London and New York: George Allen, p. 562 (footnote 1).

Sabbattini, N. (1994) *Pratique pour fabriquer scènes et machines de théâtre (1638)*, Canavaggia, M., Canavaggia, R. and Jouvet, L. (trans) Neuchâtel: Ides et Calendes.

Salem, E. (1991) 'The Influence of the Lighthouse of Alexandria on the Minarets of North Africa and Spain', *Islamic Studies*, Special Issue on Muslim Heritage in Spain, 30(1/2): 149–156.

Schiffman, H. (1996) *Sensation and Perception: An Integrated Approach*, New York, Chichester, Brisbane, Toronto, Singapore: John Wiley.

Schivelbusch, W. (1988) *Disenchanted Night: The Industrialization of Light in the Nineteenth Century*, Davis, A. (trans), Berkeley and London: University of California Press.

Schneiter, A. (ed.) (1997) 'Sunflower Technology and Production', *The American Society of Agronomy*, 35: 1–19.

Scorsese, M. (Director) (2010) *Shutter Island* [Film], Paramount Pictures.

Scott, J. (1998) *Seeing Like a State: How Certain Schemes to Improve the Human Condition Have Failed*, New Haven, CT: Yale.

Sechrest, L. (2004) 'Public Goods and Private Solutions in Maritime History', *The Quarterly Journal of Austrian Economics*, 7(2): 3–27.

Serres, M. (2008) *The Five Senses: A Philosophy of Mingled Bodies*, London: Bloomsbury.

Shanks, M. (1998) 'The Life of an Artifact in Interpretive Archaeology', *Fennoscandia Archaeologica*, 15: 15–30.

Sharpe, W. (2008) *New York Nocturne: The City After Dark in Literature, Painting and Photography, 1850–1950*, Princeton, NJ: Princeton University Press.

Sharples, J. (2004) *Liverpool: Pevsner Architectural Guide*, New Haven, CT: Yale University Press.

Shepheard, P. (1997) *The Cultivated Wilderness Or, What is Landscape?* Cambridge, MA: MIT Press.

Sheridan, M. D. (1938) *Longstone Light*, [Radio] 5 September 1938, British Broadcasting Corporation.

Shimizu, J. (2010) *Claisen Flask*, published on 6 July 2010, kopenhagentv, https://youtu.be/D18UyFJhqCQ (Accessed 30/1/2018).

Shire, W. (2013) 'Home', in Triulzi, A. and McKenzie, R. (eds) *Long Journeys: African Migrants on the Road*, Leiden: Brill, pp. xi–xii.

Shoichet, K. (2015) 'Will Cubans who Climbed Lighthouse Get to Stay in U.S.?', *CNN*, 28 June 2016, http://edition.cnn.com/2016/06/15/us/florida-lighthouse-cuban-migrants/ (Accessed 15/1/2017).

Shoreline Management Plan (2010), *Suffolk Shoreline Management Plan 2, Sub-cell 3c, Policy Development Zone 6 – Orford Ness to Cobbold's Point*, Suffolk Coastal District Council/Waveney District Council/Environment Agency, January 2010, Version 9, www.suffolksmp2.org.uk (Accessed 23/6/2015).

Sinclair, I. (2011) *Ghost Milk: Calling Time on the Grand Project*, London: Hamish Hamilton.

Singh, T. (1994) *Sikh Gurus and the Indian Spiritual Thought*, second edition (reprint), Patiala: Punjabi University Press.

Smeaton, J. (1814) 'Smeaton's Narrative of the Building of the Eddystone Light-house', *The London Review and Literary Journal*, 66: 37–40.

Smedley, C. (1932) *Grace Darling and Her Times*, London: Hurst and Blackett.

Smith, A. Mark (2014) *From Sight to Light: The Passage from Ancient to Modern Optics*, Chicago: Chicago University Press.

Smith, J. (1869) 'The Sacrament – A Saint of God – The Eternity of our Religion – Matrimony' in *Journal of Discourses*, 12: 346–351. Remarks delivered on 10 January 1869, in the Tabernacle, Salt Lake City.

Smithson, H., Gasper, G. and McLeish, T. (2014) 'All the Colours of the Rainbow', *Nature Physics*, 10: 540–542.

Spalding, F. (2009) 'In the Nautical Style: John Piper', in Fiegel, L. and Harris, A. (eds) *Modernism on Sea: Art and Culture at the British Seaside*, Oxford: Peter Lang, pp. 135–143.

Spark, M. (2011 [1961]) 'The Curtain Blown by the Breeze' in *The Complete Short Stories*, Edinburgh: Canongate Books, pp. 64–82.

Stedman, M. L. (2012) *The Light Between Oceans*, London: Transworld Publishers.

Steinberg, P. (1999) 'Navigating to Multiple Horizons: Towards a geography of ocean space', *Professional Geographer*, 51(3): 366–375.

Steinberg, P. (2001) *The Social Construction of the Ocean*, Cambridge: Cambridge University Press.

Steinberg, P. (2011) 'The *Deepwater Horizon*, the *Mavi Marmara*, and the Dynamic Zonation of Ocean-Space', *The Geographical Journal*, 177: 12–16.

Steinberg, P. (2013) 'Of Other Seas: Metaphors and materialities in maritime regions', *Atlantic Studies*, 10: 156–169.

Steinberg, P. and Chapman, T. (2009) 'Key West's Conch Republic: Building sovereignties of connection', *Political Geography*, 28: 283–295.
Steinberg, P., Nyman, E. and Caraccioli, M. (2012) 'Atlas Swam: Freedom, capital, and floating sovereignties in the Seasteading vision', *Antipode*, 44: 1532–1550.
Steinberg, P. and Peters, K. (2015) 'Wet Ontologies, Fluid Spaces: Giving depth to volume through oceanic thinking', *Environment and Planning D: Society and Space*, 32: 247–264.
Steiner, G. (1989) *Real Presences*, London: Faber.
Stevenson, A. (1831) *The British Pharos, or, A list of the lighthouses on the coasts of Great Britain and Ireland, descriptive of the appearance of the lights at night. For the use of mariners*, second edition, Leith: W. Reid & Son.
Stewart, M. (nd) 'People, Places and Things: Lampadedromia', *Greek Mythology: From the Iliad to the fall of the last tyrant*, http://messagenetcommresearch.com/myths/ppt/Lampadedromia_1.html (Accessed 10/11/2016).
Strang, V. (2004) *The Meaning of Water*, Oxford, New York: Berg.
Strang, V. (2015a) *Water: Nature and Culture*, London and Chicago: Reaktion/Chicago University Press.
Strang, V. (2015b) 'On the Matter of Time', *Interdisciplinary Science Reviews*, 40(2): 101–123.
Strausfeld, N., Ma, X., Edgecombe, G., Fortey, R., Land, M., Liu, Y., Cong, P.-Y. and Hou, X. (2016) 'Arthropod Eyes: The early Cambrian fossil record and divergent evolution of visual systems', *Arthropod Structure and Development*, 45(2): 152–172.
Suchmann, L. (1997) 'Centres of Coordination: A case and some themes', in Resnick, L., Säljö, R., Pontecorvo, C. and Burge, B. (eds) *Discourse, Tools, and Reasoning: Essays on Situated Cognition*, Berlin: Springer-Verlag, pp. 41–62.
Suetonius (2007) *The Twelve Caesars* / Gaius Suetonius Tranquillus, Graves, R. (trans); revised with an introduction and notes by Rives, J. B., London: Penguin Classics.
Talbot, F. A. (1913) *Lightships and Lighthouses*, London: William Heineman, https://archive.org/stream/lightshipslighth00talbuoft#page/n7/mode/2up (Accessed 24/1/2018).
Tanner, B., Bower, R., McLeish, T. and Gasper, G. (2016) 'Unity and Symmetry in the De Luce of Robert Grosseteste, in Cunningham, J. and Hocknull, M. (eds) *Robert Grosseteste and the Pursuit of Religious and Scientific Learning in the Middel Ages*, London: Springer, pp. 3–20.
Taylor, H. and Taylor, J. (1980) *Anglo-Saxon Architecture*, 2 Vols, Cambridge: Cambridge University Press.
Taylor, J. (2001) 'Private Property, Public Interest, and the Role of the State in Nineteenth-Century Britain: The case of the lighthouses', *The Historical Journal*, 44(3): 749–771.
The Children's Newspaper (1938) 'The Heroine of Longstone Lighthouse', *The Children's Newspaper*, September 10, p. 7.
The National Archives (1961–1962) 'Dover Straits: Separation and routing of ships', *National Archives Board of Trade file: BT 243/177*.
The National Archives (1971) 'Reappraisal of ships routing and Traffic Separation Scheme for Straits of Dover', *Foreign Commonwealth Office files: FCO 76/253*.
Thomas, D. (2010) *The Collected Poems of Dylan Thomas*, New York: New Directions.
Thomas, G. (2008) 'The Symbolic Lives of Late Anglo-Saxon Settlements: A cellared structure and iron hoard from Bishopstone, East Sussex', *Archaeological Journal*, 165: 334–398.

Thornton, P. (2015) 'The Meaning of Light: Seeing and being on the battlefield', *Cultural Geographies*, 22(4): 567–583.
Thrift, N. (1996) *Spatial Formations*, Sage: London.
Tolkien, J. R. R. (1955) *The Lord of the Rings*, London: Allen and Unwin.
Tomblin, D. (Director) (1967) 'The Girl Who Was Death' [TV], *The Prisoner*, Everyman Films, Incorporated Television Company.
Tracy, S. (1986) 'Darkness from Light: The beacon fire in the Agamemnon', *The Classical Quarterly*, 36: 257–260.
Truax, B. (2001) *Acoustic Communication*, Westport, Connecticut and London: Ablex.
T. S. (1942) 'At the Central', *The New York Times*, 29 June 1942. Available at: www.nytimes.com/movie/review?res=9C06E1D9173EE13BBC4151DFB0668389659EDE (Accessed 24/1/2018).
Tuan, Y.-F. (1977) *Space and Place: The Perspective of Experience*, Minneapolis: University of Minnesota Press.
Tufft, B. (2015) 'Migrant Crisis: Greek soldier saved 20 people singlehandedly off Rhodes Beach', *The Independent*, 26 April, www.independent.co.uk/news/world/europe/migrant-crisis-greek-soldier-saved-20-people-singlehandedly-off-rhodes-beach-10205175.html (Accessed 24/1/2018).
Tuke, T. (1617) *A theological discourse of the gracious and blessed conjunction of Christ and a sincere Christian*, London.
Turner, T. (1674) *The case of the bankers and their creditors stated and examined by the rules of lawes, policy, and common reason*, London.
Turpin, T. (2009) 'Fireflies: Torchbearers of the Insect World', in *What's Buggin' You Now? Bee's Knees, Bug Lites and Beetles*, West Lafayette, IN: Purdue University Press, pp. 75–76.
Tyndall, J. (1867) *On Sound*, London: Longmans, Green and Co.
Tyndall, J. (1874) *Address, etc. delivered to the British Association at Belfast, 1874*, London: Taylor & Francis.
Tyndall, J. (1900 [1872]) *Fragments of Science*, New York: P. F. Collier, http://archive.org/details/fragmentsofscien02tynd (Accessed 13/10/2016).
Underwood, T. (2014) Comments on planning application DC/14/0206/FUL, 15/2/2014, www.eastsuffolk.gov.uk/planning/planning-applications/publicaccess/ (Accessed 25/11/2014).
UNESCO (nd) *Kairouan*, World Heritage Centre, UNESCO, http://whc.unesco.org/en/list/499 (Accessed 25/11/2016).
Vall, N. (2007) 'Regionalism and Cultural History: The case of North-Eastern England, 1918–1976', in Gareth Green, A. and Pollard, A. J. (eds) *Regional Identities in North-East England, 1300–2000*, Woodbridge: Boydell Press, pp. 181–208.
van der Werf, S., Können, G., Lehn, W., Steenhuisen, F. and Davidson, W. (2003) 'Gerrit de Veer's True and Perfect Description of the Novaya Zemlya Effect, 24–27 January 1597', *Applied Optics*, 42(3): 379–389.
van Zandt, D. (1993) 'The Lessons of the Lighthouse: "Government" or "Private" Provision of Goods', *Journal of Legal Studies*, 22: 47–72.
Varnel, M. (Director) (1941) *The Ghost of St Michael's* [Film], Ealing Studios.
Venturi, R., Brown, D. and Izenour, S. (1972) *Learning from Las Vegas*, Boston: MIT Press.
Verity, H. (2000) *We Landed by Moonlight: Secret RAF landings in France, 1940–1944*, revised edition, Manchester: Crécy.

Vernon, M. (1962) *The Psychology of Perception*, London: University of London Press.
Victor, B. (1761) *The History of the Theatres of London and Dublin from the Year 1730 to the Present Time*, 2 Vols, London: Printed for T. Davies.
Wahlquist, C. (2016) 'Bright Idea: Toilet rolls light the way for flying doctors in lieu of runway flares', *The Guardian*, 12 August 2016, www.theguardian.com/australia-news/2016/aug/12/bright-idea-toilet-rolls-light-the-way-for-flying-doctors-in-lieu-of-runway-flares (Accessed 20/9/2016).
Warke, P., Smith, B. and Lehane, E. (2011) 'Micro-Environmental Change as a Trigger for Granite Decay in Offshore Irish Lighthouses: Implications for the long-term preservation of operational historic buildings', *Environmental Earth Science*, 63: 1415–1431.
Watson, C., Clancy, L. and Brew, K. (2011) 'Skelligs Calling', *Documentary on One*, [Radio] RTÉ Radio 1, 31 October 2011, www.rte.ie/radio1/doconone/2011/1101/646886-radio-documentary-skelligs-calling-michael/ (Accessed 13/3/2017).
Watt, R. (1991) *Understanding Vision*, London, San Diego, New York, Boston, Sydney, Tokyo and Toronto: Academic Press.
Welander, D. (1953) 'Never Fades the Name of Jesus', in *The Song Book of the Salvation Army*, New York: Territorial Headquarters.
Whealan-George, K. (2012) 'That Used to be Us: Through the eyes of the aviation industry', *Collegiate Aviation Review*, 30(1), https://commons.erau.edu/ww-economics-social-sciences/2 (Accessed 29/1/2018).
Wheeler, W. (nd) 'The History of Fog Signals', *United States Lighthouse Society*, http://uslhs.org/history-fog-signals (Accessed 10/8/2016).
Whenham, J. (2001) 'Laurenzi Filiberto', *Grove Music Online*, Oxford Music Online, www.oxfordmusiconline.com.ezphost.dur.ac.uk/grovemusic/view/10.1093/gmo/9781561592630.001.0001/omo-9781561592630-e-0000016115?rskey=dIe9Qh&result=2 (Accessed 26/1/2018).
Whitelock, D. (ed.) (1979) *English Historical Documents, 500–1042*, Vol. I, London: Methuen.
Whiting, A. B. (2011) 'Sir James Jeans, *The Universe Around Us*, fourth edition, 1944', in *Hindsight and Popular Astronomy*, London and Singapore: World Scientific Publishing, pp. 231–246.
Wiedemann, D., Burt, D. M., Hill, R. and Barton, R. (2015) 'Red Clothing Increases Perceived Dominance, Aggression and Anger', *Biology Letters*, 11: 20150166.
Wilkinson, J. (nd) 'History of Wrecking', *Keys Historium*, Historical Preservation Society of the Upper Keys, www.keyshistory.org/wrecking.html (Accessed 14/3/2017).
Williams, R. (2008) 'Nightspaces: Darkness, deterritorialisation and social control', *Space and Culture*, 11(4): 514–532.
Woolf, V. (1927) *To the Lighthouse*, London: Hogarth.
Woolf, V. (1977) *The Letters of Virginia Woolf*, Vol. 3, Nicholson, N. (ed.), London: The Hogarth Press.
Woolf, V. (1985) *Moments of Being*, New York and London: Vintage.
Woolf, V. (2004) *To the Lighthouse*, London: Vintage.
Wordsworth, W. (1984) 'Elegiac Stanzas Suggested by a Picture of Peele Castle, in a Storm, Painted by Sir George Beaumont', in Gill, S. (ed.) *William Wordsworth: A Critical Edition of the Major Works*, Oxford: Oxford University Press, pp. 326–328.
World Heritage Ireland (nd) 'Skellig Michael', *World Heritage Ireland*, www.worldheritageireland.ie/skellig-michael (Accessed 13/3/2017).

Yass, C. (2011) *Lighthouse*, [35mm film]. Commissioned by De La Warr Pavilion, Bexhill-on-Sea, East Sussex, and produced with funding from Arts Council England, Alison Jacques Gallery and Galerie Lelong.

Yeginsu, C. and Hartocollis, A. (2015) 'Amid Perilous Mediterranean Crossings, Migrants Find a Relatively Easy Path to Greece', *New York Times*, 17 August, www.nytimes.com/2015/08/17/world/europe/turkey-greece-mediterranean-kos-bodrum-migrants-refugees.html (Accessed 10/12/2016).

Young, R. (1988) 'Quartz Etching and Sandstone Karst: Examples from the East Kimberleys, Northwestern Australia', *Zeitschrift für Geomorphologie* NF, 32(4): 409–423.

Index

Please note that page numbers in italics refer to the image on this page.

Abrams, M. H.: poetry as 'mirror' to poetry as 'lamp' 52
Ackermann, K. 93; industrial architecture 93; *see also constructive intelligence*
Adziogol *see* Adziogol Lighthouse
Adziogol Lighthouse 90, *90*, 94; *see also* hyperboloid; Shukhov, V.; Stanislav Range Front Light
Aeschylus: *Agamemnon* 135; *see also* Athenian torch race
affective and sensory effects of light 162
aid to navigation *see* navigational aid
Airy, G. 107, 108; Astronomer Royal 107; production of dioptric lenses 107; *see also* Chance, J.; Whitby lights
Albion Beach 175; porcelain 175; *see also* Albion Lighthouse; Mauritius
Albion Lighthouse 175–177; Bollywood movies 176; British colonial administration 177; colonial origins 176; *see also* Albion Beach; colonial history; Mauritius
Aldhelm 70, 72; *enigmata* 70; the lofty lighthouse 70
Alexandria Pharos *see* Pharos Lighthouse
Alhazen 40; synthesis of optics 40; theory of intromission 40; *see also* optics; Ptolemaios of Alexandria; visual ray
all-seeing Eye of God 42
Almagest 40; celestial motions 40; *see also* Ptolemaios of Alexandria
altered or transcendental state *see* altered state
altered state: of being 37, 39; of mind 38
ambiguous 179, 184, 198; ambiguous beams 161–163

American lighthouses: 1789 Lighthouses Act 170
arc lamp 80, 81; *see also* Davy, H.
arc lights *see* arc lamp
archipelago 171, 172; increase in maritime disasters 172; western 172, 173; *see also* Dutch East Indies
Argand lamp *see* Argand oil lamp
Argand oil lamp 51, *79*, 86, 161; luminously stable 87
Armfield, M. 217; *see also* Grace Darling; Smedley, C.
Arnold, M.: light imagery 53
art: celebration of light 24; Central Desert Aboriginal art 37; cutting edge 200; representations of the lighthouses across the arts 207; Trobriand canoe paintings 37
artificial illumination 190; baleful effects 190; *see also* light pollution
artists 179, 187, 188; video and film 227
asylum seekers 179, *180*; *see also* migrants; refugees
Athenian torch race 38, 135; *lampadedromia* 38, 135; signal beacons 135; *see also* Aeschylus; Plato
Atlantic Wall 126, 199; *see also* Skagen Odde; Tungenes Fyr
Attenborough, D. 27, 30; living light 36; *see also* bioluminescence
attractive light: attract prey 27; warn off predators 27
Austen, J.: darkness 52; gothic parody *Northanger Abbey* 52

automation 117; deterioration since 120; and the removal of keepers 117; wholesale 117
avian decimation 190; *see also* bird death

Baafuloto 168; *see also* emergency beacon; NASA
Bacon, R.: *Optics* 238
Ballantyne, R. M. 190; *see also* Bell Rock Lighthouse; *The Lighthouse*
Bangka Strait 172
Bardsey Lighthouse 192; station for migrating birds 192; *see also* bird death
Barentsz, W. 6; *see also* Nova Zembla
Barrow, J. 178, 179; lighthouse as a memorial 179; *see also* the Hoad; Sir John Barrow Monument
Barton, R. 20, 21; *see also* evolutionary effects of light; red; seeing red
Bascular Lighthouse 123; *see also* lighthouses of Skagen Odde; *vippefyr*
Batavia 172
Bathurst, B. 30; opportunistic 'salvaging' 30; *see also* wreckers
Beachy Head Lighthouse: East Sussex 226
beam of light *see* light beam
beam of the lighthouse 1, 47, 163, 204; bird-friendly 192; intensity 161; multiple meanings 163
beams of lasers *see* laser beams
Bede 71; synod of Whitby 71; *see also* Whitby
Bell Burnell, J. 30, 31, 35; *see also* Little Green Men; pulsars
Bell Rock Lighthouse 93, *100*, 190, 213; account of the construction 99; *see also* Stevenson, R.; Turner, J. M. W.
Bellerofonte: decor 66; engraving 63, 64; Teatro Novissimo 63beryl 8; emerald 8; provide helium 8; red and infrared light 8
beryllium 8; product of nuclear fission 8
Betjeman, J. 95; *see also Shell Guides to Britain*
binary *see* dualism
Binney, T.: hymn 48
bio-hydro-geological cycle 91
biofuels 11; *see also* microalgae
bioluminescence 27, 28, 36; communication 29; defence 29; interaction among organisms 28; to prey or communicate 190; used offensively 29; *see also* Attenborough, D.

bioluminescent reaction 34
bird death 190; Bell Rock Lighthouse 190; curtailing 191; death tolls from Long Point Lighthouse 191; Statue of Liberty's lamp 191
Birmingham Lunar Society 51
Bishop Rock 93; *see also* Walker, J.
Blake, W. 15, 52; illuminated books 52
Bliss, P.: hymn 46
body of the lighthouse 3, 139–143; *see also* homologue
bonfires 166; *see also* landing aids
Border Protection 185; miniature paintings 185; *see also* Copland, S.
Both, P. 175, 177; Dutch East India Company 175; shipwrecks 175; *see also* Albion Beach; Albion Lighthouse; Mauritius
boundaries: borders and 184; life and death 23; light and dark 23
brass band *155*, 156, 157; *see also Foghorn Requiem*
brass players *see* brass band
Braun, G. and Hogenberg, F.: map of Rhodes 62, *63*
Brewster, D. 106; *see also* lighthouse reform
Buddha: Eye of the World 42; *see also* Buddhism
Buddhism 42; *see also* Buddha
burglar alarm 27, 29; *see also* bioluminescence; dinoflagellates

Cambrian period 17; explosion 16, 18; first eyes 17; marine ecosystems 17; *see also* Cambrian Radiation
Cambrian Radiation: explosion 17; *see also* Cambrian period
Cap de la Hève 100, 101
Cape Bruny Lighthouse *219*
Cape Grecale Lighthouse: Lampedusa 187
Cape Otway Lighthouse: Australia 184
cathemeral 20; *see also* evolutionary effects of light
Cats, J. 56, 57; *see also* emblem books; *Proteus*
Chance, J. 107, 108; chief manufacturing partner 107; report on the adjustment of lenses 108; *see also* Airy, G.
Chania Lighthouse 66, 67
character 36, 195; each lightship had its own 129; of fog signals 147; unique

identifier 36; *see also* optical signature; pulse of light
Christian liturgy 48; *see also* hymnody
Church of Jesus Christ of Latter-day Saints 49; *see also* Mormonism; Smith, J.
Claisen flask 200; installation at Tungenes 200; *see also* Shimizu, J.
Clayton, M. 34, 36; *see also* entrainment; synchronicity
Cloak and Dagger Squadrons 167; *see also* special duty flights
Cloch foghorn 149–154; complaints 150, 154; Cowall District Committee 150; decommissioned 154; dispute 151; local soundscape 151; primary account 150
Cloch Lighthouse: Dunoon 150; foghorn 150
Clyde Lighthouse Trust 150, 151; *see also* Cloch foghorn
coastal communities 4, 203
Cockell, C. 189, 191, 192; expedition to Sumatra 192–193; *see also* moths; Moth Machine
collision: *Brandenburg* 110; *Paracas* 110; *Texaco Caribbean* 110; *see also* Dover Strait
colonial history 175, 177
Colossus of Rhodes 3, 59, *61*, 60–66, 69; earthquake 65; not a lighthouse 66; sun god Apollo 60; *see also Deidamia;* torchbearers; Torelli, G.
commemorate 163
Commissioners of Irish Lights 104; *see also* governance of lights
Commissioners of Northern Lights in Scotland 104, 106; *see also* governance of lights; Stevensons
communication: image of the light beam 44; intentional 30
constructive intelligence 92, 93; *see also* Ackermann, K.; Smeaton, J.
control towers 131, 137
conversation *see* interdisciplinary conversation
convex lens 87; eye 21
Copland, S. 185; *see also* Border Protection
Corduan Lighthouse: France 94; pre-modern 94
Cosin, J.: Bishop of Durham 48; hymn 48
cosmic lighthouses 31, *32*, 33, 34; *see also* pulsars
cremation: 'hidden symbol' of light 48; Hindu 48; purifying flame 48

Crowhurst, D. 189; *Teignmouth Electron* 189; *see also* Dean, T.; *Disappearance at Sea*
The Crown: construction and ownership rights 104
cultural heritage 3, 142, 143, 233, 246
cultural history 142
Cuthbert, St: death of 72, 73; *see also* Bede
cyanobacteria 16, 115–116; photosynthetic 115

Danish lighthouse authority 123; lighthouse tax 123
Danish lighthouses 122; ordered to extinguish their illumination 125; strategic military and commercial location 122
dark biosphere 28, 29; bioluminescence 28; predators 28; prey 28
dark ocean: mapped and governed 111
dark oceanic biosphere *see* dark biosphere
dark sky parks 76; marine 191
darkness 51, 74, 75; alternative meanings 75; demi-monde 75; disaster 23; dystopian 235; necessitated the development of competencies 75; primeval 233
Davy, H. 80; *see also* arc lamp
De colore 39; *see also* Grosseteste, R.
De iride 39; *see also* Grosseteste, R.
De luce 39, 238; *see also* Grosseteste, R.
de Mare, E. 95; *the Sailor's taste* 95; *see also* nautical gaiety
de Veer, G. 6; report 6; *see also* Nova Zembla
de Vos, M. 62; engraving 62; *see also* Colossus of Rhodes; van Heemskerck, M.
Dean, T. 187–189; *see also Disappearance at Sea*
decay 157, 159; manage decay 243; processes of 116
decor 60, 64, 66; *see also* Colossus of Rhodes; Torelli's decor
Deep Sea Pilotage Authority 170; *see also* Trinity House
Deidamia 65, 66; dedicatory epistle 65; prologue 60, 63; Teatro Novissimo 60; *see also* decor; Herrico, S.; Torelli's decor
deities: celestial architecture 136; celestial and solar 136; source of shining spiritual light 142

deities and saints: haloes 142; rays of divine light 142
Deligiorgis, Antonis 179; rescuing Nebiat, Wegasi 183, *183*
deterioration 117, 118, 120; causes 118; condensation 120; following automation 117; salt 118; stone breakdown 118; *see also* ventilation
diaphone: contemporary 154; engine-powered 154; steam-powered 150, 152, 153
diatoms 13; *see also* protist microalgae
Diego Garcia 175, 177; strategic importance 177; US military base 175; *see also* Mauritius
dinoflagellates: warning light 27; *see also* burglar alarm
diode valve 81
dioptric lens systems 107
Disappearance at Sea 187–189; 16mm films 188; soundtrack 188; *see also* Crowhurst, D.; Dean, T.
discharge lamps: mercury vapour 82; sodium 82
disciplinary boundaries: transgression 245
disciplinary scales 246; multiple 246
disciplinary specialism 2; *see also* disciplinary territories
disciplinary territories 2; *see also* disciplinary specialism; territoriality
diurnal 20; colour cues 20; *see also* evolutionary effects of light
divine light 48
Diwali 39; Deepavali 39; *see also* Festival of Lights
Douglass, J. 93, 113; *see also* Wolf Rock
Douglass, W. 93; *see also* Fastnet II
Dover lights *see* Dover *pharos*
Dover *pharoi see* Dover *pharos*
Dover *pharos* 70, 71, 72; church 71; *see also* Roman lighthouse
Dover Strait 110, 111; *see also* pinch points; Traffic Separation Scheme
Drummond, T. 106; testimony 105; *see also* lighthouse reform
du Maurier, D.: novels 30
dualism 22, 110; challenging 76, 182; land and sea 182; life and death 23; light and dark 22, 23, 76; safety and danger 22, 182; social thinking about light 246
Dubh Artach Lighthouse 213; *see also* Stevenson, R. L.

dues 104, 105; *light dues* and *user fees* 169; moneymaking scams 169; reductions 105; *see also* tolls
dune drifts 123; *see also* sand dunes
dunes *see* sand dunes
Dungeness Lighthouse 94, 191; brutalist 94; Dungeness New Lighthouse *95*; foghorn 147; fully-automated 94; *see also* bird death
Dutch East Indies 172; better lighting 172; insufficiently lit 174; *see also* archipelago; East Indies

early lighthouse lamp technology 86–88; *see also* lighthouse technology
early medieval: English description of a lighthouse 70; lighthouses 69; sea travel 73; *see also* Aldhelm
early modern period 54, 202; lighthouse imagery 50
East Indies 171; Dutch expansion in the 171
Easter 48; candles 48; newly kindled fire 48
Eddystone Lighthouse 51, 86, 92, 93, 99, 198; built by Henry Winstanley 51, 93; burnt down 51, 93; destroyed by a storm 51; first wooden 91; John Smeaton's 92, 241; washed away 93; *see also* Rudyard, J.; Smeaton, J.; Winstanley, H.
Edison, T. 77; bamboo fibre 81; *see also* filament lamps
Egyptian gods: Imentet and Ra *42*; Ra 42; Horus 42; *see also* sun gods and goddesses
Eilean Glas Lighthouse: foghorn 195; Scalpay 195
Eilean Mor: breeding colony 205; Flannan light 205
El Jadida's mosque 69; five-sided lighthouse 69; pentagonal minaret 69
electric illumination *see* electric lighting
electric light *see* electric lighting
electric lighting 74, 77, 78, 81; fluorescent tube 82; light without smell 80
Elie Ness Lighthouse: Firth of Forth 122
emblem books 56; poetry and prose 56; *see also* Cats, J.; Hugo, H.; Quarles, F.
Emblemes 56; *see also* emblem books; Quarles, F.
emergency beacon 168; *see also* Baafuloto; NASA
emergency landings in the dark 167; *see also* night landing

emergency runway lighting: toilet rolls 167; *see also* night landing; Royal Flying Doctor Service
emigrants 184, 199; *see also* migrants
Empedocles: four elements theory 40; *see also* visual ray
enlightenment 24, 44, 50, 91; images of 45; metaphor of 69; metaphorical image of 142; scientific 50; spiritual 23
The Enlightenment 51, 74; light as rational and secular 53
entrainment 35; circadian rhythms 35; musical 36; regular external stimulus 35; therapeutic uses of light 38; *see also* Clayton, M.; Huygens, C.
The Epicurean: novel 67, 101; *see also* Moore, T.
erosion 125, 158, 159; coastal 125; tidal 12
Euclid: *Optica* 40; *see also* optics; Ptolemaios of Alexandria
eukaryote (protist) microalgae *see* protist microalgae
evolution 10, 16, 17, 19; biological 22; cultural 22; cultural evolution of lighthouses 246; eye 5, 16; sunlight and radioactivity 10
evolutionary effects of light 20
extraterrestrial intelligence 36; lighthouse 137; shipping guides 109; vessel 137
extremophiles 10; origins of life 10; other energy sources 10 *see also* Greenwell, C.; life on Earth
Eye of Providence 43; all-seeing eye 43
Eye of Sauron 44

false lighthouse: trope of moralising antithesis 56; *see also* false lights
false lights 30, 164, 234; gothic fiction 234; tourism 234; *see also* false lighthouse; wreckers; wrecker's light
The Fame of Grace Darling 216; *see also* Pienne, Y.
Faraday, M. 81, 106–108, 147; consultant on lighthouse management 106; optical glasses 106; safety and regulation 170; *see also* arc lamp; Tyndall, J.
Fastnet II 93; *see also* Douglass, W.
fata morgana 6; *see also* refraction; van der Werf, S.
fen-fires 165; *see also* false lights
Festival of Lights 38–39; *see also* Diwali; Hanukkah

filament lamps: 1881 International Electrical Exhibition 81; incandescent 81; tungsten 81
film and television 218–219; British 223; children's television 219, 220, 221; featuring lighthouses 223; lighthouses 227; locations for various British horror movies 219
fire 37, 48; negative and punitive role 48; purification and illumination 48; visual importance 48
fire and firework effects 61; Renaissance stage 61; *see also* lighting effects
fireflies 29, 30, 34–36; photophores 34; *see also* bioluminescence; Ruskin, J.; synchronicity
fires: mislead sailors 164; *see also* false lights
First World War 162, 163, 212; veterans 218
Flannan Isle 204, 223; *see also* Gibson, W. W.
Flannan Isle light 205; automatic 205; *see also* Flannan Isles Lighthouse
Flannan Isles Lighthouse: Outer Hebrides 223
flash code 36; *see also* fireflies; language of light
Fleming, J. A. 81; *see also* diode valve
fluorescent lamps 82
fog signals 149
foghorn 195; auditory pulse 195; silenced 195; sonic extension of lighthouses 151; sonic motif 153; steam-powered 152; symbolic and emotional nature 155
Foghorn Requiem 147, 153, 154–157; audience 157; collaboration with coastal communities 156; performance 156–157; symbolic performance 156; *see also* Souter Lighthouse
foghorn tests 148; *see also* Tyndall, J.
foghorns 147, 153; decommissioning 154; maritime industrial history 154; restored 154; testing 147–149; time signatures 195; *see also* soundscape; Tyndall, J.
Fox, G. 49; *see also* Quakers
Fox Talbot, W. H. 53; negative-positive process 53; *see also* Moore, T.; photography; Romantic writing
Fraggle Rock 4, 220; Germany 221; United States 221; *see also* Henson, J.
Freemasons 50; initiation ritual 50; Sons of Light 50; *see also* visible and inner light

Fresnel, A. 7, 84, 85; intense beams 7; rule of adjustment 108; wave theory of light 86; *see also* Fresnel lens
Fresnel, L. 106; early British lamp production 107
Fresnel lens 78, *85*, 83–87, 100, 161, 192, 244; technological development of the lighthouse 98; *see also* Fresnel, A.
Fresnel structures 86
function: aid navigation and trade 168; changed dramatically 244; critical 4; strategic 244; terrestrial warning 73; traditional 131
function and form: inversions of 235
functions of lighthouses: subverted 30

Galloper in a bottle *130*; *see also* lightships
gas light *see* gas lighting
gas lighting 77; declined 80; demonstrated publicly 80; Theatre Royal 52
gas mantles 80; street lighting 80
Gay, J. 51–52; *Trivia* 51; uprooted lighthouse 51; *see also* Eddystone Lighthouse
Geissler, H. 82; *see also* Geissler tubes; Rühmkorff induction coil
Geissler tubes 82; *see also* Geissler, H.
General Lighthouse Authority 113, 170; *see also* Trinity House
Gibson, W. W. 204, 205, 223, 224; *see also Flannan Isle*
Godrevy Lighthouse 208, 209, 212; *see also* Woolf, V.
Gough, O.: composer 156; *see also Foghorn Requiem*
governance: light and 169; regulation of lighthouses 170
governance of lights 104
GPS 166, 244; human error 154; navigation 154; pulsars 33, 34
Grace Darling 214–218; character 215; death from tuberculosis 217; in popular culture 213; memorial museum 215; *see also* Longstone Lighthouse; SS *Forfarshire*
Graham, J. 239; premier performance 239; *see also The Light*
Great Mosque of Kairouan 68, *68*; ancient lighthouse design 68; *see also* Kairouan minaret
Greene, G. 224; *see also Flannan Isle;* Gibson, W. W.
Greenwell, C. 10; *see also* extremophiles

Grey Lighthouse 125; decommissioned 125; international bird station and observatory 125; rotating apparatus 125; *see also* lighthouses of Skagen Odde
Grosseteste, R. 39, 238; High Medieval Renaissance 238; refraction 39; wave theory of matter 238; work on sound 238; *see also De colore; De iride; De luce*
Grove, W.: platinum 81; *see also* filament lamps
guide books 165; light beacons 165
guiding light 69, 111, 166
guru 48; shine 49; *see also* Sikhism
Guru Nanak 49; *see also* guru; Sikhism

Hanukkah 38–39; *see also* Festival of Lights; Judaism
Haselden, R. 230, *230*; *see also* Phare
Hauksbee, F. 82; *see also* mercury-in-glass barometer
haunted lighthouses 219, 224, 227
hazards 74, 110, 111, 169; hidden 131; invisible 110
heliotropism *see* solar tracking
Henson, J. 220; *see also* Fraggle Rock
heritage: climate change 121; policy of non-intervention 116; heritage structures 121
Herrico, S. 65, 66; *see also* Deidamia
Hewitt, P. C. 82; *see also* discharge lamps
Hildegard of Bingen, Saint *44*, 45; enlightening visions 45; migraines 45
Hill, R. 21; *see also* red; seeing red
hilltop beacons 131, 135
Hinduism 42, 48; power in relation to light 48; third eye of Shiva 42; *see also* Diwali; Festival of Lights
Hindus *see* Hinduism
The Hoad 177, 178, *178*; replica of Smeaton's Tower 178; Ulverston 177; *see also* Sir John Barrow Monument; lighthouse-as-memorial
Højen Lighthouse 125; closure 125; *see also* lighthouses of Skagen Odde
Holocaust 39; annual collective remembrance day 39; *see also* Judaism; memorial candles
homologous *see* homologue
homologue 2, 4, 91, 141, 142, 144, 146, 213, 245; homological forms 244; lighthouse as a person 141, 207; looking, seeing and perceiving 207; *see also* body of the lighthouse

Honfleur 100
Hopper, E. 231; *see also* modernist painters
The Horsburgh: Singapore 172
Hugo, H. 56, *57*; *see also* emblem books; *Pia Desideria*
Huygens, C. 25, *25*, 26; pendulum clocks 35; pendulums 36; *Traité de la Lumière* 25; *see also* entrainment; light ray
Hvalnes: brutalist 94; Iceland 94
hydraulic lime mortar 91, 92; *see also* Eddystone Lighthouse; Smeaton, J.
hydrotheological cycle 24
hymnody 46; Christian hymnody, liturgy and poetry 47
hyperboloid 90; *see also* Adziogol Lighthouse

IAS *see* Institute of Advanced Study
iconic lighthouse form 96, 170; *see also* Smeaton, J.
identity 142; collective sense of 34; community 3, 142; cultural 146; loss of 154; maritime 135; place 142
illumination 26, 47, 50, 74, 75, 77, 109, 163; expansion 99; global distribution 74; industrial age 77; metaphors of 51; modernity and progress 77
Industrial Revolution 94, 100, 149, 151, 154; new technologies and infrastructures 170; symbols of 96
infrastructure 81; as a public good 103; coastal 169; material and social order 23; of mobility 202; state 100
inner light 49, 50; ethical guide 49; *see also* Mormonism; Quakers
Institute of Advanced Study 2, 3, 239, 245; annual research themes 2; Durham University 2, 245
interdisciplinarity 2; embedded as a practice 3
interdisciplinary 236, 245
interdisciplinary conversation 1, 2, 3; about light and lighthouses 245
interfaces 89; geo-biotic 116; marine 115; natural world and human endeavour 89
interior space 4, 94, 224, 225; ambiguity of the lighthouse 219
island lighthouses 214; *see also* Longstone Lighthouse

Jablochkoff, P. 80; *see also* Jablochkoff Candle

Jablochkoff Candle 80, 81; Avenue de l'Opéra 81; Victoria Embankment 81; *see also* Jablochkoff, P.
Jains 39; *see also* Diwali; Festival of Lights
James, P. D.: detective thriller 213; *see also The Lighthouse*
Jesus: beacon of light 46; light of creation and salvation 47; *see also* light of the world
Jewish tradition *see* Judaism
John's Gospel 46, 47
Judaism 38; light in the Holy of Holies 38; pillar of fire 46; *see also* Hanukkah; Holocaust; Passover; Shabbat; Shiva

Kairouan minaret 69; defensive purpose 69; Roman lighthouse at Salakta 69; *see also* Great Mosque of Kairouan
Kajita, T. 31
kaleidoscope 127, 235; *see also* Rubjerg Knude Lighthouse
keeper *see* lighthouse keeper
Kepler, J. 6, 7; *Paralipomena* 6; supernovae remnants 31; *see also* Nova Zembla
Kilpper, T. 67, 187; human rights 187; *see also Lighthouse for Lampedusa*; refugees
Korakas Lighthouse 186; *see also* Lesvos; refugees
Koslofsky, C. 74, 75; *see also* mystical Christian theology
Kurdi, Aylan 179, 184; *see also* refugees

La Corbière: Jersey 115; steel-reinforced concrete 115
la Hève *see* Cap de la Hève
Lampyridae 35; *see also* fireflies; torchbearer
land-based lighthouses *see* shore-based lighthouses
landing aids 166; approach lighting 166; radio beacons 166; rotating lights 166; torches 167
landscape: coastal 117, 121, 154; darkened 162; exterior punctuation 4; negotiated settlement with the 242; revision of the 241; urban 97
Langley, W.: 'plein air' painters 234
language of light 36, 139; *see also* fireflies; flash code
languages of light 30, 246

lantern 123; *see also* lighthouses of Skagen Odde
Lanterna: Genoa 94; pre-modern 94
laser beams 163, 200; aligned 7; parallel 200
lasers *see* laser beams
LED *see* light-emitting diode
lenses 84; development of lighthouses 84; microscopes and telescopes 84; spectacles 84, 86
Lesvos 186; *see also* Korakas Lighthouse; refugees
Lethbridge, T. C. 205, 206; *see also* Skellig Michael
LGM *see* Little Green Men
Lichtarchitektur 163; Nazi rallies at Nuremberg 163; *see also* searchlights
life on Earth 10; light 243; light from the Sun 27; photosynthesis 239
The Light 239; premier performance 239; *see also* Graham, J.
light: as metaphor and as technology 51–54; metaphor of understanding 238
light and matter 7, 8
light and sound 128, 163, 194; therapies using hypnosis 38; waves 5
light beam 7, 9, 162, 164; high-security prisons 162; malign use 163; multiple meanings 161; nocturnal mobility 162; parallel 84; prisms 100; *see also* beam of the lighthouse; Fresnel lens
light beams 163; *see also* commemorate
The Light Between Oceans: film 218; novel 218; *see also* Stedman, M. L.
Light List 195; *see also* character
light messages 189; encoded 246; to non-humans 189
light of the world 42, 46; deities 247; I am the Light of the World *141*; *see also* Jesus
light offshore 109–112
light pollution 75, 190, 191; busy waters 75; malign effects 190; negative impacts 76
light ray 25; property of light waves 25; *see also* Huygens, C.
light signallers 30; marine 27
light signalling 72; human 30
light source 7, 16, 25, 26, 84; celestial 42; distinguish one light source from another 165; LED 82; redirect 85; water behaves like a 38
light vessels *see* lightships

light-emitting diode 38, 82, 113, 235; LED light system 192; red 82; white light 38, 82
The Lighthouse: novel 191; *see also* Ballantyne, R. M.
The Lighthouse: detective thriller 213; *see also* James, P. D.
The Lighthouse: poem 54; *see also* Longfellow, H. W.
The Lighthouse: novel 213; *see also* Moore, A.
Lighthouse: film 228–230; *see also* Royal Sovereign Lighthouse; Yass, C.
Lighthouse (East) 229; *see also* Yass, C.
lighthouse at Cadiz 168
lighthouse at Cape Reinga 144–146, *145, 146*; automated 145; New Zealand 144; sacred sites 145, 146; territorial statement 145; UNESCO World Heritage Site 146; *see also* Powell, Blue
lighthouse construction 106, 113, 199; modernist aesthetic 92
lighthouse control 105; centralisation 105; *see also* lighthouse reform
lighthouse design 51, 178; British 91; post-medieval 92; post-war 94; see also *secular lights*
lighthouse film 224, 225; British horror films 226–227; ghosts and madness 225; *see also* film and television
Lighthouse for Lampedusa: video 187; *see also* Kilpper, T.; refugees
lighthouse islands *see* island lighthouses
lighthouse keeper 87; daily logbook 196; disappear 204, 223, 224; duties 195; mad 223, 224; polysemic 244; position of trust 218; traditional notions of the family 222
lighthouse movies *see* lighthouse film
lighthouse of Alexandria *see* Pharos Lighthouse
lighthouse reform 104–106; recommendations for reform 105; scientific expertise and 103–109; *see also* lighthouse control
Lighthouse Relief 186, 187; Swedish NGO 186; *see also* refugees
lighthouse resilience 117–121
lighthouse technology 7, 104; enabling lighthouse technology 83–86
lighthouse's location *see* location of the lighthouse

lighthouse-as-memorial 179; *see also* Barrow, J.; the Hoad; Sir John Barrow Monument
lighthouses in the Bible 45–47
lighthouses of outer space 30, 136; *see also* pulsars
lighthouses of Skagen Odde 122–127; control of Skagen's lighthouse 125
lighthouses of the insect world 30, 35, 36; *see also* fireflies
lighting effects 60; *see also* theatre history
lighting technologies 78; lagging 105; maritime 109
Lightpole 3, 141; *see also* homologue; The Spooky Men
lightships 125, 128–130, 244; and buoys 112; decommissioned 127, 129; Formosa Banks 173; heritage sites 129; introduced into the Thames Estuary 128; reworked as art 129; *see also Galloper* in a bottle
light-signalling: codes 131; species 246; *see also* character
limelight 52–53; in the limelight 53, 80; unfit for lighthouse installation 106
lit archipelago 171–175; *see also* Dutch East Indies; East Indies
literature 4, 51, 153, 199, 207, 218, 245; darkness in the gothic novel 52; early photography and 53; Mauritian 176; storytelling and 207
Little Green Men 31, 33, 136; *see also* Bell Burnell, J.; pulsars
Liverpool Airport *132*, 132–135; hotel 132; Speke 132
Liverpool's control tower 132–134; control tower-cum-lighthouse 133; landmark 133, 135; *see also* Liverpool Airport
Liverpool's first airport *see* Liverpool Airport
Liverpool's tower *see* Liverpool's control tower
location 104, 114, 122; for dramatic intrigue 213; perilous 93; too remote for a lighthouse 128; unprotected 89
location of the lighthouse 3; ambiguity 233; between land and sea 23
Long Point Lighthouse 191; less intense light 192; *see also* bird death
Longfellow, H. W. 54; *see also The Lighthouse*
Longships Lighthouse: Longships, Cornwall *117*; *see also* Turner, J. M. W.

Longstone Light: radio play 217; *see also* Sheridan, M. D.
Longstone Lighthouse 213, *215*; *Disappearance at Sea II* 188; Farne islands 213; *see also* Grace Darling; Perlee Parker, H.
Lumière: Durham 239
Luxor Hotel: Las Vegas 163; *see also* searchlights

maintenance 116, 196, 197, 243; damaging 243; space of work and 220; structural and material failure 116
marine environment 196; dark 74; impact upon other species 189; movement of people through 131
marine illumination 191; technological developments 244; technologies of 109; *see also* light pollution
mariners' aids 54; *see also* navigational aid
maritime architecture 168; *see also* maritime infrastructure
maritime heritage 92; Britain's maritime heritage 96; nostalgic emblems 91; nostalgic vision 96
maritime infrastructure 171; *see also* maritime architecture
maritime space 109; map and govern 111
material culture 42, 139, 144; biomimicry 139; human agency 139
material properties 3; of light 5, 245, 246
material relatives 3, 131, 132, 135, 138, 142, 246; cat's eyes 131; miniature scale 144; smaller 143; street and porch lights 131; torch 131
materiality 114; of lighthouses 114–116
Mauritius 175; military significance 176; *see also* Albion Beach; Albion Lighthouse; colonial history
McDowall, C. 239; *see also The Skies in Their Magnificence*
memorial candles 39; *see also* Holocaust; Shiva
mercury: pool of liquid 87; mercury pump 81; *see also* rotation
mercury-in-glass barometer 82
Messrs. Chance Bros. and Co.: glass company 107; Great Exhibition of 1851 107
microalgae 11–14; biotechnology 11; light reactions 12; light is a necessary evil; photosynthesise 11; RuBisCO 12–13; *see also* biofuels; phytoplankton

migrants 179, 180, *180*, 182, 185; Cuban 185; maritime migrant 184; *see also* asylum seekers; refugees
Mill, J. S.: government's duty to build lighthouses 102; laissez-faire capitalism 102
minaret of Kairouan *see* Kairouan minaret
minarets 67; early minaret design 67; lighthouses and 67; place of light 69
modern lighthouse 91–96
modern picturesque 95; *see also* Piper, J.; Richard, P.; Nash, P.
modernism 94; and nostalgia 96
modernist 91, 94; aesthetic 92, 211; architects 94
modernist painters 231; *see also* Hopper, E.; Piper, J.; Ravilious, E.
monstrance 42, *43*
Moody, D. L.: hymn 46
Moore, A.: novel 213; *see also The Lighthouse*
Moore, T. 67, 101; Romantic writer 53; *see also* Fox Talbot, W. H.; *The Epicurean*
Mormonism 49–50; First Vision 49–50; *see also* Church of Jesus Christ of Latter-day Saints; inner light; Smith, J.
Morphy, H. 24; Aboriginal Central Desert dot paintings 24; Nuba body art 24; *see also* shine
Morse code 30, 133, 166, 167, 235
Moth Machine 192–193; destroyed 193; moth collecting aircraft 192; *see also* Cockell, C.
moths 189, 192; attracted to light 27, 192; collecting 192–193; day-night cycle 191; death tolls 191; *see also* light pollution
music 236, 237; culturally and communally possessed 237; light-inspired 239; performative 237; science 236, 238, 239; science of light 238; wonder 241
mystical Christian theology 75; *see also* Koslofsky, C.

NASA 35, 168; exoplanets 35
Nash, P. 95; *see also modern picturesque; Shell Guides to Britain*
Nash Point: Wales 154; *see also* diaphone
National Trust 155, 156, 158; Orfordness Lighthouse 158, 159; Souter Lighthouse 154

nautical gaiety 92, 95, 96; *see also* de Mare, E.; *unadorned functionalism*
nautical network *see* network of lighthouses
navigational aid 69, 112, 166, 176, 177; replaced lighthouses as 142–143; stars and the Moon 109; *see also* mariners' aids
navigational guide *see* navigational aid
Nebiat, Wegasi 179, 183, *183*, 184; *see also* Deligiorgis, Antonis; refugees
network: of beacons and watchtowers 72; of lighthouses 102, 169, 170, 240; of maritime rule 168
New Testament 46; divine light 48; light of salvation 47
Newlyn Art Gallery 234, 235; context-responsive artwork 234
Newlyn school 234; representations of women 234
Newton, I. 25; kinematic force 90; *Optica* 238; straight rays 26
night landing 166–167; cars 167; headlights 167; in Albury 167; *see also* emergency runway lighting
nocturnal 20; *see also* evolutionary effects of light
non-human agencies 114, 121–122, 127, 194, 243
North Ronaldsay Lighthouse *1*
Northern Lighthouse Board 150, 151; *see also* Cloch foghorn
Northern Lights *see* Commissioners of Northern Lights in Scotland
nostalgia 233; nautical 96; sound of the lighthouse 147
Nova Zembla 5, 6, 7; expedition 6; *see also* Kepler, J.; van der Werf, S.
nyctophobia 75

offshore lighthouse 89, 117, 185; inaccessible 121; island-based lighthouses 118
offshore stations *see* offshore lighthouses
oil lamp 79; circular wicks 79; concentric circular wicks 80
Old Testament 48; burning bush 48; divine light 48
On Fog Signals 147; *see also* Tyndall, J.
On Sound 148; *see also* Tyndall, J.
optical signature 164; locally distinctive 87; unique 87, 165; *see also* character
optics 24, 40, 84–85

Orfordness Lighthouse 158; decommissioned 158; erosion 158; National Trust 158; Suffolk 158; Trinity House 158

Orfordness Lighthouse Company 158; architectural life-support 159; National Trust 159; *see also* Orfordness Lighthouse

ownership 103–105; corrupt 103; de-privatisation 105; private versus public ownership 104

parabolic mirror 124; concave 87; *see also* White Lighthouse

parliamentary commission 103

Parliamentary Commission on Lighthouses: first meeting 107; report 106

parliamentary committees 105; Britain's lighthouses 103

passive ventilation 118–119; *Bernoulli's Principle* 118–119; *Stack Ventilation* 118, 119; *see also* ventilation

Passover 38; *see also* Judaism

Peace Column 163; Iceland 163 *see also* commemorate; searchlights

Penlee lifeboat disaster 233; *Solomon Browne* 234; *see also* Tater Du (or Black Rock) Lighthouse

Perch Rock Lighthouse 235; messages naming those lost at sea 235; New Brighton 235

Perlee Parker, H. 214, *215*, 216; *see also* Grace Darling; Longstone Lighthouse

phallic 198; life-generation 246; material requirements 142; statement 142; vertical prominence 222

Phare 230, *230*; box of matches 230; sculpture 230–231; *see also* Haselden, R.

Pharos at Alexandria *see* Pharos Lighthouse

Pharos Lighthouse 40, 59, 67, 78, 83, 102, 187, 243; art, architecture and language 67; Islamic symbol of enlightenment 69

Pharos *see* Pharos Lighthouse

phenomenological engagements *see* phenomenological experiences

phenomenological experiences: of light 3, 37; of numinous light 44; with light 246

photic zone 17

photography 53; *see also* Fox Talbot, W. H.; Romantic writing

photosynthesis 11, 13, 14, 16, 239; liability 12

phototropism 15, 16; *see also* solar tracking

physicality 78; of lighthouses 89–91

phytoplankton 11, 13, 14; mixotrophic 13; see 14; zooplankton 13; *see also* microalgae

Pia Desideria 56, *57*; engravings 56; symbolic lighthouse 56; *see also* emblem books; Hugo, H.

Picard, J. 82; *see also* mercury-in-glass barometer

Pienne, Y. 216; *see also* Grace Darling; *The Fame of Grace Darling*

pinch points 111; *see also* Dover Strait

Piper, J. 95, 231, *231*; *see also* modernist painters; modern picturesque; *Shell Guides to Britain*

plankton 34, 76, 190; smallest of lighthouses 34

plants 11; diurnal changes in light 14; photoperiodic 14; see 14

Plato 38; fire within the eye 40; *Timaios* 40; *see also* Athenian torch race; visual ray

Point Arena Lighthouse: California *83*

politics of lighting 173; *see also* East Indies

polyzonal lenses 107; *see also* Skerryvore Lighthouse; Stevenson, A.

postcards 233; vintage 231

Powell, Blue: artwork 146, sculpture *146*; *see also* lighthouse at Cape Reinga

predator 17, 22; early Cambrian oceans 18; emit red light 29; visual 18

prey 17, 18; counterillumination 29

primates: trichromatic colour vision 20; visual systems 20

Probst, G. B. 62; *see also* Colossus of Rhodes

Prologue, John's Gospel 49; *see also* John's Gospel

Proteus 57; *see also* emblem books; Cats, J.

protist microalgae 13; *see also* diatoms; microalgae

proto-modernist 93; Smeaton's lighthouse 94

Ptolemaios of Alexandria 39, 40; *see also Almagest*; optics; Pharos Lighthouse

public good 102, 103, 104, 169; art, for Turner 102; lighthouse as 99

pulsars 30, *32*, 31, 33, 36, 244; identity 33; navigating system 33; profiles 33; spin rate 33; *see also* Bell Burnell, J.; cosmic lighthouses; Little Green Men
pulse of light: unique 109; *see also* character

Quakers 49; political and spiritual resistance 49; *see also* Fox, G.; inner light
Quantum Electro Dynamics: theory of 8; *see also* light and matter
Quarles, F. 56; multi-tasking lighthouse 56; *see also* emblem books; *Emblemes*
Quillebeuf-sur-Seine 100

radar 166
Radcliffe, A.: darkness 52; gothic novels 52
Radio City 98, *136*; commercial radio station 98; light to mark significant moments 98; *see also* St John's Beacon
Raffles Light 173
Ravilious, E. 231; *see also* modernist painters
ray of light *see* light ray
Rectitudines Singularum 73
red 20–21; badge of status 20; colour bias 21; combat sports 21; dominance in sport 21
reform of Britain's lighthouses *see* lighthouse reform
refraction 5, 6, 7, 39, 239; light refraction technology 131; *see also* fata morgana
refugees 67, 179, 181, 183, 184, 185–187; media coverage 186; refugee crisis 179, 180; refugee policy 179; *see also* asylum seekers; migrants
reinforced concrete 115; Achilles heel 115
replicas 143, 144; mini-replicas 144; scaled-down 144; *see also* souvenirs
revolving lens 189
rhythmic light pattern: unique 195; *see also* character; rhythms of the lighthouse
rhythms 99, 194–197, 212, 244; everyday schedules 194; human and non-human 194; light and sound 194; sonic 195; tides 197; tourism 197
rhythms of the lighthouse 194–197
Richard, P. 95; *see also modern picturesque; Shell Guides to Britain*

Richborough monument 70; *see also* Roman Britain; signal station
rituals 38, 39, 136; birth, life and death 50; involving light 37; light, sound and rhythm 34; purification 48; valorisations of light 245
Roman Britain 70, 73; *see also* Dover *pharos*
Roman Empire: earliest lighthouse in the British Isles 169; Portus Dubris (Dover) 169; *see also* Dover *pharos*
Roman lighthouse: Dover 70, *71*; *see also* Dover *pharos*
Romantic writing 53; *see also* Fox Talbot, W. H.; photography
rotating devices 78
rotating light 165, 184; airport beacon 166
rotation 87–88; focusing mechanism 87; rotation systems 87–88
Round the Twist 221
Royal Academy 102–103
Royal Flying Doctor Service 167; flares 167; night landing 167; *see also* emergency landings in the dark; emergency runway lighting
Royal Institution 147, 170
Royal Society 106
Royal Sovereign Lighthouse 227, 228; *see also Lighthouse*; Yass, C.
Rubjerg Knude Lighthouse *126*, 126–127, 235; engulfing dunes 127; foghorn 127; tidal incursion 127; *see also* kaleidoscope; lighthouses of Skagen Odde
Rudyard, J. 51, 113; timber and masonry 93; *see also* Eddystone Lighthouse
Rudyerd, J. *see* Rudyard, J.
Rühmkorff induction coil 82; *see also* Geissler, H.
runway lights 166; *see also* landing aids
Ruskin, J. 34–36, 101, 102; *see also* fireflies

salt 118; accumulation 120, 121; condensation 120; stone breakdown 120; *see also* deterioration
salvation 47, 49–50, 56, 183, 185; and disaster stories 46; light of 50; symbols of enlightenment and 45–47
sand drift 122, 127
sand dunes 126, 127, 164
Sanda Lighthouse: Argyllshire 195; foghorn 195

Seaham Lighthouse: County Durham *xxiv*
seamarks 129; lightships 128, 129
searchlights 162, 163, 169; First World War 162; less malign uses 163; Second World War 162; Warsaw's Palace of Culture 162; *see also* state control
secular lights 92; *see also* lighthouse design
seeing red 21; *see also* Barton, R.; Hill, R.
sense of place 197; destabilising 185; lost 202; outdated 202; relational 203
separation schemes *see* Traffic Separation Scheme
Sermon on the Mount 46, 47; *see also* light of the world
Shabbat 38; *see also* Judaism
Shell Guides to Britain 95; *see also* Betjeman, J.
Sheridan, M. D. 217; radio play 217; reformist agenda 217; *see also* Grace Darling; *Longstone Light*
Shimizu, J. 200, 235; art and science 200; Japanese light artist 200; sound and light 200; *see also* Claisen flask; Tungenes Fyr
shine 24, 26, 27; cross-cultural importance 24; health and well-being 24; loss 24; *see also* Morphy, H.
shipwrecks 151; Dutch East India Company 175; economic opportunity 123; loss of property and life 105; Skagen's peninsula 123; Souter Lighthouse 156
Shire, W. 181, 184; poem 183; *see also* refugees
Shiva 39; *see also* Judaism; memorial candles
Shoal Lighthouse 185; ambiguous 185; Florida Keys 185; not considered US soil 185
shore-based lighthouses 89, 91
Shukhov, V. 94; *see also* Adziogol Lighthouse; hyperboloid
signal station 70; *see also* Roman Britain
signalling using lights *see* light signalling
signature *see* optical signature
Sikhism: Deepavali 39; iconography 49; light and enlightenment 48; *see also* Diwali; Festival of Light
Sikhs *see* Sikhism
Sir John Barrow Monument 178; *see also* Barrow, J.; the Hoad; lighthouse-as-memorial

Skagen Odde 122; dunes 122; important site for migrating birds 125; Sand Drift Act of 1857 122
Skagen West Lighthouse 125–126; modernist 126; *see also* lighthouses of Skagen Odde
Skellig light 206; ghosts and poltergeists 206; unmanned 206
Skellig Michael 204–206; 'beehive' stone huts 206; documentary 206; seabird colony 206; *see also* Lethbridge, T. C.
Skerryvore Lighthouse 107, 198; *see also* polyzonal lenses
The Skies in Their Magnificence 239; *see also* McDowall, C.
sky-tower 96–98; grand projects 96; iconic 97; urban 98; *see also* St John's Beacon
Smalls Lighthouse: Welsh coast 223
Smeaton, J. 51, 93, 94, 113, 170, 241; father of civil engineering 93; hydraulic lime mortar 91; iconic lighthouse shape 92; oak tree 92, 241; *see also* Eddystone Lighthouse
Smedley, C. 215–216; founded the Grace Darling League 215; *Grace Darling and her Times* 215; radio and television plays 216; *see also* Armfield, M.
Smith, J. 49, 50; darkness 49; pillar of light 49; *see also* Mormonism
Snell's law 85; *see also* optics
solar tracking 15, 16; *see also* phototropism
soundmark 149, 154, 195; *see also* foghorns
soundscape 151, 153, 154, 195; 19th-century 147; coastal 151; drastic change 153; industrialized 152; marine 149; of place 203; *see also* foghorns; soundmark
source of life: light 24; *see also* spark of life
source of light *see* light source
Souter Lighthouse 154, 156, 157; decommissioned 155; first purpose-built electric lighthouse 154; *see also* diaphone; *Foghorn Requiem*
Souter Lighthouse Foghorn 156, 157; *see also Foghorn Requiem*
Souter Point *see* Souter Lighthouse
South Foreland Lighthouse 147; extreme acoustic phenomena 148; *see also* foghorn tests; Tyndall, J.

Southeast Asia 171, 174; Dutch and British colonial administration 168; history of lighthouses 174; introduction of steam 171
Southeast Asian *see* Southeast Asia
souvenir replica *see* replicas
souvenirs 3, 144; souvenir lighthouses from Helsinki *143*; *see also* replicas
spark of life 26
special duty flights 167; flarepaths 167; French resistance 167; Lysander 167; torches 167; *see also* Cloak and Dagger Squadrons
Spectra 163; centenary of the First World War 163; *see also* commemorate; searchlights
Spermaceti candles 77
spiral staircase 216, 221; image of mental instability 224
The Spooky Men 3, 39, 139, 141; *see also* homologue; *Lightpole*
spotlights: Paris Opera 162; superseded by luminaires 162
Sprengel, H. 81; *see also* mercury pump
SS *Forfarshire*: disaster 214; *see also* Grace Darling; Longstone Lighthouse
St Abb's Head Lighthouse 188; *Disappearance at Sea* 188
St John's Beacon 91, 97–98, 136, 137; closed space 98; Liverpool 97; the Tower 137; *see also* homologue; sky-tower; Little Green Men
St John's Market 97; *see also* St John's Beacon
St Anthony's Lighthouse: Cornwall 220; *see also Fraggle Rock*
stairs that spiral *see* spiral staircase
Stanislav Range Front Light *90*; *see also* Adziogol Lighthouse
state control 162, 169; inefficient 103; lighthouses in Britain and the USA 168
state power 198, 199; lighthouse as an extension of 103; material and symbolic expression of 168
Statue of Liberty 59; *see also* torchbearers
Stedman, M. L.: novel 218; *see also The Light Between Oceans*
Stevenson, A. 99, 106; coastal beacons 99; implementation of polyzonal lenses 106–107; 'Regulations' 216; testimony 105; *see also* lighthouse reform
Stevenson, D. A. 151; letter 153; *see also* Cloch foghorn

Stevenson, R. 91, 93, 99, 113; testimony 105; *see also* Bell Rock Lighthouse; lighthouse reform
Stevenson, R. L.: *Kidnapped* 213; novels 30; *Treasure Island* 213
Stevenson, T. 108
Stevensons: development of lighthouse construction 106
stonework 115; microbial life 115; weathers 116
street lighting 77; London 51; Wembley 82
Sumburgh Head: Shetlands 154; *see also* diaphone
sun gods and goddesses 42, 247; creative power of light 42
sunflower 15–16; *Helianthus annuus* 15; hormone auxin 16
surfeit of light *see* light pollution
Swan, J.: carbonized cotton 81; *see also* filament lamps
symbol: lighthouse as 47, 245; place-symbol 197; religious 45; symbol of a symbol 209
symbols and structures of power 171
Symphony of Lights: Hong Kong 163; *see also* searchlights
synchronicity 34, 35, 35; neurological and a social response 38; *see also* fireflies

tallow candles 51, 77, 79, 86, 123; replaced 52
Tater Du (or Black Rock) Lighthouse 234; *see also* Penlee Lifeboat Disaster
Taylor, J. and Hulse, R. 31; double pulsar 31; theory of gravity 31; *see also* pulsars
technologies: colonial governance 174; maritime control 174; optical 7, 165; surveillance 3, 131, 170; to build lighthouses 89; using light beams 7
television *see* film and television
territorial: limits 142; markers 164, 170; ownership 142
territoriality: disciplinary 3; geographical 3; *see also* disciplinary territories
theatre history: trope of the lighthouse 60
theatres of London 52
theatres of war 162; *see also* searchlights
Theodoric of Freiburg: solution of the rainbow 238
time-space compression 201, *201*
To the Lighthouse 4, 207–213; disruptions to hetero-normativity 222; novel 139–140, 208, 209, 210; *see also* Woolf, V.

tolls 169, 170; construction and maintenance of new lighthouses 169; *see also* dues
tools of empire: lights as 174
topophilia 153; sentiment and sound 153; Yi-Fu Tuan 153
torchbearer 35; *see also Lampyridae*
torchbearers 59; *see also* Colossus of Rhodes; Statue of Liberty
Torelli, G. *61*, 60–66; 17th-century conception of Rhodes 62–63; Teatro Novissimo 60; *see also* Colossus of Rhodes; *Deidamia*; Torelli's decor
Torelli's decor 63, 65
Tour d'Ordre 70; Charlemagne 71
Tour Soleil 162; Bourdais 162; *see also* searchlights
tourist attractions *see* tourist sites
tourist destination *see* tourist sites
tourist sites 76, 145, 244; souvenir shops 76
Traffic Separation Scheme 111; light 111; *see also* Dover Strait
Tribute in Light 163; World Trade Centre 163; *see also* commemorate; searchlights
trilobites 17, *19*; compound eyes 17; *see also* Cambrian period
Trinity House 103, 104–109, 113, 129, 168, 169; 1566 Seamarks Act 169; 1819 Reciprocity Treaty 170; growing authority 170; multi-functional organisation 170; Royal Charter 169; Quincentenary 114; *see also* General Lighthouse Authority
Tungenes Fyr 198–200; decommissioned 199; international artists 200; Norway 198; restored 199; *see also* Shimizu, J.
Tungenes Lighthouse *see* Tungenes Fyr
Turner, J. M. W. 99–103, 188; Bell Rock Lighthouse 99, *100*; coastal lights 100; French lights 101; painter of light 231; painter of *lights* 99; Royal Academy 103
Turner's Annual Tour: book of engravings 100; *see also* Turner, J. M. W.
Tyndall, J. 5, 108, 147–149; as a lighthouse *140*, 141; experiments 147; foghorn testing 147–148; report 148, 149; sound signals 147; *see also* Faraday, M.; homologue; *On Fog Signals*; *On Sound*
Tyndall effect 5; *see also* Tyndall, J.

unadorned functionalism 92, 96; *see also* nautical gaiety
understandings of place 202; changing mobility 202; relational 202; undermine 200
unmanned 244; *see also* automation
utilitarian 92, 93

van der Rohe, M. 94; *see also* modernist architects
van der Werf, S.: computer model 6; Dutch expedition's observations 6; *see also* Nova Zembla
van Gogh, V. 15; *see also* sunflower
van Heemskerck, M. 62; engraving 62; *see also* Colossus of Rhodes; de Vos, M.
van Rijn, Rembrandt 26; luminous effects 26; natural light 26
ventilation 118–119, 121; stratification of air *119*; ventilation slats 118; *see also* deterioration; passive ventilation
Victorian paraffin lamps 80
vippefyr 123, *124*; replica 123; *see also* Bascular Lighthouse; lighthouses of Skagen Odde
visible and hidden light 50; aesthetics and ethics 47, 48, 50; *see also* visible and inner light
visible and inner light 50
visual ray 39, 40; causality 42; *see also* optics; Ptolemaios of Alexandria
volunteer 186, 187; compassion 186; crew 234; rescue 179
von Welsbach, C. A. 80; *see also* gas mantles
Voyager 32, 33; crossed the heliopause 32; golden record 33; message in a bottle 33

Wadden Sea 164; intertidal zone 164; lighthouses 164, *165*
Walker, J. 93; *see also* Bishop Rock
watchtower 69, 70, 72
water-resistant cement *see* hydraulic lime mortar
Welander, D.: hymn 47
Whitby 71; *in sinus fari* 71; *see also* Bede
Whitby lights 107, 108; prior to any adjustments 108; *see also* Airy, G.
White Lighthouse 123; art exhibitions 124; *see also* lighthouses of Skagen Odde; parabolic mirror

Whiteford Point: Gower Peninsula 9
Whiteside, H. 113
Winstanley, H. 51, 113; octagonal wooden structures 93; *see also* Eddystone Lighthouse
Winzer, F. A. 80; *see also* gas lighting
wisdom 237; acquisition of 44; disciplines that inherit the tradition of 237; Natural Philosophy 237
wish image 132; Benjamin, W. 133; *see also* Liverpool Airport; Liverpool's control tower
Wolf Rock 93; *see also* Douglass, J.
wonder 236, 241; and the lighthouse 240–242; newly-present 241, 242; role of the imagination 242

Woolf, V. 4, 207–213; Godrevy Lighthouse 208, 209, 213; letter to Fry 210, 212; novel 139; queer time 222; *see also To the Lighthouse*
Woolf's lighthouse 210; pier glass in *Middlemarch* 210
Wordsworth, W. 52
wrecker's light 55; *see also* false lights
wreckers 29, 30, 164, 224
wrecks *see* shipwrecks
Wyatt, J. 113

Yass, C. 228, *229*; film 228; *see also Lighthouse*; *Lighthouse (East)*; Royal Sovereign Lighthouse

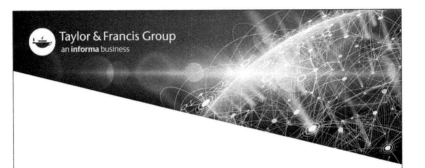